'Combines a sweeping narrative with impressively detailed analysis of the factors behind Rome's imperial conquests and internal turbulence. An invaluable resource'
Catherine Steel, Professor of Classics, University of Glasgow

'Potter presents this epic tale afresh with insight, erudition and remarkable detail. His approach stands out for its clear-eyed exposure of the bloodshed, suffering and persistent strife that led eventually to the Republic's self-destruction and the unexpected emergence of Pax Romana. Here is a book that should jolt generous admirers of ancient Rome to rethink their viewpoint'
Richard Talbert, Kenan Professor of History, University of North Carolina, Chapel Hill

'Potter has written a characteristically crisp, vibrant, and provocative new account of a turbulent and fascinating period in Roman history. Highly recommended'
Carlos Noreña, author of *Imperial Ideals in the Roman West*

'As a portrait of an old and vast representative republic deteriorating into an autocracy, Potter's book is easily, even alarmingly, lucid'
Open Letters Review

DAVID POTTER is Francis W. Kelsey Collegiate Professor of Greek and Roman History, and Professor of Greek and Latin at the University c̶ ̶ ̶ ̶ ̶ ̶ ̶ ̶ ̶ ̶ ̶ ̶ ̶ ̶ scholarly articles, and the books *Cons*   and *The Victor's Cro*   *um.*

THE ORIGIN OF EMPIRE

ROME FROM THE REPUBLIC TO HADRIAN
(264 BC–AD 138)

DAVID POTTER

P

PROFILE BOOKS

This paperback edition published in 2021

First published in Great Britain in 2019 by
PROFILE BOOKS LTD
29 Cloth Fair
London EC1A 7JQ
www.profilebooks.com

1 3 5 7 9 10 8 6 4 2

Typeset in Garamond by MacGuru Ltd

Printed and bound in Great Britain by CPI Group (UK) Ltd, Croydon CR0 4YY

A CIP catalogue record for this book is available from the British Library.

ISBN 978 1 84668 388 6
eISBN 978 1 84765 443 4

For Veronika Grimm and John Matthews

Contents

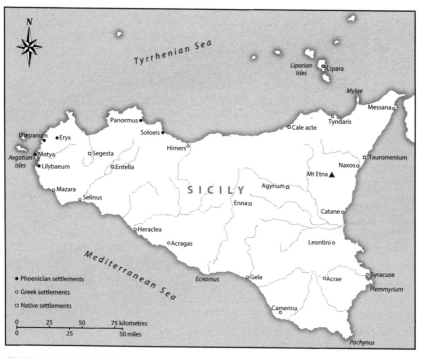

THEATRE OF WAR 264–241 BC

ITALY IN THE WAR WITH HANNIBAL

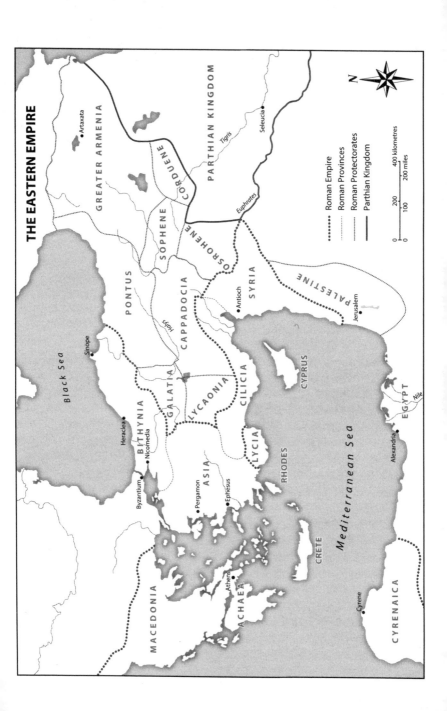

THE EASTERN EMPIRE

N

Black Sea

Artaxata

GREATER ARMENIA

CORDUENE

PARTHIAN KINGDOM

Tigris

Seleucia

SOPHENE

OSROHENE

Euphrates

PONTUS

Sinope

Halys

CAPPADOCIA

Antioch

SYRIA

BITHYNIA

Heraclea

Nicomedia

Byzantium

GALATIA

LYCAONIA

PALESTINE

Jerusalem

CILICIA

ASIA

Pergamon

Ephesus

LYCIA

CYPRUS

RHODES

EGYPT

Alexandria

Nile

MACEDONIA

Athens

ACHAEA

CRETE

Mediterranean Sea

CYRENAICA

Cyrene

· · · · · · Roman Empire

· · · · · · Roman Provinces

- - - - Roman Protectorates

——— Parthian Kingdom

0   100   200   400 kilometres
0   200   400 miles

THE ROMAN EMPIRE UNDER HADRIAN

Aral
Sea

Caspian Sea

Black Sea

anube

A

Byzantium

BITHYNIA

ARMENIA

PARTHIA

MESOPOTAMIA

Pergamon

Smyrna

ens

Ephesus

CILICIA

Antioch

Palmyra

Tigris

Ctesiphon

SYRIA

Euphrates

Mesene

RETE

CYPRUS

Emesa

The Gulf

Jerusalem

ICA

Alexandria

Petra

ARABIA

EGYPT

Nile

Red Sea

NOTE ON THE
ABBREVIATIONS
IN THE TEXT

❦

Historians of the classical world depend on a wide variety of evidence in addition to the texts that have come down to us through the manuscript tradition. Many authors are known to us only through quotations in later authors. We call these quotations 'fragments', so the abbreviation Fr. that appears in the text will be referring to the quotation in an edition of the fragments of an author only known in this way. We also use collections of documents preserved on non-perishable materials (inscriptions) or papyri. The abbreviations for these works that appear in the text appear below, with explanation of what these collections mean.

AE   *L'Année épigraphique* (the annual publication of recent
      discoveries of inscriptions)

FGrH F. Jacoby *et al., Die Fragmente der griechischen Historiker*
      (Leiden, 1926–9)

FRH   T. Cornell, *Fragments of the Roman Historians* (Oxford, 2013)

GC   J. H. Oliver, *Greek Constitutions of Early Roman Emperors
      from Inscriptions and Papyri*, Memoirs of the American
      Philosophical Society n. 178 (Philadelphia, 1989)

ILLRP A. Degrassi, *Inscriptiones Latinae Liberae Rei Publicae* (*Latin
      Inscriptions of the Free Republic*) (Göttingen, 1957)

ILS   H. Dessau, *Inscriptiones Latinae Selectae* (*Select Latin
      Inscriptions*) (Berlin, 1892–1916)

RDGE   R. K. Sherk, *Roman Documents from the Greek East* (Baltimore, 1969)

RGDA   *Res Gestae Divi Augusti* (The deeds of the divine Augustus) with A. E. Cooley, *Res Gestae Divi Augusti: Text, Translation, and Commentary* (Cambridge, 2009)

RS   M. H. Crawford, 'Roman Statutes', *Bulletin of the Institute of Classical Studies Supplement 65* (London, 1996)

SCP   *Senatus Consultum Pisonianum* (D.S. Potter and C. Damon, 'The Senatus Consultum de Cn. Pisone patre', *The American Journal of Philology* 120 (1999): 13–42)

SVA   H. Bengston, ed., *Die Staatsverträge des Altertums* vol. 3 (Munich, 1975) (an invaluable compendium of evidence for treaties)

WT   Writing tablet from R. S. O. Tomlin, ed., 'Roman London's First Voices: Writing Tablets from the Bloomberg Excavations, 2010–14', *Museum of London Archaeology Monograph Series 72* (London, 2016)

INTRODUCTION:
THE PATH TO EMPIRE

O ur story begins in the late summer of 264 BC, when a Roman army is poised to cross the straits of Messina from southern Italy into Sicily. It ends just outside of modern Tivoli, about twenty miles east of Rome, where the Roman emperor Hadrian died in AD 138. His palace, whose vast remains impress visitors to this day, was meant to evoke the world he ruled. His empire ran from northern England (the wall he built there marked one limit of the empire) through southern Germany to Turkey, around the eastern rim of the Mediterranean to Morocco in the west. The Roman Empire was then, and remains still, the most successful multi-ethnic, multi-cultural state in the history of Europe and the Mediterranean. But it would have surprised many of the people we will be meeting in this book to hear that everything was so rosy. For many of them, life was a struggle, and the ability to carry on in the face of adversity was a quality that the Roman people saw as being particularly their own. Rome's greatest poet would celebrate this idea when he penned the line 'so great was the labour to found Rome'. That was true both of the mythic tale he was writing about the city's foundation, and the real story of the way the Roman Empire came into being.

This book ends with the death of Hadrian because he embodies the process of imperial integration that made Rome successful in his own right. He was born of an Italian family that had emigrated to Spain and lived there for centuries before returning to Italy. His reign was also the period during which Cornelius Tacitus, the greatest of Rome's historians – who will also often act as our guide – was writing his history, so it is fitting that we should be able to see how his world shaped his views.

1

Romans of Hadrian's time would look back at the crossing into Sicily as the first step in the acquisition of their empire. They would also look back on the state that sent the army to Sicily as being radically different from the one they lived in. In 264 BC there was no Roman emperor. One of the two central topics of this book will be the process of transformation which led to the creation of the office of emperor, and an entire imperial government. The other will be the way that the empire was acquired. These subjects are inseparable.

To tell the stories of Rome's rise to empire, we will have to establish a baseline by looking at how Rome ran in 264 BC, and to do that, we will need to consider some Latin terms. Many are the roots of common English words, but the specific Latin meaning is not often very well understood through its English derivative. Taking time to understand the Romans in their own terms will allow us to move more easily between their world and ours.

The Roman state was formally known as the *res publica populi Romani*, or 'public matter of the Roman people'. Although the English word 'republic' is derived from it, the Roman *res publica* was unlike any modern state, in that full membership – only men could be full members – carried with it the implication of physical ownership of state property. In 264 BC, this collective property included land spread throughout Italy. The members of the Roman community expressed their will through public assemblies in which they annually elected the magistrates who would be charged with overseeing their affairs. The same assemblies passed laws governing how those magistrates should act. In this way, while the people were sovereign, their elected officials constituted the government, and members of this government tended to be drawn from the highest aristocracy. Crucially, the offices occupied had powers defined by statute, and were both term-limited and revocable. The form of the Roman democracy, in which elected magistrates acted on behalf of a sovereign people that seemed to be politically inactive so long as it was satisfied with the way its officials behaved, has come, through the work of political theorists from Jean Bodin to Thomas Hobbes, to shape modern theories of representative democracy.

Roman magistrates usually had colleagues of the same rank and the Roman people conferred upon them administrative authority in the form of *imperium* and/or *potestas*, as well as religious authority or *auspicium*. *Imperium*, or 'supreme military and administrative power', is the root of the word 'empire', and was exercised in a *provincia*, familiar to us in the English word 'province'. *Potestas* is the root of the word 'power', and a person who had *potestas* had the power to compel someone else to do something. While 'auspicious' in its modern use implies an anticipation of favourable outcomes, Roman *auspicium* was less purely positive. It meant the power to interpret divine signs – especially, but not limited to, those revealed by the actions of birds – and meteorological phenomena. No public business could be conducted unless the auspices were favourable.

In 264 BC, the word *provincia* did not yet mean a geographically defined administrative district, but rather 'a task for which a magistrate should use his *imperium*'. These tasks, assigned by the Roman people, began one mile from the sacred boundary (*pomerium*) of the city of Rome. Within the city, magistrates would exercise their *potestas* according to regulations set by the popular assemblies. One of the important limitations on *potestas* of any sort was that a magistrate could not impose a capital sentence upon a Roman citizen unless that citizen had been condemned by vote of the citizen body or was subject to military discipline.

At the beginning of our story, the Roman *res publica*'s rise to dominance in the Italian peninsula had only recently been confirmed in a series of wars between 295 and 272 BC. Rome's pre-eminence was now based on three factors: its system of alliances with individual Italian communities; its aggressive seizure of prime real estate; and its sophisticated military system drawing upon, by ancient standards, vast reserves of manpower and a relatively stable financial model.

The Roman alliance system rested upon the shared interests of Roman aristocrats and the leaders of allied Italian communities. In constructing their alliance system, the Romans depended on two basic instruments, the *foedus* (treaty) and *deditio in fidem* (handover [of self] into the faith [of the Roman people]). In the fourth century BC, it was quite common for a state that was having trouble with its neighbours to make a *deditio in fidem* to the Romans. If the Romans accepted the *deditio*, then they were under a firm obligation, before the gods, to protect the city. The Roman obsession with being seen as 'the people who dealt in *fides*' is evidenced by coins minted during the 270s BC at the city of Locris in southern Italy (a recently acquired ally), showing the goddess Pistis (Faith) crowning the goddess Roma (the personification of the Roman community).

The Romans' determination to be seen to 'do the right thing' was built

*1. Silver coin issued by Locris in
275 reflecting the city's connection
with Rome. The portrait is of the
god Zeus (the Greek version of
Roman Jupiter) while the scene
on the reverse shows the goddess
Good Faith crowning the goddess
Roma, a graphic illustration of the
importance of the concept of* fides
(good faith) in Roman diplomacy.

into the way that they declared war, and the way that they celebrated victory. Roman declarations of war were made according to rules laid down in a quasi legal/religious procedure connected with the *'fetial'* priests (the term *fetial* indicated something done following a set procedure). According to this procedure, a representative of the Roman state (originally a *fetial* priest in person) would go to a place that had committed an offence against Rome and demand restitution. If none was forthcoming, the priest would return to announce that war would be declared as a result, and then, a few days later, that war was declared. The priest was a witness of the justice of Roman claims before the gods. With victory won, the commanding general might celebrate with a triumph, a procession through the city, ending at the temple of Capitoline Jupiter, Rome's biggest temple for its most important god. The celebration was a symbolic statement of divine support. Quite often, by the end of the fourth century BC, the victorious general would erect a new temple with some of the plunder won from the victory to celebrate the divine personifications of qualities the Romans felt to be characteristic of themselves (courage, honour, etc.). By the time this book opens, the heart of Rome, surrounding the route the generals took to celebrate their triumphs, was well stocked with such self-congratulatory commemorative buildings.

In addition to violence and diplomacy, another tool of Roman dominance were colonies, which came in a variety of sizes and shapes. Some were small, limited to Roman citizens, and looked much like military camps. These tended to be located in places where their population could provide early warning of developing hostility. Others, however, although also small, incorporated members of the local population. In parts of Italy where there were no urban centres (such as Samnium, in the south central Apennines), Romans would be given land as individual settlers organised around rural centres called *conciliabula*, or 'gathering places'. Still others could be very large. Such colonies, which mingled Romans with non-Romans, came to be known as Latin colonies and could consist of 2–6,000 people. They were called 'Latin' because the members of the colony, even if they had once been Roman citizens, assumed a lower level of citizenship than the citizens of Rome, based upon the relationship between Rome and the other cities of Latium, the area of Italy in which Rome had been founded. Latin rights enabled men to do business in Rome, to marry Romans, and, if they were local officials, to acquire or reacquire full Roman citizenship. What Latins could not do, that Roman citizens could, was vote in Roman elections. So why would a Roman citizen want to become a Latin? The reason was economic – the promise of more property than he had. For non-Romans, inclusion in a colony on an equal footing with former citizens was usually a step up in status and gave the common people in communities allied to Rome a vested interest in Rome's success.

The inclusivity of Latin colonies is connected to the single most important difference between Rome and most ancient states, as well as between Rome and modern imperialist states. This was the attitude towards citizenship. In Rome, citizens were the children of families endowed with citizenship, but people could also become citizens if they were the freed slaves of Roman citizens, if the Roman people voted to make them citizens, or if a Roman magistrate known as a censor enrolled them on the list of citizens. Many of the most important families of Rome had come from other communities, and this openness helped Rome absorb potential rivals.

The attitude towards citizenship was not the only unusual feature of the Roman system. Two others in the early third century BC were that Rome had only the most nebulous of coinage systems, and it did not collect tribute from subordinate states. Even when Rome had become

2. Struck around 265 on a Greek standard this coin links Rome with Hercules (shown on the reverse) who was widely worshiped in Italy with the myth of Rome's foundation by Romulus and Remus who were suckled by a she-wolf.

the dominant state in Italy, coins which conveyed a very clear 'Roman' message by carrying images of the god Hercules on the front and the birth of Romulus and Remus (the mythical founders of Rome) on the back, were not minted in Rome. They were circulated in Campania, the area around the bay of Naples, which had a much more robust tradition of coinage stemming from the fact that many of the cities there (of which Naples is the most famous) had strong Greek roots. Roman coinage, minted in Rome, was simply not user friendly. It consisted of heavy bronze bars, weighing slightly less than five pounds, which seem to have been used for large-scale transactions; silver and bronze coins copied from coins circulating in southern Italy; and bronze discs, weighing nearly a pound.

There are two more points that we need to explore before we move on to a brief survey of what would happen to Rome after 264 BC. The first is the way that its elections worked (we will be coming back to these voting practices quite often). The second is the structure of the government (another topic we will be coming back to quite often).

The way that Romans voted depended upon whether the election was for a magistracy that would have *imperium*. These were the two chief magistracies: the consulships (of which there were two) and the praetorship. In theory, the praetor (of which there was only one in 264 BC) would stay in Rome in years when both consuls went to war. The praetor and the consuls were elected by the *comitia centuriata*, the Roman voting assembly in which citizens voted through groups called centuries. In 264 BC the 193 centuries were divided into three groups. The first group, made up of eighteen centuries, were cavalry (known formally as the 'cavalrymen with a public horse'); the second group of 170 centuries were infantry; the third consisted of four 'unarmed' centuries plus one century of *proletarii* – that is, people whose duty to the state was to 'bear children' as they did not have enough property to be classified as *assidui,* 'the settled' or 'the landowning', who made up the membership of the other centuries. The *assidui,* who were liable for military service as infantrymen and to pay tax (*tributum*) when they were not serving, were divided into five classes. Assignment to a class was based on the amount of property a person owned, with the first class being the wealthiest, and having the most centuries (eighty), the second, third and fourth classes having twenty centuries each, and the fifth class having thirty. To win an election, a person had to collect the votes of the majority of centuries, which meant that the wealthiest citizens – who were distributed through the eighteen cavalry centuries and the eighty centuries of the first class – could usually decide an election. In elections for the two annual consulships, the first person to reach a majority ninety-seven centuries was declared the winner of one consulship, then the second place votes were counted and the person with the most second place votes was declared the winner of each century until, again, the magic number of ninety-seven was reached. Even if there was some division of opinion among the wealthy, it is unlikely that voters in the lower census classes cast many meaningful votes in these elections.

There were also magistrates who only had *potestas*. These included the two aediles who were charged with managing the city, the ten tribunes and the quaestors, who administered the treasury and assisted officials with *imperium*. They were elected by the assembly of the thirty-three tribes of Rome. Voting in the tribal assembly worked on the same principle as voting in the centuries, so that whoever won a majority seventeen tribes would win the office he was seeking. On the other hand, as the tribal assembly took no account of census qualifications, the votes of the poor had potentially a great deal more weight.

It was a fundamental rule of the Roman constitution that only elected officials could sponsor laws, and that those laws were voted on in the assembly that had elected them. The result of this was that, at least in theory, very different sorts of laws could be passed. Those favouring the lower classes could pass through the tribal assembly where voting was not weighted in favour of the wealthy and those favouring the interests of the upper classes could move through the assembly of the centuries. In practice, either assembly was quite capable of passing laws of all sorts. The most striking thing about the way Romans voted on laws is that they very rarely voted anything down. The likeliest explanation for this is that the people who wanted to pass a law spent a good deal of time canvassing public opinion to make sure that their measure would pass before they even brought it to a vote.

There is also one exception to pretty much everything we have said so far about the way the Roman system worked. This was the position of dictator. A dictator had supreme political power while he was in office and he was not elected. He was appointed by the senior official in Rome when it was determined that a dictator was needed. Sometimes these needs were rather mundane, such as running elections for consulships. At other times he was appointed to solve a major emergency. When the dictator had accomplished his task, be it running an election or winning a war, he would step down.

This system of magistracies was the result of major reforms that had begun in the middle of the fourth century BC. Before these reforms, the only men who could obtain magistracies with *imperium* or the major priesthoods were those whose families were enrolled in the patrician order, which seems to have formed in the early fifth century BC and consisted of the major clans, or *gentes*, who defined Rome's political order. By the mid-fourth century BC it was clear that this sort of restrictive arrangement was problematic, and the reforms of the 360s BC resulted in the opening-up of one of the two chief magistracies to plebeians (as non-patricians were called).

Gradually priesthoods, too, were made available to plebeians, but these constitutional changes were only part of the story. The relaxing of the old rules also made it possible to incorporate leaders of other Latin communities directly into the governing aristocracy of Rome. The great patrician families could use their influence with electoral assemblies to promote the families of important dependants to high office. The major families of this period were the Valerii, the Claudii, the Fabii (a clan that claimed roots in the area going back to well before the city's foundation), the Aemilii, the Cornelii and the Manlii. The Fabii facilitated the rise of a series of Latin clans to high office, such as the Fulvii and Mamilii from Tusculum (near

3. This coin of 54 BC shows the legendary founder of the Roman Republic, Brutus, accompanied by his attendants (lictors, bearing axes bound by rods) and an assistant. The image conveys the idea of the consul's imperium.

the modern town of Frascati), the Otacilii from Malventum (modern Benevento) and the Atilii from Nomentum (modern Mentana). The Aemilii seem to have sponsored the Genucii, a Roman family that were rich but certainly plebeian, the Licinii, also Roman and rich, as well as the Plautii from Praeneste (modern Palestrina).

Magistrates were assisted by small staffs, and spent much of their time overseeing the activity of people with whom the state contracted for basic functions, ranging from repairing streets, roofing temples, supplying horses for state-sponsored chariot races to providing supplies for armies on campaign, transporting grain to market or collecting *tributum*. As the Roman state did not have a sophisticated monetary system, it is unlikely that these public contractors were especially influential or were able to become wealthy from the work they did for the government. Wealth at this period lay in land and major aristocratic clans were supported by large landholdings, though the limitation of these holdings to around 300 acres for each nuclear family was one feature of a major political reform that had taken place about a century before the Roman invasion of Sicily. The other major source of money for aristocrats was war booty, which, even though they were expected to share it with their men and with the state, would still have provided an important supplement to inherited wealth.

The Roman state we have been exploring so far was not very different from many other Italian states, which typically had aristocratic governing councils, sovereign assemblies and citizen armies, which they could supplement by hiring mercenaries (Rome was not immune to the use of mercenaries) and where magistrates worked with contractors to keep things running. This Roman state looks nothing like the Roman state that Hadrian would leave behind in AD 138. The process of change would really begin at the end of the third century BC. Before that, Rome muddled through a very long war with Carthage, a state in North Africa that had strong interests in Sicily and was strongly opposed to Rome having any presence on the island.

Rome continued to function largely as it had before 264 BC until it fell into a life and death struggle with a Carthaginian army commanded by a man named Hannibal, who invaded Italy from a family fiefdom in Spain in 218 BC. The struggle with Hannibal forced Rome to become more efficient (and even to acquire its own coherent coinage system). The war also embroiled Rome in the politics of the eastern Mediterranean.

The Roman victory over Hannibal and Carthage in 201 BC left Rome in control of Spain, and on the brink of war with the kingdom of Macedon in northern Greece. A rapid victory over Macedon (the war lasted from 200 to 197 BC) led to a war with another kingdom based in the eastern Mediterranean, that of the Seleucids. Another rapid, and total, victory over the Seleucid king Antiochus III (the war lasted from 192 to 188 BC) left Rome as the dominant power in the Mediterranean and opened sources of wealth, previously undreamed of, especially to its contractors. These contractors came to form a very powerful interest in Roman politics and it now becomes reasonable to think of them as forming a specific 'contractor class'.

The vast and rapid increase in available wealth led to political dislocation. Romans would later trace the failure of the traditional Roman form of government to the actions of a series of individuals from the second half of the second century BC through the middle of the first century BC. While it is somewhat simplistic to associate large-scale political movements and social change with individuals, as the Romans did, it is none the less convenient, which is why in this book there are so many chapters that have an individual's name in the title. The first of these people is Tiberius Gracchus, who challenged the dominance of the Senate, asserting the sovereign power of the Roman people in 133 BC. His brother Gaius Gracchus weaponised the contractor class against the office-holding classes in 122 BC by giving them control over a law court where cases could be brought against magistrates for corruption in office. Gaius Marius, a military hero who was himself the product of the politically active contractor class, would save the state from an external foe, but he had no interest in finding a solution to the complicated fractures that were running throughout Roman and Italian society as a result of the unequal divisions of the profits of empire.

A civil war broke out between Rome and its Italian allies in 91 BC, which was largely over by 88 BC, as Rome had granted the main request of the rebels (to become Roman citizens) in 90 BC. The most troubling aspect of this war, in some ways, was the appearance of large-scale military contracting, which would come to dominate Roman politics in the next half century.

The most vicious of the military contractors in this period was Lucius Cornelius Sulla, who, after a bloody civil war in the late 80s BC, established himself as dictator, a position which he reinvented to give himself all power for as long as he wanted. Sulla's failure to build a cohesive following led to the rapid breakdown of the political system he had tried to impose. In the next generation, one of his former officers, Gnaeus Pompey, achieved great prominence well before he held political office through both his ability as a general and his willingness to spend his own money to pay his own armies. Pompey's prominence would be challenged in the 50s BC by Gaius Julius Caesar, who used the resources he obtained by conquering Gaul (modern France and Belgium) to build up what was essentially a privately controlled state. He used the resources of this state to invade Italy, defeat Pompey and set himself up as dictator in the 40s BC.

After Caesar's assassination on 15 March 44 BC, Rome fell into a long period of civil war from which Caesar's adopted son Augustus, who would become the first emperor, emerged victorious in 31 BC. It was Augustus who initiated the transition of Roman government from the fiscal–military contracting system that had grown in the second century BC into a bureaucratic state. The story of the century after his death in AD 14 is dominated by the continuing development of an effective government that could provide mechanisms for the integration of former subjects into the governing groups at Rome – and occasionally offer lessons in the ways that narcissistic, bullying chief executives with short attention spans and bad tempers could be managed (there were several rather colourful emperors in these years).

The great secret of Rome's imperial success was that it allowed former subjects to become administrators and, ultimately, even emperors. No other imperial state has ever achieved the degree of integration between former administrators and former subjects that Rome did – but that, too, is not something that could have been imagined in 264 BC.

PART I

WAR (264–201 BC)

THE INVASION OF
SICILY (264 BC)

Reggio Calabria, on the southernmost tip of Italy, is a beautiful place. In the early evening a quickening breeze chases away the afternoon heat that has flattened the sea, and reawakens the small whirlpools along the shore. To feel this breeze today is to share an experience with Appius Claudius, consul of Rome in 264 BC.

Because of what he did at the end of that summer, Appius Claudius would obtain an additional last name, or cognomen, by which he is now distinguished from the many other members of his powerful aristocratic clan. He is known as Appius Claudius Caudex, 'the blockhead'. This is somewhat unfair. From what we know, he was scarcely either the most inept or the most obnoxious member of a family that would play an important role in Roman life for the better part of a millennium. In 264 BC he was confronted with a series of problems that other leaders have dealt with no better.

Appius Claudius was in Reggio Calabria because of a diplomatic crisis stemming from a Roman sense of obligation to a people known as the Mamertines, a group of Campanian mercenaries who had seized control of the city of Messana (now Messina) in Sicily, just across the straits from Reggio.

The Romans felt obligated to the Mamertines because the Mamertines had played an active role in the war that had confirmed Roman control over southern Italy between 280 and 275 BC. This war had begun as a conflict between the Romans and an alliance controlled by the southern Italian city of Tarentum. Realising that they were overmatched by the Romans, the Tarentines had imported a powerful army led by king Pyrrhus of Epirus in western Greece. Pyrrhus was an able general who had inflicted a couple of bloody defeats on the Romans in the first two years of the war (although these victories had cost him heavy casualties as well, hence our expression 'Pyrrhic victory'). In the end, however, Pyrrhus had been unable to bring the Romans to the peace table, and by 277 BC the Tarentines had run short of money with which to pay him. He had then hired out his army to the Syracusans, based in south-east Sicily, for a war with the Carthaginians. When the Syracusans, too, ran out of money, that war ended. Pyrrhus returned to Italy and the Mamertines helped the Romans by attacking him on the way. Pyrrhus then fought a third battle against the Romans, was badly beaten and returned to Greece, where he died in battle a few years later. Tarentum's surrender to Rome in 272 BC marked the completion of the Roman conquest of Italy south of the Po valley. Then the Mamertines got into trouble.

In 267 BC a general named Hieron of Syracuse crushed the Mamertine army, and now, after an interval during which he became king Hieron II, looked to finish them off. Faced with destruction, the Mamertines made a *deditio in fidem* to Rome – that is, a formal handing-over of themselves into the good faith of the Roman people, to whom they also claimed kinship as fellow worshippers of the god Mars, the father of Romulus, the founder of Rome. (We will see further instances of this sort of diplomacy anon.)

Unfortunately for pretty much everyone involved, the initial Mamertine response to the threat from Syracuse had been to ask Carthage rather than Rome for help. Such an appeal may have seemed initially attractive as the Carthaginians both had a long history of antipathy towards the Syracusans and, most recently, had been allied with the Mamertines against Pyrrhus. The problem with the Carthaginians, as the Mamertines were soon to discover, was that they wanted a good deal more control at Messana than the Mamertines were comfortable with. It was the arrival of a Carthaginian garrison that convinced the Mamertines to try their luck with Rome. Tricking the Carthaginian garrison commander into leaving, they dispatched their envoys to Rome asking that their protection be declared a *provincia*. This was done in July 264 BC.

The appeal caused confusion and ill will. The Carthaginians, who had always enjoyed good relations with Rome, thought that they had an understanding whereby Rome would stay out of areas that were important to them, such as Sicily. The Romans were uncertain how to respond: they recognised that they had a responsibility to the Mamertines, but they were already committed to a war that was not going well against a rebellious city in southern Etruria (roughly modern Tuscany) and were leery of fighting wars in two very different places at the same time.

There was considerable debate in the Senate as to whether to declare the relief of the Mamertines a *provincia* and, when the Senate could not reach a decision, Appius Claudius summoned a meeting of the *comitia centuriata*. The *comitia* duly voted him the *provincia*. What the *comitia centuriata* was *not* doing when it agreed to make 'aid to the Mamertines' a *provincia* was declaring war on either Carthage or Syracuse. Rome only ever went to war in self-defence. Self-defence could, of course, be more or less broadly defined, but in this case Rome would only declare war if the Carthaginians and/or the Syracusans attacked the Roman army once it had arrived in Sicily.

The dismissal of their garrison from Messana had so thoroughly irritated the Carthaginians that they had crucified its unfortunate commander. The prospect of a Roman intervention annoyed them even more, and before the Romans had even voted to send Appius south, the Carthaginians had already made a treaty with Hieron so as to keep them out.

We can reconstruct the events that followed Appius Claudius' arrival only with difficulty. The reason for this difficulty is that some of our evidence comes from texts that have only been preserved in summary form, or through scattered quotations in other authors, known as 'fragments' (shown abbreviated to 'Fr.' after a quotation in the text). Other evidence comes from an author who was so overwhelmed by his own prejudices that he could only read the accounts that he had through the lens of later debates.

We have three sources that matter. One is the long *Historical Library* written by a man named Diodorus in the middle of the first century BC. The scope of the work extended from early Egypt and Mesopotamia to the lifetime of Diodorus' contemporary Julius Caesar; in composing this massive work, Diodorus used material borrowed, not always carefully, from earlier writers. In this case, he used the work of an earlier Sicilian historian named Philinus, who detested the Romans. Sadly, we do not have Diodorus' whole story because this part of his work is known to us only indirectly through quotations in later historians. Our second source is Cassius Dio, who wrote an 81-book history of Rome from its foundation to his own time in the early third century AD, which is also now known only from summaries. Our most detailed account, that of the second-century BC Greek historian Polybius, is marred by the fact that, against all available evidence, he presumed the Romans started the war for reasons of grand strategy.

In Polybius' view the Romans were not inclined to help the Mamertines because they were terrible people, and because assisting them would be inconsistent with their earlier decision to punish another group of Campanian mercenaries. These men, who were in Roman employ, had seized Rhegium (the ancient name for Reggio Calabria) from its citizens during the war against Pyrrhus. What Polybius, who simply disliked mercenaries, did not perceive was that the Romans viewed the Campanians in Rhegium very differently from those in Messana. The Campanians in Rhegium had broken faith (*fides*) with Rome, whereas the ones in Messana had not – a point whose significance was obvious at the time, even if regarded as debatable. Confronting a Roman ambassador who had come to discuss the Mamertine situation, Hieron, in Diodorus' account, opined that everyone would recognise how bogus were Roman claims to deal in *fides* if they were seen supporting creeps like the Mamertines.

For Polybius, the important thing in the Roman decision-making process was not *fides* but the perception that Carthaginian power was closing in on Italy and that, inevitably, Rome would have to fight Carthage. That being the case, it was better to do so sooner rather than later, as Carthage was growing stronger by the day. But Polybius' view was based on a false appreciation of Carthaginian power – namely, that it had been stronger in 264 BC than it was in 218 BC, when the great Carthaginian general Hannibal launched the Second Punic War (be warned that Hannibal was a common Carthaginian name and we will encounter other Hannibals who have no relation to this one in the next few pages). Carthage, thanks largely to the activity of Hannibal's family in Spain during the previous thirty years, was vastly stronger at that time than it had ever been. Later Romans – that is, Polybius' contemporaries – were, however, interested in claiming that Carthage had been a perpetual and powerful menace long before Hannibal's time. They wanted to believe this in order to justify their contention that they had to destroy Carthage (which they managed to do in Polybius' lifetime and with his active participation). That is why Cassius Dio knew a Roman version of the story in which:

> These [the Carthaginians] were in no way inferior to them [the Romans] in wealth or in the excellence of their land; they were trained in naval science to a high degree of efficiency, were equipped with cavalry forces, infantry, and elephants, ruled the Africans, and held possession of Sardinia as well as the greater part of Sicily; as a result, they had conceived hopes of subjugating Italy. Various factors contributed to increase their self-confidence, but they were especially proud because of their independence, since they elected their king under the title of a yearly office and not for permanent rule; and, feeling that their efforts were expended in their own behalf, they were full of enthusiasm.
>
> (Dio, *Roman History* 11.8 (Loeb translation adapted))

Recent archaeological work has refuted the notion that Carthage at this time was a massive power, controlling the western rim of the Mediterranean. We now know that there was no vast Carthaginian empire, but rather there were numerous trade networks involving merchants of Phoenician descent, of which some, but not all, centred on Carthage. Carthage itself controlled a string of cities along the north coast of Africa, some cities in Sicily, and the islands of Sardinia and Corsica. In terms of military might it was usually hard-pressed to hold its own against Syracuse, which, as the events of late 264 BC were about to reveal, was itself no match for even a single Roman army, much less the two armies the Roman state ordinarily fielded every summer.

The Romans accepted the Mamertine *deditio* after the Carthaginian garrison had been withdrawn; the Carthaginians made their alliance with Syracuse sometime before August 264 BC, when the Roman army began to assemble at Rhegium. No one knew quite what would happen, but it appears that some Carthaginian ships sank some Roman ones. After the attack, Diodorus reports a Roman embassy to the Carthaginians complaining about the attack, pointing to the possibility that the result would be war, and lecturing them on Roman military history. Both sides seem to have been aware that an effective blockade of the strait of Messina would be impossible because the Carthaginian fleet, stationed twelve miles away at Cape Peloras, was too distant to mount effective patrols, and the Syracusans had no naval presence in the area worth mentioning. All the Romans needed to do was load up their ships one evening and head for Messana.

Although now allied against the Roman invaders, the Carthaginians and the Syracusans had a long history of mutual antipathy, meaning they were unable to coordinate their response to the enemy. Appius took advantage of this by attacking first the Syracusans and then, when they had withdrawn home in defeat, the Carthaginians. He scattered their land forces, and their naval power had no impact. Fighting on through the winter, causing his men great hardship – it is likely this is why he became known as 'the blockhead' – he reduced the Syracusans, whom the Carthaginians made no effort to help, to impotence. In March 263 BC, after the new consuls took office, they came south, crossing into Sicily without Carthaginian interference. More than sixty cities handed themselves over to Rome's *fides* and Syracuse surrendered. It was only now that the Roman armies turned on the Carthaginians. Given the well-established Syracusan hostility towards Carthage, as well as what would later appear to be their enthusiastic support for the Roman war effort, it is quite likely that the Roman commanders now turned against Carthage with the encouragement of King Hieron, who had paid the Romans a large sum as a war indemnity.

2

WAR BY LAND AND SEA (263–241 BC)

With the transformation of Syracuse from enemy to ally, the war in Sicily entered a new phase. There is, however, little evidence that the Roman Senate understood exactly what the implications of that change were, and every sign is that it took the Roman state a long time to understand just how different this new war was from those that had gone before. Polybius speaks of the Romans becoming 'thoroughly entangled in the affairs of Sicily' (1.17.3), an image evocative of entrapment and captivity that is spot on.

One of the most important indicators of the Romans' lack of comprehension of the difference between this war and previous wars is the way that they filled the consulship throughout the war. This is important because sources written after the event were composed with that same sense of historical inevitability that led them to characterise their presentation of the start of the war as being driven by considerations of grand strategy. When we see who was actually selected to do the fighting, we get quite a different sense to the way things seemed at the time.

The consuls of 263 BC were Manius Valerius Messalla and Manius Otacilius Crassus. Valerius Messalla was, like Appius, a patrician from a very ancient and powerful family, and it is one of the curious features of the Roman war effort that people like Valerius Messalla are rare among the consuls, whereas members of the recently arrived aristocracy are plentiful.

Of the thirty-eight men who held consulships during the war years, only eleven – two of whom were brothers – had a consular father or grand-father, whereas six were the first members of their families to reach the office.

While Roman leadership included fewer of the old guard, it tended to involve people who were supported by a nexus of coeval relatives. One of the consuls of 261 BC was the brother of Otacilius Crassus, while his co-consul was a cousin of his brother's co-consul. A consul of 262 BC was the brother of the consul of 265 BC; two brothers, Cornelii Scipiones, succeeded each other as consuls for 260 and 259 BC; in 258, 257, 256 and 254 BC one of the two consuls was a member of the clan Atilius. Their prominence at this point might be to do with the family's close connection with Campania, whence, quite possibly, came a good deal of support for the war. In total, nearly half of the thirty-eight consuls elected during the war had a brother or cousin who was also a consul at that time.

Another oddity is that, unlike during the war with Pyrrhus and later the Second Punic War, when people who had proven themselves before the hostilities started to return to office, only two men who had been consul before 264 BC were elected once war broke out. Indeed, during the war years people were rarely re-elected. A conclusion that may be drawn from this is that the Romans did not feel seriously threatened by the Carthaginians.

Wars waged as family affairs by men of limited ability will not be waged efficiently – the swings in Roman conduct during the war against the Carthaginians betray the absence of any coherent design. They may also betray the influence of Sicilian politics. Sicilian cities, caught for generations between Syracuse and Carthage, looked to Roman power to break the long-standing cycle of conflict. One way the Greek states com-municated with each other was by drawing on mythological traditions that could be reconstructed to suggest associations with the distant past. It was a style of diplomacy that could also work with Rome. Romans were used to listening to this sort of thing. Pyrrhus had given them a dose of it, pointing out that his ancestor, the Homeric hero Achilles, was greater than Aeneas, the Trojan prince who was remembered as one of the founders of Rome. Now that the Romans were in Sicily they found that the city of Segesta, in the south of the island, was summoning them via its connec-tion with Rome through Aeneas.

It was perhaps easier for Rome to deal with the Greeks of Sicily because many of the troops the Romans sent there were either Greek or Campanian. That the cities of Campania minted heavily during these years is highly suggestive – in some cases, the only coins that can be attributed to a given city date from this time. There is not so obvious a trend in Apulia, Lucania or Bruttium, areas that had minted very heavily during the Pyrrhic war, and no activity at all among the cities north and west of Rome. Cities coined when they needed to, and there was generally a close correlation in the third century BC between a decision to mint more money and a war in the neighbourhood. Given the long history of Campanians going off to fight in Sicily, it comes as no surprise that the region should be especially interested in this conflict.

The war with Syracuse ended in the summer of 263 BC. The war with Carthage picked up steam as soon as the Segestans decided that their mythical connection with Aeneas was more important than their actual connection with Carthage. When they declared their interest in joining the Roman alliance, they massacred their Carthaginian garrison. The next year saw fierce fighting between the two powers, and both Roman consuls concentrated their efforts on capturing Agrigentum (modern Agrigento) on Sicily's south coast. The victory at Agrigentum – facilitated by the Syracusans, who furnished the Roman army with supplies throughout the difficult campaign – led to a major change in Roman policy: they would carry the war to Africa, and for that they would need a fleet.

The decision to build a major war fleet can be associated with the sudden pre-eminence in Roman politics of the Cornelii Scipiones and the Atilii – there was at least one member of these clans in office between 260 and 257 BC – and some Syracusan encouragement. Big fleets were not a feature of Italian naval warfare, and Roman aristocrats had left the occasional mustering of fleets to their allies. Some of these allies had significant experience of naval raiding – in the eastern Mediterranean Italians were regarded as notorious pirates – but they did not have the sort of infrastructure needed to launch a major battle fleet from scratch. That would change, virtually overnight, as the Romans started to build a fleet.

The basic battleship of the fifth and early fourth centuries BC had been the trireme. The classic trireme, best known to us from accounts of warfare in the eastern Mediterranean, was around 120 feet long. It had twenty-five rows of three banks of oars on each side, carrying a crew of around 200 men. The basic tactic employed by these ships was to either disable an enemy vessel with the bronze ram that it carried on its prow or grapple and board the enemy's ship. In the middle of the fourth century BC the Syracusans had begun tinkering with this design, developing ships on which there would be five rowers to each bank of oars (two each per oar on the upper two banks). These ships were called quinquiremes. The advantage of a quinquireme was that it could crash into another ship with greater velocity, could carry more marines for boarding, and was generally more stable than a trireme.

Given that a quinquireme was basically an overgrown trireme, the two ships could be used somewhat interchangeably in a battle fleet. It also appears, thanks to the fantastic discovery of a group of rams from ships sunk off the Aegetes islands (now the Egadi islands), off the west coast of Sicily), in what would prove to be the decisive battle of the war we are presently discussing, that the warships used by both the Romans and the Carthaginians were on the small side when compared to ships used elsewhere. These triremes (almost all the rams are from triremes) were about ninety feet long and so probably carried crews of around 150 men; the quinquiremes might have carried another hundred. That would mean that a fleet of around a hundred triremes and quinquiremes would employ somewhere around 20,000 men and be roughly the same size as the standard army that a consul commanded each year.

The new fleet, whose rowers were trained on benches set up along the beach while their ships were in construction, was launched in summer 260 BC. The consuls that year were Gnaeus Cornelius Scipio and Gaius Duillius. Scipio initially held command at sea, and Duillius on the land, where Carthaginian forces were attempting to regain territory lost in earlier years. After Scipio managed to get himself captured by the Carthaginians during an ill-advised raid on their base on the Lipari islands, Duillius, who was busy driving the Carthaginians away from Segesta, took charge of the fleet. Equipped with novel boarding devices, the Roman ships encountered the Carthaginians off the Sicilian city of Mylae and inflicted a total defeat. The record of Duillius' accomplishments this year, preserved on an inscription recopied in the first century BC, is one of the most important documents of the period. The text tells us:

> [As consul Duillius] delivered the [Segestans, allies of the Roman
> people, who were being besieged by the Carthaginians], and after nine
> days, all the [Carthaginian] legions and their chief magistrates fled

4. The inscription recording Duillius' achievements, carved on one of the columns erected in the forum to commemorate his victory, offers important contemporary evidence for his campaign in 260 BC and the nature of warfare in the period. The surviving text comes from a restoration of the monument in the first century BC.

their camp in full daylight, and he took the [city] of Macela by force. In the same magistracy, he was the first consul [to succeed] at sea with ships, and he was the first to prepare naval forces and ships, and with those ships he defeated all the Punic fleets and the great forces of the Carthaginians in battle on the high sea, in the presence of [Hannibal], their dictator; he captured, along with his allies, one septireme, and [thirty quinquire]mes and triremes, and [sank thirteen]. He captured thirty-seven hundred pieces of gold and one hundred thousand [?] pieces of silver … and in his triumph [he gave] the Roman people the booty and displayed numerous free Carthaginians before his chariot.

(*ILLRP* 318)

The septireme mentioned here is a ship the Carthaginians had captured from Pyrrhus (its existence reflects the fact that eastern kings liked big ships). Aside from this titbit, which Romans in the know would have enjoyed, Duillius tells us a good deal about the way the Roman aristocracy approached the war. He opens by pointing out that he rescued a Roman ally from the Carthaginians, and reprises the value of *fides* enunciated by Appius when he first crossed the straits. In reporting the action at Mylae he makes clear, as our later sources do not, the role that Rome's allies, who had greater nautical experience than the Romans, must have played in the operations. The emphasis on the plunder that he distributed in his triumph underscores the profit motif which was important to Roman thinking about war. Finally, and perhaps a bit more disturbing, is the way he presents the Carthaginians, describing the commander of the fleet as holding the very Roman office of dictator, and the chiefs of the land army as 'the highest magistrates', as if they were Romans. If Duillius and his fellow aristocrats thought that the Carthaginians would understand what they, the Romans, considered to be the norms of conduct, or that their political system was fully comprehensible in Italian terms, they were seriously mistaken.

The year after Duillius' triumph saw further Roman victories on land and sea, which inspired yet another of our surviving pieces of third-century Latin, in this case the funerary epitaph of Gnaeus Scipio's more competent brother:

> Lucius Cornelius Scipio, aedile, consul, censor. Most people of Rome agree that this one man, Lucius Scipio, was the best of the good men. This man, son of Barbatus, aedile, consul and censor, took Corsica and the city of Aleria and dedicated a temple to *Tempestates* [Storms] in return.
>
> (*ILLRP* 310)

Here we see the connection between military glory and piety, marked by the dedication of a new temple as a reminder of an individual's personal success – a characteristic that we associate with earlier generations. Unfortunately, as with Duillius' triumph, Scipio's victory, while impressive, did not bring peace any closer.

Despite their successes, neither Duillius nor this Scipio would be employed again in a military capacity. In Duillius' case he celebrated his victory both by erecting a temple to the god Janus near the point where triumphal processions entered Rome, a column near the Senate House, decorated with the rams taken from ships he had captured and a statue of himself. He held two further offices: the censorship (Scipio was his colleague); and then, in 231 BC, the office of dictator in charge of running the consular elections. Having obtained a glory undreamed of in his generation, and being of a rare competence, his disappearance from the public stage suggests that he was aware that, as a man with no consular ancestors, he should not seek further laurels for himself, considering it more appropriate to leave the stage to men of greater nobility, even if they were of lesser ability. Scipio also made this choice. He was noble enough, and people who stopped by the forum could see his house just as they could see Duillius' monument. It was unfortunate that the aristocratic ethos of the time meant potentially limiting the participation of the able. There were plenty of less talented men now ready to step into their places.

In 258 BC both consuls took to the sea. Sulpicius Paterculus seized the island of Sardinia and defeated a Carthaginian fleet, while Atilius Caiatinus, the first of a number of men from this prominent family of Campanian origin to hold the consulship, likewise won some successes in Sicily. It was a year later that Roman ambitions, possibly fuelled by Syracusan strategic advice, reached a new level. It was thought a good idea to invade Africa with a single consular army (roughly 20,000 men), reproducing an operation that had been reasonably successful for the Syracusans in a war they had fought with Carthage around 310 BC. The leader would be a cousin of Caiatinus', Gaius Atilius Regulus. The plan may have sounded better in theory than it was in practice, for it relied upon a series of false assumptions about North African politics and what exactly the Carthaginians would be willing to put up with. It also ignored a basic difference in aims. In 310 BC, the Syracusans had been trying to distract the Carthaginians from an attack on Syracuse itself by raiding their homeland. In this case the Romans were trying to do something more dramatic. They were hoping to make Carthage surrender.

To launch an invasion, the Romans would need a big fleet, which was duly constructed even as the Carthaginians were assembling a large force of their own. Polybius gives a generous description of the battle of Cape Ecnomus off Sicily in 256 BC, in which Regulus thoroughly defeated the Carthaginian fleet. For Polybius it was the largest naval battle in ancient history, with hundreds of quinqueremes on both sides, involving 290,000 men all told. Such a picture accords with his view of the relative strength of the two powers, Carthage being on a par with Rome and both being greater than any of the powers in the eastern Mediterranean. But the truth is likely more prosaic. Regulus was trying to transport his 20,000 men. Most of his warships were probably triremes, of which it is unlikely that he had many more than a hundred – of the smaller, western size – or that the Carthaginian fleet was much larger. This would mean that the actual number engaged was between a quarter and a fifth of what Polybius claimed. If not unparalleled, a battle involving around 60–70,000 men was still enormous by ancient standards, when the numbers were limited by logistics and the average warship could carry food for no more than a few days.

The rest of the campaign was not so successful. Regulus landed in North Africa, ravaged the territory of Carthage and its allies, but lacked the resources to besiege the city itself. In the winter his consular colleague left for home, reducing his forces even further. These facts also suggest that the Romans had no clear idea of how to bring the war to an end, for when the Carthaginians approached Regulus about a peace treaty, he insisted that they make a *deditio in fidem*. With small states in Italy, all of which were aware of the terms of a *deditio*, this would have been unexceptionable, and states familiar with the system could manipulate one in their interests. Duillius' inscription, which interprets Carthaginian offices in Roman terms, suggests that Regulus was simply acting as any Roman might have acted under the circumstances. But the Carthaginians were appalled. They regarded Regulus' attitude as unspeakably arrogant, broke off negotiations and hired a new army of mercenaries.

When Regulus advanced against the Carthaginians the following spring, the new Carthaginian army, commanded by Xanthippus, a competent general from the Greek city of Sparta, made short work of his troops. Xanthippus anticipated Regulus' tactics – a full-scale assault on the centre of his line – perfectly. Instead of receiving the attack, Xanthippus broke the Roman advance with a charge of elephants – one of the few times elephants played an effective role on the battlefield – while his cavalry drove off the weak Roman cavalry and encircled their shattered infantry formation. Regulus was captured and was either tortured to death or died in harsh captivity.

We will see Hannibal using variations on these tactics in the Second Punic War. Good generals learned how to use the basic aggressiveness of their Roman counterparts against them. Polybius, usually inclined to write favourably about the Romans, observed that:

The Romans generally rely on force in all matters. They think it is necessary to finish everything they start and that nothing is impossible once they decide upon it. They often succeed because of this impulsiveness, but sometimes they conspicuously fail, especially at sea. On land, acting against humans and their affairs, they are usually successful because they are employing force against people with similar capacities, though there are some exceptions. But whenever they try to contend with and subdue the sea and the weather by force they fail spectacularly.

(Polybius, *Histories* 1.37)

The event Polybius is referring to here occurred in 253 BC, a couple of years after Regulus' surrender, when a storm struck a Roman fleet returning from a raid on North Africa. This was the second massive shipwreck that the Romans had suffered. The first had taken place in 255 BC; both were the consequence of the admirals ignoring the advice of their more experienced pilots. It is, however, unlikely that many Roman lives were lost on these occasions: the consuls in command in 255 BC who returned with survivors of Regulus' disaster celebrated triumphs for earlier naval victories, and one of the consuls who lost the fleet in 253 BC was re-elected in 244 BC. Most of the casualties were probably from southern Italy and Sicily; the Romans would react very differently when the losses struck closer to home.

One outcome of the storm in 253 BC was that the Romans stopped raiding Africa, and there are signs of unrest at various levels. Both consuls continued to be sent to Sicily, but for the next few years they contented themselves with operations on land, restoring morale among troops made jittery by reports of the power of the Carthaginian elephants. One notable success was the capture of the base at Lipara in 252 BC, where they discovered a memorial to the fourth-century BC war against the Gauls. But that was ancient history – in the here and now men were refusing to serve. The censors of 252 BC removed 400 people from the ranks of the 'equestrians with the public horse' for disobedience in Sicily, and Rome's south Italian allies may have been declining to participate in naval operations commanded by Romans. This would explain why the fleet sent to Sicily in 249 BC had a large component of men from central Italy.

This fleet was probably the one that originally sported the sunken bronze rams that have already taught us so much about the nature of the fleets in this war. Beyond what they have already told us, we may learn something from them about the way business was done in Rome. The bronze that went into the rams had been 'approved' by Roman magistrates, some by a single quaestor, some by two, others by two members of a board of six. The 'approval' process is a well-known feature of the standard central Italian public/private partnerships that provided the sinews of war; the variations in the boards that did the approving suggest that the fleet was being assembled at speed. The contractors themselves would, at this point, have been charged with basic tasks such as manufacturing the rams from bronze provided to them by the state. Such people had a vested interest in the war, which provided their livelihoods. They were small business people who worked directly on the projects upon which they had bid – others would have built the ships that carried the rams, or cut the wood that was used, made the nails or created the cordage.

One of the consuls in 249 BC was a cousin of Appius Claudius Caudex called Publius Claudius Pulcher, who was heavily defeated that year by a Carthaginian fleet off Drepanum (modern Drepana), on Sicily's west coast. Many of his ships were captured and taken into service by the Carthaginians, which is why Roman ships ended up being sunk as part of a Carthaginian fleet a few years later. Despite some successes on land, Pulcher's consular partner, who lost a fleet in a storm, committed suicide (another version attributes his suicide to a guilty conscience for violating the auspices when he lost his fleet). One of Rome's most experienced magistrates, Atilius Caiatinus, was made dictator and sent to Sicily to stabilise the situation. His primary achievement appears to have been arranging a prisoner exchange with the Carthaginians.

The disasters of 249 BC were blamed on the consuls, and Publius Claudius was put on trial for his life. A later anecdote, possibly apocryphal, suggests that heavy loss of Roman citizen lives was connected with his trouble. According to this story his sister, annoyed by crowds in the street, was heard to say that she wished her brother would be consul again so that he could rid the city of riffraff.

Claudius' trial probably began in 248 BC, with his impeachment before the *comitia centuriata* for *perduellio* (high treason). That charge was probably connected with the belief that Claudius had angered the gods just before the battle began. When he had been told that the sacred chickens – whose movements while eating provided the auspices – would not leave their cages and eat, he had ordered them to be tossed overboard, saying, 'If they won't eat, let them drink.'

The aristocracy seems to have been deeply split about what should happen to him, as trials of magistrates for what was in effect incompetence were very rare. Military and naval defeats were usually blamed on accidental misreading of divine will, or failures on the part of soldiers. In this case Claudius had been outsmarted by an able Carthaginian admiral who had trapped the Roman fleet against a hostile shore when Claudius had attempted a surprise attack on his anchorage.

The tribunes who brought the initial case against Claudius were thwarted by other magistrates who claimed that the gods had sent adverse signs when they convened the *comitia* for the trial. This effectively meant that the possible death sentence was ruled out when the trial was moved to the *concilium plebis*, to which patricians were not admitted, and it was there that Claudius was finally convicted and sentenced to pay a large fine. In 247 BC, the people voted that no more fleets should be raised, in a sure sign that war weariness was setting in.

Incipient war weariness may explain the establishment, in the year of Appius' consulship, of new 'secular' games, following the instructions of a Sibylline Oracle. The Sibylline Oracles were books, written in Greek, that purported to contain the wisdom of the ancient prophetess known as a Sibyl. They were consulted by the Board of Ten for Making Sacrifices, the priestly college that was in charge of the oracular books. The ritual, performed at the Campus Martius, the great plain outside the walls of the city proper, had to do with the notion of long life and the orderly passage of generations, reaffirming the community's survival as the rite was to be celebrated only once every *saeculum* (the longest lifespan in a generation). This year in particular, a rite stemming from the idea of continuity may have been just what was needed. The census taken in 246 BC reveals for the first time in this war a decline in the number of Roman citizens. It may be an indication of growing unease that, two years later, the Senate decided that two new colonies should be founded, at Brundisium (Brindisi), on Italy's east coast, and Fregenae (Fregene) in Etruria.

New religious rites and discontinued naval operations were also a sign that no one had a clear idea how Rome might extricate itself from a war that was now centred on Lilybaeum (modern Marsala) on the tip of Sicily closest to Africa. The current Carthaginian general Hamilcar Barca was exceptionally able and had held at bay consular army after consular army.

If he could not be cut off from the supplies being shipped to him from North Africa, the war could not be ended. Meanwhile, on his instructions, Carthaginian ships were being sent to raid southern Italy.

For 242 BC the Romans decided that radical change was needed. A second praetor was appointed, and a new fleet was raised, although it would not be ready until the end of the year. The delay was connected with money problems. The fleet was only built after the Senate adopted a form of financing, borrowed from Greek city states, whereby wealthy individuals paid for the construction and equipping of the warships. Such an arrangement is further proof that Rome's southern Italian allies had had enough of fighting, and drowning, around Sicily.

Still, nothing happened. People were restless, and in the new year a revolt against Roman authority broke out in the region of Falisci, on the border between Latium and Etruria, which continued for more than a year. The Roman state's decision, taken that year, to increase the number of tribes from thirty-three to thirty-five, leading to an expansion of the territory occupied by Roman citizens, looks like an effort to clamp down on further unrest. Then what must have seemed like a miracle occurred. News arrived of a decisive victory off the Aegetes islands and the destruction of a Carthaginian fleet.

The Carthaginians were in no better shape than the Romans. Beyond the squadrons used for raiding Italy, they were unable to keep much of a fleet of their own in operation, or to raise an army beyond what was needed to defend their Sicilian territory. When the final naval battle of the First Punic War occurred in the late winter of 241 BC, their battle fleet included old Roman triremes captured at Drepanum.

Details of the final campaign are sparse. The date can be determined (March 241 BC) because both the men who were responsible for the success, Gaius Lutatius Catulus and Quintus Valerius Falto, a consul and praetor respectively in 242 BC, were operating under continuing authority at the time of the battle. In terms of the battle itself, Polybius says Catulus trapped the Carthaginian fleet as it was sailing from the Aegetes with supplies for the Sicilian garrison. Thus laden, these ships were no match for the Romans. What exactly Falto did is less clear, but the fact that he celebrated a triumph suggests there may have been a second battle to complete the Roman victory.

When Catulus sailed to North Africa in the battle's wake, Carthage's city council felt it had no choice but to negotiate a peace treaty. Catulus, evidently mindful of what had happened to Regulus, did not insist that the Carthaginians make a *deditio in fidem*.

The terms Catulus delivered to Carthage were of his own devising. As a holder of *imperium* he had the authority to make large-scale policy decisions, with the proviso that they would later be approved by the *comitia centuriata* back in Rome (this would also have applied had he insisted on a *deditio in fidem*). He told the Carthaginians that they would have peace on the following conditions: they evacuated Sicily; they swore not to wage war on Hieron, the Syracusans or the allies of the Syracusans; they returned all Roman prisoners; and they paid an indemnity of 125,400 pounds (57,200 kilos) of silver over twenty years.

As delivered, the terms attest the importance of the Syracusans to the Roman war effort, as well as the Roman perception that the Carthaginians needed a lot of money to fight their wars. A payment of nearly 1,300 pounds of silver each year would have been a substantial, but not impossible, burden on a state like Carthage. But the Roman people thought it inadequate and refused to ratify the terms as presented, possibly because Senate members did not reach consensus before the process began. A board of ten, headed by Catulus' brother, was sent to negotiate new terms. But the ambassadors changed only the terms of the indemnity, halving the payment period and adding 57,000 pounds of silver to the total, while also insisting that the Carthaginians evacuate the islands between Sicily and Africa – although this still left them with Sardinia and Corsica, which they had retaken from the Romans during the war. The Carthaginians accepted the new terms, which were duly ratified by Rome.

Any residual resentment the cash-poor Carthaginians felt concerning the revision of the treaty terms would be compounded when they found themselves at war with the mercenary army from Sicily, already suffering from arrears in compensation, that was dumped on their doorstep by the treaty terms. A war 'distinguished by far greater savagery and disregard for convention than any war in human history' (Polybius, *Histories* 1.88.7) ensued between Carthage and the mercenaries, which lasted until 238 BC.

As that war ended, Carthaginian mercenaries on Sardinia declared their independence. When, in response, the Carthaginian administration prepared an expedition against them, the mercenaries made a *deditio* to Rome, which duly sent a message to Carthage explaining that the two states would be at war if the Carthaginians proceeded against the mercenaries, who were now under Rome's protection, while also demanding another

57,000 pounds of silver as a yet further indemnity. Carthage believed it had no choice but to agree to these demands, which would in the long run prove to have been exceptionally stupid. The consuls responsible for this outcome were Publius Valerius Falto, brother of Catulus' colleague at the battle of the Aegetes, and Tiberius Sempronius Gracchus. While the family of Falto would provide no more consuls, Gracchus' descendants would shake the *res publica* to its core.

The events of 238 BC convinced some in Carthage that they needed to rebuild their strength. In 237 BC the governing council allowed General Hamilcar Barca to leave with an army for Spain, in order to build as powerful a dependency as he could there. Hamilcar understood that he would be ruler of this new realm in alliance with, rather than in subordination to, the government of Carthage. The stage was set for what would become Rome's most decisive war ever, to begin some twenty years hence. Before then, however, Rome would take other decisions, and other actions, that would only make this next war more difficult for itself.

3

ROME AND ITALY
(240–217 BC)

❦

On 9 September 1943, a huge armada of warships steamed into the bay of Salerno. In the face of heavy German opposition, it began to unload a joint American/British army that was to join up with a further British force that had crossed the straits from Messina to Reggio.

One of the initial American landing beaches was at Paestum. The city, whose ancient ruins now amaze the modern visitor, was founded in the sixth century BC by Greek settlers who had come from Sybaris, a powerful state established on Italy's south-western coast by Greek immigrants at the end of the eighth century. These settlers named their new city Posidonia, in honour of the Greek god of the sea, and in time they invented connections with the Trojan War in order to cast an aura of respectable antiquity over their home. In their case, the connection would be with the Greek hero Diomedes, who had thoroughly thrashed the Trojan warrior Aeneas in a famous scene from Homer's *Iliad*. Before 450 BC they completed three great temples around the edges of the city's public area, the Athena temple on its north side and temples to Hera and Poseidon on the south side. Just outside the walls there was a shrine to the goddess Aphrodite, the goddess of love, whose image was influenced by that of the Carthaginian goddess Astarte.

Classical Posidonia was at a crossroads, but in the late fifth century descendants of the original Greek settlers lost control of their city to their Italian neighbours the Lucanians, who named the place, in their own language, Paestum. The fullest description of this event survives in the work of Strabo, a Greek from Amasia on the Black Sea, who wrote a *Geography* in the first quarter of the first century AD. Describing southern Italy, he depends on Timaeus, an early third-century BC historian from Sicily, who reported that, after the Trojan War, Greek settlers had taken over much of Italy and Sicily. In his time, however, he says, all these cities, excepting only Naples, Reggio and Tarentum (modern Taranto), had become 'utterly un-Greek'. They were occupied by Italic peoples – Campanians, Lucanians and Bruttians. Strabo, now speaking for himself, goes on to say that the places held by the Campanians were Roman 'since they [the Campanians] became Romans' (Strabo, *Geography* 6.1).

The significance of this statement for understanding the creation of Roman Italy is hard to overstate: it was still possible to recall the different peoples in Italy and their individual histories, even though by Strabo's time they had all been Roman citizens for more than a century. For Strabo, legal citizenship and cultural identity were not the same thing. Just as people will identify now as Scottish as well as British, people in Roman Italy could identify as Campanian *and* Roman. Their histories were in their names, their foods, their accents, their habits.

The ruins of Paestum reveal to us how Strabo came to his understanding of Magna Graecia, or 'Great Greece' as southern Italy had come to be known. In 273 BC Rome had taken control there, founding a Latin colony. Romans had been moving into the area for a while, and the number of newcomers arriving at this point would have been substantial. The colony was rapidly becoming a focal point for the integration of the community into the Roman state, as Lucanian families rose to positions of local leadership.

The link between Latin Paestum and old Posidonia is evident in the city's street plan, which preserves its public space between the two great temples to the south and Athena's on the north side; and in the preservation of the *agora* (the Greek market and public meeting place) along with the new Roman-style forum – also a market place and administrative centre. A temple on the forum's north side provided a focus for the worship of the Roman trinity – Jupiter, Juno and Minerva – but it pales, even today, in comparison with the great temples of the Posidonian past. The old council house, perhaps used in the 270s–260s BC as a debating hall, was also maintained, along with a new Roman one.

The Latin colony had probably been located at Paestum because the

Roman state was interested in gaining a harbour to the south of Campania. Paestan ships show up in later Roman narratives, and it is quite likely that the region played a major role in the conflict with Carthage. With the war's end, peace came to south central Italy and, significantly, the cities that had been bankrolling the war in Sicily now stopped issuing coins. Suddenly the demand shifted to the cities of north central Italy, an area that had never produced a significant coinage. These places minted heavily for the next twenty years, clearly demonstrating the shift of Rome's attention away from the south towards the Po valley – the land inhabited largely by Celts and a prime breeding ground for the mercenaries who had made up a large part of the Carthaginian army in Sicily. The fact that Rome itself still did not produce a significant coinage illustrates the symbiotic aspect of Roman warfare in Italy.

The First Punic War had interrupted developments on Italy's east coast stemming from the final campaigns against Rome's Italian rivals a few decades before Appius Claudius crossed the strait of Messina. In the years after the decisive battle at Sentinum (295 BC), which stabilised Roman control of central Italy, three colonies were established on the Adriatic coast. One, Sena Gallica (Senigalia), has become better known through excavations revealing a site with a substantial history before the arrival of the Roman colonists in either 290 or 284/3 BC. A major building from the first phase of the site suffered violent destruction before the end of the fourth century BC, which may explain why the Romans appear to have constructed a city on a new plan whereas at Paestum they had simply moved into the existing site. The other colonies were at Castrum Novum (modern Guilianova) and at Hadria (modern Adria), both of which had substantial prior histories and rather successful economies – amphorae made from the local clay were much in demand in the Aegean world.

The Adriatic colonies, like Paestum and the important *colonia* at Fregellae, implanted on the border of Samnite lands in the late fourth century, were places where the Romans had come not so much as occupiers but as allies. The cities offered Roman protection to the surrounding communities; they symbolised Rome's willingness to be drawn into local disputes and to stand by those who had shown good faith. This was something even remembered by Strabo in the first century, who tells us that the people of the region had engaged in their own wars with the Gauls before joining with Rome.

If the Adriatic colonies were founded as protection, the same could not be said of a much larger colony, founded in 268 BC: Ariminum (modern Rimini), just south of the river Rubicon, which marked the notional boundary between the Gallic lands to the north and the Umbrian lands to the south. Ariminum had about 6,000 settlers and the cults they brought with them tell interesting stories. The gods who featured most prominently here were not those of Paestum, or any of the Roman trinity. The main cults at Ariminum, as in other northern *coloniae* such as Cosa (near modern Ansedonia in Tuscany) and Alba Fucens (near modern Avezzano in the Abruzzo), were Apollo and Hercules.

Hercules had long been popular in northern Italy: it was believed he had visited the site of Rome before Aeneas ever set foot there. He had also dismembered a brigand and established an altar in Rome's Forum Boarium. The Fabian clan had a strong interest in north central Italy, and were connected with the cult of the *ara maxima*, as Hercules' altar was known.

The worship of Hercules was not simply to be associated with any particular Roman family or even, more generally, with Rome. The god was far more widely cultivated. Hercules had been very good at dealing with barbarians and defending civilisation against outside threats. He was an excellent god to have around, for instance, if you were concerned about the Gauls. So was Apollo. As the Pyrrhic war was raging in Italy in the late 270s BC, a band of Gauls had invaded Greece. One group ended up in what is now central Turkey (the modern Turkish capital of Ankara originates from one of their settlements). Another had tried to loot the great shrine at Delphi, where Apollo gave oracles. He had, so the story went, driven the Gauls back, albeit with human assistance.

The cults of Hercules and Apollo mirror an important aspect of the developing soft power of cultural discourse. Earlier Roman coins linked images of Romulus with Hercules as a way of expressing Rome's connection with Italy's broader cultural history (see p. 6). In addition to these coins, numerous bronze mirrors – a few from Latium, but mostly from Etruria and Praeneste – show us how Greek stories had generally become part of the cultural currency. On some there are images of myths that originated in the Greek world, sometimes with captions revealing the way these stories had been domesticated in central Italy. Heroes appear with members of the Italian pantheon, or demons from the underworld, depicting versions of a tale that are not necessarily the same as they might be in a Greek context. Many other mirrors depict a nude winged female, known as a Lasa, who served Turan, the goddess of love. Others show two young men, usually armed, who are the divine twins, Castor and Pollux, the 'Discouroi' (or 'Divine Boys') in Greek. These two were the brothers of Helen of Troy, of whom one, Pollux, had been fathered by Jupiter, who had assumed the form of a swan in order to impregnate his mother Leda. The other, Castor, was the son of Tyndareus, who was also Helen's father. At Pollux's request they shared his immortality, spending half the year in heaven and the other half on earth. Their importance to Rome is attested by the prominent location of their temple in the heart of the forum. They came to symbolise self-sacrifice, success in war and the bonds that hold people together.

Mirrors and cults, along with various allusions to Rome's history during the First Punic War, reflect a reasonably well-developed cultural world with a well-established tendency to domesticate foreign ideas. Later Romans would, however, see the years after the end of the Carthaginian war as a first flowering of a sophisticated Latin literature that drew inspiration from the Greek world. This was not because there had previously been a cultural void, but rather because they now developed the practice of making archival copies of texts – another practice adapted from the Greek world, where it had just become established as a feature of being an important place. Prior to the fourth century BC, Athens had been by far the most active place when it came to preserving its literary record. Now great royal capitals of the eastern Mediterranean – most famously, Pergamon and Alexandria – established pre-eminent libraries. Keeping a record of what was being produced would now become something that Romans felt they, too, should do, especially if it was something that had been produced for public consumption.

For later Romans the crucial figure was Livius Andronicus, allegedly brought to Rome as a young slave from Tarentum in 272 BC, then freed. In 240 BC the aediles, one of whose duties was to oversee the Roman games (*ludi Romani*), asked Livius to compose both a tragedy and a comedy for the event. He did so, and was remembered as the first person to compose in both genres for the same occasion; he seems to have acted in them, too. Livius also produced a Latin translation of Homer's *Odyssey*, probably inspired by the fact that in contemporary thought Odysseus' wanderings had taken place around Sicily and Italy. People believed, for example, that the Roman colony of Circeii (modern Monte Circeo) was founded on the spot where once had lived the great witch Circe, who turned men into swine (there are some bronze mirrors that survive showing a local adaption of this tale).

None of Livius' works have survived; what we know of his achievements comes chiefly through quotations from later authors, but it appears that he drew heavily – as the visual evidence indicates had been done for some time – on Greek mythology for his plays' themes, and on contemporary Greek comedies, which were a bit like modern sit-coms with stock characters and predictable plot lines.

Livius' success was later seen as a watershed event. Little that was written before Livius survived for later Romans. Marcus Tullius Cicero, the politician and all-around man of letters whom we will be meeting in much more detail towards the middle of this book, produced an invaluable history of Latin oratory recalling that the speech Appius Claudius (father of the consul of 264 BC) delivered on the theme of not making peace with Pyrrhus had survived, as had one of Appius' henchmen's deeply controversial work on the Roman calendar. There were vague memories of heroic songs, none recorded for posterity; but records were kept by individual priests, especially by the augurs, to help them interpret the signs offered by the gods. As a result, later generations were able to find out what the signs had foretold before the battle of the river Allia in 387 BC. This was useful, since that disaster opened the door for the brief Gallic occupation of Rome a few days later. It is also likely that there had been plays on Roman themes that had increased people's sense of their own past.

The earliest plays on Roman themes that survived long enough for later writers to quote a few lines from them were the work, not of Livius, but of his contemporary Naevius. Naevius was from Campania, and the bulk of his oeuvre consisted of plays on both tragic and comic themes. His most memorable work, however, was a poem in seven books about the war with Carthage. Using, as did Livius, the traditional Saturnian metre for Latin verse, he mimicked the style of contemporary Greek poets to add depth to his story, including a long flashback telling how Aeneas came from Troy and the story of Romulus' birth. What, sadly, we cannot know for certain is whether he also included the story of Aeneas meeting Dido, Carthage's legendary founder. We do know that he mentioned the prophetic Sibyl, whom he placed near the bay of Naples.

That a new literature based on ostensibly foreign literary forms should germinate in a successful imperial state would seem strange, on the face of it. And if Greek had been truly foreign to Italy, strange would not be too strong a word. But foreign it was not. The use of Greek myth for diplomatic purposes as well as on coins, and a taste for Greek forms generally throughout Italy from the sixth century BC onwards, reveal that Italian culture was already based on a fusion of indigenous and imported artistic elements. What would be much harder to imagine in light of what we can see on the ground would be a Latin literature that did *not* have a strong element of Greek borrowing. The events of the 240s BC represented not a great cultural shift, but rather, a new facet to an ongoing process. Rome had become the Italian capital rather than merely a regional centre, the chief city of Latium.

Almost immediately after the war with Carthage ended, there had been a significant change in the structure of Roman politics, facilitated by a change in the organisation of the *comitia centuriata* in 241 BC. This reform folded the eighteen centuries of 'cavalry with a public horse', who had previously voted before everyone else, into the first class and aligned the first class's other seventy centuries with the thirty-five tribes so that there were now thirty-five centuries of 'juniors' (men up to the age of forty-six) and thirty-five centuries of 'seniors' (those over forty-six). The same division was also imposed on the other four census classes so that the one hundred centuries in the second to fifth classes were divided into fifty centuries each of 'juniors' and 'seniors' (the four centuries of artisans and the *proletarii* were left as they were). The mortality rate in the ancient world was such that most people did not survive their early fifties if they even lived that long, meaning that the 'senior' centuries would be much smaller than the 'juniors'. Given that it was a fundamental tenet of ancient thought that older people were wiser than young people (which pretty much meant 'more conservative'), this reform appears to have been aimed at loading the electoral deck in favour of traditionalist politics and preventing a radical interest group from securing a series of elections to the consulship, as arguably had happened at the beginning of the war with Carthage.

If the intention of the electoral reform was to calm things down and strengthen the traditional aristocracy, it worked. Newer families, with some exceptions, now found that the old nobility was closing ranks around the state's chief magistracies. Only thirty-nine men held consulships – of whom seven held office twice – between 240 BC and 219 BC, the year it became clear that Spain's Carthaginian state had become a menace to

Rome. Fourteen of these individuals were the sons of consuls, and seven more had a recent consular relative; the twenty-two patricians among them came from only nine families and, even more striking, seventeen came from the six 'major clans'. Only five men without consular ancestors would reach the consulship during this period.

The collection of Roman blue bloods who dominated the polls for the five years after 240 BC did remarkably little. Except for the annexation of Corsica and Sardinia, no records of significant military action survive. Even the wars in Sardinia and Liguria, the area of north-western Italy around modern Genoa, scored badly – the only triumph took place in 236 BC. In 235 BC the consul Titus Manlius Torquatus celebrated his own triumph over the Sardinians, and, in a gesture that proclaimed peace on earth, joined his consular colleague Gaius Atilius Bulbus in closing the doors to the shrine of the god Janus. The peace was rather short-lived, and the next few years involved yet more conflict, including a Ligurian campaign in 233 BC headed by the consul Quintus Fabius Maximus Verrucosus, who vowed a temple to Honos (Honour) just outside the Porta Capena, on Rome's southern boundary.

Nearly two decades later Fabius Maximus would be celebrated as the saviour of Rome for the leadership he provided in the next great war against Carthage that would start in 218 BC. Now, however, his term in office coincided with the beginning of the tribunate of Gaius Flaminius, who passed a bill – against, according to Polybius, strong senatorial opposition – providing for the division of land north of Ariminum in the Po valley for settlement by Roman citizens. The negative tone of Polybius' story about the *lex Flaminia* may have been shaped by the unfortunate fact that Flaminius was responsible for a major disaster during the Second Punic War. In actuality, significant pressure must have been building up for new settlement in the north; otherwise, he could never have passed the bill. That land distribution was directly involved with the expansion of Roman power; rather than a revolutionary act, the *lex Flaminia* is intimately associated with the way Romans conceived the exercise of state power.

The crucial document, a law enabling us to understand how public land – *ager publicus* – was defined in Roman Italy, was composed in 111 BC, some 130 years after the passage of the *lex Flaminia*. The purpose of this later law was to end a period of massive change in land distribution. The law is mostly concerned with actions taken under tribunician laws of 133

BC and 123 BC, but there are significant references to aspects of the administration of public land that go back a good deal further. These include
the division of land between what was good for pasturage and what was
good for other kinds of farming, and the public status of all the land along
Roman roads throughout Italy. On the administrative side, it is notable
that there was no central administration, beyond that implicit in the
power of the censors, governing the land even though this land established
a formal presence for the Roman state throughout the peninsula. What
was done with the land was the result of gradual negotiation between
Rome and the states from which it had been taken.

The acquisition of new *ager publicus* was also a feature of the Romans'
overseas expansion. When they ultimately destroyed Carthage in 146 BC,
ending the Third Punic War, land that had once belonged to that city had
been taken over by Rome, even though there was no direct Roman administration in North Africa at the time. From the law of III BC we might well
infer that there were similar arrangements in Sicily, Sardinia and Corsica,
stemming from *deditiones* made by communities in those regions. So ines-
sential were magistrates to the administration of these territories that no
new posts were created after the annexations of Sicily and Sardinia. It was
only after 228 BC, possibly because both consuls had been overseas the year
before, that two new praetors were elected, expanding the number from
two to four. By that time even more public land had been acquired – in
the area known during Antiquity as Illyria (Croatia, Bosnia, Montenegro
and Albania, today).

Given that the expansion of Roman power virtually coincided with the
acquisition of public land, Flaminius' dealing-out of the land along the Po
is pretty much in line with the way the Roman state had traditionally acted,
and Polybius' blaming him for what would be a major war in Italy might
not have been wholly fair, especially as that war broke out seven years after
the *lex Flaminia*. That the distributions were made to individuals suggests
the areas in which they were settling were thought to be protected against
alien incursion; furthermore, there were two Gallic tribes in the eastern Po
valley, the Cenomani and the Heneti, that were allied with Rome against
their powerful neighbours in the west, the Senones and the Boii.

The Roman settlers were probably occupying lands that Rome had
acquired at the time it founded Sena Gallica and Ariminum, while the
avoidance of any new colonial settlement could reveal a desire not to
provoke the western tribes. If Polybius had examined the matter more

closely, he might have noted that land distributions did not just happen of their own accord. Since the Senate would have had to appoint a commission to deal with the actual distributions, one way to torpedo a bill it disliked was to foul up the appointment of commissioners, who tended to be senior senators requiring funds so as to do their jobs. The consuls of 232 BC, who would have taken the lead in making these appointments, cannot have been hostile to the enterprise.

Before there would be any Gallic war, there would be a war in Illyria. Polybius sees this conflict as entirely provoked by a couple of failed states. One was the piratical realm of Illyria, ruled first by Agron, then by his ill-tempered wife Teuta, who assumed the regency for his child – by another woman – when he died in 231 BC. The other was Epirus. The Epirotes had employed Gallic mercenaries whom the Romans had sent home, after they had wreaked mayhem in Sicily, to garrison the city of Phoenice. In 230 BC these Gauls handed Phoenice over to an Illyrian pirate fleet. Having failed to recover the city, the Epirotes had called upon the services of the Aetolian and Achaean Leagues (the two main powers in western Greece, who were usually at odds with each other). Their forces drove the Illyrians out from Phoenice, at which point the Epirotes betrayed the two leagues, making a new alliance with the Illyrians that allowed them to raid more easily to the south.

This turned out to be a bad idea. Italian merchants suffered and complained to Rome, whereupon Rome reacted by sending envoys to Teuta. Polybius says that Teuta found the Roman ambassadors deeply offensive and ordered for them to be murdered. The next year, a gigantic Roman fleet showed up in Illyrian waters, accompanied by a somewhat mysteriously separate army, which took a number of *deditiones*, chased Teuta into the hinterland and installed one of her treacherous subordinates, Demetrius of Pharos, in her place.

Polybius claims this Roman intervention was an epochal event brought on by the folly of people who had no idea what it would be like to encounter a Roman army. The problem with his story is that in most of its details it is probably wrong. He writes on the basis of Greek sources that showed a limited grasp of Roman institutions, and he was writing for a Greek audience, so it was not in his interest to change a well-known story in favour of one that depended upon actual facts. In Polybius' view it was the Greeks who got themselves into trouble rather than the Romans who started it.

A more likely explanation is that the Greek city of Issa, presumably well informed about how to manipulate the Roman Senate, offered to make a *deditio in fidem*. But the Roman ambassadors sent to explore the issue were intercepted by Illyrian pirates and murdered, along with an Issan counterpart. Rome did not take kindly to the murder of its ambassadors, so dispatched both consuls the next year to deal with the pirates. At this point the two stories come together: the Romans received a number of *deditiones* and went home, leaving Demetrius of Pharos in a position of influence.

With *deditiones* came even more *ager publicus*. One of the rare surviving contemporary documents from this region records the existence of public land on the island of Pharos after the Roman intervention. The key point that this text reveals is that, as Polybius and our other source, the second-century AD writer Appian of Alexandria, imply, the Romans were simply settling the Illyrian situation in the way they would have dealt with a similar situation in Italy.

Roman interventions could be exceptionally brutal. It was not unknown for Roman generals to order the killing of every living thing in a town that was being stormed. Hence the need, after the exercise of hard power, to project soft power. Here Polybius helpfully informs us that Rome sent embassies to many states in the Greek world explaining its actions. These embassies were well received by and large, and in 228 BC Roman participants were accepted as honorary Greeks to compete in a major athletic festival. Thus 'Flat Foot' (Plautus) won the main running race at the Isthmian Games, held near Corinth, in that year.

We have evidence of Roman efforts to introduce themselves elsewhere, specifically in a text from Chios, a Greek island off the coast of modern Turkey. The people of Chios thanked a local man for putting up pictures illustrating Rome's martial excellence and attributing that excellence to the fact that the Romans were descended from the war god – something that had been slowly dawning on the peoples of the eastern Mediterranean. In the wake of Pyrrhus' defeat, a truly appalling poet called Lycophron wrote a mini-epic that he claimed to be the revelations of the Trojan princess Cassandra who, having witnessed her brother Paris heading off to snatch Helen of Troy and bring ruination upon their city, foresaw that the descendants of Aeneas (that is, the Romans) would become powerful in war.

Much, if not all, of what Lycophron has to say about Italy (which is actually quite a bit) is probably based on the same history by the Sicilian Timaeus that Strabo would later use. That probably reflects the fact that people in the eastern Mediterranean had started to become a bit more interested in Italy even before the Romans started crossing the Adriatic and were looking for what passed for the best available book on the topic.

The years after the return of the expedition to Illyria were reasonably peaceful. No triumphs are recorded, which suggests that there were no large-scale military operations. But discontent was building, and in 225 BC the Gallic tribes of the western Po valley, the Taurisci, the Boii, the Insubres and the Gaesatae, decided to invade Italy. Given that Polybius' explanation for this uprising – as the consequences of the *lex Flaminia* – is plainly inadequate, it is unfortunate that we know nothing about the internal politics of the tribes themselves, or about their kings Aneroëstes and Concolitanus. The one certainty – and this conclusion can be drawn from the thoroughly inadequate Roman response to the invasion – is that the initiative lay with the Gauls.

Indeed, the military dispositions for the year suggest that Rome was poorly informed as to Gallic intentions. One consul, Gaius Atilius Regulus, was sent to Sardinia at the beginning of the campaigning season, while his co-consul, Lucius Aemilius Papus, was sent to Ariminum on the Adriatic. Since the Gauls came down from the western end of the Po valley through the Apennines, neither was in the right place, and the enemy advanced as far as Clusium (modern Chiusi), a mere ninety miles from Rome, before an army commanded by one of the praetors caught up with them. The Gauls defeated this force but then decided that, since by now they had enough plunder, they might as well go home.

Aemilius Papus caught up with the Gallic army around Faesulae after it had turned for home, while Regulus arrived at Pisa soon afterwards. Then the two Roman armies trapped the Gauls in a pincer movement at Telamon, in Etruria. The outcome was a massive Roman victory.

For the next three years, both consular armies campaigned in the Po valley. One of the consuls for 223 BC was none other than Flaminius, who had also been praetor in 227 BC, which suggests that most Romans, possibly even most senators, found him acceptable. In 222 BC, refusing a plea for peace, the consuls once again marched into the Po valley, defeating a coalition including tribesmen from the Rhône valley. Then, after some tricky manoeuvring during which a Gallic army managed to slip in behind

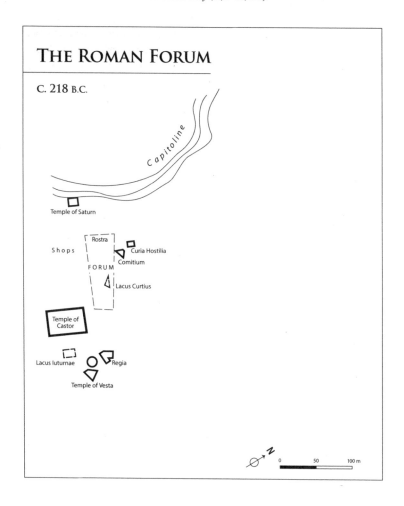

THE ROMAN FORUM

C. 218 B.C.

Capitoline

Temple of Saturn

Rostra

Shops

Curia Hostilia

FORUM

Comitium

Lacus Curtius

Temple of Castor

Lacus Iuturnae

Regia

Temple of Vesta

N

0   50   100 m

them, the Romans advanced towards Mediolanum (Milan). One of the consuls for this year, Marcus Claudius Marcellus, killed the commander of the Gallic force opposing him, winning the *spolia opima*, the award for generals who killed their opposite number in single combat. He was, according to Roman memory, just the third man to do so. Since the first had been Romulus, who did not exist, we may reasonably suspect that the award was largely invented for Marcellus. He may also have inspired Naevius to write a play about the event; upon his return he dedicated a temple to Virtus (masculine virtue). In the wake of these victories, which brought active fighting to an end, Rome sent a golden bowl to Delphi (famously hostile to Gauls) and distributed plunder from the campaign to allied cities.

The campaigns of 225–2 BC are of immense importance, not merely because of what did not happen – Rome could have been sacked – but also because the Gauls were the aggressors. The Roman state had organised what was essentially a defensive war, in Italian territory, to protect its allies. The celebrations of 222 BC indicate both Rome's sense of the importance of its image as a foe of barbarism in the broader world (hence the dedication at Delphi) and the importance of the alliance system within Italy (hence the distribution of plunder). The campaigns displayed the positive value of Rome to its allies, which would not be forgotten in what would soon be Rome's darkest hours.

4

HANNIBAL

❧

J ust as the situation along the Po river was heating up, the Roman Senate
sent an embassy to meet with the recently elected leader of what was fast
emerging as a powerful state in Spain. Disinterest or, quite possibly, embarrassment on the part of later historians has buried the reasons for this Roman
mission. All we know is that its members struck a treaty with Hasdrubal,
son-in-law of the recently deceased Carthaginian general Hamilcar Barca,
by which the Romans agreed to have nothing to do with Spain south of the
Ebro river. In return, Hasdrubal agreed that he would not cross the Ebro
bearing arms. As his armies and allies were well south of the river, the treaty
may well have been something of a non-event. It was certainly one that had
no direct bearing on relations between Rome and Carthage.

Hamilcar's achievements in the decade after he left North Africa were
extraordinary. Before his arrival in Spain and his establishment of a new
capital for himself at Acra Leuke (near modern Alicante), the Carthaginian presence had been limited to a few trading posts linking Spanish
trade networks with others in North Africa. In no sense had there been a
Carthaginian empire in Spain. By the time Hamilcar was killed in battle,
probably in 229 BC, he had built up alliances across south-eastern Spain
and, significantly, in doing so had given Spanish chieftains a voice in the
direction of the new state. When Hasdrubal succeeded Hamilcar, he was
'proclaimed general by the people and the Carthaginians', we are told, and,
after avenging Hamilcar and marrying the daughter of a Spanish king, he
was declared 'supreme leader by all the Spaniards' (Diodorus, *Historical*

5. This coin, minted in Spain between 237 and 227 shows the god Melqart on the obverse (often identified with Hercules) and an African war elephant on the reverse. Some scholars think that Melqart's features suggest those of Hamilcar.

Library 25.12). He then paid a visit to Carthage to stabilise his relationship with the government there. Crucially, what Hamilcar had created was not a Carthaginian state in Spain, but rather a Spanish state run by Carthaginians.

Hasdrubal continued expanding his kingdom until his assassination in 221 BC, when he was succeeded by Hamilcar's son, Hannibal (born in 247 BC). Hasdrubal had founded several new cities, transferred the political centre of his realm to 'New Carthage' (modern Cartagena, south of Alicante), assembled a large elephant corps, and built a powerful army. And as his realm had not yet come close to the Ebro, there was no ostensible reason why hostilities should break out between his domain and the Roman Republic. But many would still have known Hamilcar's reason for moving to Spain in the first place – that is, to build a force that could fight Rome – and Hannibal had sworn that he would never abandon his father's hatred of the Romans.

The Rome that Hannibal would face was still very much the Rome that had entered the First Punic War. It was led by men who shared the value system of their ancestors, and whose views of international relations were conditioned by the terms of the fetial procedure and other central Italian customs. But that would all begin to change as a result of the bloody confrontation with Hannibal that was soon to be set in motion.

Roman codes of behaviour seem to have been well known outside of

Italy in the wake of the war with Carthage. The way that Rome was drawn into the politics of Illyria shows that the locals there had some idea of how to manipulate Roman tendencies, and the events of the two years after Hannibal took over from Hasdrubal show that this information was available to people living as far away as Spain. So it was that, as Hannibal secured his power, people in the city of Saguntum (now Sagunto) realised that they were in very big trouble indeed. And, unwilling to be incorporated into Hannibal's kingdom, they sent envoys to Rome offering to make a *deditio in fidem*.

The Senate responded with caution. Spain was conveniently distant, and before sending an army more than a thousand miles overland it made sense to evaluate the situation coolly and calmly.

An embassy comprising two senior senators was dispatched at the end of 220 BC to meet with Hannibal. The meeting was not a success. Hannibal had been brought up to believe that the Romans were utterly faithless, and the acceptance of the *deditio* by the rebellious mercenaries on Sardinia was proof positive of this. Polybius suggests that the Roman envoys were to Hannibal like a red rag to a bull, and there is no reason to disbelieve him. Their arrival would simply have confirmed to him the notion that if he did not move on Rome, and as soon as possible, the Romans would find an excuse to attack *him*.

Later historians would build the fate of Saguntum into a major issue. Seventy years after the fact, when senators were arguing the case for a war of blatant aggression, historians would assert that Carthage was perpetually treacherous and that the destruction of Saguntum had violated earlier treaties with Rome. Given that the Carthaginians had been so faithless in the past, went the argument, they must be so now, and it would be right to declare war in response to alleged attacks on Rome's allies in North Africa.

In hindsight, Polybius' view that the Romans should have declared war on Carthage when they realised what was happening in Spain, thereby forestalling the invasion of Italy, makes sense. But such a decision would not have been in keeping with the Roman belief that war could be declared only if the other side could be shown, before the gods, to have violated an existing agreement. There was no majority in the Senate willing to provoke Hannibal by accepting the Saguntine *deditio* and, unless it was accepted, there was no just cause for war. Acceptance might also appear to be an act of bad faith, as there was no way that Rome could provide any sort of adequate defence of the place.

Very different from the situation in Spain was that east of the Adriatic. There, a problem had arisen that the Romans, operating in accordance with their traditional moral compass, could understand. One upshot of the expedition of 229 BC was that, thanks to his timely betrayal of Teuta, Demetrius of Pharos had acquired a great deal of authority. In the next few years he entered the ambit of the kings of Macedon: first Antigonus Doson, who died in 221 BC; and then Philip V, who succeeded Antigonus at the age of sixteen. Philip immediately became embroiled in a war 'against the allies' – Sparta, Elis and the Aetolian League. In the summer of 220 BC Demetrius took a fleet, in support of Philip, well south of the line established by the Romans as permissible for an Illyrian.

Rome's allies were not forbidden to have other allegiances. To be Rome's ally did, however, mean that the interests of those other allies could never supplant the interests of Rome. By aiding Philip, Demetrius broke this golden rule; furthermore, he may have raided territories that had made *deditiones* to Rome in 229 BC. As far as the Senate was concerned, these were transgressions that could not go unpunished. Even while Hannibal laid siege, then waste, to Saguntum during the summer of 219 BC, a Roman army showed up in Illyria. Demetrius fled into exile. And Philip may have come away with the impression that to be in true control he might have to find a way of cutting the Romans down to size. This is certainly what he would attempt, a couple of years later, to the ruin of his kingdom.

Back in Spain, Hannibal was gathering his forces with a view to invading Italy. Years later, on leaving Italy to return to Spain, he erected a column spelling out his dispositions outside the modern Calabrian city of Crotone. He sent about 16,000 men to defend North Africa – and, quite possibly, his own standing in Carthage – leaving about 14,000 under the command of his younger brother Hasdrubal, to defend Spain.

Hannibal arrived in Italy at the head of an army of 20,000 infantry and 6,000 cavalry. Given their intense loyalty to him over the years, it is likely that most of those who had begun the trek saw it through to the end, their five-month ordeal culminating in a fifteen-day crossing of the Alps. Polybius' declaration that Hannibal had left Spain at the head of more than 100,000 men can be traced to a historian who could not resist exaggerating. Given difficulties in procuring supplies, functional ancient armies rarely exceeded 50,000 – the size of Alexander's when he invaded Persia – and would more commonly number around the 20,000 that made up a standard consular army at this period. Typically, Rome would have expected to put two such armies into the field, roughly half of which were made up of Roman citizens; as in 225 BC, there might also have been a third army commanded by a praetor. Given the number of men that he brought into Italy and the likelihood of some losses along the way, it is a reasonable assumption that Hannibal left Spain with around 30,000 men.

In describing the strength of Roman Italy in 225 BC, the contemporary Roman historian Fabius Pictor had provided a list of Roman Italy's manpower resources, setting the number of men eligible for military service at around 800,000. This is not a totally implausible figure, but it must be stressed that in any given year Rome could not hope to field more than a fraction of that number. When, over the next few years, it would enlist up to 100,000 a year, the resources of the state would be stretched to their limits.

The size of Hannibal's army offers an important clue to what he was planning to do and how he expected to succeed. Arriving in Italy during the autumn of 218 BC, he immediately began recruiting Gauls from among the tribes still smarting from the defeats of a few years before. These were people who could be counted on to harbour hostility towards Rome. According to the text of a treaty he struck with Philip V after his victories in 217 BC, Hannibal never expected to destroy Rome. Rather, he intended to make it too weak to continue playing a dominant role in Italian politics, and to deprive it of its allies. On paper this was not an implausible plan, but the reality would prove to be far more complicated than Hannibal had imagined.

Although his plan proved impractical, Hannibal was well prepared for the coming war. He had studied the tactics of the great generals of the past, he understood logistics, he had a sound knowledge of the way Roman aristocrats approached the world, and he was conscious of the need to control the recording of events. Alexander had taken his own historian with him for the campaign against Persia, and Hannibal, too, equipped himself with a couple – Sosylus and Craterus, Greeks both, whose works would be composed in Greek (still the lingua franca of the Italian peninsula). It is probably to them that we owe details of the campaign, such as the inflated numbers at the start, the clever stratagem Hannibal devised to transport elephants across the Rhône, and the miraculous crossing of the Alps. Sosylus embellished his account with an imagined meeting of the Senate at which war was solemnly debated and declared.

After Saguntum's destruction Roman envoys were dispatched to

Carthage to demand that something be done about Hannibal, who by that time would have ensured that most of the troops around Carthage had come fresh from Spain. The story of the leading Roman ambassador telling the Carthaginian senate that he carried peace and war in the folds of his toga is certainly a later fantasy, perhaps influenced by – or influencing – the appallingly rude conduct of a Roman ambassador to a Greek king in 167 BC (see p. 99). By that time Roman dealings with other states had taken on a brutal frankness. This time around they were told to go away.

It is Fabius Pictor who tells us what really happened. Rome did nothing, aside from send ambassadors, until Hannibal crossed the Ebro. It was only then that the Senate voted that the treaty had been broken.

How quickly did Hannibal reach Italy? We are told it took him five months to travel from the Ebro to the Alps, and then a further fifteen days to cross the mountains – so not an especially speedy journey, but fast enough to catch the Romans off guard. Hannibal would have known that the consuls for 218 BC, Publius Cornelius Scipio and Tiberius Sempronius Longus, had not been able to start levying troops until they took office on 15 March, and even then they might not have been certain that it would be necessary. The fact that two large *coloniae*, planned the previous year, were sent out to Placentia and Cremona in the spring may suggest that there was greater senatorial interest in the Gauls and the Po valley than in Spain.

The boards assigned to the settlement project included several senior officials who, predictably, alienated the Boii, who then attacked the colonists. The fact that the consuls were not assigned Gaul as a *provincia* suggests that Polybius and Livy are correct in stating that the Boii attacked the colonists only after it became known that Hannibal was on the march. This may also suggest that the consuls were not assigned *provinciae* until the Romans were satisfied that they knew what Hannibal was up to (although a praetor and some legions had been sent into the Po valley). None of this indicates that there was a clear plan of action when the consuls took office. Nor is it easy to see how a newly enacted law limiting the size of ships that senators could own fits into the picture. But it may have been to do with contracting for military supplies, ensuring the work would be spread outside the senatorial order. If so, perhaps it was simply a measure intended to build solidarity behind a war effort.

Once it was clear that Hannibal was on the move, the consuls positioned themselves to resist him, hastily changing plans as they did so.

Scipio had been assigned Spain, while Longus was told to invade Africa. When, having sailed from Pisa, Scipio discovered that he had missed Hannibal at the Rhône by three days, he turned swiftly around to defend the Po valley and sent his brother ahead to Spain with part of the army. Longus abandoned the African plan, to make his way north at high speed. He reached Ariminum by early October.

Almost immediately, Hannibal's passage of the Alps became the stuff of legend. Polybius complains that Sosylus and Craterus had divine beings show up to lead the way. Later historians confused things by inventing obstacles of all sorts. What we actually know, however, is less dramatic. He was welcomed by Gallic tribes still bitter from their defeats in previous years and the new colonies. It is unlikely that the first they heard of Hannibal was when he appeared on their doorsteps: Polybius says messengers had inspired the earlier attack on the colonists. Hannibal would have then taken either the St Genève or the Mont Cenis pass over the Alps. He ended up at the city of the Taurini, most likely near modern Turin.

Scipio was outnumbered and, while waiting for Longus to arrive, he tried to shield Placentia, near the juncture of the rivers Ticinus, which flows south from the Swiss Alps, and Trebbia, which rises in the Ligurian Alps. A cavalry action ensued on the banks of the Ticinus, in which the Romans were badly beaten. Scipio was wounded and, in one account, was rescued by his 17-year-old son, also called Publius Cornelius Scipio (and who is the source for this story); others said it was a slave who saved the consul's life. The one incontrovertible point that emerges is that Roman aristocrats placed considerable stress on personal demonstrations of martial valour, no matter what their command responsibilities. As far as we know, Hannibal would engage in personal combat only a very few times, if at all, during this war.

After a difficult retreat marked by acts of treason on the part of his Gallic auxiliaries, Scipio reached the Trebbia and made camp. On arrival, Longus assumed operational control while Scipio convalesced. At this point there was no real hierarchical command structure on the Roman side, in that the two consuls had equal *imperium*; and neither of the praetors, Manlius and Atilius, appears to have been coordinating with them. Their *provincia* was 'fighting the Gauls', which they had been doing since the summer. The consuls could not give them orders. Hannibal, conversely, could expect that when *he* gave an order it would be obeyed, and this allowed him to make rather more elaborate battle plans than his rivals.

When Longus joined Scipio, the numbers on each side were relatively equal. Pressure was on Hannibal, who needed a big victory to convince the Gauls to remain enthusiastic in his cause, while losing as few as possible of the men he had brought from Spain. Towards the end of December, he got his chance. Encamping at some hours' distance from the Roman camp – west of the Trebbia and just south of the Po – he stationed a body of cavalry under the command of his younger brother Mago, to wait in ambush. He then provoked Longus – much of what Hannibal would accomplish derived from his ability to trigger the Roman commanders' aggression – to lead his army out of camp before breakfast on a cold wet day. The Romans marched for several hours and then, drenched from the chilly waters of the Trebbia, lined up to face Hannibal's main force which, warm and well fed, was waiting for them. When the two sides were fully engaged, Hannibal gave the signal for Mago to attack. The sudden appearance of the new troops to their rear shattered Roman morale, and the army fell apart. It is testimony to the extreme toughness of the average Roman soldier that some 10,000 of them managed to fight their way out of the trap and reach Placentia. They may well have left as many, or more, behind as casualties or prisoners. The rest of the army fell back to the original camp.

After Trebbia, Longus remained around Placentia with his surviving troops, while Scipio gathered his forces to join his brother, commanding the Roman fleet at Pisa, to begin the invasion of Spain. On 15 March two new consuls took office in Rome: Gnaeus Servilius Geminus and Gaius Flaminius. The campaigning season of 217 BC would ultimately decide the course of the war, though Hannibal may be forgiven if, in the glow of his success that spring, he missed the point.

Flaminius, the mover of the land bill in 235 BC and the successful commander in 223 BC, was a Hannibalic dream come true. Impulsive and aggressive, he took over the army that had served under the praetor Atilius Serranus in 218 BC and took up station at Arretium (today's Arezzo). Hannibal, meantime, privy to plenty of first-hand information about routes through Italy, released his non-Roman prisoners and planned a march along the river Arno into Umbria and Etruria, hoping to persuade Rome's central Italian allies that the Romans could not protect them. What he succeeded in doing was to convince these people that he was no different from their ancestral enemies from the Po valley. The fact that he supplied his now largely Gallic army by pillaging the countryside only served to consolidate their viewpoint.

Leaving aside later legends concerning the passel of ill omens that greeted Flaminius' rise to office, there was not actually all that much that he could do about Hannibal, who was well ahead of him and had a bigger army. Hannibal took his time, which is why, on 24 June 216 BC, Flaminius caught up with him near Lake Trasimene, the large stretch of volcanic water that lies between Cortino to the north and Perugia to the south. Hannibal may well have noted that Flaminius tended not to scout out his advance in detail, and so on that misty morning he drew up his army in ambush above the lakeside path that he suspected Flaminius would take. And Flaminius did indeed take that path, leading his army into the ambush, from which neither he nor all but a few of his men would emerge. Roman losses were about 10,000 dead and 10,000 captured – a defeat more total than any the Romans had ever previously sustained. Another state might well have done what Hannibal expected them to do: negotiate.

But instead of negotiating, the Romans elected a dictator, Fabius Maximus. The election was a variation on standard procedure, which required that a consul appoint a dictator: such appointments had been relatively common in the fourth century BC, when there was a shortage of magistrates, then later was largely limited to solving short-term domestic needs. Once in place, Fabius recognised that he had to do two things. First, avoid losing another Roman army. Second, get Hannibal out of central Italy as fast as he could. His strategy was very similar to that of the Athenian politician Pericles, as described by Thucydides, in the Peloponnesian War: to take no risks and 'win through in the end'. It would not be surprising if Fabius had read Thucydides, for the style of warfare he was about to undertake was as un-Roman, and ultimately as unwelcome, as could be imagined.

Before Fabius' plan was finally accepted, there was considerable debate and discontent. His own lieutenant, Minucius Rufus, complained about his dilatory habits, and Carthaginian depredations across Italy. Rufus was ultimately made co-dictator, but would be saved from a military disaster of his own only by Fabius' timely intervention.

Hannibal had at this point no answer for Fabius' strategy – with the Romans cutting off his raiding parties he could not adequately supply his army, who were living off the land they passed through from one day to the next. He kept away from the heart of Roman Italy, recrossing the

Apennines into the Picenum region and making his way south. Although he would find allies and his greatest military success in the south, Hannibal was cut off from the Po valley, and had to leave the crucial central region of Latium to Rome. Latium, and Etruria, would provide the wealth and manpower that would enable Rome to win through. That, however, would only come after another spectacular Roman disaster.

The Roman people had tired of Fabius' tactics. The two consuls elected for 216 BC, Gaius Terentius Varro and Lucius Aemilius Paullus, understood that their task was to bring Hannibal to battle and destroy him. They would come face to face in southern Italy, in Apulia, at a town called Cannae.

5

CANNAE (216 BC)

On 2 August 216 BC the combined armies of Terentius Varro and Aemilius Paullus confronted Hannibal's army on the banks of the Aufidus river (now the Ofanto) in south central Italy. Some weeks earlier Hannibal had seized the Roman supply depot at Cannae. The consuls had been dispatched from Rome and were now about to engage him in battle on the plain between the hill of Cannae and the river.

The orders from Rome and the decision to enrol double the number of citizens in the consular legions removed any strategic initiative from the consuls. Indeed, we may assume that their *provincia* now was simply defined as 'the war with Hannibal'. Aware that the consuls' forces could attack him at any time, Hannibal had found a battlefield that suited him perfectly. After two years in the field he knew that a Roman soldier stood, ideally, three feet from the men on either side, in front and behind him, which gave him the space he needed to use the sword that had become the basic killing instrument of the Roman army during the 220s BC. If the Roman soldiers were deprived of this vital space, they would rapidly lose the ability to defend themselves. This was exactly what the Carthaginians had in store for them.

On the day of the battle Hannibal probably had about 40,000 infantrymen and 10,000 cavalry. The Roman army numbered about 60,000 infantry and perhaps 6,000 cavalry. Hannibal intended to make full use of his superior horsepower, deployed on either wing of his army, while drawing the legions into a trap in the centre of his formation. There he had placed his Gallic soldiers in a convex line beyond the ranks of his

Spanish and African soldiers who were aligned on either side of them. He planned to draw the legions inwards towards the advanced Gallic line, forcing them to crowd together as they sought out their enemies. He knew that the Roman army was freshly raised, with new officers, and might not be able to maintain the level of discipline he could expect from his own men. He also thought – correctly – that the battle would open with an extended skirmish between the Roman light infantry (*velites*) and his own light troops. That would give more time for his cavalry to complete the rout of their Roman counterparts and surround the infantry. He may also have counted on the Roman commanding generals being so committed to the warrior ethos in which they had been raised that they would act more like small-unit commanders than generals.

Hannibal was right on all counts. The initial skirmishing took some time, and the Roman legionaries pressed in on the advanced line of Gauls, reducing the space available to their own front. 'The consequence was, as Hannibal had planned, the Romans straying too far in pursuit of the Gauls, they were caught between the two divisions of the enemy and were not able to keep their proper order' (Polybius 3.115.12). In the end, 'as the men on the outside were killed, huddled in a mass, they all died' (Polybius 3.116.10–11). Among the dead was not just Aemilius Paullus, the consul, but also the two consuls who had been in office at the end of 217 BC. Arguably, the men most responsible for leading the Roman army to disaster paid the appropriate price.

Varro survived the slaughter and led what was left of the Roman army – about 10,000 men – away from the battlefield. Although Varro was blamed in later tradition for what happened, his contemporaries did not see things that way. The Senate voted for a decree, thanking him for not despairing of the Republic, and ordered fresh armies to be raised. Meanwhile, Maharbal, one of Hannibal's generals, demanded to know why Hannibal did not march on Rome immediately, saying that he knew how to win battles but not how to use his victories. The situation was not that simple. Rome was a long way from Cannae, and Hannibal lacked any sort of equipment for laying siege to the city. What he needed, above all else, was for people in Italy to believe that he could guarantee their security. The treaty that he would soon strike with Philip V of Macedon indicates that he expected them to start showing up. This did not happen. Initially the only major place that defected was Arpi (near modern Foggia), a Greek foundation believed to have been founded by Diomedes.

Hannibal had begun negotiations with Philip after his victory at lake Trasimene and the resulting treaty reflects the situation that had been developing since Cannae. This referred to the Carthaginian allies in Italy – allies, it should be noted, not subjects – and to the expectation that Rome would come to the negotiating table. When, in Hannibal's words, 'the gods give victory to you and to us', he would negotiate in Philip's interest as well as his own, forcing the Romans to give up territory they had taken in Illyria (Polybius, *Histories* 7.9 and *SVA* 528). It is also clear that Hannibal, even at his moment of greatest glory, recognised that the war with Rome would have to end through a negotiated treaty.

Important as the treaty with Philip is as evidence of Hannibal's intentions, the defection of Arpi – previously an ally of Rome – is just as important in illustrating the potential problems that he faced in building his own system of alliances within Italy. Arpi brought with it into Hannibal's camp a small group of other cities that shared its interests in the region. Given that many other cities remained loyal to Rome, it is possible that the real reason for Arpi's new alliance was not so much joy at Hannibal's success as long-standing irritation with the success of its neighbours. Those who dominated Arpinate politics may have felt they were losing out under Roman control.

There were reasons why cities would have stayed with Rome. Hannibal had ravaged the region in 217 BC, not ordinarily a good way of winning hearts and minds; and even his willingness to free allied prisoners – he freed all those taken at Cannae without asking for ransom, as he did at Trebbia and Trasimene – did not endear him to the Italian population as a whole. Most places that remained steadfastly loyal to Rome were led by people with a vested interest in the status quo. For instance, at Canusium (Canosa), in whose territory Cannae lay, lived a woman named Busa, who provided aid to the survivors, most likely at the behest of the local governing group. The nearby cities of Luceria (now Lucera) and Venusia (now Venosa) also remained loyal, as did nearby Teanum Apulum (near San Paolo di Civitate).

While Hannibal looked to strengthen his position in the south, the Roman Senate went into emergency management mode. Since, to Roman minds, all success was ultimately the result of divine favour, a disaster such as Cannae must indicate the existence of a serious problem in Rome's standing before the gods. In no time at all, two Vestal Virgins (members of the college of seven priestesses who tended the sacred flame of Rome) were found to be non-virginal: one committed suicide, the other was brutally executed; and one of their seducers was flogged to death in prison. When the Sibylline Oracles were consulted as to how to apologise to the gods in order to expiate the sins of the Vestals, the gods were found to be interested in further human offerings. They demanded that a couple of Gauls and a couple of Greeks, in each case one woman and one man, be buried alive in the Forum Boarium. Then, after carrying out this rare human sacrifice, on the suggestion of Fabius Maximus, an embassy was sent to consult the oracle of Apollo at Delphi, who specialised in destroying the enemies of civilisation.

On a more mundane level, Marcus Claudius Marcellus – a friend of Fabius Maximus and praetor in command of the fleet at Ostia – was sent to relieve Varro of his command, and a dictator was appointed to hold a new levy of troops. Four citizen legions were enlisted, drawing in boys as young as seventeen, along with 8,000 slaves purchased by the state and then freed so that they could serve. An equal number of allies were called up; and later that year an additional 6,000 Romans, disqualified from citizenship for unpaid debts, were forgiven their sins (and their debts) if they joined the army. Finally, when Hannibal offered to ransom his Roman prisoners from Cannae, Rome refused to have anything to do with him. The refusal was both practical and ideological. Practically, it avoided funding Hannibal's war effort; ideologically, it illustrates the Roman tendency to blame disasters on divine displeasure, as they were already doing, and the failure of the rank and file. Rome would also refuse to employ Cannae's survivors in Italy.

Hannibal greeted the Roman response by murdering many of his prisoners and selling the rest into slavery.

As 216 BC became 215 BC, the immediate crisis passed. After a complex set of happenings, including the death of one consul in battle and the removal of another for religious reasons, Fabius Maximus was elected consul in a special election along with Tiberius Sempronius Gracchus. Fabius now began gradually to transform the Roman war effort. He would create a system of orderly command, managing the electoral cycle to make sure only men he could trust would command an army against Hannibal. It was through the systematic application of a political/military plan that Hannibal's genius would be thwarted.

The end of 216 BC marks not only an end to the first phase of the Second Punic War in Italy, but also a change in the primary source for our information about that war. Polybius' history is only partially preserved from this point onwards. Despite his faults – his tendency to view things through the lens of his political prejudices, his misogyny, his hatred of mercenaries, his interest in correcting eyewitness accounts in light of his assumptions about the way the world worked and his evident belief that he was the smartest human being that ever wrote history – Polybius did try to get things right and did read writings that were not the work of Romans. From 216 BC until 167 BC, our primary source will be Livy. Although for eastern affairs he would sometimes use Polybius' account (not always translated with great accuracy), Livy was primarily interested in what Romans had to say about their own history. What he reveals about that tradition is that it was largely the self-serving tool of the aristocracy. And he usually saw the collective wisdom of the aristocracy as correct.

In Livy's history, battles are often described with minimal eyewitness testimony, while the speeches are largely of his own composition. The speed with which Livy wrote – he filled 142 papyrus rolls in roughly fifty years – tells us that he engaged in minimal, if any, examination of contemporary documents. That said, his sources do occasionally preserve accurate accounts, or accounts whose factual core can be recovered from the rhetoric in which they are embedded. This is especially so with, for instance, the terms of treaties, basic administrative measures taken in Rome such as the numbers of legions raised each year or where they were deployed, and non-controversial domestic issues. These things all derive, ultimately, from documentary records, and it is from such parts of Livy's history that the story of the Second Punic War, where Polybius' narrative is no longer preserved, may most reasonably be reconstructed.

The pattern for the next few years of warfare was that the Romans would seek – successfully – to avoid being drawn into direct engagement with any force commanded by Hannibal himself, while Hannibal, in his quest to develop his alternative to Roman Italy, would rapidly lose all strategic initiative. As cities began to desert Rome it was up to him to defend them, but Rome's resources were simply too great for him to cover everywhere there was a Roman army. Before Cannae, there had been some 65,000 men under arms in the Roman alliance; the emergency measures taken after Cannae restored the numbers to around 58,000 by the end of the year. Between 215 BC and 211 BC there would be, on average, 75–80,000 men who were battle-ready.

Not all of Rome's soldiers would serve in Italy. The Scipios had taken about 10,000 men with them to Spain in 217 BC, and were busy building their own Spanish alliances to take on that of Hannibal's family. There was also trouble in Sicily. King Hieron of Syracuse, Rome's ally in the First Punic War, died at the beginning of 215 BC and his 17-year-old grandson Hieronymus took the throne. Heavily influenced by pro-Carthaginian advisers, he immediately opened negotiations with Hannibal, who, lacking a fleet and having better things to do, had nothing to offer him. The Syracusans then contacted the government of Carthage itself, which was more receptive, and now for the first time willing to act in support of the Italian war effort.

Hieronymus did not survive his first year on the throne. And after he was murdered, a couple of seriously pro-Carthaginian extremists took over, proclaimed a new, theoretically democratic constitution, then declared war on Rome. The Senate sent Marcus Claudius Marcellus at the head of an army of around 20,000 men to deal with Syracuse, to which Carthage offered no useful assistance. Marcellus captured the city, after a long siege, in 211 BC. He sacked it with exceptional brutality and was responsible for the collateral death of Syracuse's most famous resident, the mathematician Archimedes. It was the war's first unequivocal Roman victory.

The curious thing about the Syracusan revolt was that the government there never appears to have appealed for aid to Hannibal's ally, Philip V of Macedon. Roman diplomacy had gradually developed a coalition of Greek states to oppose Philip both on the mainland, in the Aegean and along the Adriatic coast, including the states of Elis, Sparta, Pergamum (in today's western Turkey) and Aetolia. Philip never managed to operate a fleet in the Adriatic, nor did he do anything effective for Hannibal. At the same time, the Romans showed a greater capacity than in the past to deal with people in ways that were not, strictly speaking, Roman.

The text of a treaty between Rome and the Aetolians, drawn up in 211 BC and partially preserved on an inscription, is one of the earliest documentary manifestations of this change in Rome's way of dealing with the world beyond Italy. The language of the *deditio* is completely missing; instead, the Romans agreed that if they should take any cities within a designated area of interest, they would hand them over to the Aetolians; if they should take places outside this area, then they, the Romans, could keep them; if they took cities within the region of common interest, then the Aetolians could have them; and the two signatories would enjoy joint control of places they took outside the designated area. Furthermore, the Romans would allow any of the cities taken in the designated zone to join the Aetolian League. Livy indicates that this zone included Corcyra and the region of Acarnania on the west coast of Greece (*SVA* 536).

By the time Rome struck its agreement with the Aetolians, Hannibal was watching his vision of a new Italy fall apart, piece by piece, city by city. This vision becomes clear in the agreements recorded between himself, Capua (Santa Maria Capua Vetere), Tarentum and Locris. Capua came first and, as the leading city in Campania, was by far the most important to join Hannibal during the war. The terms, agreed in the winter of 216 BC, were that no Carthaginian general or magistrate would have power over any citizen of Campania, that the Capuans would govern themselves under their own laws, and that the Carthaginians would give the Campanians 300 prisoners to exchange for 300 Campanian cavalrymen serving in Sicily (this never happened – the Campanian cavalry most likely served under Marcellus). In the case of Locris, Hannibal allowed the Locrians to live under their own laws, with the proviso that the two sides would aid each other in the war. In 212 BC Hannibal assured the Tarentines that they, too, could be self-governing, that they could have their own laws and control their own territory, and that they would not have to take in a Carthaginian garrison or pay tribute to Carthage.

Roman Italy was based on a series of independent treaties between Rome and other states, which were then enrolled on a list of places that agreed to provide troops to Rome (the *formula togatorum*), meaning that there was no independent league structure and, consequently, no way for individual states to unite to prevent Rome from doing whatever it wanted. Hannibal, by contrast, was offering a league in which the member states had collective rights, for instance, to determine the nature of their own constitutions and laws. This model was neither necessarily attractive nor relevant to Italian aristocrats, who owed their individual local standing to their relationships with the Roman state.

Hannibal was successful, however, wherever he found a deeply divided governing class, or one splintering under the impression that the Roman ship was sinking. In Capua, for example, he released cavalrymen who had been taken at Cannae, thereby opening a channel of communication between his camp and local leaders. Livy identifies a group of aristocrats who, he claims, were pandering to the common people by throwing off the Roman alliance preferred by most Campanian aristocrats, who had personal links with the Roman aristocracy. This reads like special pleading of the sort that we have already encountered regarding Flaminius' law of 232 BC, whereby an unpopular person was portrayed as a demagogue. In truth, the men dealing with Hannibal appear to have been loyal to Rome up until Cannae. Did they feel that Capua, the region's chief city, was sacrificing its interests to Rome's?

Locris was another city that very soon came over to Hannibal. Here it seems that the deciding factor was a split in the local governing class, possibly provoked by the presence of a Roman garrison. Many Locrians fled to Rhegium as soon as the city began to negotiate with Hannibal, and members of the garrison made their escape without local interference – although they were not so lucky later, when the Carthaginians caught up with them.

The situation at Tarentum was similar, with the added complexity that this city, like Capua, had a long history as a regional power. It, too, had a Roman garrison and a divided aristocracy – and, for Hannibal, it proved to be a big mistake. The garrison remained in the citadel, forcing him to leave a substantial body of men to lay siege to it. Also, the fact that Tarentum was on the opposite side of Italy from Capua compelled Hannibal to march back and forth across Italy to support his allies. As both places came under Roman siege and he could not be in two places at once, his allies were no longer safe and he was helpless in the face of strong Roman fortifications. He was not good at siege warfare – relatively small places like Nuceria (Nocera) and Casilinum (near Capua) resisted him far longer than might have been expected.

Poor preparation for siege warfare was a considerable technical drawback. What Hannibal failed to understand when trying to take advantage of local rivalries was that his allies also had their own rivals, and that their alliances with him would strengthen the Roman cause wherever the big cities were already competing for local influence. The obvious case was Naples, which remained steadfastly loyal to Rome and had been willing to take in a Roman garrison even at the time Capua rebelled, as had nearby Nola and Cumae. A Roman army, which Hannibal could not budge, was embedded outside Capua in 212 BC, then in front of Tarentum in 209 BC, which he likewise failed to eliminate.

6

Victory (201 bc)

In 211 BC the war in Italy turned decisively against the Carthaginians. In an effort to relieve the siege of Capua, Hannibal invaded the heart of Roman Italy, advancing rapidly up the route of the modern A1 autostrada, then encamping within three miles of Rome. It was spring and the annual levy was in full swing; unsurprisingly, there were plenty of willing hands to defend the city walls. When the consuls refused to be drawn into battle, Hannibal had to turn away. He had accomplished nothing.

One story that emerged was that he was especially annoyed to learn later that the land upon which he was encamped had been sold at auction while he was there. Also, having ravaged the lands behind him and lacking sufficient supplies, he had to withdraw eastwards through the modern province of Aquila, thus ending up further from Capua than he had been at the start of the campaign. When, two years later, Fabius Maximus took Tarentum, Hannibal found himself trapped in southern Italy. He had essentially become a nuisance factor, and would not be seriously engaged until he returned to defend Carthage in 202 BC. In the meantime, the main action had shifted to Spain.

As the crisis of Cannae passed, stresses both social and economic continued to surface within Rome, compelling the gradual modernisation of Roman institutions. In 214 BC, for instance, the censors had found the treasury considerably depleted, so members of the top three census classes were urged to come up with funds to pay for men to serve in the fleet. Members of the third class were expected to pay for a single man for six months, members of the second class for one man for a year, and senators for eight. Additionally, and again 'because of shortages in the treasury', the censors announced that they could not issue the usual contracts for the maintenance of temples and the supply of horses for the circus and other public events. Fortunately for the Roman state, the usual recipients of these contracts were willing to forgo payment until the end of the war. Furthermore, cavalrymen and unit commanders (centurions) waived their salaries, doubtless placing some significant social pressure on those inclined to take the money. Given that centurions were selected by the men with whom they served and that they tended not to be, as they would be later, of significant means, this was a genuine sacrifice.

There had been problems before this. In 216 BC the censors rounded up people associated with a quaestor of that year on the grounds that they had plotted to flee Italy in the wake of Cannae, and had ordered that they be reduced to the status of the poorest citizens and removed from their tribes. The same sanctions were imposed on the 2,000 men who were found to have evaded military service since the outbreak of the war; they were enlisted and sent to serve in Sicily with the survivors of Cannae. The level of public sympathy with these measures may have been less than Livy allows, as Metellus, the disgraced quaestor, was elected tribune in 215 BC (and henceforth made life miserable for the censors).

In 212 BC, faced with a shortage of young soldiers, the Senate reduced the minimum age for enlistment below seventeen, and set up two boards of three (triumvirs) to scour the area around the city for recruits. That year there was a massive scandal involving war contractors whose routine robbing of the state had been covered up by the Senate during 213 BC. In 210 BC, when faced with another shortfall in revenue, senators made up the deficit from their own resources, and the state took out loans from individuals, due to be repaid in three instalments over the next decade. It also leased out some of the land taken from Campania – the first time, apparently, that the Roman state tried to monetise *ager publicus*. At some point, possibly also in 210 BC, a law was passed limiting the amount of worked gold and silver senators could keep in their possession.

In 209 BC twelve Latin colonies informed the Senate that they could no longer furnish recruits; two years later maritime colonies – ordinarily responsible for contributing men for the fleet – refused to send men to participate in the year's land campaign, so slave 'volunteers' were recruited to form two legions. In 204 BC there may still have been difficulties, as

6. The new Roman coinage, a victoriatus, minted on the standard of a Greek drachma is on the left (it takes its name from the image of Victoria crowning a trophy), a denarius showing Castor and Pollux is on the right.

the censors conducted a thorough review of the population of the Latin colonies (we are not told what the result of this was) and in their search for new revenue streams leased out salt pans on *ager publicus*.

The shortages in 214 BC and 210 BC may be linked with the transition to a new system of silver coinage, initiated either when Fabius Maximus and Marcellus were consuls in 214 BC or the following year, when Fabius Maximus' son was consul along with Tiberius Sempronius Gracchus. This move followed a misguided effort to debase the silver coinage and the steady reduction in the quality of bronze coins, the medium for daily transactions. One of the new coins, the denarius, valued at ten asses (the basic bronze coin), would become the standard coinage of Italy: it was issued along with another silver coin, the victoriatus, based on the Greek drachma. Records of the number of dies used in minting these coins – our only real indication as to how many there might have been – suggest that the uptake of the new currency was gradual, and the large number of victoriati would suggest that it was not obvious which would become the standard (or indeed if there would be a standard coinage at all) for some time.

In the discontent and worry generated in the wake of Cannae, financial issues were just one concern; ongoing religious controversies were another. About 213 BC, the people of Rome were particularly hungry for fresh news from non-government sources about the future. Livy attributes this desire to ignorant folk crowding in from the country, but his narrative implies that there was far more to it than that: he refers to predictive apparatus being set up in the forum itself. But the Senate, wishing to preserve the monopoly on divine communication, cracked down on this development, removing the apparatus and ordering that anyone in possession of books of prophecy or prayers, or works discussing forms of sacrifice – presumed to advertise channels of communication with divine spirits – should hand them over to the Senate by 1 April.

One of the books that the praetor Marcus Aemilius Lepidus claims to have acquired at this point offered the prophecies of a seer called Marcius. These he passed on to his successor, Publius Cornelius Sulla (ancestor of an individual who would change the Roman state for good in just under a century and a half). Sulla decided to publicise them, pointing out that as the prophecy predicting the battle of Cannae had come true, it was altogether likely that the order to set up a sacrifice to Apollo 'according to Greek rituals' if they wanted to get rid of Hannibal should be obeyed. This decision prompted the public consultation of the Sibylline Oracles, whereby it was discovered that the Sibyl was in agreement. The Games of Apollo, the *ludi Apollinares*, were duly instituted in 212 BC. A year later, the Senate decreed that the games should be vowed afresh annually; then, after an epidemic in 207 BC, it was decided that they would be held every year on the dates the epidemic had struck (for a week, starting on 5 July).

The *ludi Apollinares* were not the only new games to be introduced during these years. In 205 BC, after a fresh outbreak of epidemic and with the war still dragging on, popular agitation led to another consultation of the Sibylline Oracles. This led to envoys being sent to king Attalus of Pergamum – a staunch ally against Philip V – asking for an image of the goddess known as the Great Mother (*Magna Mater*), or Cybele. He duly sent back an image of the Great Mother, and a new festival, the Megalensian Games, was founded in her honour. A large temple, also in her honour, was built on the Capitoline Hill overlooking the Circus Maximus. At roughly the same time the Roman ambassadors who had visited Delphi the year before to announce a major victory pronounced that Apollo promised an even bigger victory in the near future. The combination of oracles appears to have helped calm the situation (oracles sought by the state tended to favour the established order).

Fabius Maximus dominated Roman public life for ten years after Cannae. It is therefore reasonable to see the patterns that emerge during these years as mirroring his principles. The first of these was a desire for coherence. In this decade, Rome did indeed pursue a consistent strategy, and magistrates subordinated their interests to those of the state. The currency reform brought stability to state finance, and the handling of religious uncertainties looks like it, too, was directed towards bringing about order. Roman citizens were told that they had a duty to fight their enemies, Roman aristocrats that they had an even greater duty to set an example of good behaviour in the struggle. Fabius Pictor produced the first history of Rome, and in 207 BC Livius Andronicus was summoned to compose a hymn in praise of Juno 'the Queen'. The war against Philip V, with its 'internationalist' approach to building an effective coalition, went hand in hand with an interest in advertising the state's links with the god Apollo. There was less room for individual heroics and a great deal more stress on collective responsibility as Rome staked out a new position on the world stage.

The one person who does not fit well with the pattern of Fabian Rome is the man who would bring the Second Punic War to an end. This was Publius Cornelius Scipio, who saw himself as the divinely guided agent of Rome's salvation. There is reason to think that Fabius Maximus could not stand him, which may be why he was allowed to raise what was in effect a private army of 10,000 men from his family estates and wage what was initially a private war in Spain. Scipio went to Spain in 210 BC, taking over the command that his father and uncle had built up since 218 BC, and which had been nearly undone the previous year when the two of them had died in a major defeat of their forces, well inside the zone of Carthaginian control.

The first Roman invasion of Spain, which began in 218 BC with the arrival of Gnaeus Servilius Geminus at Emporion, well north of the river Ebro, had been executed on a shoestring, even after Scipio (by now fully recovered from his wounds at Ticinum) turned up with his brother. Nevertheless it had been reasonably successful, as the Scipios accomplished two things. One was to begin the process of breaking down Spanish alliances with the Carthaginian regime; the other was to prevent Hasdrubal, Hannibal's younger brother, from reinforcing the Italian campaign. Moreover, the Scipios had opened negotiations with one of the most important rulers of the Numidians, Carthage's powerful North African neighbours, aiming to detach him from his alliance with Carthage. What is unclear is why, in 211 BC, the brothers, supported by 20,000 Spanish mercenaries, advanced deeply into Carthaginian territory. The mercenaries betrayed them, marching off home, leaving the Scipios, who had divided their command, to face much stronger Carthaginian forces. The surviving Romans were rallied by a surviving officer, and the position stabilised when the praetor, Gaius Claudius Nero, brought two additional legions to northern Spain. In the meantime, the Carthaginians were dividing their command so as to restore their control over the tribes that had gone over to Rome, seizing hostages and generally alienating their allies. This is when, at the end of 210 BC, the younger Scipio turned up.

On arriving in Spain and realising that the Carthaginian forces were still widely scattered, Scipio conceived a plan for announcing his presence with panache. In the spring of 209 BC he launched a surprise attack on the Carthaginian capital, Carthago Nova, where were housed much treasure and 500 hostages taken from Carthage's Spanish dependants. The plan depended on speed and on avoiding a protracted siege that would enable the Carthaginian armies to concentrate on his position. From detailed intelligence Scipio knew that at low tide it was possible to cross the edge of the harbour and enter the city from the sea side, where defences were weak. It was typical of Scipio to disguise his planning with claims of divine inspiration, so he told his men that he had been shown the weakness in the Carthaginian defences by the god of the sea, Neptune, himself. Distracting the defenders with an assault on the main fortifications, he sent 500 specially chosen men across the harbour. They entered the city unopposed, seized unguarded sections of the walls and opened the way for their colleagues. Scipio promptly ordered a massacre of the population, to continue until the citadel surrendered. He believed that terror could supplement divine inspiration.

With the capture of New Carthage and the hostages now returned to their people, Hannibal's Spain began to unravel. In 209 BC Hasdrubal decided that it was time to take what he could of his army to Italy, where he might help Hannibal restart the war. But before he left, he wanted to defeat Scipio. The encounter between the two armies took place at Baecula, near today's Santo Tomé in the valley of the Baetis river. Polybius, relying now on eyewitnesses, provides an account – which has been confirmed in its most significant particulars by archaeologists studying the site – of the Roman assault on the Carthaginian position located on a steep plateau.

The battle of Baecula ended almost as soon as it started. Hasdrubal saw that his men were no match for the Romans and hurriedly retreated with as many of them as he could, along with his elephants and his money, into northern Spain, picking up reinforcements as he went. After the battle, Spanish tribes tried to proclaim Scipio their king – possibly in a formal invitation for him to assume a position like that of their previous Carthaginian overlord. Scipio refused, pointing out that Romans did not have kings.

For much of 207 BC the Roman and Carthaginian armies took no direct action against each other, though Scipio appears to have been at work stabilising his own alliance system, and began to cast his eyes towards North Africa. Among the captives at Baecula was the nephew of a Numidian king named Masinissa. Scipio sent him back to Masinissa, opening a line of communication that would result in the king agreeing to become an ally of Rome in 206 BC. A few months before that happened, though, Scipio defeated the remaining Carthaginian forces in Spain at the Battle of Ilipa, in the far south of Spain. He then returned to Rome, where he was elected consul for 205 BC.

Spain remained under the control of lieutenants whom Scipio had left in post with a significant number of troops. There was no formal administrative structure for these areas, and relations with local groups were mainly based on individual treaties, as in Italy. Furthermore, while it seems that the Romans took over the management of the wealthy silver mines, they had no systematic way of getting the silver back to Rome or using it to pay Scipio's men on the ground. Before he left, the army mutinied because it had not been paid. He managed to control his troops, but the problem of administrative incompetence remained.

It was time for a change of strategy. Hasdrubal had reached Italy in 207 BC, but his communication with Hannibal had been intercepted by the Romans, with the result that one of the consuls slipped away a significant part of his army to join his colleague without Hannibal noticing. The two of them brought Hasdrubal to battle, along with some Gallic allies he had raised after he crossed the Alps, near Sena Gallica on the Metaurus river. Hasdrubal's army was essentially wiped out. The first news Hannibal had of what had happened is said to have been the delivery of his brother's severed head. With Hasdrubal's death, any chance Hannibal might have had of renewing the Italian war perished.

Hannibal might not have been able to renew the war, but no Roman was going to fight him. Scipio had been preparing for an invasion of Africa, but in order to do that he needed a fleet and money was short. The only way round it was to end the war with Philip V, which had kept the existing fleet occupied. But that war was not going well. The Aetolians had made a separate peace with Philip in 206 BC, and lackadaisical Roman campaigning was inspiring no great effort from Rome's other allies. It had either to send massive new forces, or make peace. Since all extra forces would be needed in Africa, the only viable option was peace. This was duly accomplished through the peace of Phoenice of 205 BC. If Philip had been a bit savvier, he might have realised that from the Roman perspective this peace was more of a truce than an agreement to end all hostilities. His joining Hannibal when Rome was at its low point would not be forgotten.

Despite the peace, there remained disagreement about the path ahead. Fabius Maximus opposed the African campaign, regarding it as too risky. It was only with difficulty that Scipio prevailed in his effort to have Africa named as his *provincia*, and even then it was with the provision that he take with him an all-volunteer force. He now moved south, reconquering Locris and taking up station in Sicily as he prepared his final move to Africa, expanding his army to include the disgraced legions of Cannae. It was late in 204 BC when he finally made his way to North Africa, where he found that his Numidian ally Masinissa had been driven from his throne by the neighbouring pro-Carthaginian king Syphax. To make matters worse, Scipio was unable to capture Utica, which he had hoped to use as a base for further operations. Unfazed, he pretended to negotiate with the Carthaginian–Numidian army that had been sent against him and encamped in an area known as the Great Plain. Having lured his enemies into a false sense of security he launched a surprise attack, destroying their camp and routing the army.

Carthage now began peace negotiations, which dragged on and on. The Carthaginians recalled Hannibal from Italy. It is not clear what happened next, but both sides agreed that negotiations were over, with accusations of bad faith on both sides. In the spring of 202 BC Hannibal led his army from Carthage to take on Scipio, who now had the support of Masinissa, who had been restored to the Numidian throne after the battle of the Great Plain.

Hannibal and Scipio met in person on 17 October 202 BC, at Zama, south-west of Carthage. Hannibal offered peace terms and a lecture on the vicissitudes of Fortune, recalling how he had excelled at Cannae but how different his situation was now. Scipio replied that he was fully aware of Fortune's fickle nature, and that if Hannibal had offered peace terms before he came to Africa the war could have been ended as he had requested, but now that the gods were punishing the aggressors they were testifying to the justice of the Roman position. Scipio laid out the terms Carthage could expect once it made a *deditio*. Polybius' account of this meeting appears to have been based on Scipio's own testimony, recalled later by his friend Laelius. As part of a very consistent portrait that Polybius offers us, Scipio speaks as the defender and representative of Rome's traditional beliefs and practices.

On the morning of 18 October, Scipio led his army out to face Hannibal. He was the first Roman general in more than a decade to invite such a confrontation. The army that he commanded was highly trained, and for once possessed superior cavalry, thanks to Masinissa. Hannibal's army was, as a whole, less competent, being comprised of three distinct groups: Carthaginian citizens; mercenaries; and the men he had brought with him from Italy. Hannibal did not have great confidence in the fighting qualities of the first two groups, which he planned to use as spear fodder to weaken Scipio's infantry with a series of attacks that would permit him to beat it with just his veterans.

First, Hannibal released a tsunami of elephants. Having anticipated this, Scipio arranged his men so that the massive creatures could be goaded through gaps, before being disposed of by his light infantry behind the main battle line. The tactic worked. His next challenge was to fight his way through what may well have been a considerably larger Carthaginian infantry. At that point, Scipio may have been on the verge of falling into Hannibal's trap. Polybius, again relying on eyewitnesses, wrote:

> As the space between the remaining troops was full of blood, death and dead bodies, the enemy's flight provided an obstacle causing some hesitation for the Roman general. The number of dead bodies, covered in blood and fallen in heaps, as well as the weapons scattered around the field, made it difficult to advance across the field in good order. However, once he had removed the wounded to the rear, and recalled those of the *hastati* [the first division of a legion] who were scattered in pursuit with a trumpet call, he set them against the middle of the enemy formation in the front of the battle line, and placing the *principes* and the *triarii* [the second and third divisions] on either flank, he ordered them to advance across the dead bodies. When these men, crossing their obstacles, were aligned with the *hastati*, the two battle lines engaged against each other with great energy and enthusiasm.
>
> (Polybius, *Histories* 15.14.1–5)

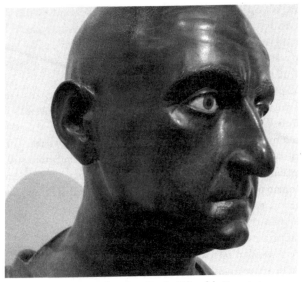

*7. This portrait bust found in the Villa of the Papyri at
Pompeii is identified as being of Scipio Africanus.*

But then Scipio got lucky. His cavalry, which had chased the enemy
from the field, returned and attacked Hannibal's men from the rear in a
sort of reverse Cannae. Hannibal fled, returned to Carthage and urged the
government to offer an immediate surrender to Rome. Despite making
some threatening noises about Carthage facing the consequences of its
habitual treachery, Scipio knew that he could not take the city without a
long siege and that he needed, above all else, to end the war. The peace he
offered to Hannibal was therefore more lenient than it might have been.
The Carthaginians would retain the territory they held in North Africa;
they would be governed by their own laws and would receive no Roman
garrison; they would return all deserters and prisoners and surrender all
their navy, except for ten triremes, to Rome; they would not make war
either in Africa or beyond without Rome's permission; they would restore
Masinissa's full territory to him, feed the Roman army for three months,
pay a massive indemnity to Rome (more than 11,000 pounds of silver a
year), and hand over a hundred hostages drawn from the city's leading
families. Hannibal ensured that Carthage agreed to these terms.

Even as Scipio, who now took the cognomen Africanus to commemorate his victory, was preparing to return home, opposition to the peace terms was voiced in the Senate. One of the consuls for 201 BC wanted the war to continue so he could get the credit for ending it. Outrage set the stage for an unusually potent demonstration of popular sovereignty.

With the consul, Lentulus, adamant about getting the command, frustrated senators passed two measures for two tribunes to put before the *comitia tributa*. The first asked the people if Africa should be a *provincia* in the coming year; the second was about the peace terms. The *comitia tributa* ordered that the *provincia* of Africa stay with Scipio and that the Senate authorise him to make peace with Carthage, which he then did. The Roman people – the 'sleeping sovereign' – were fed up and waking up.

The peace was concluded with a religious ceremony at Carthage conducted by fetial priests from Rome. This was accompanied by the burning of the Carthaginian fleet and the mass execution of the Roman deserters, whose return was a feature of the treaty.

The debate over the peace terms was symptomatic of the very deep divisions in Roman political society, to which Scipio himself contributed in no small way. He was the most famous Roman in the world, ever, Polybius would write. He had won victories no one else would have been capable of winning, and he had brought peace and a chance for Roman Italy to recover from the stresses of war. The Senate should do its best to tolerate him. In fact, Scipio had very limited experience of domestic politics, and his insistence that people be grateful for his achievements gave him a practically limitless capacity to alienate his peers. Consequently, he virtually disappeared from public life for the next decade while the Senate remained unwilling to confront his legacy. This legacy manifested itself largely in Spain, where warfare had become endemic. The administrators that Scipio had left there were still in post but with no plan for the future.

Indeed, the end of the African war did nothing for Spain. Perhaps, if action had been taken soon after the end of Barcid Spain, a solution could have been found that would not have resulted in the peninsula being swamped in blood for the better part of two centuries. If an outside power eliminates an existing power structure, it has a responsibility to come up with an alternative. But Rome did not have either the administrative structures to take on that responsibility or the desire to create them. The victory in Spain had now become a feature of the Scipio personality cult (how many times did people really need to be told about that vision of

Neptune?), but it would be up to the Senate to acknowledge his contribution by setting up new provinces and accepting what was basically a done deal in which it had no part. That was hard to swallow.

Spain's leaders had made it clear what they expected after the battle of Baecula when they had asked Scipio to be king. They wanted some sort of functioning replacement for the Carthaginian administration, which had been an effective referee between the different Spanish factions, some of whom were now calling on the Romans to massacre people they found uncongenial, exploiting the 'butcher and bolt' mentality that was the default setting for post-Scipionic administrators. Such ongoing violence required some sort of standing army. That was not something the Roman state had ever had before. Roman armies were traditionally raised for fixed terms and for specific purposes. The support for a standing army would also require some sort of bureaucracy. Within the Roman system of government, the only way this could be done would be by contracting for the required services.

Rome now had an empire, but it needed to learn how to run it.

PART II

EMPIRE (200–146 BC)

7

MACEDON

❦

Carthage was defeated, but what of Rome's other enemy, Philip V of Macedon? Even as the final peace terms with Carthage were being settled, Roman ambassadors were testing the waters to see if something might be done. The previous war with Macedon had shown that the Senate was fully aware of the diplomatic niceties of the Greek world, and that it was quite capable of turning them to its advantage. When in 201 BC the Senate sent an embassy to the king of Egypt to give him the glorious news of the victory over Carthage, it took a further step in that direction.

Polybius would say later that the Romans were shocked and appalled by the degree of diplomatic duplicity they discovered in the east – especially when they learned that there existed a secret agreement between Philip V and Antiochus III, ruler of the vast Seleucid empire whose territory extended from what is now Turkey through to the borders of Afghanistan and into Uzbekistan, to eliminate the Ptolemaic kingdom. The old king Ptolemy IV had died in 204 BC, leaving his 10-year-old son Ptolemy V as king. Philip and Antiochus planned to share out the kingdom's territories between themselves.

Philip, as we have seen, rated himself rather more highly than the facts warranted. That was also true of Antiochus, who acquired some reputation as a soldier when he led a grand tour of his central Asian domains, then suppressed a revolt in his western provinces. His true levels of ability were revealed when he tried to eject the Egyptians from the land of Palestine, which they then occupied, and lost a battle at Raphia (modern Rafah) in 217 BC.

The detailed description of Raphia that Polybius provides reveals significant features of the military establishment of both kingdoms. Both were following rather antiquated military systems which stressed the tactical centrality of a core phalanx of pike-carrying infantry. This phalanx traditionally consisted of Greeks who had been drawn by promises of pay and privileges to enlist in the service of kings who made minimal efforts to incorporate their non-Greek subjects into their armies. Given that the Seleucid and Ptolemaic kingdoms had developed out of the wreckage of the empire briefly created by Alexander the Great through the brilliant tactical exploitation of quick-striking cavalry forces, the prominence of the phalanx was a retreat into the past. But it was not recognised at the time that the military systems of these two states had ossified into inefficiency – indeed, Antiochus seems to have seen himself as a modern-day Alexander.

Who told the Romans about the two kings' nefarious plot? The answer was, among others, the Ptolemies themselves. This somewhat self-interested disclosure figured in an exchange of embassies at the end of 201 BC, at which point Philip was in no position to take action against Ptolemy, with or without the aid of Antiochus, who was currently engaged in a successful campaign to drive the Ptolemies out of southern Syria and Palestine.

Far from positioning himself to carve up Ptolemaic territory, Philip was fighting a war against the Pergamenes and Rhodians on the west coast of Turkey. After suffering a naval defeat, he was spending the winter of 201/200 BC at Bargylia (modern Boğaziçi, near Bodrum, on the Turkish coast). In the spring, he would escape and begin campaigning with a view to re-establishing his image as a figure of power, starting with raids on Athenian territory. Athens had been allied to Rome in the First Macedonian War and had a long-standing relationship with both the Attalids, who ruled Pergamon, and the Ptolemies. The raid resulted in the Athenians sending an embassy to Rome.

Although embassies from the eastern Mediterranean were successful in making the case for war to the Senate, selling the idea to the people proved more difficult. A meeting of the *comitia centuriata* was summoned to consider ordering Philip to cease his appalling behaviour and, essentially, submit himself to the authority of Rome or face war. Ordinarily the *comitia centuriata*, where voting favoured the interests of Rome's wealthier citizens, aligned reasonably well with the views of the Senate. This occasion proved to be an exception, and the measure was rejected by virtually all the centuries. At a public meeting before the vote, the tribune Quintus Baebius is said to have given an impassioned speech against the prospect of endless war, which convinced people to vote as they did. It is interesting that as a tribune, he could simply have used his power of intercession, as veto power was known, to prevent such measures from going forward. That he did not suggests there was some feeling that if tribunes were going to use this power, they should be able to demonstrate that it did represent the popular will.

The Senate was furious with Baebius. Just a few months earlier, of course, the senators who wanted peace with Carthage on Scipio's terms had asked the tribunes to intervene and get the people to vote in favour. If the senators had just affirmed the democratic aspect of the Roman state, why were they so upset? The most likely reason is that, whatever its internal divisions, the Senate preferred to put on a unified front, one that made tribunes defying senatorial will deeply unwelcome. A new vote was called, which resulted in an embassy being dispatched – even as the army was being assembled – to deliver the essential fetial warning to Philip: namely, that he must either do what the Romans wanted and cease his hostilities, or face war with Rome.

The Roman envoys found Philip in the process of encouraging the people of Abydos, a city on the Dardanelles in western Turkey, to commit mass suicide. When he rejected the Roman demand that he end his aggression, the envoys continued on their way, rallying support in the Greek world for the now inevitable confrontation. Philip hurried back to central Greece, looking for allies and gathering his army in the area of Durazzo (in modern Croatia), where he suspected, correctly, that the Roman army would land. In Rome, with the army assembled under the command of the consul Galba, further consultation now took place on the proper fetial procedure for declaring war. Since Philip was technically a dynast who resided in Macedon and had been elected king by the Macedonian people, the 'king' and the 'Macedonians' were technically separate entities, which raised the question of whether or not, since Rome was declaring war on both King Philip and the Macedonians, each needed to be told individually? The *pontifices* – the board of priests charged with oversight of the religious system – held that it was sufficient to inform the first Macedonian garrison they encountered that Philip and Macedon were at war with Rome. Trivial as this discussion might seem, the fact that it took place at all indicates the growing concern in Rome that ancestral traditions be preserved in a rapidly changing world. (Although that was going to change, and soon.)

When Galba landed in Durazzo, he accomplished very little in what was left of the year 200 BC and that part of 199 BC in which he retained command. His consular successor, Villius, achieved equally little. The consul of 198 BC, a dynamic character named Titus Quinctius Flamininus who had served under Scipio, was another matter. After the failure of negotiations at the beginning of 198 BC, Flamininus began to make serious inroads into Philip's territory. By the end of the year he had moved his army into the strategically vital region of Thessaly in central Greece, while also expanding Rome's alliances in the rest of the Greek world. At this point Philip agreed to negotiate.

The peace conference took place in the autumn at Nicea on the Malian gulf, near the Greek island of Euboea. Philip turned up with a group of courtiers, while Flamininus brought with him an impressive array of leaders of an alliance of Greek states – representatives of the kings of Pergamum, Rhodes and the Aetolian and Achaean Leagues, and Amynander, king of Athamania in western Greece (who had betrayed his previous alliance with Philip in early 199 BC).

Flamininus spoke first, telling Philip that he must withdraw from 'all of Greece', return all prisoners, hand over deserters, and give the Romans the territories in Illyria that he had seized after the peace of Phoenice. The other ambassadors delivered demands for reparations that fell within the overall Roman framework, and Flamininus allowed that what he meant by Philip's withdrawal from all of Greece was his surrender of cities he had taken outside the traditional borders of Macedonia. Polybius notes that Flamininus laughed on several occasions when Philip and the various Greek ambassadors argued back and forth. Well might he have done so. These arguments were pointless – the matter would be decided in Rome.

When Flamininus was satisfied that the outlines of an agreement had been reached, he informed the negotiators that the Senate would still need to be consulted, and recommended dispatching representatives from each side to Rome. Philip agreed. What he did not know was that, if the opportunity arose, Flamininus would stab him in the back.

Flamininus' biggest problem in his hunt for recognition and eternal glory was that he did not know if he would be reappointed as commander in Greece. If not, he might as well negotiate an end to the war and take credit for that. If he *was* going to be reappointed, it would be much better for him to defeat Philip in battle. Only, he wouldn't know which way to leap until after the embassies had reached Rome. At this juncture, though, news may have reached him of a significant change that would take effect the following year: that there would be six praetors rather than the current four, so that magistrates could be sent to govern Spain on an annual basis. One implication of this change was that there would now be two provinces in Spain, with geographically defined borders, to be called 'Nearer' and 'Farther' Spain. The decision to create the two provinces was sufficiently radical to render any other radical step in the near future unlikely. Whatever happened, there was not going to be a permanent province in Greece, so, one way or another, Flamininus would be coming home.

Fortune favoured Flamininus. His friends in Rome now learned that the consuls for 197 BC would both be assigned to *provinciae* in northern Italy. So it was that when the allied Greek embassies arrived to present their proposals to the Senate in February that year, they were now instructed to claim that Rome could not free Greece from Philip if the king was allowed to hold three fortress cities, unnamed in the previous negotiations but well known to be strategically important. When Philip's ambassadors were asked about giving the cities up and replied that they had no instructions on the matter (as Flamininus had expected), they were sent home.

Flamininus began to prepare for the spring campaign. His army met Philip's at Cynoscephalae (meaning 'Dogs' Heads') in Thessaly. They stood on opposite sides of the steep hills that gave the place its name. The battle began by accident when foraging parties ran into each other in the morning mist. Philip mustered his heavy infantry in the traditional phalanx formation of the Macedonian army – men lined up sixteen deep, armed with long pikes. On level ground, as Polybius observed, the phalanx was unstoppable. Philip's problem was that he was not fighting on level ground. Nor did it help that Flamininus had elephants, sent by the Carthaginians. Pressed back by the phalanx on his right wing, Flamininus concentrated his strength on his own left, using his elephants, which the inflexible Macedonian formations could not avoid, to break up the units facing him. As the Macedonian right wing fled, a unit commander in the Roman army took his men out of line so that they could launch an attack on the rear of the victorious phalanx on Philip's left wing.

This spelled disaster for the Macedonians. More than half were killed or taken captive. Philip rapidly agreed to terms that were not dissimilar to those offered the year before at Nicea, but with the additional provision that he give up the three cities that had been the sticking point in Rome.

The final settlement after Cynoscephalae was not quite so simple. There were numerous complaints. Flamininus was helped by a board of ten ambassadors to work out the last details, which would take several years. In 196 BC at the Isthmian Games outside of Corinth, one of the four great athletic contests in contemporary Greece, he made a dramatic announcement: that Rome would guarantee the 'freedom of the Greeks'. These words, which were totally specious – especially when uttered by the representative of a state that was holding southern Italy and Sicily by force – were borrowed from the political vocabulary of classical Greece. What 'freedom' meant in this context was the freedom of a state to govern its own internal and external affairs. But, Flamininus warned, this 'freedom' had to operate within a Roman framework. So, even as Rome was taking steps towards creating a territorial empire in Spain, its representative was announcing that it was establishing a new area of self-governing yet subordinate allies, thereby exporting the old Italian model to the shores of the Aegean. The Senate had no clear plan for the future.

8

VICTORY IN THE EAST

❦

The Roman stage had offered the opportunity for mocking foreigners well before Philip surrendered to Flamininus. Performances of comedies, written in Latin, had begun, at the latest, after the First Punic War. The first two playwrights we hear of are Livius Andronicus and Naevius, but their works have not come down to us complete. For the first full text of a Roman comedy we must wait until the middle years of the Second Punic War. This play was one of many written by Plautus, a writer of vast imagination whose work came to define for later generations the genre of 'comedy in Greek dress'. His plays allow us all sorts of glimpses into contemporary Roman minds, which appear to be anything but as orderly as Livy and Polybius would like us to believe. Romans laughed at love stories, foolish old men and all kinds of people who did not belong to polite society. Very often we can hear Roman audiences laughing at people who upset the social order, such as slaves who are smarter than their masters or young prostitutes who make fun of senior statesmen.

Plautus borrowed the plots for his plays from Greek models, along with some of the lines. But as time went on, he added more and more jokes based on contemporary material. It is because he did this that Plautus allows us today to experience an expansion of the Roman imagination, a greater sense of confidence in Rome's place in the world, and some of the increasing social ferment of his time, and how Roman society was changing.

In Plautus' earlier plays, references to things foreign that are not found in the scripts of Greek models are few. The divinity who delivers the preface to *The Rope*, for instance, simply expresses the hope that the Romans will vanquish their enemies; there may also be a passing reference to the recapture of Capua, but nothing more. War was no laughing matter while Hannibal was on the loose, but the description of a shipwreck and a storm at sea that halted a journey to Sicily undertaken by the play's main character might be plausibly amusing for a Roman audience in the absence of recent nautical difficulties of the sort that bedevilled them in the first war with Carthage. Other plays, such as *The Comedy of the Asses*, contain no reference that might be associated with contemporary politics. Only *The Brothers Menaechmus*, written as the tide was turning in the war with Hannibal, makes a somewhat risqué suggestion about the impact of the sort of art generals like Marcellus were displaying in their triumphs, art that included naked goddesses and depictions of the unions of gods with mortals. This sort of thing made people think about sex (so he suggests). That is unlikely to have been what Marcellus intended.

Political content in Plautus' plays increased substantially in the 190s and 180s BC. Sosia, a character in *Amphitryon*, describes a war that his master Amphitryon has just won in perfect Roman terms: the Argives, as his people are called – fouling up Greek identities is part of the game, since the story is set in Thebes – appear before the walls of their enemies, the Teleboans (a joke name – foreigners do sound so amusingly strange), deliver the appropriate fetial demand, are turned down, and then win the battle. Amphitryon wins the *spolia opima*, and the other side makes a *deditio*. A passing mention (not the only one in a play of this period) of the proper recording of the booty may refer to a major dispute of the 180s BC. So, too, might mentions in this play and others – which are not found in earlier texts – to the cult of Bacchus, which was rumoured, in some quarters, to involve wild orgies.

Plautus' *The Captives* is set against a conflict between the Eleans and the Aetolians – a real enough subject – with plenty of joke names for Greek cities that didn't exist. This is true of *The Persian Girl*, too, where the action depends on a war in Arabia. The play mentions a couple of generic foreign kings, Philip and Attalus, who could not have appeared in Plautus' Greek-modelled writings as they were composed before any such pairing would have been meaningful. Philip and Attalus show up also in *The Little Carthaginian*, which is striking for its somewhat sympathetic portrayal of an old Carthaginian merchant who is seeking his long-lost children in Greece. He even gives a longish speech in his native language, unparalleled in our surviving evidence for the Latin stage. There is also a passing reference to a king Antiochus, which was a stock royal name, not the real King Antiochus who was to play such a big role in the Rome of the late 190s and early 180s BC.

Even when Plautus isn't referring to real events far from Italy's shores, his language shows that people *like* Attalus, Philip and Antiochus now existed on the fringes of Roman consciousness. This is not the same as taking from old Greek plays names like Darius (the king of Persia), which must have been a direct import from an earlier script because there hadn't been a king Darius, or indeed a Persian empire, for well over a hundred years when Plautus wrote the play in which it appears, *The Pot of Gold*. The world of the later Plautus is not only self-confident, it assumes an audience with a fair share of veterans to laugh at the military language, and quite possibly at the rich officers who seem unable to take the field without their rented mistresses in tow. The place that is conspicuously missing from all this is Spain – which was no laughing matter.

The five years after the formal creation of the new provinces in Spain witnessed continued efforts to achieve some sort of administrative order. In 195 BC one of the consuls, a first-generation senator from Tusculum called Marcus Porcius Cato (later known as Cato the Elder), was given Nearer Spain and won significant victories that resulted in peace for the next few years. Then, the silver mines near New Carthage (now the Huelva province of western Spain) were put into production. By the time Polybius visited them forty years later they were producing a vast quantity of silver: he puts it at around 73,000 pounds of silver per year, or around 8 million denarii. The money went largely into the coffers of the Roman state, as did that from war indemnities. In 193 BC the income from indemnities was just under 17,000 pounds of silver a year. That sum would soon increase significantly because another war was about to break out.

For all his advertising it as a great moment in the history of Greece, Flamininus' settlement had not been an overwhelming diplomatic success. He had preserved the independent and militarily self-sufficient kingdom of Macedon, which was a wise move as Macedonia's northern neighbours were prone to raiding, and he had largely subjected the Peloponnese to the interests of the Achaean League. But in doing so he had alienated the Aetolians, who felt they had been inadequately recompensed for their aid in the wars against Philip. And with the Romans showing no obvious interest in sticking around, they were looking to introduce a new factor into local politics. That factor was Antiochus III.

The fact that Antiochus had difficulties with Rome became very rapidly apparent after the end of the Macedonian War. Flamininus' declaration of Greek freedom extended to places on the eastern Aegean coast that Philip had ruled before 197 BC and that Antiochus had swept up after the war. Antiochus was consequently anything but happy to find the Romans telling him to give up cities that he regarded as legitimately under his control. Conversely, some of these cities were delighted that they could invoke Roman aid. An inscription survives from the ancient city of Lampsacus, on the Dardanelles, which records an appeal for help to Rome because Aeneas had set out from there to found Rome.

Envoys crossed and recrossed the Aegean, but they were simply talking past each other. The Romans pressed the issue of Greek freedom, while Antiochus asserted the hereditary claims of his dynasty to land in Europe as well as the Middle East. The Roman view was that he must confine himself to the lands east of the Dardanelles, while his was that dynastic history gave him a claim to Thrace, the area along the north coast of Greece. Rome was none too happy that Hannibal, whose exile from Carthage the Senate had recently insisted upon, had found refuge at Antiochus' court. The Seleucid king had enough faith in his own military genius to employ Hannibal as an admiral.

It soon became evident that the two sides had nothing upon which to agree, a state of affairs that did not, apparently, bother the Senate. Scipio was re-elected consul in 194 BC, expecting to be given the command. That was not going to happen. There was a strong feeling that he was altogether too prominent, so negotiations carried on until, in late 192 BC, the Aetolians elected Antiochus as their chief magistrate for the coming year, whereupon he decided to invade Greece. In Rome, one of the consuls for 191 BC was assigned the war against him. In discussing the war vote, Livy says that at the beginning of the consular year a lavish eight-day festival, known as the *lectisternium*, had been held, and that the sacrifices offered then were said to be propitious for war. So the Senate elected to omit all fetial procedures and consult the people: that war vote was duly passed.

As spring, and the Roman army commanded by the consul Acilius Glabrio, arrived in Greece, Antiochus had done little of note other than have sex – so we are told – with the young wife he had married on

Euboea soon after his arrival. Was he waiting for a general outpouring of Greek feeling to strengthen his army? If so, it didn't happen. Philip V remained loyal to his post-war Roman alliance, and no other Greek states were greatly moved by the Aetolian complaints. Antiochus elected to confront the Romans at Thermopylae, the narrow pass opposite Euboea made famous by the heroic defence offered by the Spartan king Leonidas against a Persian invasion in 480 BC. Antiochus would have done well to recall what his well-read Roman opponents knew full well: the Persians had beaten the Greeks by finding a pass in the mountains from which to attack them from the rear. The precautions Antiochus took to avoid a repeat of that event proved inadequate: the Romans found the pass and his army was annihilated.

Glabrio moved on to attack the Aetolians, against whom he committed numerous atrocities. Antiochus returned home to raise a new army. The war was reassigned to one of the consuls for 190 BC, Lucius Scipio, who brought his brother Publius along as an adviser. Glabrio halted operations in Aetolia, honoured Apollo at Delphi, and went home to what he hoped would be a grand celebration of his victories. The Scipios encountered Antiochus at Magnesia, near Sipylos in western Turkey. Antiochus made numerous tactical errors; the Scipios did not.

In the wake of his defeat at Magnesia, Antiochus no longer had a functional army. Consequently, the terms of the treaty imposed on him, known as the peace of Apamea, were severe. He was ordered to: give up his ancestral lands north of the Taurus, which would largely be handed over to local dynasts or to Rome's principal eastern allies, the Rhodians and Pergamenes; destroy most of his fleet, now forbidden to sail west of Cyprus unless carrying money to Rome; slaughter his elephant corps; and pay a vast indemnity to Rome. The Scipios had already collected more than 170,000 pounds of silver from him to stop the fighting; in addition, he was to pay more than 684,000 additional pounds of silver, in instalments over the next twelve years. He was also forbidden to recruit mercenaries, or indeed take on volunteers, from people 'in the power of Rome'. This clause tells us much about the way the Senate saw the world: as divided between those who were in its power, its allies, and others. This was still the conceptual world of fourth-century BC Italy. In contrast to the remains of the Macedonian and Seleucid kingdoms (or, for that matter, the Ptolemaic), there was as yet no *imperium Romanum* operating on the principles of centralised government; no Roman empire.

The comprehensive defeat of the Seleucid king at Magnesia underscored two important facts. The first, that the post-Hannibalic Roman army operated at an extraordinary level of professional competence. The second, that the major kingdoms of the eastern Mediterranean were inherently weak. The Macedonian state, lacking the territorial and human resources of the Ptolemaic and Seleucid realms, should never have been a major player; and Philip's aggressiveness had made it impossible for him to develop the sort of alliance system that could offset this weakness. The situation was different in the Seleucid realm, and in Egypt, the wealthiest of states. Here, the refusal of Greek administrations to permit their non-Greek subjects meaningful governmental roles made it impossible for them to realise their potential. The Seleucid regime in 189 BC was far weaker than the Achaemenid, which had ruled much of the same territory before falling to Alexander the Great in the 330s BC. As Rome was becoming an imperial state, the challenge would be to find a way to avoid the errors made by Alexander's successors. The system of mutual alliances that had secured Roman strength in central Italy provided a model for the ready incorporation of non-Romans into the Roman enterprise at all levels – as soldiers, colonists, and even as senators.

But could this system, or mode of behaviour, be exported to areas that were culturally distinct? Certainly, the desertions in southern Italy and Campania, motivated by local politics though they were, showed that there was still a long way to go, even in Italy. The constant warring with the Celtic peoples in Liguria and the Po valley, as well as in Spain, suggest that there were limits to the adaptability of the Roman system.

In order to incorporate new peoples into their nascent imperial project, the Romans needed to develop a stronger sense of who they themselves were. Expansion was somewhat ad hoc, old methods such as creating new tribes having been abandoned after 241 BC; while the first general history of Rome had only been written in the last decade of the Second Punic War, and even then it was in Greek. There was a sense that something more ambitious was called for and that a way needed to be found for dealing with the massive influx of new wealth stemming from the victories in the east. Plautus indicates that Romans were beginning to see themselves differently, but that this was still a work in progress. And what role might the rest of Italy have in this brave new world? There was no obvious candidate to articulate a clear way forward. Unfortunately, the most noteworthy Roman of this time, Scipio Africanus, saw himself not as an innovator but as the representative of the old Roman virtues. There would be worse to come.

The peace with Antiochus, negotiated by Lucius Scipio in 188 BC and confirmed the next year after the arrival of a senatorial commission with his successor Manlius Vulso, led directly to a couple of scandals. These kicked off a decade marked by numerous internal and external problems as Roman society adjusted to Rome's new place at the centre of the known world. The disruptions and debates of these years raised fundamental questions about the standards of conduct expected of Roman magistrates and what were acceptable forms of personal behaviour at all social levels. The 'solutions' to these problems, often reactionary and brutal, raised the further issue of what role the Senate would now have, and where its power would lie in relation to the power of the people. Could the sovereign that had been awoken at the end of the Second Punic War be lulled back to sleep?

Magisterial behaviour was the first issue to arise from the end of the war with Antiochus. There would be various cases involving the Scipios and Manlius Vulso. One was linked to the supremacy of the Senate as a corporate body. Another was the growing and appalling habit of massacring 'barbarians' for personal profit.

The Scipio problem came about because the self-identified 'Greatest Man in the World' believed that he was answerable to no one. There was certainly a problem with his accounts because plunder, over which he did have control, had been all to easily muddled with 'indemnity', which was due to be paid to the treasury because it was theoretically money that recompensed the state for its war expenses. In Scipio's view, he had deposited such enormous sums in the treasury that arguments about whether the cash came from fund A or fund B were irrelevant, and his brother, who was technically in charge of the operation, had anyway deposited more than the requisite amount.

At first Scipio was able to get away with a dogged refusal to comply. When he was impeached by two tribunes (urged on by Marcus Porcius Cato) on the grounds that no one should be above the law, he burnt his account books in the Senate. He was then indicted and summoned to face trial in the forum before the *comitia tributa*. The tribunes had not, it seems, looked at a calendar. It was the anniversary of the battle of Zama. Not bothering to offer a defence of his behaviour, Scipio simply led the assembled people up from the forum to the Capitoline, to give thanks for his existence to Capitoline Jupiter. His enemies did not give up, however, and Scipio finally elected to leave Rome, moving to Minturnae in Campania, where he died in 180 BC. He had erected a tomb for himself there rather than be buried in his family's ancestral tomb outside the Porta Capena: this was his response to the ingratitude of the Roman people, he said. The place subsequently became a tourist attraction.

The scandal surrounding Manlius Vulso was somewhat more straightforward. When he returned from Asia Minor and applied to celebrate a triumph, members of the senatorial commission that had overseen his management of the peace process tried to deny him the privilege. Their reasons were that on the way home he had lost a battle against some Thracian tribesmen and that to solve some local disputes he had hired out the services of his army to attack various peoples in central Turkey – chiefly the Galatians, who were descendants of the Gauls who had moved there about a century before. The formal charge was making war without the Senate's authorisation. After some backroom negotiations, and a large payment to the treasury, Vulso's application for a triumph was successful.

The fight over Vulso's triumph was not the only instance during these years of arguments arising over a general's merits. Fulvius Nobilior, who had sacked Ambracia on Greece's west coast, faced challenges from a hostile consul who tried to suborn a tribune into vetoing his triumph. The claim was that Nobilior had not won much of a victory – not unfair if one were to compare his achievements with those of the Scipios. When Nobilior pointed out that he was making a large deposit into the treasury he was awarded his triumph. In both cases, the Senate was keen to ensure that the state shared the fiscal windfall. This may suggest a hangover from the issue with the Scipios, but also raised the nasty possibility that a triumph could be purchased.

And these were not the only problems. In 190 BC Minucius Thermus, who had campaigned against the Ligurians in northern Italy, was denied a triumph on grounds of inadequacy, whereas Glabrio *was* awarded a triumph – reasonably enough, given his victory at Thermopylae and subsequent successful campaign in Aetolia. A year later, however, while seeking the censorship, he was tried for having stolen some of the plunder taken from Antiochus. Cato testified about specific gold and silver vessels that he had seen in Glabrio's camp, but not in the triumph. In any event, the whole thing was ridiculous. Glabrio's real problem was that he was a first-generation senator seeking office against men who were descended from long-standing consular families. Nor did it help that he was a friend of the Scipios, and hence could be tarred with the same brush – even if, as it turned out, unfairly. The case was dropped as soon as Glabrio quit the race for the censorship, which went to Flamininus and Claudius Marcellus, son of the previous generation's hero.

Although all this does not suggest strong administrative oversight on the Senate's part, it does reflect a feeling that as the state's representative the Senate should assert its collective authority more firmly over powerful individuals. But that was not always easy: the next few decades would witness both increasing competition among the governing classes and the Senate's dwindling ability to keep it in check.

Magisterial competition included the consular desire to take commands close to home, and to be awarded engagements that offered easily won victories and/or the opportunity to build connections. In fourteen of the sixteen years between 187 BC, when the end of the war with Antiochus was declared, and 171 BC, when a new war with Macedon was inevitable, both consuls were usually assigned to Liguria. In the two remaining years of this span, one consul was in Liguria while the other was (for one year) campaigning on the other side of northern Italy; in the second year, one was in Liguria while the other was in Sardinia. Such assignments were admittedly suited to the needs of men who took office in March and typically would only be in the field for the summer months.

These campaigns did not always bring great credit to the consuls. For instance, in 173 BC the consul Marcus Popillius attacked a previously peaceful Ligurian tribe, destroyed its city and sold the survivors into slavery. The Senate ordered him to repurchase all those he had sold and then set them free. His consular colleague, Postumius Albinus, behaved not much better: angry with the people of Praeneste, he set a precedent by insisting that they pay his travel expenses to his *provincia*. That same year three cases were brought against governors of Spain for corrupt practices. A year later, when Rome's ambassadors to Greece lied to the Macedonian king Perseus, Philip's son and successor, in order that a Roman army could position itself better for the invasion of his kingdom, some in the Senate deplored the 'new wisdom' that had replaced old-style conduct. But the advocates of this new wisdom – that power could be exercised without reference to traditional moral restraints – prevailed. Gone were the days when moral obligation could seriously be considered as a reason for doing something. In foreign, as in domestic affairs, what mattered was power.

An absence of garrisons east of the Adriatic meant that the Romans behaved differently – in kind if not in manner – towards easterners than they did towards westerners. Rome's use of deliberately disruptive diplomacy to humiliate or unsettle states throughout the region was consistent from the peace of Apamea to the outbreak of war with Macedon in 171 BC. In 186 BC, for instance, Philip had taken advantage of the removal of Seleucid troops from Thrace to take control of a few cities there. Complaints flowed into Rome from the other claimant to those cities, the new king of Pergamum, Eumenes II, and from those who favoured him. The Senate sent an investigating team and, on the strength of its report, ordered Philip out. Philip removed his garrisons and murdered those he thought had complained. This, according to Polybius, 'brought forth the beginning of fatal times for the house of Macedon' (Polybius 22.18.1). Certainly, it had not been a wise move on Philip's part.

Ultimately, to dispel Roman suspicion that he was not as devoted as he could be to maintaining Roman interests, Philip sent his younger son Demetrius to Rome as a hostage. There, Demetrius made some powerful friends and, when he returned to Macedon, Philip took it into his head – probably with justification – that he was conspiring against him. He executed Demetrius, leaving his elder son Perseus as his successor. Perseus would thereafter be regarded as a potential troublemaker, a view that he reinforced in 178 BC, a year after his succession, by marrying Laodice, daughter of Seleucus IV and granddaughter of Antiochus III. Such an alliance between these formerly great powers raised instant suspicion in Rome.

The Macedonians were not the only people running into problems. Soon after the peace of Apamea, the people of Lycia in south-western Turkey, newly liberated from the Seleucids, complained about having been subordinated to the Rhodians. Irritated that ships from Rhodes had been used to transport Laodice to Macedon, the Senate concluded that what the ten ambassadors charged with overseeing the peace of Apamea had meant was that the Lycians had been given not as subjects to the Rhodians (although the ambassadors had quite explicitly said that they were a gift), but rather as friends and allies. In Greece, Roman interventions routinely undermined the Achaean League, which had been genuinely helpful in the Second Macedonian War, in its dealing with Sparta. So it seems that the Romans 'were unhappy if all matters were not referred to them and if all things were not done according to their direction' (Polybius, *Histories* 23.17.4).

By the late 170s BC, Perseus had become something of a hero to those Greeks who felt ground down by the narrow governing groups Rome supported, while those same groups, along with Eumenes of Pergamum (who was now widely loathed in Greece), complained to Rome. Embassies went back and forth, resolving nothing, as Marcius Philippus, the consul of 186 BC who now headed a diplomatic mission to Greece, made use of the 'new wisdom' against Perseus in 173 BC and lied about Rome's intention (which was to start a war with him).

Philippus acted as he did because Popillius, the consul at the time, was enmeshed in the aforementioned controversy over his appalling behaviour towards the Ligurians, which so unsettled the situation in northern Italy that Liguria rather than Macedon had to be assigned to the consuls of 172 BC. It was only in the spring of 171 BC, after further embassies from Greece – most importantly from Eumenes, who claimed that an attempt had been made on his life as he was returning home – that the Senate declared war. The excuse was the alleged attack on Eumenes.

Despite the advance preparation, the war lasted longer than it should have. When the first commander, Licinius Crassus, consul in 171 BC, was soundly beaten in a cavalry engagement, his successor, the consul Hostilius, did no better. Unable to defeat the Macedonians in battle, the Romans inflicted atrocities on civilians instead. Meanwhile, both sides engaged in diplomatic offensives: the Romans circulated a list of charges against Perseus to justify the war, while at the same time, Perseus worked to detach Roman allies, with limited success.

Even if no one was rushing to join Perseus, the lack of Roman success caused diplomatic chaos across the Greek world. The Rhodians offered to mediate between Rome and Perseus (a poor idea, given that the Rhodians were suggesting to Rome that they would not win), while the Achaean League offered somewhat feeble support.

The Roman situation improved in 169 BC when Marcius Philippus, he of the 'new wisdom', took command and laid the groundwork for his successor, Aemilius Paullus, consul for 168 BC and son of the Paullus who had died at Cannae. Operating well within Macedonian territory, the Romans encountered Perseus' army at Pydna, where the decisive battle was fought on 21 June. The Macedonians were roundly defeated. Perseus surrendered and was taken back to Italy, where, after appearing in Aemilius Paullus' massive triumph, he was placed under house arrest at Alba Fucens, in central Italy, along with his son Philip, for the remainder of their lives.

8. *The monument of Aemilius Paullus, taken over from one planned for Perseus, stood nine meters high, topped with a statue of Paullus on a rearing horse. The surviving reliefs show the struggle between Roman and Macedonian troops.*

As Perseus headed to prison, the Roman state ceased collecting *tributum* from Roman citizens. It would thereafter be supported by revenues obtained from non-citizens. In ending *tributum* the Senate was not giving up a major revenue stream, but it was issuing a powerful statement to the effect that Rome was turning away from the traditions of the past while it reasserted its dominance in the Mediterranean world. That world would now nurture its conquerors.

Ending *tributum* was not the only way Rome was defining its position for the world at large. Before his return, Paullus held a massive spectacle in Macedon apparently modelled on earlier eastern Mediterranean royal festivals. A couple of decades later the historian of a new breakaway state in Palestine, ruled by the Maccabees, would describe the Roman Senate as 'an assembly of kings'. He had understood what Paullus was saying.

Signs of disloyalty or defeatism amongst Rome's allies were not acceptable. There was some suggestion that war should be declared on Rhodes because its offer to mediate with Macedon was interpreted as a pro-Macedonian gesture. A measure to this effect was put before a popular assembly, probably the *comitia centuriata*, by one of the praetors. His action was unprecedented, as sitting magistrates did not propose major bills of this sort without prior consultation with the Senate. We will explore in the next chapter this sign of the ongoing tension between the desire of the Roman aristocracy to impose strict controls on the lower classes and the theoretical principle that the people were sovereign. There had been a somewhat similar outburst in 171 BC. On this occasion the tribunes had challenged Crassus' authority when he had begun the levy for the Macedonian War by announcing that men who had been centurions in previous campaigns would not automatically be given that rank again. On that occasion, says Livy, the angry former centurions were quelled by a speech from a long-serving officer (and it may be that a compromise was reached that this speech omits).

As regards the Rhodians, the tribunes vetoed the war vote and the business was returned to the Senate, giving rise to a speech by Cato in which he argued that guilty thoughts were not the same as guilty acts, using as his example the conduct of some of his colleagues. The Senate's declaration that the Greek island of Delos would henceforth be a free port – that is, harbour dues would not be charged – thereby drawing trade away from the Rhodian ports, must have delighted the Italian merchant community that was establishing itself there.

The ten commissioners who now arrived from Rome to oversee the peace settlement gave instructions for a complete revamping of Greece's political landscape. The kingdom of Macedon was devolved into its four constituent districts, now made self-governing; Epirus, which had supported the Macedonians, was pillaged (the number of 150,000 given by Polybius for those enslaved is a rhetorical exaggeration). Elsewhere, a feature of the peace process would be the removal of the politically unreliable: in Aetolia, this involved the massacre of more than 500 men by

Romans soldiers; in Achaea, a thousand were handed over as hostages. One of these was Polybius.

As a coda to the destruction of Macedon, a Roman embassy was sent to Alexandria where the new Seleucid king, Antiochus IV, was taking advantage of the political chaos that had enveloped the kingdom, in order to try to conquer Egypt. They met at Eleusis, not far from Alexandria. As Antiochus approached, the chief Roman ambassador, Gaius Popillius Laenas (himself a former consul and brother of the man who had been so abominable to the Ligurians), is said to have drawn a circle around him with his cane, telling Antiochus that before he stepped out of it he would have to decide whether or not to leave Egypt and accept peace with Rome. Antiochus agreed to take his army home. The scene sounds more than a bit improbable, but the outcome was beyond doubt. The next year, Antiochus tried to reclaim some shred of dignity by holding his own massive festival echoing that of Aemilius Paullus after Pydna, but adding 2,000 pairs of gladiators. As a hostage in Rome he had seen the by now popular gladiatorial shows, and wanted his own people to be encouraged to think brave thoughts by watching them – gladiators then, as later, would rarely fight to the death, but instead put on risky but stylised displays of martial arts.

So it was that, just as the gladiators moved eastwards, Polybius arrived in Rome. This was the moment at which he could claim that in only just over fifty years Rome had come to dominate the known world.

9

THE HOME FRONT

The years of Roman expansion in the east were years of turmoil and controversy at home. The great victories of the era supported the notion that Rome was 'exceptional', but what did this mean? On an ideological level, should Rome maintain the belief systems of the past, or should it embrace its new role as the dominant Mediterranean state? What did this mean for the political order? Should the Senate and magistrates still predominate, or should the people's assemblies have more say?

Then there was all the new money from Spanish mines and war indemnities. How should it be spent? Could the old social order be saved? How could the governing classes retain control if new families were acquiring the wealth to buy their way into power? The thirty years between the defeat of Hannibal and the final destruction of the Macedonian kingdom would see periods of violent repression, significant reallocations of resources around Italy, and new efforts to offer differing visions of what Rome could and should become.

One of the first signs of increasing social division was conflict in 195 BC over the repeal of the *lex Oppia*, a piece of legislation dating back to the Second Punic War, which forbade ostentatious public displays by Roman women. The theory underlying this law, as with other laws banning excessive expenditure, was that in a city where rich and poor often lived next door to each other, social cohesion was strengthened when the rich lived with moderation. While it is hard to know just who cared about the repeal of the *lex Oppia*, the objection voiced by the Roman aristocracy was that Rome's allies could display and celebrate their wealth in ways that they were denied. If the repeal was as popular as Livy maintains, it might well be that the average Roman, too, welcomed the opportunity to spend a bit more, and the fact Plautus makes fun of the debate in his *The Little Carthaginian* shows that the positions were familiar to a wide audience. The two tribunes who tried to block the repeal soon acceded to the argument that they were opposing the people's will.

Romans outside the blessed circle of the rich and powerful had become increasingly unwilling to live within the social order that had been imposed on them as a result of the war with Hannibal. It was they, after all, who had fought and died in it. Laughing at Plautus' plays, they may well have been familiar with the new cult of Bacchus – or Liber, as he was also known – the god of wine and excess who was also associated with freedom and the upset of the social order. There was no set way to worship him, women as well as men could be initiated into the rites of his cult, and a new variety of Bacchic rite was imported from Campania sometime after the Second Punic War.

It was this new worship of Bacchus, founded upon the divine revelation of a woman, that in 186 BC prompted one consul to seize on a domestic scandal as an excuse for a widespread campaign of repression against the lower classes. The catalyst was a young man who was about to be cheated out of his inheritance by his stepfather, who was manoeuvring to implicate him in disreputable activities. This young man had a girlfriend, a prostitute, who saw what was going on and informed the consul Spurius Postumius Albinus, providing him with the grisly details of the new forms of worship involving rather a lot of sex. Albinus reported the scandal to the Senate, on whose authority he began to round up people in the countryside where protection against seizure by magistrates was minimal, even for Roman citizens.

The upshot was that Livy invited his readers to visualise junior magistrates traipsing along the wooded banks of the Tiber arresting copulating couples in a desperate effort to stem the upsurge of illicit fornication. Thousands were jailed, and many then executed. All this might seem no more than the enactment of a middle-aged Roman's fantasy, were it not for the fact that Livy quotes a language very similar to that which appears in an inscription directly connected with these events that was found near Tiriolo in southern Italy. This text, while less dramatic than Livy's version, is quite revealing: 'Concerning the Bacchanals who are allies' (*ILLRP* 511).

According to this document, 'the Senate agreed that it must be decreed that' people should not wish to have a shrine of Bacchus (but if they must they should appear before the urban praetor at a meeting of the Senate at which a hundred senators were present). A woman should not join the cult (unless she presented herself before the urban praetor and a hundred senators); no one should be the leader of such a group, form a conspiracy, engage in collective business activities or celebrate the rites (unless he or she appeared before the urban praetor and his hundred colleagues); and no group should consist of more than five people. An additional provision for Tiriolo – and presumably other places – was that if a person persisted in banned behaviours after the views of the Senate had been publicised, then that person could be put on trial for his or her life.

The fact that the Senate gave orders to non-Roman citizens is hardly surprising, as the structure of Rome's power in Italy depended on, among other things, its ability to tell local magistrates when to show up with soldiers to serve Rome. In this respect, the decree simply illustrates the exercise of power in the Roman environment. Somewhat more troubling is the suggestion that the death penalty could have been widely imposed, both in Rome and elsewhere in Italy. The Tiriolo text makes clear that it might not be a question of summary execution, but still implies that the Roman state could see itself encouraging the large-scale slaughter of its own citizens and allies. If the 'Greatest Man in the World' was not immune from prosecution, then neither was anyone else.

It was not just in 186 BC that the Senate was worrying about public morality and divine anger. Livy reports that a year later 2,000 people were arrested on suspicion of conspiring to poison others, and that the praetor Lucius Postumius conducted what Livy calls a 'strict investigation' into some sort of plot concerning shepherds and slaves around Tarentum. Action was taken to quash a recurrence of Bacchanalian activity in 181 BC, and the next year the Senate initiated another investigation of alleged mass poisonings, resulting in some 3,000 arrests. These events followed an outbreak of the plague, which made it difficult to recruit enough men to suppress a revolt in Sardinia; massive sacrifices were ordered by the Sibylline Oracles, including a two-day religious holiday throughout Italy.

Meanwhile, new efforts were made to bring greater decorum to public life. One innovation was the allocation to senators of special seats at the theatre so that the less fortunate could see how their leaders behaved in public; another was the reorganisation in 179 BC of the *comitia centuriata*, probably involving the redistribution of voters into new centuries to account for the movement of people into new colonies. In 168 BC the censors reversed what had apparently been a long spell of censorial slippage on the issue, placing all freedmen in one of the four urban tribes. It would later be claimed, by a politician of rather conservative views, that this move preserved the state because it restricted their voting power.

The interest in a properly ordered state carried over to the new colonial foundations. In new Latin colonies, recipients of land tended to be graded according to census class (the more important the person, the more land they received). In 193 BC, 3,000 infantry and 300 cavalrymen were sent to form a new *colonia* at Thurii in southern Italy, where the ravages of the Second Punic War may have left many people dead and hence much land empty. Twelve acres were given to each infantryman and twenty each to the cavalry. In 189 BC, when a *colonia* had been established at Bononia (Bologna) on land taken from the Boii, the cavalry received forty-three acres while the infantry received thirty (Livy claims the Gauls had chased the Etruscans from the land). In 181 BC, at Aquileia, another big Latin *colonia* on Gallic land, the 3,000 infantrymen each received twenty-five acres, centurions received sixty-one and the cavalrymen eighty-six. Similar class-based divisions occurred in 173 BC, when land taken from the Gauls and Ligurians was handed out to individuals at a rate of six acres for a Roman citizen, two acres for an ally. At smaller places, where there may have been no threat of military intervention (or evidence of recent massacre), land seems to have been given out only to poorer Roman citizens. At Saturnia, six acres were handed to the latter, while in the same year 2,000 settlers were divided between the *coloniae* at Mutina (Modena) and Parma, each individual receiving five acres in the former, three in the latter. Three-acre plots were distributed at Graviscae, the port of Tarquinia in Etruria. The small plot size might be connected either with the perceived excellence of the land for cash products – Graviscae produced good wine – or, again, with the perceived poverty of the recipients (in the record they are accorded no military rank, and may have been members of the fifth census class).

The reforms of the electoral assemblies, while of considerable practical significance (as is gerrymandering in any era), were ideologically linked to attempts to make elections more 'orderly' and to enhance the ability of the 'right sort' of people – those who respected the Senate's authority – to get elected.

In 180 BC the tribune Villius passed a law setting minimum age limits for office holders (such a law would have disqualified the 24-year-old Scipio from his command in Spain). Whereas previously the only limit was that a candidate seeking office should have completed ten years of military service, now, in addition, he would be obliged to hold three offices – quaestorship, praetorship and consulship, in that order – and with a two-year interval between them. The tribunate of the plebs could not be a required office, since patricians could not hold it. Aedileships were limited in number, so that office was not required either. On the other hand, as aediles were expected to organise public festivals, the office could offer an invaluable stepping stone to the praetorship if the aedile's festival was successful. Concern about the competitive advantage an aedile could gain in this way is reflected in a law the consul Baebius passed the year before, in 181 BC, that defined very high expenditure on games as a form of electoral bribery (*ambitus*). That same year he passed another law stating that the number of praetors should be six and four in alternate years, the theory being that this would lessen competition for the consulship.

This last law suggests that the Roman aristocracy regarded the stability of the domestic political process as more important than ensuring a suitable number of administrators for the empire. The *ambitus* law, which forbade magistrates from soliciting money from provincials, allies and Latins to pay for games, reflected the ever-increasing importance and availability of money in domestic politics.

In 188 and 187 BC two more bills of significance were proposed, both to do with Rome's relationship with its allies. The first was a tribunician bill giving full Roman citizenship to citizens of the Latin cities of Arpinum (Arpino), Fundi (Fondi) and Formiae (Formia). The measure was initially vetoed by four tribunes who claimed that it should first have been passed by the Senate. They later withdrew their vetoes, apparently, when told that it was the people's prerogative to bestow the vote. The next year, representatives of the Latin league complained to the Senate that too many citizens were moving to Rome and being included on citizen lists there. These embassies probably resulted directly from the end of the censorship in the previous year, which would have registered the Latin immigrants as Roman citizens. The praetor re-examined the lists and expelled 12,000 people who were found not to have had fathers registered in the census.

These domestic reforms were features of a growing consciousness of what it meant to be a member of the Roman aristocracy, and an awareness of the history that lay behind the generation that was now about to control the world. It is perhaps not accidental that two of the most important contributions to defining Rome's past date to the second quarter of the second century BC. The authors of these works, once close colleagues, appear to have parted company over the fate of Scipio. One, the poet Ennius, composed a poem on Rome's past that was the first work to adapt Latin to the Greek epic metre, the dactylic hexameter; he was granted a statue on the Scipios' family tomb at Rome. The other was Cato, whose new history of Rome was the first major historical work in Latin prose.

Ennius, who had previously written plays, called his new epic poem the *Annales*, a title which simply seems to have meant 'tale of Rome through the years'. Just how many years were involved emerges from a line that is quoted from his fourth book: he writes that it was now 'more or less' 700 years since a 'venerable augury' (Ennius, *Annales*, Fr. 154–5 (Skutsch)) had predicted the foundation of Rome. The use of phrases like 'more or less' does not suggest a robust interest in precise chronology; and furthermore, given the economy of his work, suggests that he was dating the founding of Rome rather close to traditional Greek dates for the fall of Troy, as he thought that Romulus was Aeneas' grandson. In fact, Ennius has relatively little to say about Rome's mythic past. He may reach the Gallic sack of the city (390 BC) in his fourth book, he certainly deals with the war against Pyrrhus in his sixth, and introduces the First Punic War at the beginning of the seventh with a rather nasty account of Carthaginian practices such as baby-killing, as well as a clear statement that Appius Claudius had followed proper fetial procedures in declaring war on Carthage. By the end of book nine he has dispatched the Second Punic War.

At one point it does look like Ennius might be anticipating what would become a fashion in Roman historical writing – identifying years according to consuls. Histories organised in this way would also be called 'Annales', but such a view might be stretching the evidence further than is wise. The year in question is 204 BC, the year in which Scipio invaded Africa, and it may be that by using the consular date Ennius was trying to point out that this one year was especially important. For Ennius, it seems, the people who mattered most were those who would be listening to his poem. With that in mind he extended his work, originally conceived in fifteen books, to end with his friend Fulvius Nobilior's triumph over

Ambracia in 187 BC, then three books on 'recent wars' which bring the story into the 170s BC.

To Ennius (who died in 169 BC), the greatest generation of Romans was his own. It was the deeds of his generation that were set against those of the past; and it was to immortalise these accomplishments that he learned to adapt Latin to the metre of Greek epic, equating the deeds of his contemporaries with those of Homeric heroes. His sophisticated use of language was in keeping with a generation that was seeking a new definition of its relationship with a world it now ran and whose wealth was rapidly changing the way people lived. To write, though, of this generation as an epic generation must imply something about its greatest figure. There was presumably good reason for Ennius' statue being placed on the tomb of the Scipios. Although none have come down to us, it is not unreasonable to suggest that he had many kind things to say about the 'Greatest Man in the World'.

Cato had originally been a patron of Ennius, helping him gain Roman citizenship in 184 BC. Like many of the great figures of early Roman literature, Ennius was not born in Rome; he came from Rudiae in southern Italy. But his relationship with Cato may well have soured as Ennius' expressions of appreciation for Scipio soared. Cato's book *The Origins* was begun in old age, after Ennius' death. Cato may have undertaken the project with a view to writing just about Rome's earliest history and that of other Italian states, as the first three books deal with precisely that. The content was, in Roman terms, entirely 'antiquarian'; in our terms, mythological. This all changes in book four, which opens with an account of the First Punic War, presented as significant because it was the first war in which Rome commanded an Italian alliance abroad and, quite possibly, because by the time he was writing it Cato was regularly urging the Senate to destroy Carthage – something he had been encouraging ever since he visited the place in 157 BC and found that it was more prosperous than he had expected.

In writing *The Origins*, Cato stated that his purpose was to educate his son and to respond to the Roman tendency to write their histories in Greek – there were three such histories by Cato's time, the most recent by Aulus Postumius Albinus, which opened with an apology for the author's less than perfect command of the language. Cato, who had excellent Greek, retorted that it was time, then, for Romans to use their own language for writing their own histories, because it was important for people to know their own past. In composing the later books of his history, Cato stressed his own contributions by including two of his speeches: one on peace with Rhodes; the other, his speech of 149 BC prosecuting Servius Sulpicius Galba for his abominable behaviour in Spain. It is impossible to know whether this was purely self-advertisement or a reaction to the invented rhetoric that filled the pages of Greek historians. A theme that may link the two speeches with the purpose of the history is their stress on the practical application of old-time Roman morality.

Later readers, upon whom we are dependent for our knowledge of Cato's work, make it clear that his range of material was extraordinary. He gave a detailed account of Aeneas' arrival in Italy, telling how the local king Latinus gave him his daughter Lavinia in marriage, even though she was already married to a local noble called Turnus. Turnus and the Etruscan Mezentius then went to war with Aeneas and were defeated. Given land, which Cato sets at 1,667 acres, Aeneas founded Lavinium, named for his wife. Rome would not be founded for centuries – according to Cato, this happened 432 years after the Trojan War, which corrected Ennius' view about the temporal relationship between the two events. He was also unhappy with the suggestion, found in Timaeus, that the word 'Italy' derived from *vitulus* or calf, claiming instead that the region got its name from an ancient king named Italus.

In discussing other places in Italy, Cato supplies a vast quantity of geographical, mythological and other information, including on the Gauls of the north of the country. He tells his readers that the Sabines took their names from a man named Sabus, the son of a local god named Sancus, that the founder of Praeneste (Palestrina) was one Caeculus, who took his name, which literally means 'Little Blind Guy', from the fact that the young girls who found him as a baby lying on a hearth thought he had small eyes. Caeculus founded Praeneste with the help of a band of shepherds, Cato says. Polites, a wayward companion of Aeneas, founded Politorium (modern La Giostra), and Argives founded Falerii (now Civita Castellana). He also says that in the Alps lived 'white hare-like creatures, eleven-pound mice, solid-hoofed pigs, shaggy dogs and hornless cattle' (*FRH* 5 Fr. 75). In a surviving work on agriculture he shows an equally detailed interest in regional products.

Cato's interest in the founding fathers of Italian and Roman history does not end with Romulus. It appears that Book 1 of his history carries it down to the Gallic sack of Rome, at least (the war with Pyrrhus would have been the other obvious stopping point). In so doing he describes Romulus' kidnap of Sabine women to provide females for the nascent Roman community, then the war against the Sabines who wished to avenge the outrage, and how the Sabine women eventually brought peace between the two sides. He also relates the career of Marcius Coriolanus, the great warrior whose monumental ego made it impossible for him to participate successfully in political society. He went into exile and led an army of Volscians, an Italic tribe, against Rome, only stopping when his mother and other women met him at the fifth milestone and urged him to abandon his course. Cato also mentions the Roman women who contributed their jewellery to ransom the city from the Gauls. People familiar with his views on Scipio and on luxury would not have missed the contemporary relevance.

Cato's style changes when he begins to relate more contemporary history. He no longer names leading figures, whether Roman or foreign. A typical passage might mention 'a Carthaginian general in Sicily' leading his army to a certain place, at which point 'a tribune' makes a suggestion to 'a consul'. Occasional use of the first person, possibly confined to points at which Cato had been a player in the narrative, as in phrases like 'we fought', may not have violated the general rule. Thus the Second Punic War features a character who appears as 'the Carthaginian Dictator' rather than as Hannibal (*FRH* 5 Fr. 78) and passes without 'the Greatest Man in the World', who is simply mentioned as 'the Roman consul'. Cato's history stresses the achievement of a people and of a value system.

Concluding with his speech against Galba, Cato sounds something of a warning, suggesting that the moral strength that had brought the victories of the previous fifty years was not to be taken for granted. Real Roman virtue does not require displays of wealth – it is based, as Cato repeats in his work about agriculture, on a strong attachment to traditional ways of doing things. With the changes that were taking place as the new wealth flooded into Italy, those ways were changing, too. Cato's sense that the success that was undermining the qualities upon which Rome's rise was based was remarkably similar to that of a person we have every reason to believe he disliked: Polybius.

Polybius was composing his history at about the same time as Cato. He had come to Rome as hostage from Achaea after the war with Perseus. Writing over the course of the next thirty years, he provides the only contemporary account of the working of the Roman constitution, to which he attributes Rome's success. His discussion of that constitution, modelled on earlier Greek political thought, offers us a valuable insight into the way the Roman state was operating at the time.

In classical Greek political thought there were three sorts of 'good' constitution: democracy, aristocracy and monarchy. By Plato's time, in the late fifth and early fourth centuries BC, it was recognised that each 'good' constitution had an opposite. The opposite of democracy was ochlocracy (mob rule); the opposite of aristocracy was oligarchy; and the opposite of kingship was tyranny. Plato, Aristotle and Polybius believed that constitutions change from good to bad in a regular cycle. Thus monarchy becomes tyranny, which gives way to aristocracy, which declines into oligarchy and gives rise to democracy; democracy declines into ochlocracy – a descent into pure savagery – and finally the cycle begins again with the rise of another monarchy.

In introducing his analysis of the Roman constitution, Polybius says:

> The elements controlling the constitution are three ... And each part is equally and appropriately set in order and managed in every way so that no one who lives there can say clearly whether the whole form of government is more aristocratic or democratic or monarchical.
>
> (Polybius, *Histories* 6.11.11)

For Polybius, the consuls constitute the monarchical element; the Senate as a whole, the aristocratic; and the people, the democratic. The consuls are monarchical because they command the armies, and all the other magistrates except the tribunes must obey them; they run meetings of the Senate, carry out its decrees, and summon legislative assemblies of the people. They have absolute authority when in the field, and may take whatever sums they need from the public treasury, administering them with the assistance of a quaestor. The Senate controls the treasury, regulating all expenditure, except for the money handed over to the consuls; it also approves the state contracts leased every five years by the censors.

The Senate investigates crimes throughout Italy, and provides arbitration for persons or communities throughout the peninsula. It dispatches all embassies, whether they be for settling disputes or for 'offering encouragement', imposing demands, receiving submissions or declaring war. It also receives embassies at Rome. By contrast, the people confer honours and inflict punishments; theirs is the only court that can pronounce a capital sentence, and they may even try those who have held the highest office; they bestow office on the deserving, approve laws, and deliberate on matters of war and peace.

The monarchical aspect of the constitution cannot work without the aristocratic and democratic aspects, because the Senate controls the consuls' budgets and it is the people who approve and ratify peace treaties. The Senate can also decide whether to leave a man in office at the end of his term or replace him, and whether a general may celebrate a triumph; and it is to the people that the consul must account for his actions. The Senate must defer to the will of the people in the investigation of crimes, and the people can decide whether to pass bills limiting the power of the Senate. The people depend on the Senate because they profit from the contracts leased by the censors throughout all of Italy; and its members are appointed as judges in civil trials.

Although a description of the Roman constitution that omits concepts such as *imperium*, *potestas* and the class and tribal divisions of the assemblies – not to mention the consequent existence of two ways of voting – is inevitably somewhat idiosyncratic, Polybius' outline accords well with the situation in the second century BC. As for the finer details, he admits that people 'inside' the system would note what he left out. What Polybius is interested in is the way institutions of state functioned, which is why his description of, for instance, the Senate's power to investigate crimes throughout Italy and, without the passage of a *lex*, to inflict mass carnage on lower-class individuals irrespective of their citizenship status, looks very much like the kind of judicial power the Senate began to assert around the time of the Bacchanalian episode. The stress on its role in managing embassies is illustrated nowhere so well as in Polybius' own history, while the stress on its role in overseeing the state contracts that proliferated over the length and breadth of Italy had taken on particular significance by the mid-second century. The importance of such contracts is mirrored both in the accounts we have of what the censors were doing and the archaeological records.

State contracts injected masses of new cash into the Italian economy; and the increasing censorial spending reflects the increasing flow of funds as war indemnities combined with Spanish silver to strengthen the standing of the contractor class, a constituency which would develop immense political clout in defence of its own interests. This class would later become the equestrian order, but not for a while, and we should not confuse the result of a process with its inception. At this point, the people who would later form the core of the order still belonged to the eighteen centuries of 'cavalry men with the public horse', which also accommodated most members of the Senate. The change in the status of this group was the result of the retention of a traditional system of public finance in a new environment. The failure to change the traditional contract system effectively brought about the privatisation of Rome's wealth.

The upsurge in spending began during the war with Antiochus III. The censors of 194 BC showed more interest in maintaining the social order than they did in spending money. They ousted three men from the Senate for 'conduct unbecoming' to a Roman aristocrat, and evicted a few others from the equestrian centuries for the same reason. The only extraordinary expenditure was for two new buildings in Rome. The election of 189 BC was the first at which the censors leased contracts enriched by the plunder recently poured into the treasury, and that election was both especially competitive and especially nasty – as Glabrio found out, to his cost.

In 184 BC the election was again hotly contested. The two successful candidates, Cato and Lucius Valerius Flaccus, were of one mind when it came to conducting a strict review of the upper classes – they removed two former consuls – and in imposing an especially high *tributum* on members of the upper class, whose property they assessed at extremely high rates. But they also did a great deal of building, both in Rome and in Latium more broadly. Projects included paving the cisterns that served Rome's water system, cleaning sewers and constructing new ones, building roads, and building a basilica in the forum (which Cato modestly named after himself). Contractors complained that they were not paid enough, and those taking out the tax-collecting contracts protested that their profit margins were too low, but a lot of money was changing hands. The contract for sewer-cleaning is said to have been worth 57,000 pounds of silver (equivalent to the annual indemnity from Antiochus).

In 179 BC the censors launched more major public-building projects. Their request that a full year's revenue be allocated to cover them suggests that there was now a substantial surplus in the treasury. In addition to road construction and temple refurbishment outside Rome, the censors substantially improved the city's port facilities; built a new portico in the forum, the Basilica Aemilia, which housed new banking facilities;

and created a forum and a colonnade outside the Porta Trigemina near the south-eastern end of the Forum Boarium. Since these censors were following the example set by the previous two boards in both funding large projects and tossing quite a few people out of the Senate, it is hard not to see a connection between the availability of masses of new money and a new emphasis on personal morality.

That money also provided the wherewithal for ever more elaborate projects, as well as for projects beyond Rome's immediate environs. The censors of 174 BC, having expelled nine men from the Senate, issued contracts for paving Rome's streets with flint, for improving the Circus Maximus and roads outside the city, for building new bridges, new colonnades in Rome, city walls at Calatia and Auximum, and numerous other projects both in Rome and in the rest of Italy. There was also a scandal when one of the censors ordered roof tiles taken from the temple of Juno Lacinia in Locris for a self-commemorative temple he was building in Rome. That was sacrilege and he was made to put them back.

Although we glean less about building projects from the next census, in 169 BC, they were so substantial that the censors tried to have their terms extended for an extra eighteen months to oversee them. We also know that they tried to change the bidding on public contracts to prevent people who had taken out contracts in earlier years from bidding for new ones, a policy reminiscent of the principle that Crassus had applied with the centurions in 171 BC in order that newcomers would get a chance at the higher returns that came with that status. While Livy concentrates on the protests, which culminated in a tribune bringing a charge of *perduellio* (the archaic treason charge) against the censors, great pressure must also have been exerted by people who, convinced that the system was rigged in favour of existing contractors, were intent on getting a piece of the pie. The prosecution only just failed to gain the conviction of the censor Appius Claudius, thanks to his colleague Tiberius Sempronius Gracchus, who came vigorously to his defence. Gracchus was the son-in-law of Scipio Africanus, and Appius Claudius' granddaughter would marry Gracchus' son. At this point, Livy's narrative breaks off – but the future trend is clear.

In addition to the censorial outflow of cash in Rome and, increasingly, in Italy at large, there is significant archaeological evidence of new prosperity throughout Latium and the lands immediately adjacent, which may have been partly funded by censorial contracts as well as by the fact that both consular armies, when operating in northern Italy, were annually depositing about half a million denarii into the Italian economy.

Fregellae, founded as a watch post on the Samnite border, contributed at least one unit of cavalry to the army at Magnesia. It may have been their commander who commissioned the terracotta reliefs depicting fighting men and ships that have been found in a large house there. By the second quarter of the second century BC the place boasted a new shrine to Asclepius and one of the earliest bathhouses in central Italy. Various leading Fregellans figure in association with the governing aristocracy in Rome. In 177 BC the Fregellans had to petition the Senate to remove thousands of Samnites who had hopped over the border to share their lovely space.

At about the same time, a remarkable temple was built at Gabii, halfway between Rome and Praeneste. It is likely that the divinity honoured here was Juno, although the most noteworthy thing about this temple was that it was attached to a meeting place shaped like a theatre; and Gabii was indeed a creative place – in the third century BC the city had already built a very large public building that had no parallels elsewhere. At Praeneste a new Temple of Fortune, replacing an earlier shrine to Juno, was built in the 120s BC. Here some eastern influence is detectable: the divinity in question is the Greek goddess of luck, Tyche. Here, too, the sanctuary included a semi-circular meeting chamber overlooking massive terraces, which, with its spectacular view of Latium, set an impressive new standard for civic self-display. An interest in new styles may have been attributable to the Praenestians, who were coming to occupy a significant place in the Italian community on Delos. By the mid-second century BC a visiting Greek philosopher would comment that in no place was 'Fortune more fortunate than at Praeneste' (Cicero, *Concerning Divination*, 2.86). The shrine was connected with an oracle who operated by comparing the number from a dice throw with prerecorded responses (by the first century AD these dice would be made of gold).

Another oracular temple, to Jupiter Anxur, outside Tarracina, received a rather less spectacular facelift during these years, as did the Temple of Apollo – in both cases with money provided by a censor of 179 BC; while at Tivoli the ancient shrine of Hercules Victor, believed to be older than Rome itself, underwent renovation, including the addition of a semi-circular stone meeting area attached to the temple, as at Praeneste and Gabii. Praeneste also built itself a massive new city wall. At Ferentinum, where the great walls built to defend the city in its wars against Rome during the fourth century still stood, a new acropolis was under construction.

Shrines, especially those offering advice on health or on the future, had an obvious tourist appeal. The building projects of cities around Latium mirrored not only their participation in the increasing wealth of the area, but also a growing civic self-assertion. They had civic amenities that Rome still lacked. At the same time, new banking facilities established in the Basilica Aemilia in Rome reveal an ever more sophisticated system of private finance that increased the flow of money through the economy, or that part of the Italian economy most closely connected with Rome. Latium and parts of Samnium, Campania and Etruria benefitted most; southern Italy and Italy beyond the Apennines, far less. These differences would be exacerbated as the second century turned into the first.

10

CARTHAGE MUST BE DESTROYED (146 BC)

After the Macedonian War the information that has been passed down to us on the next stage of Rome's history becomes considerably patchier. Manuscripts preserve no more of Livy's history, leaving us with only short summaries of his work produced in the centuries after he stopped writing, and quotations from Polybius in later authors become ever more sporadic. Without a full text of either author we are left to put things together from a variety of sources, including: Appian of Alexandria's histories of the wars in Spain and Africa (composed in the second century AD); the lists of triumphs and consuls inscribed towards the end of the first century; many quotations, though again no complete texts of historians writing during these years; the comedies of Terence (six plays, all performed in the 160s BC); and Cato's astonishing book on agriculture, *De Agri Cultura*. We also have evidence for an increasing volume of silver coinage pouring from the state mints, and even more evidence of changes in the cityscapes of central Italy.

One distinctive feature of our lists of triumphs is the absence of many from Spain in the fifteen years after Perseus' defeat; indeed, there were few triumphs overall, even though consuls were routinely given commands in Liguria and Sardinia, and occasionally on the east coast of the Adriatic. The list of consuls shows quite a high percentage of individuals from families outside the important clans of the fourth and third centuries BC, a function of new wealth spreading through the highest class.

In foreign affairs, Roman envoys continued to travel the eastern Mediterranean. Among other commissions, they were sent to mediate the quarrels of the increasingly dysfunctional Ptolemies in Egypt, and to weaken the power of the Seleucids, who were soon to be embroiled in their own dynastic civil wars. The Seleucid instability strengthened a new dynasty that was beginning to move south from its central Asian base and that would ultimately take over the eastern Seleucid provinces and play a major role in Roman history. The new dynasty traced its descent from a man named Arsaces (hence its members were known as Arsacid), and its people were called the Parthians.

In the late 150s BC there was to be a great deal more violence. Trouble would break out in Spain, North Africa and Macedonia, and the Roman response would be brutal in every case. In Italy, rising income disparity sharpened existing divisions between rich and poor, Roman and non-Roman. At the root of the discontent lay the question: 'Why should I fight and die hundreds of miles from home to make someone else richer?' As there was no good answer to this question, protest against the authority of the Senate increased and hostilities between tribunes and magistrates intensified.

In 155 BC the praetor governing Farther Spain took his army into what is now the border area between Spain and Portugal (Lusitania to the Romans), where he was defeated. His successor did a bit better, but the next year the Senate sent a consul, as fresh trouble broke out in what is now Soria province in north-western Spain. The problem, apparently, was some ham-fisted intervention in what was effectively a civil war between local tribes, the Romans choosing to support the Belli and the Titi against the Aravacae. Possibly in response to the problems in Spain, the Senate changed the state of the official year from 15 March to 1 January for people entering office from 153 BC. If the purpose of this change was to enable governors to get to their provinces before the beginning of the campaigning season and thus be better prepared, it was not initially a great success. The consul of 153 BC, Quintus Fulvius Nobilior, suffered a serious defeat, and the war continued.

The next governor, Marcellus, the consul for 152 BC, was more successful in his campaigning, but he decided to have the tribes negotiate a settlement with the Senate. Unfortunately for him, ambassadors from the Belli and the Titi, well primed with arguments likely to convince the Senate, spoke first. If the Aravacae were not severely punished for their deeds, they explained, the Senate's mercy would encourage others to rebel. The ambassadors of the Aravacae were prepared to submit to some form of penalty, but thereafter expected to have their previous relationship with Rome restored. Not pleased to find that Marcellus favoured this approach, the Senate told him (though at least not publicly) that it expected him to take a harsh line with the Aravacae. The duplicity of the senatorial response was reminiscent of their conduct towards Perseus, and it would be seen again within the year. There was not much that Marcellus could do, since Spain was about to pass to Lucius Licinius Lucullus, the consul for 151 BC. The Aravacae were, however, spared more trouble. Having learned that they could not trust Romans to be honest, they found that they could trust them to be dishonest. They bribed Lucullus to attack someone else.

Before Lucullus could attack anyone, however, he had to raise an army. That proved harder than anticipated as there was widespread resistance to his recruitment efforts. People talked of the endurance and bravery of the Spanish enemy. Young men simply did not want to enlist, and Roman aristocrats who might have been willing under other circumstances showed no inclination to sign up as military tribunes.

This was not the first time the issue of service in Spain had arisen. In 184 BC, when the retiring Spanish governors had wanted to bring their men home, the incoming governors had tried to prevent large-scale demobilisation. With some difficulty, a compromise had been reached: namely, that men who had completed their terms of service were allowed to leave. In 151 BC, the situation was far worse because Lucullus was plainly trying to fill his army with men who had already done significant military service; and because these men were unwilling to serve, the tribunes imprisoned the consuls until the terms of the levy were changed. The crisis was solved when it was agreed that the men should be enrolled via the lot system, and, according to Polybius, when the young but influential Scipio Aemilianus volunteered to serve as a military tribune. This encouraged other nobles to follow suit. It may also have been around this time that it was established by law that no one could be forced to serve abroad for more than six years; and an additional measure may have been introduced limiting the right of magistrates to obstruct tribunician legislation by claiming that they were watching the heavens for favourable signs.

The new army departed. Scipio stayed for a year, and no doubt participated in the atrocity Lucullus committed against the Caucaei, a Spanish tribe he attacked when he found that Marcellus had negotiated an end to the war before he, Lucullus, could get there. Despite their surrender, Lucullus ordered the tribe's massacre. A year later, Servius Sulpicius Galba did the same to a tribe in Lusitania. Appian, who records these events in some detail, was plainly disgusted by both men, but that was with hindsight. Lucullus was never prosecuted, and Galba was not convicted, despite Cato's best efforts, when his theatrical efforts to elicit pity from the assembly trying his case made them forget they had before them a mass murderer. The next year, a law was passed establishing a special tribunal for trying corruption cases.

The Scipio Aemilianus who assisted Lucullus in getting his army to Spain was the biological son of Aemilius Paullus (the victor over Perseus) who had been adopted by Scipio Africanus' son (who had died young). Scipio Aemilianus was also Polybius' most important Roman patron. So important was this relationship for Polybius that when the surviving Achaean hostages were allowed to go home in 150 BC, he decided to remain in Rome, and went to Spain to observe the silver mines in operation. Two years later, Polybius accompanied Scipio Aemilianus to North Africa. Scipio would be remembered as the greatest Roman of his generation, largely because he sacked two major cities and massacred their populations. One of those cities was Carthage.

In 150 BC war broke out in North Africa between the Numidian king Masinissa, the by now aged friend of Scipio Africanus, and Carthage. Masinissa trounced the Carthaginians, who complained to Rome. Unfortunately for them, most of the Senate agreed with Cato that Carthage should be destroyed. The history of the earlier encounters between the two states, especially as regards the origins of the Second Punic War, had by now been so thoroughly rewritten that many people – Polybius included – believed that the key issue was the Carthaginian sack of Saguntum, and could no doubt produce lists of other Carthaginian acts of bad faith.

The Carthaginians were at a loss as to what to do. They were all too well aware of the Senate's hostility towards them and may also have known that an order had been issued before the end of 150 BC to levy an army for service in North Africa. When the army was preparing to embark, the Carthaginians sent an embassy to Rome offering to make a *deditio*, which was accepted. Lucius Censorinus, consul of 149 BC, gradually escalated Rome's demands until, having forced the Carthaginians to hand over most of their arsenal, he ordered them to tear down their city and resettle ten miles inland. The Carthaginians refused, rearmed and prepared to resist.

The war did not go as expected. Carthage was still a large city, very hard to besiege, and its citizens were desperate. As the siege dragged on, Rome now also became embroiled in a war in Greece. In what would prove to be the first of a number of royal impersonations, a man named Andriscus, having been turned away by the Seleucid king Demetrius, went to Thrace, raised an army and announced that he was Philip, son of Perseus (the real Philip having died at Alba Fucens about a decade earlier). He took over the four Macedonian republics and managed to defeat a Roman army supported by the Achaean League. A year later, a second Roman army appeared under a competent commander, the praetor Quintus Caecilius Metellus, who made short work of Andriscus. Meanwhile, in defiance of orders from Rome, the Achaeans prepared for war with Sparta.

In 147 BC Scipio Aemilianus was elected consul and sent to take charge of operations in Africa. More efficient than his predecessors, he pressed the siege hard and by the end of the year Carthage was in desperate straits. In Greece, repeated Roman embassies charged with challenging Sparta's subordination to the Achaean League increased ill feeling and enhanced the influence of a group of anti-Roman politicians in that league. Polybius attempted to mediate, failed, and went to join Scipio at Carthage. Mobs insulted a Roman ambassador in Corinth.

It is never a good idea to insult a Roman ambassador. It is an even worse idea to declare war on Rome if one has no army to speak of. But this is what the Achaean League effectively proceeded to do by sending a small force north to Thermopylae. Metellus destroyed the League's men in a couple of battles, then held back until a fresh army under Lucius Mummius, consul for 146 BC, turned up outside Corinth. The Achaeans put up limited resistance. The city was destroyed. A commission was sent from Rome to regulate the affairs of Greece, which would be left more or less free – though with a large patch of *ager publicus* where Corinth had been – while a new province was established in Macedonia. Mummius' 'appropriation' of a great number of artworks, some of which ended up in the hands of allies, later became notorious.

The sack of Carthage had taken place a bit earlier in the year. The city's population had been reduced to starvation by the time Scipio launched his final assault, and many chose suicide over death at Roman hands. The city's former territory was divided between neighbouring cities that had assisted Rome, and a large area of *ager publicus* was leased to, among others, people liable to pay *stipendium* (tribute) to Rome. These may have been former settlers on land around Carthage, as well as those who had deserted the Carthaginian cause during the war. Some treasures, items taken by the Carthaginians in their earlier wars against the Sicilians, were returned to their owners. One of these items was the bronze bull in which the legendary Sicilian tyrant Phalaris had roasted his victims alive. Scipio is said to have asked Phalaris' subjects whether they were better off under their own tyrants or the – theoretically more merciful – rule of Rome. Scipio's approach to Carthage's treasures was notably different from how Mummius handled Corinth's, and harked back to the earlier Roman practice whereby allies would see actual benefits accruing from Roman triumphs.

A year before the sacks of Carthage and Corinth, Rome had occasion to celebrate the secular games, first held during the crisis of the First Punic War. The Sibyl had specified that they should be celebrated once each *saeculum*. So, in a theoretical lifetime, Rome had progressed from a regional power to the greatest force in the Mediterranean. As the year of the games would be marked by mass destruction on a scale not practised back in the third century BC, it might also have been observed that Rome was not adjusting especially well to the changes that had taken place in the interim. Indeed, Polybius says that Scipio, weeping as Carthage burned, reflected on the fates of nations and quoted lines from Homer's *Iliad*:

> There will come a day when sacred Troy will perish
> And Priam and his people will be slain.
>
> (Polybius, *Histories* 38.22, quoting *Iliad* 6.448–9)

Scipio knew that Rome was a Trojan foundation, and by the time he wrote these lines Polybius seems to have been aware that political society in Rome was standing on the verge of an internal crisis. He was to be proved right.

PART III

REVOLUTION
(146–88 BC)

TIBERIUS GRACCHUS
AND THE SOVEREIGNTY
OF THE PEOPLE

O ne Roman writer, looking back over the century following the
destruction of Carthage, would attribute the chaos of the times
to the moral effect of losing a great rival. This same writer, Sallust, from
whom we will be hearing a good deal, would also claim that the Roman
state had been torn apart by the ambitions of two brothers, tribunes of
the plebs in 133 BC and 123/2 BC respectively. His contemporary, Cicero,
would agree with him. Both had all too rosy a view of Roman society in
the first half of the second century BC. The greatest generation, which had
beaten Hannibal, had given way to the greedy generation.

The governing classes of the 180s BC had shown themselves willing and
able to countenance the mass execution or incarceration of thousands of
Romans and Italians engaged in Bacchanalian behaviour on the charge
of un-Roman activity (free thinking being an aspect of Bacchic beliefs).
While Scipio Africanus had negotiated to leave Carthage a viable entity,
this latest generation had allowed Rome's magistrates to behave with
extraordinary brutality in the provinces. The massacres in Spain in the
150s BC had started wars that were to rage for decades, while the ongoing
conflicts in Liguria were giving Roman magistrates further opportunity
for shameful behaviour. The ruin of Epirus after 167 BC was no different

in theory than the slaughter of Spaniards after their surrender – both constituted an irresponsible exercise of power. The sacks of Corinth and Carthage in 146 BC were aspects of the Roman aristocracy's increasing willingness to countenance violent oppression.

Looking to other areas of Roman life, it is significant that the edgy plays of Plautus and Naevius – who was once tossed into prison for negative comments about an aristocratic family – were giving way to the staid comedies of Terence. Stage performances increasingly competed for the public's attention with other forms of entertainment, provided in the form of massive and expensive 'public gifts' to the Roman people. While chariot-racing remained the primary event at state-sponsored events, *ludi* ('games'), gladiatorial combat and beast hunts were the stuff of these 'gifts' (*munera*), offered by aristocrats on self-commemorative occasions. They were supplemented with new acts and actors brought in from the east. The Roman aristocrat was now seen as an individual who drew the resources of the world to himself. Regularly coming to Rome were famous Greek intellectuals seeking to impress senators by expounding the latest rhetorical theories, or demonstrating their mastery of new philosophic doctrines. Eastern art filled senatorial houses and the public spaces. To all of this the Roman people were nothing more than spectators.

This world of ever-growing opulence for the few was also one in which some people were raising questions about what it all meant. In these years, as more Romans took to writing histories, a concentration on the theme of 'who we are' in this changing world became apparent. The outcomes of debates on the subject were not purely academic – objections to the calculations used to fix a date for celebrating the secular games in 146 BC brought about their celebration again in 126 BC.

Debates between writers in these years show that fundamental questions remained as to what the true traditions of the community really were. Two writers of this new generation, Cassius Hemina and Lucius Calpurnius Piso Frugi, stand out as representing quite different views. While almost nothing is known about Cassius Hemina, Piso was certainly famous in his own time: he was consul in 133 BC (though out of town for its most dramatic moments), and then censor in 120 BC. Although Piso is the first author who we know for certain called his prose history *Annals*, it was probably Cassius who first devised what for Rome was to become the standard style of historical writing: the chronicle organised around the annually elected magistrates, a form that had been used by Greek states' local historians for some time. Roman history was thus, at its heart, parochial – but with a twist, since Roman foundation myths signalled that all the world's most interesting people had at some point been to Rome.

To compose *Annals* in the true sense, one needed a list of all the magistrates since the expulsion of the kings of Rome in the early sixth century BC. The first list may actually be Cassius' work, since it is clear that Piso was working from one that someone else had drawn up (he argued that a couple of consuls on this list were false additions). How did Cassius make his list? Certainly the issue of 'false' magistrates shows that the list had no single 'official' source, while the inclusion of omens in the standard account of a year suggests that one source could have been books composed by augurs and other priests to record the meanings of signs. Other entries (of triumphs, for instance) might have been suggested by famous families, while the state's public records would have offered the texts of laws and treaties. Whatever its original sources, Piso built upon the foundation the list provided to create a way of telling the annual history of Rome, each year opening with the names of the magistrates taking office, followed by an account of domestic affairs, then of wars, and then of more domestic affairs.

As for Cassius Hemina, it appears that he followed Cato's lead in showing great interest in the origins of Rome's earliest traditions, then speeding through Roman history after the expulsion of the kings down to his own time. It took him only two books to reach the Second Punic War, which he described at length in the third of the four (or perhaps five) books of his history; the last event that we know he covered was the celebration of the secular games in 146 BC.

As a self-professed modern intellectual, Cassius followed Ennius in proclaiming his devotion to the doctrines of the fourth-century Greek thinker Euhemerus, who had declared that the gods were mortals who had been given divine honours for their amazing accomplishments. Euhemeristic observations in Cassius' early history include the view that Faunus – often considered a native Italian divinity with prophetic powers – was actually a man whom Evander, the oldest Greek settler in Latium, had met when he arrived there and called a god.

Similarly, Hercules was really a robust farmer of Greek extraction, who had likewise lived in Latium but before the arrival of Evander; while the Greeks who allowed Aeneas to pass freely through their ranks because they so respected him created the concept of sacrosanctity – the inviolability of a person. Sacrosanctity in Cassius' time applied chiefly to the tribunes of the plebs, who were not to be struck, let alone beaten over the head and killed. Cassius has Romulus and Remus elected by the people, using Cato's date for the city's foundation; he also has Servius Tullius, Rome's penultimate legendary king, create market days, and Rome's last king, Tarquinius Superbus, invent crucifixion.

In his second book Cassius devotes his attention to the Gallic sacking, suggesting that it was people not living up to their beliefs that had caused the disaster. He reports with evident approbation a young member of the Fabian clan who celebrated an ancestral cult while the Gauls were in Rome, and also a meeting of the Senate to discuss irregularities in consulting the will of the gods associated with disasters, including Rome's capture. Cassius also has *proletarii*, members of the lowest census class – not ordinarily called up for service because they could not afford weapons – enlisted for the war against Pyrrhus, and approves the arrival in Rome of the first Greek doctor. He also mentions people who were 'expelled from *ager publicus* because of their plebeian status' (*FRH* 6 Fr. 41). Given what he says elsewhere, it is improbable that he recorded this with approval. A historian who has Romulus elected, Tarquin invent crucifixion, and the technical error that caused the Gallic sacking to be senatorial in origin, is unlikely to have suggested that history would justify senatorial domination.

Piso took a different line. Contrary to Cato, he believed that the name 'Italy' derived from a word meaning 'calf'; contrary to Cassius Hemina, he believed in the gods. He liked people who were conciliatory, pointing out that Romulus founded two festivals to celebrate the alliance with the Sabines that followed the war they had fought after he had stolen their women. He also says that the *lacus Curtius* in the forum was named for a Sabine warrior, and that Tarpeia, who gave her name to an area where the bodies of criminals were exposed to public view, was maligned when called traitor: she did not mean to betray the Capitol to the Sabines – it was all an accident – which is why she received libations and a shrine on the great hill. He thought that Numa, Rome's second king, worked wonders; that Servius Tullius did a fine job initiating the census; but that Tullus Hostilius, the third king, was rightly struck by a thunderbolt for ritual impropriety.

Piso noted miraculous events, and deplored the new extravagance: the expensive personal luxuries Manlius Vulso brought back with him from

Asia Minor were unacceptable (Romulus had been a more restrained partier). Piso recorded miracles at many periods of Roman history, while praising a simple farmer who proved that his success on the land was achieved not through sorcery but by hard work. He knew the original number of the books containing the religious lore of the pontiffs, and details about the history of the tribunate in the fifth century. He praised aristocrats for their noble deeds, especially one Servilius, who murdered an individual named Maelius for trying, without justifiable claim, to make himself king. He also expressed approval for the censors' decision to melt down a statue of Spurius Cassius – executed because he proposed to distribute public land to the common people – that stood in front of a temple he had dedicated.

Piso's views on people seeking monarchical power resonate with the event for which his consulship (in 133 BC) was later to become most famous. This was the passage of a bill by the tribune Tiberius Gracchus appointing a board of three to distribute *ager publicus* in generous allocations to individual Roman citizens throughout Italy, as well as doubling the customary amount of land that a family could legally own. Gracchus also sponsored a bill taking over the properties of King Attalus III of Pergamum, who had willed them to Rome at his death.

The debates that rocked Rome as Gracchus moved his bills were linked with those of the previous decades. They began with the question: what makes a good Roman? In his work on agriculture Cato had written that good farmers made the best soldiers. His book was for his fellow aristocrats, ostensibly advising them on how to maximise the returns from their farms (all of which would have fitted within the pre-Gracchan property-holding maximum of 350 acres). They needed to know the best local markets, he told them, and where to buy the best tools, how to manage their slaves, the right prayers to say. The implication was that farming was better for them than profiteering from provincials, and that the appropriate values for a Roman aristocrat were thrift and professionalism.

Cato's statements about agrarian virtue appeared at about the same time that Polybius was (wrongly) attributing an economic decline in Greece after 167 BC to population decline. Given that these two arch-conservatives thought this way, Tiberius Gracchus' proposal that Rome needed to morally regenerate itself through a return to traditional agrarian values was not especially new, nor self-evidently 'left-wing'. And he was certainly responding to some very real worries. Indeed, when he first proposed his land bill, it probably seemed the least of Rome's problems. Scipio Aemilianus, who would later express much hostility to his adoptive cousin's legislative programme, was away from Rome, busy attacking the Spanish city of Numantia which had inflicted a series of embarrassing defeats on the Roman armies. And Rome would soon learn that the property that Attalus had bequeathed was embroiled in a very nasty civil war. The consul Piso would spend most of his term in Sicily completing with great brutality – he was a keen crucifier – the suppression of a revolt that had broken out three years before. The Sicilian revolt was said to have been caused by the extreme cruelty with which slave owners were treating their slaves. But it went further than that, as the common people – who felt oppressed by the rich – made common cause with the slaves, who were ruled by a man named Eunus who specialised in giving oracles and set up a quasi-Seleucid-style court to govern the rebellion. News of his rebellion had briefly sparked a slave revolt in both Rome and, more seriously, Attica. Social unrest would also be significant in Asia Minor, where utopian hopes of a better future would reinforce a civil war that was to begin at about the same time that Gracchus was taking office.

To a contemporary observer, the big problem of the 130s BC might have seemed not the impoverishment of the Italian peasantry, as Gracchus was claiming, but the unwillingness of people throughout the Mediterranean world to tolerate Roman rule, or the rule of their clients.

In a famous speech, reported to us in fairly similar terms by two later sources, Gracchus introduced his legislation by declaring that the Roman peasantry had been driven from its lands by the rapacious rich. They had replaced the small farmers needed to man the armies of future conquest with gangs of slaves imported from abroad. The beasts of Italy all had their lairs, but not so the men who had fought Rome's wars; while the dangers of slave labour were evident to all from the ongoing crisis in Sicily. The only way to save Rome was to repopulate it with citizen farmers, providing them with land from the *ager publicus*, which already belonged to the state. He proposed to distribute it in plots of about twenty-three acres to individuals, probably *proletarii*, who would make a modest payment but would not be allowed to sell the plots (hence preventing a mass takeover by plutocrats). People who already occupied public land in excess of the 350-acre maximum would be allowed to lay permanent claim to an additional 350 acres without, it seems, having to pay.

Gracchus makes no claim that there were no men on the land because they had been dragged off to fight in endless wars around the Mediterranean. In fact, this would have been a demonstrable falsehood since, even with the war in Numantia, the total number of Romans and Italians under arms was at its lowest in nearly a century. Indeed, one reason for the economic dislocation was that not enough people were in the army and so channelling money back to their families at home. Less well off parts of Italy may also have suffered as many of the young peasant population, generally quite mobile, were moving to Rome and participating for a time in the urban economy before returning home.

One striking aspect of the 130s BC is that, despite a decline in the number of men in service, massive amounts of silver coinage were minted. The number of obverse dies (the ones containing the image for the top of a coin, which have to be changed out more often than the reverse dies because they break more readily) in a given issue allows some impression of its relative size, and the issues of the 130s BC were generally much larger than those of the 140s BC. Over 1,700 obverse dies have been identified as dating between 138 BC and 134 BC, as opposed to 319 between 145 BC and 139 BC; and, from 141 BC, the number of men responsible for minting increased from one to three.

Thus, money supply was not a problem. Military service was not a problem. The problem seems to have been leadership.

The war being waged around Numantia was one sign of what was wrong. It had begun in the mid-140s BC, inspired by Viriathus, a survivor of the massacre ordered by Galba back in 150 BC. Viriathus had won a major victory over a Roman army in 140 BC, and in 137 BC a new army commanded by the consul Mancinus had been forced to surrender at Numantia. Tiberius Gracchus, who had negotiated the terms, was not pleased when the Senate repudiated the treaty, returning a bound and naked Mancinus to the Numantines. They gave him back.

The surrender of Mancinus, followed by another bad loss two years later, raises questions about how well Roman armies had adapted to their new mission as garrison troops. Traces of Roman siege works uncovered by archaeologists at Numantia allow us some glimpses of just what this process of adaptation might have entailed. One thing that's clear is that the legions increased in size from around 4,000 men to around 5,000, but the command structure remained very much as it had been for centuries. This meant that legions did not have their own commanders but were led by a committee of six tribunes, all young men. Overseeing these was the quaestor – with no one between him and the commanding general. Given this lack of basic experience in the officer corps, operational command and control must have been exercised through the centurions, who were still, at this stage, elected by their men. This did not make for a strong command structure, especially for the generals, who would have to deal with legions they had only partially raised. It may also help to explain why Rome's military efforts were so ineffective, and hence why the Spanish wars became so deeply unpopular.

Every change of command was essentially a political rather than an operational process, which could make it hard to alter the way things were done. Scipio Africanus had experimented with new formations called cohorts, which were deeper and larger than the traditional Roman maniples of 120 men, but the camps at Numantia suggest that these were only reintroduced to the army in Spain when Scipio Aemilianus showed up. A further feature of the Spanish armies was that the cavalry was now all recruited from provincial sources – members of the Roman upper classes were no longer willing to go to war in a place that promised no quick loot.

As the wars dragged on, it became apparent that something needed to change. And it did. Political radicalism was the air as the decade of the 130s BC opened. In 140 BC, tribunes had tried to prevent Quintus Pompeius, consul during the previous year, from leaving for Spain because of complaints about the levy, and in 138 BC two tribunes who disapproved of the consuls' conduct of a levy had them arrested. Also in 139 BC, a praetor had tried to ban astrologers from Rome for 'misleading' the Roman people. It is against this background of unrest that two laws were brought in that fundamentally changed Rome's political landscape – by introducing secret ballots. The first ballot law, passed in 139 BC, introduced secret ballots for elections; a later writer would describe this law as one which 'separated the people from the Senate' (Cicero, *Concerning Friendship* 41). The second law, passed in 137 BC, introduced written ballots for public trials. This followed a couple of scandalous acquittals and it would appear that Scipio Aemilianus was behind the measure. It is even possible that Scipio had supported the measure introduced by his good friend, Gaius Laelius, in which it was proposed that *ager publicus* be distributed to the poor. Laelius dropped the measure in the face of strong senatorial opposition. That was in 140 BC.

Given that roughly the same land bill had been discussed seven years before, and the affinity of Gracchus' thought with that of Cato, Gracchus cannot be seen as a particularly revolutionary thinker or more obviously 'anti-senatorial' than any other tribune. Furthermore, the proposal in his bill that the people who received land should pay rent perpetuated the occasional practice of monetising *ager publicus* that had begun during the Second Punic War, while the provision to double the maximum size of a landholding was an outright giveaway to the rich. Neither provision suggests that Gracchus saw the bill as a present to the downtrodden. It may be that he genuinely believed there was a connection between moral worth and labour in the fields; that he believed that what he was doing was both morally right and fiscally sound. The problem was that, in doing what he thought was right, Gracchus might awaken the 'sleeping sovereign' by asserting the latent principle that the Roman people controlled the Roman state.

Gracchus was not just any tribune. He was Scipio Africanus' grandson. Scipio's daughter was noteworthy in her own right, as was Gracchus' father Tiberius Sempronius Gracchus, whom we have already met as consul in 177 BC and as one of the controversial censors of 169 BC. The younger Gracchus' other connections included his father-in-law Appius Claudius Pulcher, who had been consul in 143 BC and censor in 136 BC, while Appius Claudius' biological brother, adopted into the aristocratic clan of the Licinii Crassi, was the father-in-law of Tiberius' younger brother Gaius. Tiberius could also count on the support of Publius Mucius Scaevola, Piso's colleague as consul in 133 BC, who was a leading lawyer and possibly a historian in his own right. In 141 BC, as tribune, he had prosecuted the ex-praetor of 142 BC for corruption in office, winning a conviction before the *comitia tributa*.

People pondering Tiberius' friends and family might have been less concerned with the problem of Italian land than with the possibility that some of the most powerful men in the world would form a 'board of three for judging and assigning lands' (*triumviri agris iudicandis assignandis*). The board would determine both what land was available for distribution and who would get it. There would be no appealing their decision. This might well look more like an aristocratic coup d'état than an effort to save Rome (or, given the leadership issues they had recently been having, an aristocratic coup d'état aimed at saving Rome).

The Senate refused to pass a decree supporting Tiberius' bill – perhaps not a complete surprise, but in an era when the power of the people had been openly discussed and tribunes had routinely presented themselves as the people's defenders against the abuses of magistrates, neither should it surprise us that Tiberius took his measure directly to them. When the tribune Marcus Octavius – said to be in league with individuals who occupied far more than their legal share of public land – vetoed the bill, Tiberius summoned a meeting of the people, with a view to removing him from office on the grounds that his conduct was not in their interests.

In the past half century tribunes faced with similar charges had tended to give in, and since Polybius had written that the tribunes were subordinate to the people, Tiberius Gracchus' view had precedent behind it. Despite this, Marcus Octavius did not budge. Gracchus begged him to withdraw his veto when seventeen of the thirty-five tribes – just short of a majority – had voted for his removal, but he remained firm. He was removed from office only when the vote of the eighteenth tribe was counted. A version of the speech that Gracchus gave justifying what had happened survives. If this accurately reflects what he said – and it is certainly consistent with reports about his speech promoting the land bill, with its appeals to a sense of Roman history – then it shows us how important the developing historical consciousness of the governing class was becoming in public discourse:

> ... if a tribune annuls the people, he is no tribune at all. Is it not dreadful that a tribune should have power to arrest a consul, while the people cannot deprive a tribune of his power when he employs it against the body that bestowed it? The people elect both the consul and the tribune. And surely kingship, besides taking all power to itself, is also consecrated to the divine by the greatest sacred powers; and the city expelled Tarquin for his wrong-doing, and because of one man's arrogance the power that had founded Rome was overthrown. Again, what institution is as sacred and holy at Rome as that of the virgins who tend and watch the undying fire? And yet if one of them errs, she is buried alive, for they do not retain the sacrosanctity that is given them for their service to the gods to commit acts of impiety against the gods. Therefore, it is right that a tribune who acts unjustly towards the people should not retain the sacrosanctity that is given him for service to the people, since he destroys that which is the source of his own power. And if it is right that he becomes tribune with a majority of the

votes of the tribes, then is it not even more just that he be removed by the votes of all of them?

(Plutarch, *Tiberius Gracchus* 15.4–7)

With Octavius out of the way, Tiberius summoned an assembly to vote on his land law; people are said to have come from all over Italy to support it, and it passed. Tiberius Gracchus, his brother Gaius Gracchus and Appius Claudius were elected as the board of three.

The people had the power to legislate, but the Senate had the power to control funding for public activities. Polybius had written: 'It is obvious that supplies must always be provided to the legions; without a decree of the senate, neither grain, nor clothing, nor pay can be provided' (Polybius, *Histories* 6.15.4). The Senate refused to give Tiberius the customary rent allotted to officials on public duty and fixed his expenses at less than a denarius.

News now came that Attalus III had died and wished to leave his property to Rome. News may also have arrived that a civil war was already raging in the north of Attalus' kingdom, as a man named Aristonicus, following in the footsteps of Andriscus who had claimed to be the son of Perseus, was after the throne. Aristonicus raised an army in Thrace, proclaimed himself the true heir of Attalus and invaded the kingdom. The Senate hesitated over Attalus' bequest: it had refused a gift of this sort from Ptolemy VIII, who had left Cyrenaica to Rome. Tiberius announced that he would put two bills before the people, one accepting Attalus' bequest and dedicating it to the work of the land commission. The other concerned the cities of Asia, apparently stating that the people rather than the Senate would decide what was done with Attalid revenues in the future.

Popular power as Tiberius exercised it certainly existed, for Polybius, who was with Scipio Aemilianus at Numantia while all this was going on, could point to places where it had been used. Unfortunately for Tiberius, others who might have been in Polybius' audience or who had encountered Greek political theory elsewhere would be aware that demagogues can become tyrants, and Tiberius, with his well-practised eloquence and flair for the dramatic, fitted the model of demagogue to a T. What he was also able to do that others could not, or could not be bothered to do, was organise rural voters, possibly using the tribal offices at Rome.

In the late summer of 133 BC a fresh quarrel between Gracchus and the

Senate came to a head. Gracchus wanted to be tribune again. Although the *lex Villia*, which set limits on when people could stand for office, banned self-succession only for holders of *imperium*, there was no immediate precedent for his move. On the first day, confused as to what should happen, the tribune who had convened the electoral assembly dismissed it after the voting had begun. The next day a fresh assembly was convened, this time on the Capitoline, which limited the number of voters – quite possibly to those who could be recognised as Gracchus' supporters. Simultaneously the Senate was meeting in the Temple of Fides, also on the Capitoline, debating what to do. Rumour reached the Senate that violence had broken out at the election – and possibly that Gracchus was trying to make himself king. At this point, although Mucius Scaevola, presiding, refused to take any official action, Gracchus' cousin Scipio Nasica gathered together a group of angry senators who, armed with clubs made from bits of broken furniture, attacked the electoral assembly. When the fighting ended, Gracchus' body was discovered near the entrance to the Temple of Capitoline Jupiter.

Tiberius Gracchus' murder was greeted with confusion and some shock. The praetor Popillius seized the initiative against his supporters, exiling some without trial and quite possibly executing men of low status, also without trial. It was significant, given that tribunes were sacrosanct individuals whose murder was an act of gross impiety, that no one was ever prosecuted, though Scipio Nasica was told to leave town and sent as a member of an embassy of five to organise the province of Asia. He was murdered at Pergamum in 132 BC. Scipio Aemilianus, who opposed Gracchus' legislation, may have complicated matters by circulating an oracle to the effect that a new state leader would come from Spain.

Despite efforts at intimidation, the tide turned against Gracchus' enemies. The land commission got down to work, with Crassus taking Gracchus' place. Elected consul for 131 BC, Crassus was then chosen to replace Scipio Nasica as *pontifex maximus* (head of the board of priests). In 131 or 130 BC the tribune Papirius Carbo passed laws formally allowing a person to hold successive tribunates of the plebs, and for the use of the secret ballot at legislative assemblies. Interestingly, there was no return to the massive coin issues of 138–34 BC; we can identify around 580 new obverse dies for the period 133–30 BC, which suggests that the actions of the commissioners were in fact placing no great strain on the treasury.

It might have seemed that business had returned to normal. The land commission functioned without causing any momentous changes, or so it appeared. Rome acquired a new province, which no one yet had realised would prove immensely profitable. But Asia would prove immensely profitable, thereby playing a major role in the ongoing economic transition of the governing class, and many Italians were deeply offended by the activities of the land commission. More importantly, Gracchus had shown that it was possible to circumvent traditional patterns of behaviour through direct appeal to the people, and to circumvent traditional government by inventing new administrative groups that were not dependent upon the standard offices of state. In the long run this discovery would provide the mechanism through which the traditional government of Rome would be transformed.

12

GAIUS GRACCHUS
AND THE RISE OF THE
CONTRACTORS

Scipio Aemilianus returned home having destroyed Numantia, whose population committed mass suicide. Meanwhile, the Sicilian revolt finally ended in 132 BC. At Numantia, Scipio had drawn on connections he had made throughout his career, including those with the Numidian kingdom. Masinissa had died during the siege of Carthage, but his son Micipsa had sent men to fight on the Roman side. One of these men was Jugurtha, Micipsa's nephew, whom we will be meeting in a very different role in a few years' time. For now it is enough to note that, in recognition of his service, Scipio recommended that Micipsa adopt him as his son – which he did. Jugurtha is said to have made many friends among the Roman aristocracy while he was there. We can only speculate whether one of those friends was Gaius Gracchus.

Scipio settled down to what he expected to be a long and influential career. Marcus Tullius Cicero, the greatest literary figure of the first century BC, envisages him on his estate in 129 BC debating the nature of the Roman constitution with friends. As behoves a friend of Polybius, Scipio is imagined as supporting a balanced constitution, but also as showing a strange interest in monarchy. He also, Cicero says, deplored the actions of Tiberius Gracchus. This was no Ciceronian fantasy, for as complaints came into Rome from Italian communities outraged by the actions of the board of three, Scipio took it upon himself to represent their interests in the Senate. He then, quite suddenly, dropped dead.

Scipio Aemilianus' death in 129 BC deprived Rome of its one genuinely talented soldier just as it was becoming clear that the situation in Asia was a great deal more complex than anyone had realised. Crassus had been sent out in command of an army in 131 BC, and had been defeated and killed by Aristonicus early in 130 BC. It would be two more years before Aristonicus was finally out of the picture – largely coinciding with the Roman army developing alliances with Greek cities in the region. The leaders of those cities regarded Aristonicus, who was given to spouting utopian notions of social equality, as a threat to their comfortable oligarchic societies. What also emerged was a province based, for the first time, on a functioning eastern kingdom, with tax collection mechanisms that could easily be taken over by the new regime. It plainly rankled with those who would have liked a piece of the action that in the initial post-war settlement the revenues were paid through the governor. The governorship of Asia became a popular career option.

The issue of Asian taxes was but one that caused concern among thinking Romans as the 120s BC wore on; another, rather closer to home, was the relative standing of Italians and Romans when it came to land distribution. Since it was largely Italian-occupied *ager publicus* that was reclaimed by the commissioners, there was considerable unhappiness. In 125 BC, something went very wrong at Fregellae, some of whose inhabitants were said to have been conspiring against Rome. The urban praetor of that year, Lucius Opimius, promptly led an army south, destroyed the city and removed some of the population. A new city, Ferentina Nova, was founded a year later, probably for the Fregellans who had not been 'guilty of conspiracy'. Opimius' action – recalling earlier acts of brutality throughout Italy and recently inflicted on the people of Sicily – reveals that whatever guilt the imperial upper classes might have felt after Tiberius Gracchus' murder was gone.

The destruction of Fregellae provides the background for the tribunate of Tiberius' brother Gaius Gracchus, whose turn it was to take centre stage in 124 BC. Running for office and intent on advertising his moral rectitude, he left the electorate in no doubt that he believed insufficient action had been taken against his brother's murderers and that the state was in serious need of reform. Openness, honesty and fairness for all Romans formed the core of Gaius' political programme, a far more sophisticated one than had been put forward by any domestic politician, and one that was also accompanied by some clear thinking about how to exploit the resources of the empire more efficiently. Although he used his brother's fate as a rallying cry, Gaius was not Tiberius. Whereas Tiberius' programme had looked backwards to a fanciful golden age, Gaius' looked forwards.

Gaius Gracchus was not without his supporters. Documents from this period indicate that he was working with several like-minded individuals whom he could trust to pass legislation to forward his agenda. Unlike his brother, who aspired to create a powerful aristocratic faction, Gaius was keen to establish a group dedicated to the notion of effective, more inclusive government that would reflect the expanding political community of the contractor state.

It is to one of Gaius' supporters that we owe our best evidence for his time in office and for the political spirit of the age. Marcus Acilius Glabrio, tribune in 122 BC, would pass a law of specific significance for Gaius' plans, concerning extortion. This law, partially preserved on a bronze tablet which was once owned by Cardinal Pietro Bembo, a sometime lover of Lucrezia Borgia, states that any citizen, Latin, ally, foreigner or anyone in the 'disposition, sway, power of friendship of the Roman people' could bring an action to recover property stolen by a Roman magistrate, before a new court presided over by a praetor. The praetor would appoint a Roman patron for the complainants, and draw up an annual list of 450 persons from which a jury of fifty could be empanelled for a trial. There were provisions setting strict time limits within which a trial must take place and allowing for the prosecution to call up to forty-eight witnesses. The possibility of jurors misbehaving was taken very seriously, and there were detailed instructions on how to cast a ballot at the end of the trial. These ballots were to be handed out by the praetor, marked 'a' (*absolvo*) on one side and 'c' on the other (*condemno*). Each juror would delete the letter he didn't want. The ballots would be counted publicly by two jurors. In the case of a guilty verdict, the praetor would sequester the defendant's property immediately and appoint a board to determine the proper payment to the complainant. Specifically, the praetor should beware of collusion between the prosecution and the defence. If the prosecution was successful, the plaintiff would receive Roman citizenship if he wanted it.

The most noteworthy aspect of Acilius' law was his definition of the

*9. A portion of the bronze tablet recording lex Acilia setting up the
extortion court in 122 BC. This section of the text includes provisions
to investigate collusion and for the granting of citizenship.*

group from which jurors would be chosen: namely, from the eighteen
centuries of 'cavalrymen with the public horse' who were *not* also senators
or the immediate relatives of senators. This exclusion clause enabled leading
members of the contractor class, who tended to be members of the eighteen
centuries, to pass judgement on magistrates. One of the crucial political
conflicts of the next three decades would be the magistrates' efforts to wrest
control of the court from the contractors, and to prevent the potentially
vast increase in membership of the contractor class which would inevitably
follow if the Italian aristocracy were given Roman citizenship. The political
interests of the Italian aristocracy, already linked economically with the
state contractors, would complement their political interests, too. Just as
the contractors sought political power through the law courts, the Italian
aristocracy would seek admission to the Roman state.

The long-term implications of the extortion law may not have been
obvious to Glabrio or to Gaius, but it is clear that they thought the
problems facing Roman society extended well beyond the corrupt

behaviour of magistrates. Underlying the law's provisions for openness was the conviction that Roman society was continually undermined by influence-peddling on the part of its dominant class, and that the only answer to this was to expose all the state's activity to public scrutiny. In the year before his election to his first tribunate, Gaius complained that secrecy violated the traditions of Rome, noting that no one had been tried for his brother's death, whereas in 'ancient times' if a man was arraigned on a capital charge a trumpeter would stand in front of his house and summon him with a blast. And no judgment could be rendered until this had been done.

The concern to create a fairer society runs through the rest of the legislative record for this year and the previous one. The first two laws of 123 BC had looked to what Gaius regarded as offences linked with his brother's murder: one banned a man who had been removed from office from seeking further office; the other stated that a magistrate who banished a man without trial should be liable to prosecution. This looks like an attempt to prevent the sort of magisterial mass slaughter that had occurred in 133 BC and before. Other laws forbade the enlistment of anyone under seventeen, and eliminated the requirement that soldiers buy their own equipment. There was also a land law that prohibited the dividing-up of some *ager publicus*, and one setting up two new colonies in southern Italy. Then there was the grain law.

Gaius' bill, guaranteeing a subsidised supply of grain for Romans in Rome, was to prove as influential over the course of the next century as the extortion law. Rome had long had a tradition of subsidising the price of grain in times of crisis, but the system was somewhat rickety. The aediles controlled the distribution of funds for the subsidies, while some of the wealthiest families in Rome controlled the warehouses where grain – even grain that was collected as tax from the province of Sicily – was stored. Any assumption that there might be collusion between the owners of the storehouses and the aediles, especially given the well-attested dishonesty of members of the clan Sulpicius (owners of one of the main storehouses), cannot be proven, but it is clear that individual aediles would have had to rely on personal and family connections to acquire grain when needed. There had been a number of bad years before 123 BC, and we have direct evidence of a Metellus using his family connections in Macedonia to acquire a large shipment. Gracchus' law changed all that. First off, he set the price of grain at roughly a denarius and two-thirds for a monthly ration set at just over forty-three litres. Second, he stated that every free Roman male was eligible to receive grain at this price. (There is a story that he found Calpurnius Piso, who had previously praised the violent suppression of people trying to 'buy' the Roman people with these bills, in the queue to take his distribution, apparently to make the point that the bill was wasteful because it let people like him have cheap food.) Third, Gracchus established state-run granaries. From here on out the management of Rome's grain supply would be an issue of fundamental importance. At the time, it fitted very well with Gracchus' efforts to ensure transparency in important spheres of government activity.

The legislative programme of 122 BC included, along with the one setting up the extortion court, a law establishing a colony at Carthage (drafted by Rubrius, a colleague). What is not clear is when Gaius passed critically important laws turning the collection of taxes in the province of Asia over to the *publicani* (public contractors), and ordering that before each consular election it should be determined which provinces were to be awarded to which consuls.

Gaius aimed to change the way business was done in Rome quite fundamentally. Correcting some obvious injustices – such as that in a state that could afford such massive building projects soldiers had to provide their own equipment – the thrust of his legislation was to limit the Senate's discretionary powers and to expand participation in the business of government. It is unlikely that he also introduced a law expanding access to citizenship to all Italians and allies, as our sources allege, or a law doubling the size of the Senate. Such bills may merely have been rumoured at the time. Both would seem to run counter to the motive underlying the extortion law – to keep the senators out of the action – not to mention that law's assumption that non-Romans might not actually want to be Romans.

Given the radical nature of his programme, it is scarcely surprising that Gaius Gracchus made himself a lot of enemies in Rome. They waited, though, to launch their attack until he was away in North Africa, where he was one of three officials sent to establish a new colony, created by Rubrius' law, which would allot very generous amounts of land to settlers on the site of Carthage. With Gracchus away, the tribune Livius Drusus passed another law – this one establishing twelve new colonies in Italy – so as to convince people that they did not need Gracchus to safeguard their welfare, while also suggesting that Gracchus might be in favour of the aforementioned measure to grant citizenship to non-citizens. This was a wildly unpopular idea to ordinary Romans, who were not at all keen to share the goods of empire now beginning to trickle in their direction. Also doing the rounds was a rumour that Gracchus, or his close associate Fulvius Flaccus, had murdered Scipio Aemilianus.

On his return from North Africa, probably during his campaign for a third tribunate, Gracchus put on something of a performance in the forum, tearing out the front rows of seats in the amphitheatre, in which the senators normally sat, so that 'everyone' could enjoy the spectacle. This failed to improve his standing, and he was not re-elected. Lucius Opimius, the butcher of Fregellae, topped the poll for the consulship.

As he took office in 121 BC, Opimius announced that he would repeal Rubrius' law. At a public sacrifice on the Capitoline in early January, a scuffle broke out in which an assistant at the sacrifice was killed. Gracchus was blamed. The next day, as the Senate convened in the forum, Gracchus and his supporters occupied the Temple of Diana on the Aventine, a shrine now associated with the plebeian movement of Rome's earliest days. After a failed exchange of envoys between the Aventine and the forum, Opimius, who had already brought archers into the city, had the Senate pass a decree that he should take whatever actions necessary to ensure that the state came to no harm.

Opimius understood this as an invitation to murder Gaius Gracchus and his allies. His archers duly attacked Gracchus' men on the Aventine. In the mêlée that followed, Gracchus, Flaccus and some 3,000 others died. Opimius ordered yet more people to be arrested, charged them with being Gracchus' supporters, then had them strangled in the state prison in the forum. Their property was confiscated and their bodies thrown into the Tiber. The families of the deceased were forbidden to mourn them in public.

As Opimius triumphed over Gaius Gracchus, his consular colleague Quintus Fabius Maximus joined the previous year's consul, Gnaeus Domitius Ahenobarbus, on campaign in southern France. Via their victories there they established what was to become the Roman province of Transalpine Gaul, and Domitius Ahenobarbus built a road across southern France linking northern Italy to Spain. Though no one could have guessed at the time, the new province's exposure to tribes from central France and further north, and the opportunities that this would offer to an ambitious governor, would spell the end of the traditional form of Roman government. It is more than a little ironic that in the year that the cause of the Roman people suffered what may have seemed a terminal setback, fresh seeds of the Roman oligarchy's destruction were planted deep in France's soil.

During the next few years the strength of reaction against Gracchan-style populism shattered the balance that Polybius had seen as the constitution's strength, leaving in its place an unrestrained oligarchy, dominated by the ever-wealthier leading families of the nobility – as they were now starting to call themselves. Between 121 and 109 BC five members of the Caecilii Metelli clan held the consulship, while a sixth was the husband of Caecilia Metella, who was a sister of three of these men and cousin of the other two. Also, a niece of Caecilia Metella married Marcus Aemilius Scaurus, consul of 115 BC, who for a while was regarded as the Senate's unquestioned leader, or, as Cicero put it, a man 'by a nod of whose head the world was governed' (Cicero, *On Behalf of Fonteius* 24.1). That seven members of one family, by birth or marriage, should hold consulships within thirteen years was unprecedented.

The most important aspect of Gaius Gracchus' tribunician career was the shift of power away from the Senate to the contractor class. Contractors soon found that collecting taxes in wealthy Asia opened limitless opportunities for profit – if people needed money to pay their taxes, the Roman banker was available to make a high interest loan. The Roman governor, who was liable to prosecution before a jury of a tax collector's business associates, was unlikely to step in. The influx of new money, which the state could not touch, would rapidly shape the political landscape in ways that it is most unlikely that Gaius Gracchus, who seems a genuinely honest and decent man, could ever have imagined.

13

A CRITIC'S VIEW

⬥⬥⬥⬥⬥⬥

The key to the Gracchan land bills had been that the plots distributed by the triumvirs remained *ager publicus* and could not be sold off by their appointed settlers. It was a law partially preserved on the flip side of Cardinal Bembo's bronze tablet that permitted the sale of this land in 111 BC. Such a provision allowed for exactly the circumstance Tiberius Gracchus claimed to have been at the heart of Rome's difficulties: the expropriation of peasants' land by wealthy landowners who were newly free to create ever larger estates. It is now, at the end of the second century BC, that we see shifts in Italy's economic situation, with large sums of money generated by public contracting supporting new private fortunes. The obvious signs of these changes were the development of large estates centred on private villas, and expensive private houses incorporating aspects of Greek urban architecture along with masses of art copied from Greek originals.

Roughly speaking, two styles of housing characterised Roman upper-class dwellings before the second century BC. In the countryside, there was the 'Attic-style' farmhouse, well-constructed but of relatively simple design. In the city, the average house (which might have shops on its street front) would be accessed through a formal entryway leading into a central court, or atrium, backed by another room, the *tablinum*, with wings of private space on either side. In the earliest variation of this style, evident by the early third century, a four-sided colonnade (a peristyle) – a feature borrowed from Greek public buildings – would be added to the atrium, with a water feature (*impluvium*) as its centrepiece.

In the second half of the second century, enlarging houses by means of the addition of 'public' architecture became much more common among Rome's wealthier classes. There had always been those who could afford gigantic expensive residences on the outskirts of Rome or on the Palatine, but it was the development of a new building material, cement, that facilitated not only architectural innovation but also a new style of interior decoration that allowed features typical of public buildings to be created within the domestic space. Before 100 BC there was at least one house on the Palatine that had a peristyle surrounding an interior garden, and Cicero visualises Scipio Aemilianus and his friends in 129 BC debating the ideal Roman constitution within the confines of a peristyle court at his house in Tusculum.

By the first quarter of the first century, grand mansions such as the Villa Arianna and the Villa San Marco at Stabiae, and the Villa of the Mysteries at Pompeii, were taking shape. This expansion in size was accompanied by the growing use of imported Greek furniture (fancy dining tables, sometimes singled out as extravagances in our sources, seem to have been particular favourites); by changes in the organisation of private space, such as the moving of cooking areas and latrines as far as possible from a house's public areas; and by ever larger slave staffs. In rural households, despite Tiberius Gracchus' complaints, slaves were fewer – being both expensive and economically inefficient – as tenant farmers inhabited much of the land administered by a country villa.

We can gain some impression of how much money was passing through the hands of Roman aristocrats and the contractor class during these years. The figures that we get, while admittedly impressionistic – derived as they are from reports of excessive prices for cooks, bribes and such like – give us some impression of the scale of the new wealth. So while the statement that the wealthiest man of the era had a fortune of about 16,000,000 denarii, or that Marcus Aemilius Scaurus (who boasted of having made a vast fortune despite a small inheritance) paid 175,000 denarii for a new cook (celebrity chefs, although always slaves, were highly valued) are exaggerated, other numbers look real. An impecunious consul, for instance, did take a bribe of 8,400 denarii from a Spanish tribe (presumably he thought this was a lot of money), and Polybius says that Scipio Aemilianus had a personal fortune of just over 400,000 denarii and controlled an additional 336,000 denarii, which he used to pay the dowries of his two aunts (the mothers, respectively, of the Gracchus brothers and of Tiberius' murderer, Scipio

Nasica). Polybius thought that was a lot of money even though it was less than the wealth of a senator of middling means – our friend Cicero – by the first century BC.

Polybius' estimate for the annual revenue from the Spanish silver mines of around 8,000,000 denarii probably represents about one-fifth of Rome's total annual revenue. Given that the minimum value of a senator's estate was 100,000 denarii, the property controlled by the 300 members of the Senate, even at this point, might have amounted to a good deal more than 30,000,000 (while Scipio's estate was exceptional for the time, it is likely that most other senators had considerably more than the minimum census requirement). The income generated from these estates, at an expected rate of return of around 5 per cent, would mean that a very conservative estimate for the annual income of the Senate as a body was more than 1,500,000 denarii.

An estimate of senatorial income as equivalent to somewhat more than 5 per cent of the state's annual revenue is probably conservative, but it still gives us a sense of the plausible. It is also interesting that Polybius says that aristocrats were very precise in managing their money, desiring to make a profit at every turn (which is both a bit worrying when talking about government officials and suggests that Scaurus' claims about how he got rich from being a senator would not have appalled his contemporaries). But for all that members of the aristocracy were interested in profit, none of the sums we have been talking about would have been sufficient to raise an army at private expense – which we will see a number of people do once we come to the end of the 90s BC and further on into the first century BC.

The influx of new silver had stimulated the development of an increasingly sophisticated banking community, multiplying the impact of the new revenues in a complex environment in which several different coinage systems were used in different parts of the Mediterranean. To accommodate the differences in coinage systems, large-scale business transactions were made through the exchange of bank drafts using exchange rates developed by the banking community (there was absolutely no regulation by the state).

Bankers tended to be people on the make, not aristocracy, but individuals heading in that direction. Their individual clients ranged from merchants to men of moderate means needing to tide themselves over in difficult times. Unlike the average Roman aristocrat, the average person, in Italy or elsewhere, did not have a wide margin for error. Other borrowers, however, would be communities, and these, being in theory more solvent, were a magnet for Italian bankers.

As the eastern Mediterranean opened up after the annexation of Asia, the Italian community, consisting largely of merchants as well as bankers, expanded rapidly. Some intended to move out of Italy and move up in society, with no intention of returning. For example, a text recording a remarkably lacklustre festival in Lycia, an area of southern Turkey beyond Asia's frontier, mentions one Roman who, when entering a winning horse in a race, had himself announced as a citizen of Telmessus, the Lycian city where he had settled. Others looked to return home and ascend the social pyramid.

Of course, Italians were scarcely novelties in the eastern Aegean in the second century BC. A vessel from Brundisium (Brindisi) is recorded as having picked up a famous third-century Achaean politician on Andros in the western Aegean and ferried him to Egypt via the west coast of Turkey, where the shipmaster had business. Delphi had long been important, both for its oracle and for its architectural significance – Aemilius Paullus had erected a large monument there, to celebrate his victory over Perseus. In Thessaly, merchants appear to have followed the victorious path of Flamininus' army and installed themselves in communities where they were identified by the locals as the 'toga-wearers'. Italian merchants were involved in the export of grain from northern Greece to Italy, where it was incorporated into the subsidised grain distributions Gaius Gracchus had regularised. But it was the island of Delos that became the major centre, both for Italian settlers and as a focal point for trade with the new province of Asia and the surrounding lands. Its development had begun well before Asia's annexation, when in 167 BC it was declared a tax haven in order to divert trade away from Rhodes.

Although technically belonging to Athens, Delos had a long history as a religious and commercial centre, and the Athenian administration was decidedly non-interventionist. The Italians who came to Delos are traceable to this day via the remains of their houses and public buildings, as well as numerous inscriptions revealing a community of bankers and traders in luxury goods flourishing alongside and interacting well with the Greek community. Wherever they were from – and most of the Italians we see on Delos came from Latium, Campania or Apulia – they mixed easily with each other, tending to self-identify as 'Romans' no matter what their actual citizenship. The goods they shipped west fed an increasingly sophisticated life of luxury, but the stress needs to be on 'increasingly', since what we see on Delos, and then in Italy, is not new – Plautine characters doused themselves in the same eastern scents as did diners of this era – but the massive expansion of a phenomenon that had previously attracted a narrower audience.

A vigorous critic of the new normal was a man named Lucilius, whose work (like so much only preserved in quotations from later authors) created the Latin genre of satire. Lucilius, who wrote a lot, and fast, had been a friend of Scipio Aemilianus. He was no fan of Opimius – he thought the destruction of Fregellae was a case of factional oppression – but nor was he was a supporter of the Gracchus brothers. His subject matter was broad: he could envision a gladiatorial combat from the gladiator's perspective; he wrote a poem about the siege of Numantia in a positive vein, but also poems critical of Roman conduct in Spain. He could write about sex, philosophy and food, as well as literature. He used Greek technical terms in his verse treatments of rhetorical theory, noted bankers' aptitude for making huge profits, and praised those who were content to live the simple life, but he also commented without obvious sympathy on people who received subsidised grain. He suggested that tax collecting in Asia could be a challenge, possibly because the locals would try to cheat you.

Lucilius' poetic range, venturing well beyond the conventional forms of epic and drama, and his willingness to address contemporary issues head on, are perhaps linked with the emergence around this time of more explicit political memoirs. Cato had included two of his own speeches in his history, and Gaius Gracchus had gone further in composing a memoir in which he explained his brother's decision to introduce the land law. There followed in the next decade a three-volume memoir by Marcus Aemilius Scaurus. A decade later appeared a further series of self-serving volumes in which aristocrats asserted that their contributions to Rome's greatness had been misunderstood.

It was in Lucilius' lifetime that historical writing in Rome took a gigantic leap forwards in terms of its complexity, if not its accuracy. It was probably in the 120s BC that Gnaeus Gellius completed his history of Rome, in at least ninety-seven books. It took him fifteen books – the whole of Cato's *Origines* comprised just seven – to reach the Gauls' sack of Rome, and thirty-three more to reach Cannae. Some of this may be due to rhetorical expansion – a fondness for inventing long speeches and putting them in the mouths of the long-since deceased – and some of it from what seems to have been a genuine interest in the traditions of foreign lands. But that cannot explain everything, and local archives and other sources probably provided extra details, especially for the fourth and third centuries BC. It is likely to have been Gellius who vastly expanded the history of Rome's relationship with other states in Italy. The contemporary relevance is clear: people were raising questions about who had the right to land and who might claim particular precedence.

The cities of Italy were not ready to sweep their own histories and customs under the carpet in a desire to be assimilated to Rome. Rather, they wished to commemorate both their distinct non-Roman pasts and their current relationship with the imperial city. A visitor to the Umbrian city of Iguvium (modern Gubbio), for instance, would have found that the rites for the local divinities, especially the dominant trinity of Trebos Iovios, Marte Grabovios and Vofionos Grabovios, were celebrated in Umbrian. If she had moved on into Etruria, she would have noted that the Etruscan language was widely used even though individuals would have been using new, Roman forms of their names. In Pompeii, officials were inscribing the record of their activities in the local southern Italian language of Oscan: Maras Atinius *kvaísstur* (quaestor) used money from fines to finance his building work, as had Minaz Avdiis, son of Klípís, and Dekis Seppiis, son of Úpfals *kvaízstur* (see M. H. Crawford, *Imagines Italiae*, Pompeii, 650–51 n. 21; 647, n. 19).

At Abella (modern Avella in Campania), if our traveller was there around the year 100 BC, she would have observed a *kvaísstur* agreeing to a contract for the construction of a public peristyle with statues, erected when one Maiieís Stattieís held the traditional office of *meddíx*, 'leader' (M. H. Crawford, *Imagines Italiae*, Abella, 893–5, n. 2–3). If this putative visitor had then journeyed further south, into Lucania, she would have seen that Oscans were still using the local alphabet when writing in their native language. And at Potentia, Herennius Pomponius, during the five-year censorship of Lucius Popidius and in accordance with a decree of the local senate, erected statues 'of the kings' – the god Jupiter and the local goddess Mefitis (M. H. Crawford, *Imagines Italiae*, Potentia, 1365, n. 1).

Offices like that of *kvaísstur* were plainly taken over from the Latin quaestor, and there is other evidence of communities modelling their constitutions on those of Roman colonies. A second-century BC inscription from the city of Bantia, where Oscan was the native language, preserves a section of a civic constitution related to, but not dependent upon, Roman practice. There is mention of a senate that could prohibit the meeting of an assembly (*comono*), if more than forty members were present and agreed to it and if a magistrate was willing to swear in public that this was in the state's best interest. Magistrates could hold trials before the people, and fine those who behaved poorly at trials (maximum fine: 125 denarii); trials could not conflict with assembly meetings; and the defendant would have an opportunity to appear. Censors could draw up a list of citizens, and rules to be followed by office holders: to be a censor one must have been a praetor; and to be praetor, a quaestor. There was a board of three and a single tribune of the plebs (an office that a person who had already held higher office could not hold). The shared concepts such as the ranking of offices in ascending order, the importance of the censor and the existence of tribunes does not make the Bantian constitution a mini-Roman constitution. The fact that it was written out coherently was in the tradition of Greek cities and Roman colonies rather than of Rome, which had no written constitution.

Just as the record of inscriptions in the Italian cities reveals constitutional innovation and a vigorous and diverse linguistic culture, the archaeological record reveals many kinds of personal and public celebration and leisure activities. At the same time it shows that the driving forces behind these developments were not always Roman. Thus, at Volterrae in Etruria, the ruling classes continued pretty much as they had for centuries, dominating the peasant population and occasionally building some reasonably modern villas for themselves. This was very different from nearby Luna and Genoa, where there was a more distinct Roman presence, in the one case because the city had a citizen colony, in the other because Rome used it as a military base. In the southern Apennines, by contrast, Roman tastes do not explain why the worthies of Monte Vairano in the Samnite highlands liked importing wine from Cnidos and Rhodes. And since Rome itself did not yet have a stone theatre, one Gnaeus Statius Clarus' massive new stone temple–theatre at Pietrabbondante owed nothing to Roman influence. The temples at Pietrabbondante were somewhat unusual in that they were set in a rural landscape. Samnites still weren't building themselves cities; and evidence for contacts with the east and for the availability of large sums of money that is provided by sites like Pietrabbondante shows that this was a matter of choice. The Samnites were not living in some sort of primitive disconnect from the rest of the Mediterranean.

To see what may have been a model for the theatre at Pietrabbondante, visit Pompeii. Like the masters of Pietrabbondante, this town's leaders still communicated in Oscan, but they preferred an urban environment with opulent houses for themselves, impressive temples and entertainment venues. In the south-west of the town, between what are now known as the Herculaneum and the Vesuvian Gates, was a series of large houses, the grandest of which, the House of the Faun, covers some 31,000 square metres (the size of a royal dwelling in the eastern Mediterranean) and was once the home of the great mosaic depicting Alexander the Great in action against Darius III (now on display in the National Archaeological Museum of Naples). The owner did himself live like a king, and his idea of glory was plainly shaped by his knowledge of eastern history. Nearby, and nearly as grand, was the House of Pansa. Other buildings, while not nearly so splendid, were still places of substance. But if the images were Greek, the language in which their owners expressed their appreciation for them was Oscan, the official language of government.

Although Pompeii's cultural buildings, including the two theatres and two gymnasia, were Greek in inspiration, it is more than likely that the dominant language of performance was again Oscan. It is also worth noting that these buildings were all in place well before the most 'Roman' ones were built – the Temple of Jupiter and the Roman-style council house (*curia*) on the forum's north side. Very different was the scene at Paestum, further south, where political life had been centred, for the last century, on the generously proportioned forum, with its Roman-style temple but theatre-like council house. Here Greek and Roman cities co-existed, with the Roman city in the heart of the Greek one, and the whole being the sum of the two.

Other measures of cultural interaction were shared dining habits and personal hygiene practices. By the end of the third century BC public baths, in Rome and elsewhere, were becoming major centres for informal exchange; there was a pleasant bathhouse at Fregellae, for instance, and the Stabian baths at Pompeii were also in use before the first century BC. Another marker of cultural interaction was the spread of the ubiquitous 'black gloss' tableware, based on Etruscan models and produced in regional potteries from the fourth century BC to the first. Then, too, there was the practice of dedicating Etruscan-inspired terracotta body parts in the temples: the main shrine to the Greek healing god Asclepius, for instance, at the Latin colony of Fregellae was filled with such items. This, clearly, was no more a Roman-inspired habit than was the use of black gloss pottery, but the taking-up of the habit throughout Italy was Roman-facilitated, and that is significant.

The power of Rome enabled cultural exchange networks to link regions of Italy with one another but also to enhance their connections with the broader Mediterranean world. The development of Italian communities was a direct result of the influx of cash from the Roman fiscal–military complex. At the same time, the contractors who helped steer new money into peninsular Italy were not the passive recipients of imperial largesse. The material record reveals a heightened sense of regional identity that was not dependent upon Roman models.

14

MARIUS: POLITICS
AND EMPIRE

━━◆◆◆━━

As a witness to the ferment of his age, the poet Lucilius noted problems with the leadership in Rome. Not obviously committed to either the defence of oligarchy or the notion of popular power, he mocked the representatives of both. And as time passed, he may have become somewhat disillusioned with the governing group. In one poem he attacks the man who would be consul in 113 BC, one of the dominant Metelli; in another he remarks that Rome lost battles, but not wars; later he mentions the evil deeds that senators concealed. He observed that Opimius was a creature of the Numidian king Jugurtha, whose wide-ranging contacts in Roman society stemmed from his service with Scipio at Numantia. It was Jugurtha's appalling treatment of a community of Italian merchants at Cirta in 112 BC that spelled the end of the oligarchic regime that had grasped the Roman political scene by the throat for a decade after Opimius' massacre of Gaius Gracchus' followers.

The North African war that broke out in 111 BC between Rome and Jugurtha stemmed from the inability of the Roman aristocracy to take effective action against a man with whom many of them were personally acquainted. After a couple of desultory campaigns, the war would descend into embarrassment and scandal, none of which might have been enough to rattle the oligarchy, had it not been for a series of other failures and scandals that were happening at the same time. In fact, the surrender in

110 BC of a Roman army to Jugurtha, who let them decamp as he tried to negotiate a peace agreement, was in actuality the least serious defeat among several in recent times. In 119 BC the governor of Macedonia had been defeated and killed by the Scordisci, a Celtic tribe, invading from the north; the same tribe beat an army commanded by Gaius Porcius Cato (grandson of the Cato we have met several times), who was then convicted of corruption in office; in 113 BC the consul Gnaeus Papirius Carbo was badly beaten in southern France by a migrant tribe, the Cimbrians.

The troubles in Gaul, and with Jugurtha, reveal a fundamental problem with imperial statecraft. There was no intelligence service. To predict the behaviour of a man like Jugurtha, the Roman Senate depended upon personal contact either with the ruler himself or through the resident Italian communities. If it became suspected that the ruler might be acting against Rome's interests, the way forward might depend upon the willingness of the target of inquiry to receive an investigatory embassy – precisely the sort of embassy that in the past had caused stress throughout the eastern Mediterranean.

The more complex a state's political organisation, the easier it was to spy on. A complex society would have had numerous contacts in Rome, which might well have surfaced in Senate meetings, supplying some degree of knowledge about the area in question. North of the border, in Gaul or in the Balkans, areas populated by often unstable tribal societies, there were many fewer avenues of contact and those that there were did not necessarily possess any entrée to information networks in Italy. In less developed kingdoms like Numidia, conversely, the problem was that the most important links would be via the court – links that were relatively few at the Roman end. The arrival of a people like the Cimbrians could take a Roman governor very much by surprise, whereas in dealing with Numidia the 'experts' were compromised by their personal relationships with Jugurtha himself. Indeed, as late as 111 BC the law allowing people to sell their Gracchan allotments included clauses referring to large swathes of public land in Africa having been leased to neighbouring states since 146 BC; while others reflected on the abortive Gracchan colony or a sudden interest in encouraging new settlement. The inclusion of these terms suggests that the previously nebulous Roman interest in the area was changing as the crisis erupted; the policy had been to leave things the way they were, until the Roman state discovered it had an interest in encouraging Romans to move into the area.

It is against the background of failure, intrigue and structural weakness that, in 112 BC, a junior senatorial commission sent to prevent Jugurtha from taking over the kingdom that the Senate had guaranteed to his adoptive brother, failed. Jugurtha drove his brother from the throne. A rather more senior Roman embassy, responding to an appeal from Jugurtha's brother, asked Jugurtha why he had not done as he had been told. If, after the departure of that embassy, Jugurtha had managed to restrain himself from torturing his brother to death and slaughtering the Italian merchants with whom his brother had sought refuge at Cirta, it is possible that this would have been the end of the affair.

As it was, the massacre at Cirta changed the dynamics of the situation. A tribune, Manlius, informed the Roman people that a small senatorial faction was supporting the crimes of Jugurtha, and demanded action. It is doubtful that the average Roman cared all that much about a community of merchants in North Africa – more likely, Manlius was addressing his complaints to members of the contractor class, who would have had a vested interest in the Senate not allowing their peers to be slaughtered. And it was probably pressure from people with political clout that encouraged the Senate to declare Numidia a province for a consular army in 111 BC. Even then, Jugurtha, who had observed that in Rome everything was for sale, might have succeeded in side-tracking the Romans. But his distribution of largesse to important senators when he arrived in Rome to finalise a new settlement gave the game away. The stink of corruption was now so great that the Senate lost its grip on the situation. Another tribune, Memmius, called upon the Roman people to reassert control, and the settlement was rejected.

The new campaign was even worse than the previous one. The consul of 110 BC commanded an operation that could generously be described as desultory and, when he returned to Rome to conduct the elections, Jugurtha forced the surrender of his army. Now a commission was empanelled, on the motion of a tribune named Mamilius, to look into the whole business. Opimius, who had once been on an embassy to Jugurtha, was convicted along with several other senior senators of having taken bribes, and was forced into exile.

Mamilius' investigation was the second major judicial inquiry in four years. In 113 BC there had been another investigation of scandals involving Vestal Virgins. Three were charged with having had illicit sexual encounters at the end of 114 BC, after the Senate allowed that the report of a young girl being struck by lightning while riding her horse was a sign of divine displeasure with the Vestals – if a virgin was struck by lightning, the theory went, Jupiter must be angry with Rome's official Virgins. The *pontifices*, who investigated the matter, found only one guilty and had her executed. There was a suggestion that favouritism had something to do with the decision, and a special commission was appointed the next year that found the other two girls guilty and ordered their execution, too.

Since Vestal scandals invariably involved the most important families of Rome – in order to become a Vestal Virgin the girls had to be patrician and their parents had to have married by an archaic formula – it is striking that they tended only to happen at points when the state was having other difficulties, such as after Cannae. It is somewhat improbable that Vestals only had sexual encounters during times of national emergency. More likely, given that contraception, although primitive, could sometimes be achieved, there were more than a few post-virginal Vestals over the years. Accidents were probably covered up: a Vestal would 'become ill' and go off to a country estate for a few months. A prosecution was first and foremost a political act designed to question the integrity of the governing class.

Vestal scandals, tribunician investigations of corruption and failure on the battlefield all weakened the hold of the Metelli and their associates on power, even as yet another Metellus, Quintus Caecilius Metellus, took office as consul in 109 BC. He duly pursued Jugurtha into the heart of his kingdom, but now a new actor appeared on stage.

Gaius Marius, from Arpinum, had been tribune in 119 BC when he moved a bill limiting the possibility of people observing how others were casting their votes in elections. After this, he barely managed to get himself elected praetor in 115 BC, but none the less proved himself an effective governor (of Farther Spain) in 114 BC. He married a member of an obscure patrician house that claimed descent from the ancient kings of Alba. This was a sign both that Marius was becoming a person of some note and that old families, possibly aided by new fortunes made in the east, could re-establish themselves in political circles. In 109 BC he accompanied Metellus to Africa, where he announced his intention to run for consul, claiming that he had been told this was part of a divine plan. But Metellus told him that he had no business standing for the office.

Metellus' disapproval did not stop Marius. He returned to Rome in 108 BC, having tested the waters for his candidacy, and was elected consul for 107 BC. A tribune then moved a bill abrogating the provisions of Gaius Gracchus' law on consular provinces (the one stating that consular provinces for the coming year had to be selected before the new consuls were elected), removed Metellus from his North African command and gave it to Marius.

Marius left for Africa, taking with him drafts of new soldiers, among them men who had failed to meet the basic census qualification for recruitment (the so-called *proletarii*). A later writer saw this as a decisive break with tradition, creating a situation where soldiers would be motivated by greed to serve their general first, the state second. This view is overstated. There were not a lot of men in Marius' new drafts, and certainly not all were *proletarii*. The personalisation of commands depended on many factors, of which recruitment was but one – more important than class would be the fact that armies were recruited from districts with which their general had close connections, and that some generals could afford to pay their men a higher rate.

Marius is said by the historian Sallust to have boasted of his military prowess, giving this as the main reason why he should be elected. Marius did prove to be an excellent soldier, and the fact that Sallust highlighted this trait, together with the unpopularity of the arrogant Metellus, as reasons for his election shows that he believed that politics could be based on genuine issues. The Roman people could not control who ran for office, but they did have a free say in who would gain it, even in one of the bleakest periods of oligarchic domination. Given that in the previous few years several consuls who lacked consular ancestors had been elected, it is perhaps an exaggeration on Sallust's part, mirroring the well-attested attitudes of his own time, to say that the governing oligarchy, which referred to itself as 'the nobility', would have regarded the consulship as 'polluted' if it was held by a 'new man'. It would, however, have been no stretch at all for Marius to have claimed that he had torn the office from their hands as a prize of war.

Lucilius says that there were plenty of people who were fed up with the 'nobility', and its control had already been challenged by the Vestal scandal, Memmius' assault and the Mamilian commission. The nobility's cause was not helped by the disparate military records of Marius and his consular colleague, a member of the aristocratic clan of the Cassii Longini. Whereas Marius was competent in the field, this Cassius was badly beaten in battle against a tribe belonging to a confederation known as the Helvetians, which occupied territory in the region of what is now Switzerland.

Marius drove Jugurtha from his realm in 107 BC and brought the war to an end the next year when the ruler of the kingdom to which Jugurtha had fled turned his unwelcome guest over to Marius' quaestor, Lucius Cornelius Sulla. The surrender must have taken place late in the year, as Marius remained in North Africa during 105 BC. While he was there, one of the consuls of 105 BC fell out with the consul of 106 BC, both of whom were commanding armies in southern France awaiting the return of the Cimbrians, now accompanied by a new tribe, the Teutons. Because the consuls would not cooperate, and because it was not clear whether a consul could give a former consul orders, the two botched their encounter with the Cimbrians and the Teutons so badly that on 6 October both armies were destroyed near Arles. The other consul of 105 BC passed measures to recruit new troops and held an election in which, although he was still in Africa, Marius was elected consul for 104 BC.

Marius would be consul from 104 to 100 BC, a five-year span of office that was even more unprecedented than the domination of the Metelli during the previous decade. Marius does not, however, seem to have spent much of that time in Rome; he was too busy fighting. And although he possessed limited command experience before the Jugurthine war, Marius had studied the art of war and held views regarding the way the Roman army could be modernised.

The crucial elements of the new Marian organisation were the use of a system based on ten cohorts rather than maniples; of a single style of armament for a whole legion, all of whose members would now be armoured (or 'heavy') infantrymen; and of allied auxiliaries in place of the *velites* (light infantry). Legions would now have individual identities for as long as they were in service, and their own standards (ultimately these would all become eagles). Within the legion, the administrative structure would be based on the centurions who commanded the cohorts; increasingly, these centurions were local leaders in the regions from which the legions were recruited. Unlike the army that fought Hannibal, in which the levy threw together men from different towns who would then elect their own officers, the units of this army represented specific regions from which most of their members came. Indeed, contrary to what Sallust believed, it was not the proletarisation of the army that was the most important transformation in these years, but the regionalisation of recruitment.

Marius moved immediately to southern France, where he took over the army that had been raised under an emergency decree by Rutilius, the consul of 105 BC who had not disgraced himself on the battlefield, and schooled by gladiatorial trainers in swordsmanship. Marius continued this hard training, instituting regular twenty-mile marches. He also redesigned the basic missile of the legionaries, introducing the *pilum*, a heavy javelin whose metal head was attached to its wooden shaft in such a way that the head would bend if stuck in an enemy shield. Having decided to hold off direct encounters with the Cimbrians and Teutons until he was confident in his men, Marius' first engagement did not come until 101 BC, when he took on the Teutons in a couple of battles. The first was at a crossing on the Rhône where he inflicted a major defeat on one part of their force. The second, even more decisively, was at Aquae Sextiae (Aix-en-Provence), where his new *pila* were particularly effective in halting a mass charge uphill – imitating Hannibal's tactics at Ticinum, he had a force attack the enemy from an ambush. The next year at Vercellae he intercepted the Cimbrians, who had penetrated northern Italy as a result of incompetence on the part of Lutatius Catulus, his consular colleague. He destroyed them.

Thanks to the distortion of his record at the hands of Catulus and his former quaestor Lucius Cornelius Sulla, Marius was later seen as a decidedly anti-establishment figure. It is hard to reconcile this with the fact that his consular colleagues included the sons of the consuls of 131, 129 and 126 BC, as well as the descendant of the Lutatius Catulus who had won the battle of the Aegetes islands. True, in 104 BC his co-consul was, like him, a man with no known senatorial ancestors, but Marius seems otherwise to have been a man of conservative opinions. Indeed, so far from being anti-establishment, Marius was in fact very keen for the establishment to acknowledge his military achievements and make him a member.

In his quest for acceptance, Marius displayed a bit of a tin ear. He recalled Africanus' claims to divine guidance by advertising the services of a Syrian prophetess named Martha, who established her credentials by properly predicting the outcomes of gladiatorial combats and who accompanied him on campaigns. He then added a prophetic priest of Cybele, one Battacus, to his train. (Neither were good establishment types.) In 104 BC he celebrated his triumph on 1 January so that he could attend

10. Catulus' temple of Today's Fortune monumentalises his version of the battle of Vercellae.

Senate meetings in his triumphal garb. (That was gauche.) He also carried a large cup (*cantharus*) bearing images of the god Bacchus, depicted as a conqueror of the east. Did all this divine display mean that the people should see Marius as the new Africanus, or possibly even as a modern-day Alexander (he had exploited this same image)?

Marius also expressed delight when people greeted him as Rome's third founder – after Romulus and Marcus Furius Camillus, the hero who had saved Rome from the Gauls after the sack in 390 BC. But his claims to mythic heroism and divine inspiration won Marius even fewer friends among the aristocracy, if such a thing were possible, than Scipio's had. Catulus held up his claims to divine guidance to ridicule in his memoirs, asserting that Marius' army had been led astray at Vercellae by a divinity, thereby leaving him, Catulus, to win the battle by himself. He then dedicated a temple to 'Today's Fortune', to make the point even more obviously.

Marius was not the only Roman magistrate to make his mark during these years. Even as he held the line against the Cimbrians and Teutons, others were playing a significant role in developing the eastern empire, notably by creating a new province, Cilicia, in what is now southern Turkey. This was the consequence of what had been perceived as a problem with pirates. A new law – probably proposed by Valerius Flaccus, Marius' consular colleague – reveals the detailed instructions being issued to provincial governors in February 100 BC. The law, some of whose provisions restate existing regulations, announces Rome's interest in ensuring safe passage of the seas for Romans, Latins and 'nations friendly to Rome'; instructs that the garrison of Macedonia be reinforced; states that no one shall take an army outside the borders of his own province; that Rome will not interfere with the subjects of foreign kings; that the governor of Asia will keep out of Lycaonia (in southern Turkey); that allied kings shall not harbour pirates; that the decree will be published throughout the east by the governor of Asia; that embassies will be received at Rome; and that new boundaries will be established by the governor of Macedonia in the wake of a recent war. Lastly, the law sets out the powers of the governor of Macedonia, and states that magistrates shall do as they are told.

The law on the praetorian provinces details the way the Roman state was dealing with the eastern Mediterranean, and the manner in which the Senate managed state business in what was otherwise a rather chaotic year. It also reveals that the state now envisaged the empire as having fixed boundaries that people should not cross; probably in 115 BC, Gaius Porcius Cato, then praetor, had been the first to pass a law prohibiting a governor from taking his army outside the boundaries of his province. The definition of a *provincia* could thus now be territorial as well as meaning 'a task for which a magistrate should use his *imperium*' (for instance, the war with Jugurtha). Finally, it reveals the way enemies of the nobility sought to constrain the actions of magistrates.

In a speech that Sallust claims represented the sort of thing Memmius was saying in 112 BC, he had the tribune point out that the Roman people, in the years after Gaius Gracchus' murder, had allowed the treasury to be pillaged; that kings and foreign nations had so enriched the nobility that a handful of men possessed the greatest wealth and glory. The nobility had, he said, delivered the sovereignty of the Roman people, all things human and divine, to their enemies, while flaunting priesthoods, consulships and triumphs as if they were actual honours rather than stolen goods. The tribune's solution was not riot or insurrection, but due judicial procedure.

Just how serious the situation had become, and the extent to which the hostility between the contractor class and the Senate was focused on the courts, emerged in 106 BC when the consul Caepio passed a law placing senators back on the juries of extortion courts after delivering a speech full of comments on senatorial virtue and the vice of the current jurors. That law was rapidly repealed. The view that statute and the threat of prosecution should constrain magisterial action appears in the law of 100 BC and in other contemporary laws, which also used 'oath' clauses whereby magistrates were forced to swear that they would do what the people commanded. The law of 100 BC contains just such a clause, ordering that within five days of the law's passage all magistrates except tribunes and governors (because they were too far away) were to 'swear by Jupiter and by the ancestral gods to do all the things that have been laid down in this statute and to see to it that they are put into effect and not to do anything contrary to the statute ...' (*RS* 12 Delphi Copy Block C, 13–15).

We do not know who first thought of including oath clauses in legislation, but there were two domestic politicians at this time whose opposition to the nobility was widely known. They were Lucius Appuleius Saturninus and Servilius Glaucia. As tribune in 103 BC Saturninus, a splendid orator and a vigorous supporter of Marius' election to the consulship of 102 BC, introduced a land bill which gave extremely generous allotments of African land to Marius' veterans (presumably those who had fought in the Numidian war), essentially offering a legionary what a cavalryman would have received under the earlier Gracchan law. He also passed a new law defining treason as an act that diminished the majesty (*maiestas*) of the Roman state and provided that the accused be tried before a non-senatorial jury. There was violent opposition to the land bill, and a tribune who tried to veto it was driven from the forum. Probably as a consequence of the new *maiestas* law, another tribune indicted the consul of 106 BC, Quintus Servilius Caepio – one of the two responsible for the disaster at Arles in 105 BC – for treason (there was also a suggestion that he had misappropriated a substantial amount of Gallic treasure). He fled into exile.

Signalling that neither side could gain complete control of the political arena, and possibly in response to Saturninus' recent behaviour, two Metelli (the consuls of 113 and 109 BC) were elected censors for the next year, and they did their best to perpetuate the polarisation of Roman politics by attempting to expel Saturninus and Glaucia from the Senate. Glaucia was elected tribune the next year, and passed a revamped extortion law, restoring the non-senatorial juries. This new law, taken with the *maiestas* law, reveals the sense of corporate identity that the contractor class had developed and could assert through control of these juries.

Having passed these bills, Glaucia presided over turbulent elections for the tribunate of 100 BC, in which Saturninus was elected after the sudden, allegedly violent death of a previously successful candidate. Glaucia himself was elected to the praetorship for the next year. More violence ensued.

Claiming that he was acting in the absent Marius' interests, Saturninus now moved a series of new bills. One followed Gracchus's precedent in guaranteeing a low price for grain, to be subsidised by the state; another involved the settlement of veterans. When Marius returned, he celebrated a magnificent triumph in near-regal style, with his son riding one of his chariot's horses.

It was around this time that Marius' sister-in-law had a child. Marius' brother-in-law was Gaius Julius Caesar, which would also be the name given to the son born on 13 July 100 BC. The baby Caesar's grandmother was from the family of the consul of 118 BC, which also claimed royal descent, and his mother was of the Aurelii Cottae, a politically successful clan which usually allied itself with the nobility. The family also seems to have become exceptionally wealthy in recent years, which may explain its prestigious marriage alliances – the Julii could claim that they were descended from Aeneas, but that would not do much without the money to back it up, and that they now had. The significance of the new arrival would not be recognised for many years.

Even if he had been inclined to speculate about his nephew's future, Marius would not have had much time to do so. There was trouble brewing. With Marius presiding over the Senate, Saturninus brought in a second agrarian bill, dealing with land that Marius had taken from the Cimbrians and declared *ager publicus*. This bill included an oath clause, which the Metellus who had been Marius' commander in North Africa refused to swear, possibly because he took the view that the law had been passed illegally. He disappeared into exile.

At the tribunician elections in December, Saturninus murdered an incompatible candidate, then used more strong-arm tactics to secure re-election. This was too much for Marius, who took the extraordinary step of asking the Senate to authorise the same use of force that it had authorised Opimius to use against Gaius Gracchus. In this case, though, convincing Saturninus and his immediate supporters to surrender, he seems to have stopped short of murder. Imprisoned in the Senate House, however, they were slaughtered by a mob led by members of the Senate, over which Marius could exercise no control.

Marius did not stand again for election.

15

Civil Wars (91–88 bc)

M arius retired from public life at the end of his consulship. Phenom-enally wealthy, he was able to enjoy an attractive residence with a view over the bay of Naples.

Marius may have been out of sight, but he was not out of mind. The forces that had supported his rise to power were still active, shaping issues great and small. One important open question, at least for symbolic purposes, was whether or not the Metellus who had been consul of 109 bc, and who had taken the name Numidicus in an effort to claim that he had won the Jugurthine war, should be allowed to return from exile. Marius opposed this in 99 bc, but Metellus' son persisted in his efforts on behalf of his father, who was allowed back in 98 bc. Metellus' return could be taken as a sign that the warring factions were looking to make a truce. If that was the case, it must be admitted that truces conceal rather than solve underly-ing problems. The latent strife between the Senate and the contracting class manifested itself towards the end of the 90s bc in a pair of unfair convic-tions of former magistrates. Such actions also masked the fact that members of the contractor class were making themselves deeply hated throughout the empire as they used their access to power to bully provincials.

Another issue that continued to be important was the make-up of the governing class. Three men with no consular ancestors, one of them a friend of Lucilius, were elected consul in the years between 99 and 91 bc; this was highly unusual, and several other consuls came from well outside noble circles (only one Metellus was elected during these years). Several had strong connections with Marius, including the consuls of 91 and 90 BC, relatives of Marius' brother-in-law.

The expansion of access to office was good for some, but that access was uneven and resulted in even more unequal access to the benefits of empire. One sign that inequality in the distribution of the goods of empire continued to be an issue was that Italians were continuing to move to Rome in considerable numbers. Relatively lax scrutiny on the part of the censors of 96 BC triggered a backlash from the consuls of 95 BC, who ordered all Italians to go home, then set up a court to prosecute those making bogus claims to citizenship. This move may have been more symbolic than effective, but it alienated the leaders of the Italian communities. The situation worsened when the censors of 92 BC attempted to rid the city of people referred to as 'Latin *rhetors*', whose crime was to teach advanced rhetoric to people who would not ordinarily gain these skills.

Expulsions exacerbated the latent tensions between Rome and the Italian leaders. Some believed that the only way to gain equal access to power was by becoming Roman citizens, whereas others felt they would be better off if Rome was simply wiped off the face of the earth. These opposing opinions reflect the fact that different regions of Italy had had different experiences of the benefits, or otherwise, of Roman rule.

From the Roman point of view, potential office holders were not interested in increasing competition by adding lots of new potential candidates from all over Italy. With newly enriched Roman families stepping into the competition, winning was already becoming hard enough for the old elite. For the average Roman citizen, an expansion in the citizen body should not have made much of a difference, but many seem to have been convinced by the specious argument put abroad by various magistrates that more citizens would mean less access to the benefits that they were already enjoying. People who believed (with no evidence to support such a view) that immigrants were bad for their own prosperity were going to oppose the measures to allow Italians to become Roman citizens.

The tensions between Rome and the Italians came to a head in 91 BC, when a new tribune, Livius Drusus (son of Gaius Gracchus' antagonist), introduced a radical series of bills. One offered new subsidies for grain; a second promised new land distributions through the establishment of new colonies; a third would have doubled the size of the Senate while removing members of the contracting class from juries. The grain and land bills passed. Drusus became a land commissioner under his own law.

Later in the year he proposed extending citizenship to all Italians, perhaps using his position as a land commissioner to organise the leaders of the Italian communities. Consequently there was now a vociferous demand for citizenship from Italian aristocrats, many of whom perhaps thought that there would be a fast track into the Senate if Drusus' proposal to double its membership found approval. It did not. After the measure failed, Drusus warned the consuls that there was a scheme afoot to murder them when they left the city to celebrate the festival of Jupiter on the Alban Mount (the so-called Latin festival). He was promptly killed.

Drusus' Italian confederates responded to his murder – which the Roman political establishment seemed none too keen to investigate – by raising the standard of revolt. Livy, in describing a Latin revolt against Rome in the fourth century BC, may have been influenced by the experience of this later rebellion, to which he devoted several books of his history – all now lost – detailing the movements of secret embassies from city to city to gather support. He also, as we can see from the summary of one of his lost books, blamed the war's outbreak on Drusus, whose activities he deplored. Diodorus preserves the text of an oath that leaders of the revolt had sworn to Drusus, so Livy's take on things may not be completely eccentric. Livy was certainly not alone in preferring to blame an individual for some disaster when, in truth, no one person could be held responsible for the deep social divisions that were the actual root cause of the trouble.

Among the rebels, it does seem that there was a plan for unified action, and some agreement as to what would spark a call to arms. This was provided by an incident at the city of Asculum (now Ascoli Piceno), where a praetor sent to keep an eye on suspicious activities in the area was assassinated.

The Italian revolt, largely Umbrian at first, took Rome more by surprise than it should have. It should have been obvious that people in the less urbanised parts of Italy, especially to the east of the Apennines, were very unhappy. That lack of anticipation meant that there were no Roman armies in Italy when the revolt broke out, and, to make matters worse, the consuls of 90 BC, Lucius Julius Caesar and Rutilius Rufus, were not experienced soldiers. As both sides began arming in the opening months of that year there was general confusion in Rome, where it was believed that treason was afoot and that members of the aristocracy had encouraged the revolt for their own ends. A tribune called Varius set up a commission to try senatorial leaders believed to have plotted with the Italians. The model for the commission was presumably the one set up to try those accused of aiding Jugurtha twenty years earlier, but the proceedings under this one appear to have been very arbitrary, thereby complicating the war effort with political theatre.

While Varius provided distractions at home, Rome's fortunes varied on the battlefield. Lucius Caesar won a victory in Campania, but Rutilius ignored advice from Marius, now returned from retirement, and died, defeated, on a north Italian battlefield. Of the consuls elected for 89 BC, one, Pompeius Strabo from Picenum – a centre of the revolt – had demonstrated some military competence during the summer of 90 BC. The other was Cato the Elder's great-grandson, Lucius Porcius Cato. Before the new consuls could take office, Lucius Caesar passed a bill giving citizenship to any Italian community that would stop fighting Rome. It was a stroke of political genius, splitting the Italians in two, between those who wanted equality with Rome and those who wanted to destroy it.

The war would continue, but the tide turned decisively in favour of the Romans, despite hardships at home, including a debt crisis (presumably caused by unregulated lending as well as the enormous expense of raising an adequate army). When one of the praetors of 89 BC tried to alleviate the situation of debtors pressed by creditors with liquidity problems of their own, he was lynched by a mob of bankers. No action appears to have been taken against them. The incident illustrates not just the fiscal stress of the war years, but also the general breakdown of civil relationships in a Rome where the wealthy were used to getting their way and the state imposed minimal restraint on their conduct.

Arguably, things now were going better on the battlefield than on the home front. The Senate began to draw on more established talent: Marius retrieved the situation in the north after Rutilius' death; and his former quaestor, Sulla, who had been praetor a few years earlier, took command of the army in Campania. Generally, the campaigning season of 89 BC went well, despite the loss of another consul, Cato, in battle. Strabo celebrated a triumph after capturing Asculum, then appears to have released his prisoners – and kept the plunder for himself. Sulla's success in central Italy convinced many Romans that, though well past the age at which he might ordinarily have expected the office, he would make an ideal consul for next year. At the same time, new laws were passed to ease the path of willing Italians to citizenship.

By the time Strabo, who had been sole consul for most of the year,

*11. This portrait of Sulla, on a coin minted by his grandson in
54 BC, is the most realistic surviving image of the man.*

presided over the consular elections, it was obvious that the Italian war
was not Rome's only problem – even, that it was possibly the lesser of two
evils. There was now a war in the east against an energetically homicidal
enemy, Mithridates VI, king of Pontus.

Mithridates, whose Persian name means 'Given by Mithras' (a Persian
divinity), presented an alternative to Rome in a variety of ways. In cultural
terms, he represented a world in which Iranian traditions fused with
Greek, which was an increasingly significant development on the fringes
of Roman Asia. To the south, in the kingdom of Commagene, kings would
build massive monuments expressing their devotion to an Iranian–Greek
pantheon; to the east, a new power had arisen under King Tigranes of
Armenia, who was now aspiring to end the Seleucid kingdom of Syria as
well as to control northern Mesopotamia and the highland territory north
of the Taurus.

To Tigranes' south and east was a greater power, stretching from central
Asia to the Persian Gulf. This was the Parthian kingdom, which had begun
to pick apart the Seleucid territories in central Asia, then to do the same
in Iran and Iraq during the second century BC. The Parthians spoke a form
of western middle Iranian, a term that distinguishes that language from
the archaic Persian of the Achaemenid empire that Alexander the Great
had destroyed and the more recent forms of the language that emerged
after the seventh-century BC Arab conquest. They also communicated in
Greek, and allowed Greek and Iranian cities to co-exist throughout their

realms. If the Parthian stress was Iranian first, Greek second, Mithridates' form of cultural expression was Greek first, Iranian second.

Mithridates' enmity towards Rome stemmed from persistent Roman efforts to keep him from taking over the kingdom of Bithynia in northwest Asia Minor, which would have placed him in a dominant position along the coast of the Sea of Marmara and given him a border with Roman Asia. Most recently the Senate had confirmed Nicomedes IV as Bithynia's king. A year later, with Mithridates' support, Nicomedes' half-brother had taken the throne, at which point a Roman embassy, led by Manius Aquillius, consul in 103 BC and governor of Cilicia, ordered Mithridates to allow Nicomedes to have his kingdom back. This was in the year 90 BC. What happened next cannot be explained as a rational act. In the spring of 89 BC, with war raging in Italy, the governor of Asia, Gaius Cassius, encouraged Nicomedes to invade Pontic territory. Mithridates destroyed Nicomedes' army with no difficulty, then invaded Roman Asia. He defeated the Roman armies, and is said to have ordered molten gold to be poured down the throat of Manius Aquillius, whom he had captured.

Mithridates' plan was to put a stop to Roman control of the eastern Mediterranean, so he sent an army into Macedonia and a fleet across the Aegean to occupy Athens. At the same time, now sporting a cloak that he claimed had once belonged to Alexander the Great (one of his heroes), Mithridates sent his agents to Asia promising an end to Roman oppression, and to the domination of local politics by men backed by Rome. The poor, the debt-ridden and the discontented rose in support, and keenly answered his call to murder all the Italians in their midst. There is no accurate count of those who died; the best evidence says simply that there were thousands of victims.

The mass murder of civilians and the takeover of what were now important provinces demanded an immediate response from Rome. As the Italian war was winding down, assisted by new laws granting citizenship to those who made peace, it was clear that one of the consuls of 88 BC would receive the command against Mithridates while the other tidied up in Italy. It was Sulla, whose army had been besieging Nola (now a suburb of Naples), who was given the Mithridatic war. The other consul, Pompeius Rufus, was Sulla's son-in-law, and both men owed a debt to the oligarchs whose power had been in abeyance since Marius' first consulship. That Sulla rather suddenly married Caecilia Metella, thus linking himself with what was still Rome's most potent political clan, confirms this.

The crowds in Rome greeted the news of Sulla's marriage with derision. The general opinion was that he was marrying well above his rank – which posed a problem. As both he and Pompeius Rufus could more easily be seen as the products of circumstance rather than powerful politicians in their own right, they were hardly in a position to resist the aggressive intervention of a certain Sulpicius, tribune. Sulpicius filled the streets with gangs of supporters – allegedly, 600 men whom he described as his 'anti-Senate' – to press for new radical laws.

One of Sulpicius' laws changed the terms under which Italians were being admitted to Roman citizenship. The laws in effect since Lucius Caesar's *lex Julia* of 90 BC had placed new citizens in new tribes that were additional to the thirty-five tribes that had previously provided the framework for the tribal assembly. Sulpicius' aim was to increase the voting power of the new citizens by redistributing them across the original thirty-five tribes, at the same time presenting bills to limit senatorial debt, recall the men exiled by Varius' commission, and to transfer the command against Mithridates from Sulla to Marius. Sulpicius' measures were passed, and his thugs forced the consuls out of the city. This was simply one step further down the path to the disintegration of civil society, where bankers could get away with murdering magistrates, or anyone else who annoyed them. The consuls could muster no support on their own. It was alleged that Sulla had sought refuge in Marius' house as he made his escape from a mugging.

Rufus had no army to which he could appeal, but Sulla did. A product of the post-Opimian political world, Sulla was well aware that consuls could use troops to deal with tribunes who might pose a threat to the social order. Even though all but one of his staff officers demurred, Sulla convinced his troops that it was in their interests to march on Rome to 'restore order' by murdering his political opponents. As Sulla's men stormed the city, there was no garrison to mount an effective response. Sulpicius was killed, Marius fled to North Africa, and Sulla imposed a new political settlement. This included the formal declaration of Marius, Sulpicius and their leading supporters as enemies of the state, and provided that no law could be put before the people without prior approval by the Senate. Another measure – which Sulla claimed would restore the 'true' constitution of Rome's legendary king, Servius Tullius – restricted the passing of legislation to the *comitia centuriata*; other measures limited the authority of the tribunes, whose legislative power was effectively stripped by his provisions

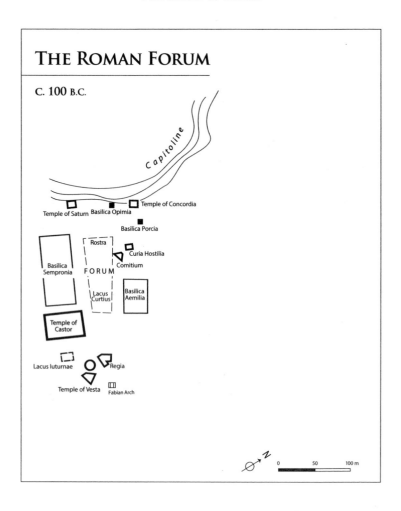

THE ROMAN FORUM

C. 100 B.C.

Capitoline

Temple of Concordia
Temple of Saturn   Basilica Opimia
Basilica Porcia
Rostra
Curia Hostilia
Comitium
Basilica
Sempronia   FORUM
Basilica
Aemilia
Lacus
Curtius
Temple of
Castor
Lacus Iuturnae   Regia
Temple of Vesta   Fabian Arch

N
0   50   100 m

concerning voting assemblies. Additional bills were passed relating to the size of the Senate, to citizen colonies and to debt payments.

Sulla's constitutional changes mirrored the ideology of Roman conservatives who argued that the essential institutions of the state had been set in place by Romulus and Servius Tullus, that tribunician power was a menace, and that the Senate properly set the direction for all aspects of public life. In an ordered society, there was consensus between all classes, a notion enshrined at the north end of the forum by Opimius' Temple of

Concordia. Indeed, if his fellow citizens had looked west from the centre of the forum towards the Capitoline they would have seen clearly the image of that society in the collection of monuments erected by generals of earlier eras as well as the ancient shrines to Jupiter Feretrius and Saturn and the Temple of Jupiter Optimus Maximus atop the hill. On the west there were further monuments to past heroes, including Duillius' column, and the *rostra* (speaking platform) standing in front of the *comitium* where Rome's most ancient voting assembly, the *comitia curiata*, met to confer *imperium* on magistrates, and then the *curia* itself and the basilica constructed by Aemilius Paullus. Straight ahead was the *lacus Curtius*, a marshy patch recalling both an ancient hero who had sacrificed himself there and the unification of the Romans with the Sabines. Then on the south side was a basilica built by Sempronius Gracchus (the father of Tiberius and Gaius), the Temple of Castor and Pollux (symbol of Italian unity) and the religious complex that housed the Vestals, along with a shrine to a nymph named Iuturna at which Castor and Pollux had appeared to announce a famous victory in the distant past, and the 'State House' where lived the *pontifex maximus* next to the ancient royal residence or Regia. But this vision of triumph and traditional stability was routinely belied by the actions of the people who frequented the space.

Sulla had fixed, so he thought, the constitution for the future. But before he could hold the consular elections for 87 BC, news came that Pompeius Rufus had been murdered by his own men when he arrived to take over command of Strabo's army in Picenum. Strabo, though he had no legal authority to do so, reassumed command; he was a good soldier and a dangerous man. Sulla, ignoring what had happened, held the elections, then took off for the east to fight Mithridates, thus revealing to all the world the depth of his dedication to his own system.

Sulla was not the only individual whose dedication to peace and social order was questionable. The two consuls for 87 BC, Gnaeus Octavius and Lucius Cornelius Cinna, both swore to uphold his revamped constitution. But Cinna, at least, was lying. Cinna, like Sulla, was a member of a patrician family that had languished for centuries in obscurity; it was only when his father became consul in 127 BC that the family had become publicly prominent. Octavius' father and grandfather had both been consuls. The civil strife that was now about to sweep across the Mediterranean was fuelled by the ambitions of two men whose families had enjoyed decades rather than centuries of prominence.

Cinna began to fight with Octavius immediately after taking office. He revived Sulpicius' law distributing the new citizens throughout the thirty-five tribes, then with a gang of armed men seized the forum. Responding in kind, Octavius brought his own armed bands of men into the forum, dispersing Cinna's and murdering many of his supporters. Cinna fled to Nola, where there was still a legion engaged in a somewhat desultory siege of the place, and sent messengers urging the commanders of other forces engaged in the final stages of the Italian war to join him. He also invited Marius to return from Africa. In the meantime, the Senate declared that he was no longer consul. In Cinna's view, as he told the army at Nola, a consul was a consul because the people had voted him as such, and the will of the people could not be undone by senatorial action alone. The men agreed to follow him. Marius, having taken advantage of the chaos to return from North Africa, landed in Etruria and raised a legion from among his veterans in the area.

Bogus appeals to constitutionalism did Octavius no good at all. He had appointed a second consul even though Cinna was still legally in post; his assertion of senatorial power against the will of the people garnered no enthusiasm. Nor could he get much help from peoples with armies elsewhere in Italy. Metellus (son of the consul of 109 BC) – who will play an important role later in our story – was then commanding an army in Samnium, but, having failed to win support for Octavius from the Samnites, who deserted him when Cinna offered them a better deal, fled to Africa. Rather late in the day, Strabo agreed to help Octavius, but he merely engaged in desultory skirmishes with troops loyal to Cinna and Marius while taking no decisive action. He wanted to be consul himself, and so would side with whoever made him the best offer – and why not? Neither side could convincingly make the case that it was observing the law, custom or unwritten constitution any better than the other.

Then Strabo died. At his funeral in Rome the people rioted; Octavius and his companions tried to take over his army but, with famine and pestilence raging in the city, support for their cause was declining. Finally, after a campaign that involved a great deal more posturing than fighting, the Senate surrendered Rome to Marius and Cinna. Octavius tried to flee, but was overtaken by a cavalry detachment led by Marcius Censorinus, a member of an aristocratic clan long dormant in the annals of the Republic that claimed descent from Numa Pompilius, the second of Rome's legendary kings.

One of the new regime's first acts was to declare Sulla a public enemy, for all that he was now on campaign against Mithridates at the head of his own fiercely loyal army.

Accounts of the events following the occupation of Rome in 88 BC are tinged with pro-Sullan commentary from the period after his bloody return, setting his massacres in the context of prior atrocities. And atrocities there were. But in the broader context of political bloodletting they seem rather low-key. There were no mass executions of Roman citizens but there were murders of some prominent men – which would have been perceived as a far greater atrocity by the aristocrats who composed the histories than the slaughter of thousands of their less well-to-do compatriots.

Some of the executions that followed Cinna's entry into the city were predictable – that of Octavius, for instance, and two Licinii Crassi, a father and son who had commanded soldiers on Octavius' behalf. Marius' nephew, Marius Gratidianus, murdered Marius' old rival and colleague (and Sulla's former patron) Lutatius Catulus. Others were less obvious candidates: the orator Marcus Antonius, for example, who in public life was past his prime. Ostensibly puzzling were the murders of Lucius Caesar and his cousin Gaius Caesar Strabo. The former, as censor in 89 BC, had begun enrolling the new citizens into the new tribes; the latter had previously been aedile and served on a land commission under a law passed by Saturninus. Neither was obviously 'Sullan', but Caesar Strabo, who had been adopted into the Julian clan, was Catulus' biological brother. That relationship may have trumped any marital connection to Marius. Their deaths are indicative not only of the deep divisions within Roman political society, but also of the fact that the political struggles of the period were fought out between coalitions uniting for temporary mutual advantage.

Bronze tablets granting citizenship to two units of Spanish cavalry for service at Asculum offer the most important hard evidence for the fluid nature of contemporary alliances. These tablets contain lists of fifty-five people who were serving on Strabo's staff, and thus, at least for the moment, primarily aligned with him. The names of four of them are too incompletely preserved for identification; of the remaining fifty-one, nine (or ten, depending on how one counts Gnaeus Pompey, Strabo's son) can be seen as active supporters of Sulla at some point in the next decade; four are notable for their connections with the younger Pompey; three, including a descendant of Opimius and a man most famous for murdering Saturninus, can be classified as generally hostile to people favouring popular power; five would be diehard anti-Sullans.

One further individual we know to have been on Strabo's staff was Cicero. He transferred to Sulla's staff in 88 BC, and seems to have played as minimal a role as he could during the next six years. Since he later became very famous, it is perhaps significant that what we know of two more members of that staff comes only through his writings. Possibly they, like Cicero, preferred a state *sans* chaos and *sans* dictator. The next decade would be hard for anyone who took this position. It would be best to lie low, which is what Cicero did.

Cinna's stance before the civil war had been to allow new citizens into all thirty-five tribes, thereby reinstating the law of Sulpicius. This he continued to do when he and Marius were elected consuls for 86 BC (Marius died almost immediately after taking office). He also appears to have negotiated final settlements with those Italians, chiefly the Samnites, who had remained at war with Rome. Then he prepared to deal with Sulla.

The greatest of the ancient historians of Rome, Cornelius Tacitus, would ask whether we are responsible for our own actions, or if the gods alone determine the course of events. The Tacitean question tracks the one frequently posed by modern historians: namely, are there great forces in history that drive events to an inevitable conclusion, or is the true skill of the historian, mastered by Tacitus, to discover the space in which individual human agency may have a determinative impact?

The Rome in which Sulla grew up was shaped by the exponential growth of aristocratic fortunes, which deepened divisions and inflamed antagonisms. The growing differences of opinion among educated Romans as to what their history meant were evident before Tiberius Gracchus introduced his land bill, and there is no inevitable thread leading from his death to Sulla's attack on Rome. But their actions, and those of Opimius, Marius, Saturninus and others, shaped the way the Roman political world would reflect the transformation of Italy. The increasing inability of politicians to find common ground or to compromise may have stemmed from a sense that the stakes were much higher than they had been in the past. Before Tiberius' time, no generation of Roman politicians had faced the challenge of figuring out how to run an empire, nor had there ever been an empire without an emperor. Without any sort of roadmap it is not surprising that there were missteps along the way, but as self-interest increasingly ruled out compromise and eliminated space for honest statesmanship, error compounded error. Hundreds of thousands of people would ultimately pay for these errors with their lives as by supporting the murderers of the Gracchi, the Senate opened Sulla's path to power.

PART IV

DICTATORSHIP
(88–36 BC)

16

SULLA TRIUMPHANT

Younger contemporaries would describe Cinna as seditious and wholly unpleasant. Cicero would add him, along with Saturninus and Livius Drusus, to a list of bad guys that started with the Gracchi. In the later collective memory of the Roman people he would be remembered as an individual interested in *dominatio* (tyranny). As an enemy of Sulla, he was by definition an enemy of the nobility. Memories and reputations, however, are complicated things which depend partly on the winds of political fortune. Seeing Cinna as an enemy of the 'nobility', rather than simply of a noble faction associated with Sulla, is problematic.

Cinna staunchly supported and enabled the cause of Italian integration into the body politic of the Roman state. This cause was not self-evidently popular, in that word's basic sense. The Roman people had several times voted against proposals to expand admission to their own privileged access to land and publicly funded amenities in Rome. Although Sulpicius Rufus, who had championed the integration of new citizens into the existing thirty-five tribes, was also tarred with the 'anti-senatorial radical' brush in later tradition, his proposal was as much pro-Marian as anti-Sullan, while the last man to propose the extension of citizenship before the outbreak of the war, Livius Drusus, would have been appalled to be thought 'popular'. He had seen the expansion of the franchise as part of a programme to strengthen the Senate's control of the state. The most radical act of the Cinnan regime was to enable the censors of 86 BC, Marcius Philippus, who as consul in 91 BC had been violently opposed to Livius Drusus, and

Marcus Perperna, consul in 92 BC, to complete the enrolment of those new citizens. They did so with some careful gerrymandering, favouring areas that had been loyal to Rome by distributing their inhabitants across a greater number of tribes than those who had made peace later on. These censors probably also reorganised the first census class, since there would now be far too many people who were eligible for entry to the eighteen centuries of 'equestrians with the public horse'. In dividing the whole first class into four groups they defined an 'equestrian order' of the wealthy non-senators – mostly consisting of those who had benefitted significantly from being able to take out state contracts – who could now have a place in any of the eighty first-class centuries.

Philippus and Perperna, who were certainly 'nobles', were not the only patricians to serve with Cinna. Another noble was Valerius Flaccus, who had taken Marius' place as consul; one of the consuls of 83 BC was a Scipio; and Marcius Censorinus, something of a menace, also had claims to nobility. Cinna would succeed himself as consul until 84 BC, when he was murdered in a military mutiny, and would have Papirius Carbo as consular colleague for his last two years in office. Cicero implies that this regime was overtly tyrannical and stayed well out of the way, in Arpinum – which was probably a good idea since he had served both Strabo and Sulla. The politics of these years involved an uneasy compromise between Cinna and his more radical supporters with others who had remained more or less neutral in 87 BC.

Sulla tended to paint all his enemies as dangerous populist radicals, even if such a characterisation did not fit the facts. His tendency to lie about his opponents (among many other subjects) is made evident by Plutarch, who composed a biography of him in the late first or early second century that largely consisted of an edited summary of the twenty books of memoirs that Sulla wrote in the last years of his life. In addition to depicting his enemies as proponents of social revolution, or, as in Marius' case, as overrated dimwits, he stressed the divine guidance he received throughout his life. Plutarch reports numerous 'wonders' which 'proved' that Sulla's actions had received divine sanction. Were it not for so many signs of divine approval, one might otherwise view Sulla as a mass-murdering traitor responsible for numerous crimes against humanity – even by Roman standards.

It is to the contemporary Greek historian Posidonius – who reproduced and even embellished the Sullan propaganda – that we owe a dramatic description of the anti-Roman regime established in Athens in the wake of Mithridates' conquest of Roman Asia Minor. The regime's leader was Athenion, a radical philosopher, who after Mithridates' triumph had been sent on an embassy to him (it was quite typical of Greek cities to employ cultural figures in this way). When he arrived at court he managed to insinuate himself into Mithridates' inner circle, and soon became acknowledged as one of the king's official friends. From there he wrote to Athens, promising debt relief, social peace and a place in Mithridates' brave new world.

Athenion followed up his letters by journeying back to Attica, where an enthusiastic crowd greeted him – allegedly bringing a litter with silver feet to transport him, in his bright-red robes, into the city. 'No Roman had insulted Attica with such a display of effeminate luxury,' wrote Posidonius (Fr. 253. 42–3), in telling evidence of the behaviour that communities throughout the Greek world had come to expect of the Romans, who were generally best known in the east for their banking and tax-collecting skills. Indeed, it may have been to drive home his anti-Romanness that Athenion set himself up in the house of an Athenian who had made a fortune doing business with the Romans on Delos.

According to Posidonius, Mithridates wrote to Athenion describing his victories over the Romans the previous year and claiming that he was acting in conjunction with the Armenian and Parthian kings, that he was in active communication with rebels in Italy, and that oracles were predicting his defeat of Rome. Indeed, as Athenion was setting up his 'independent' regime in Athens, Mithridates was dispatching armies westwards. Posidonius also tells us that Athenion failed miserably in his attempt to take control of Delos, and that the people of the island of Chios, who had been slow to surrender, had been made the slaves of their own slaves.

Even if ventriloquised by a pro-Roman agent, the voices of Rome's enemies are striking in their pan-Mediterraneanness, and so-long as Mithridates flourished there would continue to be rumours of a vast international conspiracy ranging from one end of the Mediterranean basin to the other. Other traditions preserve oracles of the sort that Posidonius refers to, predicting that a great king will come from the east to avenge past defeats. One of these is put in the mouth of a talking corpse, imagined to have uttered his predictions after the Roman victory over Antiochus III at Thermopylae. Such oracles, coming from great seers of the past, had become a significant form of social criticism in the post-Alexandrian age, enabling non-Greeks as well as Greeks to speak of their anger to an international audience. With reference to Rome, such oracles promised a saviour ('powerful Ares', the war god, in this case) who would destroy Roman power.

The Romans who had moved east in the previous decades had done much to inflame the hatred evident in these texts. In speeches that he would give over the next twenty years or so, Cicero would refer to various Roman businessmen linked with the tax-collecting firms of *publicani*, lending large sums to cash-strapped cities on terms that could only make life worse for them. The Roman financial community's untrammelled greed, backed by the threat of force and supported by juries willing to convict unpopular governors – as well as their disinclination to bring locals into the business, was creating genuine misery throughout the eastern Mediterranean. To complain with effect, provincials needed Roman patrons. Those patrons might take up their cause for domestic political reasons, but justice for downtrodden subjects was rarely a domestic issue. There was, as yet, no way for provincial political concerns to become Roman political concerns. In fact, there was no one at this time, aside from Mithridates, for people to turn to if they hoped for a better world.

Another theme of Posidonius' history is the total failure of leadership in the kingdoms founded by Alexander's successors. The Seleucid rulers were locked into endless civil war and hopelessly inferior to the Parthians to the east, who are presented as being rather interesting. The Ptolemies, on the other hand, were simply ridiculous, riven by factions of their own. King Ptolemy X Alexander I, on the throne when Mithridates began his invasion, is said to have been so fat that he could not relieve himself without help, and was despised by his own people.

Posidonius' wide-ranging interest in peoples and places enables him to get over to his Greek audience that the grass really is not greener anywhere else. Whatever happens, they will be ruled by people whom they once sneered at as barbarians. That being so, for all their faults, the Romans are the best option.

If one were to ignore the rampant profiteering that typified Roman administration, it could be possible to claim that Rome still represented social stability – and that was certainly a point that Sulla was at pains to drive home in his memoirs. According to his account, Mithridates cancelled debts and changed the citizen bodies of Greek cities by filling them with freed slaves (usually excluded from full citizenship in Greek cities), then freed more slaves so that they could become new citizens. This was seen as a bad move, making the excitable and unstable citizenry of the east even more unreasonable and uninterested in the welfare of the rich – never mind the fact that, if true, Mithridates was simply imposing a Roman model, as freed slaves automatically became citizens in Rome, and always had done.

As far as military operations go, the narratives that have survived from the period after Sulla brought his five legions into Greece, Plutarch's *Life of Sulla* and the later book that Appian of Alexandria wrote about the Mithridatic wars, are so thoroughly contaminated with Sullan material that it is hard to reconstruct the actual chain of events. That said, we know that a Mithridatic army arrived in Greece under the command of a general named Archelaus, who brought with him Aristion, Athenion's replacement as the leader of the Athenian government. On his way to Greece, Archelaus managed to capture Delos, whose Roman population seems to have anticipated his arrival by moving to Argos on the Greek mainland. When he arrived in Attica, Archelaus gathered an army from various Greek states and repulsed efforts at suppression by Gnaeus Sentius, the governor of Macedonia. All this took place in the first part of 87 BC. When Sulla arrived at the end of the year, he ordered Sentius to stay in Macedonia while he besieged Athens and its harbour Piraeus, where Archelaus was ensconced with the bulk of his forces.

Athens, whose people were by now reduced to starvation (and, Sulla says, routine cannibalism), fell first. Sulla executed Aristion, allowed his men to sack the city, massacred its inhabitants, and imposed upon the survivors a new model constitution appealing to precedents from the distant past and designed to restrict future social unrest. Piraeus fell some time later, after Archelaus had, inexplicably, managed to extricate himself and escape to Boeotia, where fresh troops from Mithridates, who had swept past Sentius, joined him.

Sulla defeated the Mithridatic armies in battles at Chaeronea and Orchomenos, then proceeded to Macedonia. But he could advance no further until his able lieutenant, Lucius Licinius Lucullus, who had been sent to raise a fleet from Egypt and Egyptian dependencies and from a few independent Roman territories in southern Turkey, returned in 85 BC. In the meantime, another Roman army, this one with a fleet and commanded by the consul of 86 BC, Valerius Flaccus, evaded Sulla and the fleets of

Mithridates to land in western Turkey by the end of 86 BC. Flaccus was murdered in a mutiny, and Flavius Fimbria, the mutiny's probable engineer, took his command.

Murderer and mutineer that he was, Fimbria was none the less the representative of the Roman state, Sulla having been declared a public enemy as soon as Cinna took power. He was also a rather good general, and succeeded in driving Mithridates out of the Roman provinces east of the Aegean. At this point, a rather desperate Mithridates realised that he was in a better position to get a deal from Sulla than from Fimbria. So when Lucullus refused to coordinate operations with Fimbria, Mithridates escaped to Pontus, and towards the end of 85 BC agreed terms with Sulla. Sulla then crossed over to Turkey and laid siege to Fimbria's army near the ancient city of Troy. Fimbria's men, who were heavily outnumbered, deserted in droves. Fimbria ultimately took flight, ending his own life by means of an assisted suicide at Pergamum.

The peace treaty between Sulla and Mithridates – essentially a compact between two declared enemies of the Roman state – provided the necessary resources to support Sulla's planned invasion of Italy. Mithridates withdrew to the kingdom he had ruled at his accession, turned his fleet over to Sulla, returned all prisoners, deserters and runaway slaves, restored people he had kidnapped to their homes, and agreed to pay Rome 'the cost of the war'. Mithridates seems to have been a bit short of the money needed to make good his promise. So, instead, Sulla stripped the assets of the cities of the province of Asia that had been guilty of participating in the massacre of Romans in 89 BC. Summoning a meeting of these cities, Sulla presented a bill for five years' taxes, payable at once, transferring 'the cost of the war' from Mithridates to them. After years of warfare, the cities were not flush, so many found themselves having to mortgage public property and resort to other emergency measures to pay what Sulla demanded. It is quite likely that much of the cash they handed over had been lent by the revivified Roman banking community, which proceeded to charge such appalling rates of interest that within a decade the total debt reached six times the initial sum.

Sulla's use of the apparatus of provincial government, especially his absorption of eastern contractors into his military regime, represents a major development within the Roman military–fiscal system. What Sulla did was essentially to privatise the contracting system to support what was, at this point, a private army. What is more, the resources he obtained from the peace with Mithridates, together with what he had extracted from Asia, provided him with a more substantial war chest than was available to Cinna.

Cinna, as far as we can tell, was nearly broke. The Roman mints had been employed to capacity during the war with the Italians. The officials overseeing them in 90 BC had run through something like 2,400 dies while at the same time lowering the coinage's silver content by 15 per cent. In both 89 and 88 BC they had used around 800 dies while improving the purity of the silver somewhat, but there was still a financial crisis, evident in the various proposals on debt in 89 and 88 BC. The number of dies dropped to less than 500 in 87 BC; just over that number in 86 BC; 600-plus in 85 BC; fewer than 400 in 84 BC; and 157 in 83 BC.

The sudden drop-off might be related not only to the high expenditure of earlier years but also to the disruption of important banking and trade connections with the eastern Mediterranean after Mithridates' invasion. At the same time people were uncertain of what anything was worth, or whether they would recover what was owed to them. In 86 BC, a measure was introduced allowing debtors to settle through payment of a quarter of the principal; a year later, Marius Gratidianus passed a law stating that all silver coins should be exchanged at face value. Happy as people might have been with Gratidianus, this didn't change the fact that the state was short of cash and the Cinnan regime was becoming associated with economic hardship.

The money minted in 90–88 BC had presumably not vanished from the face of the earth; rather, it had shifted from the coffers of the state into those of individuals. There is substantial evidence that a few had sufficiently large sums tucked away to pay for private armies when the war broke out. One of these was the young Gnaeus Pompey, who had withdrawn to the ancestral estates in Picenum after being acquitted of a charge of hanging on to money his father Strabo should have turned over to the state. Short of ordering new taxes or a round of confiscations – neither of which seemed feasible – there was no way for Cinna to recover this cash unless he was willing to make deals with people like Pompey, with whom he was plainly on poor terms.

Also, quite a number of people had left for Greece to join Sulla – scarcely a vote of confidence in the regime's stability. Others had been at odds with the regime all along. One of the most significant of these was Caecilius Metellus, who had been in command of the army operating in Samnium when Cinna attacked Rome. He fled from there to Africa, taking, no doubt, a good deal of money with him. In 83 BC he landed in northern Italy at the head of an army he had raised at his own expense. There he was joined by the son of the deceased Marcus Licinius Crassus (also named Marcus Licinius Crassus), who had spent the intervening years in Spain, at times allegedly living in a cave.

Just how much did it cost to run an army for a year? It so happens that we have extremely precise figures, seemingly taken directly from the account book of a senior magistrate by Cicero when he was prosecuting Verres, governor of Sicily, for corruption in the late 70s BC. When Verres had been quaestor in 84 BC he had been entrusted with 558, 854 denarii for the pay of the consular army in northern Italy, numbering around 9,000 men, for four months. Of this he paid out 480,854 denarii for soldiers' pay, grain and administrative salaries, before absconding to Sulla's camp with the remaining 78,000 denarii.

Cicero's evidence suggests that soldiers expected to be paid in cash. If Cinna was having a cash flow problem, that would explain both why his armies were mutinous and why it was difficult to coordinate a defence against Sulla when he landed in southern Italy during the spring of 83 BC. Also problematic was the fact that, having been educated in the art of war by Marius and having also by now clocked up many years' experience commanding armies himself, Sulla was rather a good soldier.

Cinna did not live to see Sulla's return to Italy. In 84 BC he had been taking what prophylactic steps he could to prevent that eventuality, shipping troops across the Adriatic to occupy the bases that Sulla would need to launch his invasion. It was then that his men mutinied, and killed him. The troops that had crossed the Adriatic returned to base and whatever fleet Cinna had been using disappears from the record, doing nothing to prevent Sulla landing near Brundisium (Brindisi) the following year.

It was at this point that traces of the vast sums minted to finance the Italian war began to reappear, as Italy descended into a state of regional warlordism. Private enterprise had already become established as a feature of military operations by the time of the Italian war, when we hear of Minatius Magius from Aeculanum, who 'showed such great loyalty to the Romans in this war that he captured Herculaneum in the company of Titus Didius [the consul of 98 BC who was then serving as a legate in

Campania] with the legion he himself had raised amongst the Hirpini'
(Velleius Paterculus, *Short History* 2.16.2). Magius is representative of
the class of fiscally successful individuals who found that they could
enhance their status through military contracting. The most successful of
these military contractors was young Gnaeus Pompey. Recognising that
Papirius Carbo disliked him, he assembled three legions from his own
district and fought his way south, evading those major forces also raised,
it seems, under regional leaders, to stop him. Assuming that he planned
on paying his men for a year, Pompey himself must have had something
like 2.5 million denarii in hard cash to raise the force he did – which is not
so surprising, given that his father retained the booty from his victories.
Similar sums must have been at the disposal of the men who were sent
against him, who also appear to have been local leaders.

When Pompey joined Sulla, he increased the number of Sulla's legions
to eight. There would ultimately be twenty-seven, a larger army than had
been assembled in the Second Punic War. In a deeply self-serving section
of his memoirs, Sulla claims that his enemies deployed forty legions. This
may not be a complete falsehood, although some of them deserted to
Sulla before the war ended. Allowing for some double-counting of units
that served on both sides, there were something like sixty legions engaged
in the struggle. This exceeded in magnitude all the civil wars that would
come afterwards, and represented a level of militarisation in Italy alone
that would exceed the regular strength of the Roman armies drawn from
across the entire empire in the first century AD.

It is perfectly plausible that the forces engaged in this war were
enormous: first, Italy was already highly militarised because of the Italian
war; and second, many of the armies raised against Sulla did not last
all that long in the field. But this is only part of the story. The level of
economic disruption occasioned by the conflict was vast, people throughout Italy taking advantage of the chaos to settle old scores with local
rivals. In northern Italy, for instance, we know that a man named Naevius
exploited the fact that a supporter of Cinna managed a farm owned by a
certain Quinctius in order to seize control of the property. At Larinum
one Oppianicus, despite having married his first wife's mother and having
also been found guilty of trying to poison her son, was able to return to a
position of local prominence through his adherence to Sulla's cause. Such
dramas no doubt played out all over Italy.

Such distractions aside, the main campaign began in late 83 BC after

Sulla landed at Brundisium. His plan was to divide Italy in two, thereby cutting his rivals off from support in southern Italy. To this end he advanced up the via Minucia, the great highway along Italy's Adriatic coast, defeating the consul Norbanus at Casinum before crossing the Apennines and entering Campania, where he encountered the other consul, Lucius Cornelius Scipio (Scipio Africanus' great-great-nephew), at Teanum. Military skill seems to have passed this member of the family by. He did not notice that Sulla was suborning his troops, who promptly defected to him. Sulla let Scipio go free, possibly in a gesture to his lineage rather than as an expression of hope that he would be given another command.

The desertion of Scipio's army brought the campaign to an end. Sulla spent the winter shoring up his position, assuring the Italian states that he had no intention of undoing the Cinnan arrangements over citizenship, and gathering a 'sort of Senate' around him. He recruited heavily in order to bring his army up to sufficient strength to mount two campaigns when the long winter came to an end. He would begin operations in Campania, while Metellus was sent to invade northern Italy.

Metellus advanced up the Adriatic coast, defeating an army under the praetor Carrinas, a new member of the Senate who hailed from Umbria or Etruria and who, given his importance to the war effort, had presumably played some significant role in earlier rounds of fighting. Metellus, accompanied by Gnaeus Pompey, won two battles – one at the river Aesis over Carrinas, and another at Sena Gallica, where his opponent was Marcius Censorinus, the man who had killed Octavius in 87 BC. From there he moved on to Ravenna and fought further engagements in the Po valley, defeating Norbanus at Placentia, after which the latter jumped the rapidly sinking ship and fled to Rhodes, where he would later commit suicide. The last battle of the campaign was left to Lucullus, who wrapped things up with a victory at Fidentia.

The southern campaign was longer and bloodier. Sulla opened by winning a battle at Mons Tifatum – at whose feet the Volturnus river passes as it enters Campania – over an army commanded by Norbanus (who would later head north for the defeats mentioned above) and the young consul Marius. Sulla drove them back to Praeneste, where Marius remained closely besieged, and settled into a tough fight with Carbo, who was based at Clusium. News of defeats in the north would so dishearten Carbo that he deserted his own cause and fled to North Africa.

So far Sulla, who had left substantial forces behind for the siege of Praeneste, had stayed away from Rome – a decision which had unfortunate consequences. Despairing of his inability to break the siege, Marius sent a messenger to Brutus Damasippus, then praetor, ordering him to kill any Senate members suspected of harbouring pro-Sullan sentiments. This he did. And thus did Sulla change his somewhat conciliatory policy of the previous year to one of mass murder.

It was now autumn 82 BC, and a large army had gathered under the old leaders of the Lucanians and Samnites in the Italian war, Telesinus and Lamponius, to relieve Praeneste and hold Rome against Sulla. Getting wind of this, Sulla moved his main force rapidly to Rome even as Carrinas and Marcius Censorinus linked their forces to the army from the south. On 1 November the decisive action of the war took place outside the Colline Gate on Rome's east side. Historians who bought Sulla's line on the struggle presented the forces gathered to defend the now post-Cinnan regime (including the one legally elected consul still in Italy) as devoted to the annihilation of Rome. One such historian, writing in the early first century AD, even claimed that Telesinus told his men that the 'last day had come to the Romans and that the city must be destroyed and obliterated ... the wolves who had stolen the liberty of Italy would not vanish, unless the forest in which they were accustomed to hide was destroyed' (Velleius Paterculus, *Short History* 2.27.2). In fact, the army of central Italy had arrived in the city, under the aegis of Rome's elected magistrates, to defend it from rebels. But the justice of their cause did them no good; they were comprehensively defeated in a hard-fought battle.

The day after his victory, Sulla ordered the newly surrendered prisoners (either 6,000 or 8,000 of them, depending on the source) be taken into the Circus Flaminius on the Campus Martius, where they were put to death as he addressed a meeting of the Senate in the nearby Temple of Bellona (a goddess of war). The site was chosen in part because it was beyond the *pomerium* (the city's sacred boundary), so Sulla could retain the *imperium* that he would have lost if he had crossed it. Constitutional niceties aside, another reason for the choice of this site may have been that the screams of the dying would be audible to the senators. Censorinus and Carrinas, captured a day later, were also executed; Telesinus had died on the battlefield. Marius Gratidianus was brutally tortured and dismembered by Catiline, a former member of Strabo's staff.

The massacre on 2 November was a prelude to further killing. The following day, Sulla summoned another meeting of the Senate, at which he produced a list of eighty men who, by virtue of their being on the list, were sentenced to death or proscribed (from the Latin verb *proscribere*, 'to write up'). Some senators demurred at what Sulla may have presented as a logical extension of previous practice under emergency decrees issued against Gaius Gracchus and Saturninus. But the scruples of the few did not matter, the eighty were all dead men walking.

Although Sulla remained outside the *pomerium*, his edict was posted on white boards in front of the Regia, the ancient royal palace in the forum's heart. The formal terms of the edict, in addition to announcing that whoever killed one of the men on the list would receive a reward of 14,000 denarii upon delivery of the deceased's head to the quaestor in charge, were as follows: anyone who provided information leading to the execution of one of the proscribed would receive a reward – so a slave, for instance, could be freed; all the man's property would be confiscated by the state (to be used, among other things, to fund the reward); those on the list were banned from residing in the Roman world; anyone hiding or protecting one of the proscribed would be punished; and the body of the slain could receive neither proper burial nor memorial.

The Roman state had fallen into the hands of a large-scale military contractor whose funding had been initially provided by Rome's bitter enemy. Sulla's success stemmed from a combination of his high-level organisational skills, the weakness of his enemies and his own capacity to leverage financial resources far in excess of those controlled by the government of the Roman state. He was the ultimate product of a system that had privatised government resources. The question that remained was whether he could produce a system that would make it impossible for people to follow the example he had set.

17

SULLA'S ROME

Sulla was fully conscious of the illegality of his own career, that much is clear from the stress he put on the divine sanctions for his behaviour in his memoirs, and now his stress on apparently legal processes in shaping a new regime for Rome. Sulla had an enormous sense of his own intelligence, he does appear to have been widely read and, having destroyed the Republic, he now needed to put in place a new one.

So it was that the proscription edict was followed by further constitutional manipulation. Sulla ordered that the board of augurs – the priests charged with interpreting divine signs – be consulted. The question they were to consider was whether it was legal for an *interrex* to be named in the absence of the consuls. The office of *interrex* was technically a very ancient one meaning 'temporary king', and believed to go back to the regal period when kingship was elective rather than hereditary. The augurs duly held that it would be legal to elect an *interrex*. Valerius Flaccus, the consul of 100 BC who had attempted to mediate between the factions of Sulla and Cinna a few years earlier, was selected for the job. Sulla then wrote him a letter spelling out what he expected him, as technical head of state, to do. The technical head of state did as he was told, and twenty-four days before the vote to appoint a dictator was to be held, posted a bill to that effect for consideration by the *comitia centuriata*. When the *comitia* finally assembled in early December, it passed the *lex Valeria* allowing the *interrex* to appoint a dictator whose powers – which included the writing of laws and the restoration of the state – were spelled out in considerable detail.

The procedure whereby Sulla became dictator reflected his fascination with Rome's early history and the development of its institutions. This interest had been manifest during his occupation of Rome in 88 BC, when he claimed to have restored the Servian constitution which preceded the tribunate of the plebs, and was believed to have been created to solve a political crisis during the first years of the Republic. The origin of the dictatorship, and the notion that it could be created through a legislative process, was another historiographic fantasy.

According to Livy, the first dictator whose name could be remembered was created by a decree of the Senate in 494 BC; the basic provision of this office was that no one could appeal the dictator's decision, whatever the issue. Sulla's way of creating a dictatorship was obviously quite different, but the involvement of the *comitia centuriata* may owe something to the election of Fabius Maximus to the office in 216 BC. The use of an *interrex* to pass the legislation presumably owed something to earlier practice, in that the position was resorted to for elections where there were no sitting magistrates (which is just about possible while all this was going on).

The idea that the dictator should have a specific function – such as write laws and restore the state – follows on from the custom of naming a particular purpose for earlier dictators, though these tended to be duties such as holding elections and overseeing religious rituals. In many cases the specificity of the task limited a dictator's time in office – no more need for a dictator 'to drive in the nail' (referring to a ritual concerning the Temple of Minerva) once the nail had already been driven in. In some cases there appears to have been a six-month time limit, as with Fabius in 216 BC. In others, there may have been no set time span. Other aspects of the new law, describing Sulla's actual position, appear to have been that no tribune could veto any of his bills, that there would be no right of appeal (*provocatio*) against his decisions, and that he could issue edicts that would have the force of law.

On 27 and 28 January 81 BC, Sulla celebrated a triumph over Mithridates – perhaps he thought it would be bad form to stage one for victories over the Roman state – and then brought a new bill concerning proscription before the *comitia centuriata*, which duly passed it. He also delivered a public summary of his actions and formally adopted the cognomen 'Felix' (the Fortunate), which served as a reminder of the reason for his success.

Sulla's new law on proscription was far wider ranging than the original edict. It extended the reach of his regime throughout the Italian peninsula by encouraging people to work out their local animosities by getting anyone they disliked added to the list. A new provision of the law was that the list would remain open for new additions until 1 June 81 BC. There followed, during a year when Sulla was quite often out of Rome, a number of important bills spelling out his vision for the future. These bills reshaped the Senate, reorganised the main priestly colleges, set new minimum requirements for office, dealt with the city's grain supply, excessive luxury, the settlement of his veterans, and the confiscation of land from Volterrae.

Sulla's reform of the Senate was based upon the notion, significant in Greek philosophy, that systems could shape individuals. A democracy, to use terms that Polybius had used, would shape people who behaved 'democratically', who put the interests of the common people first. An 'aristocracy' in Polybian terms was one in which members of the 'aristocracy' placed the perpetuation of their own interests first. This did not necessarily mean that governance was bad (in theory), rather that it would have a consistent direction which would (in theory) be good for everyone. What Sulla was doing through his reshaping of the Senate and setting of new expectations for its members was creating a system through which to school the 'aristocratic man' so that he could function at his best. This would create an ideal state for the future.

The reform of the Senate fell into three parts: membership, career structure and function. The most important changes in function consisted of the creation of eight permanent criminal courts whose juries would be entirely senatorial, and strict limitations on the authority of tribunes. As the new courts called for fifty-one jurors, the new system required that the Senate increase its membership to over 400. It can be assumed that, given the ongoing reduction in senatorial numbers as a result of the recent civil war and the ongoing proscriptions, more would have been needed anyway. Sulla appointed 300 new members from the equestrian order, though he seems to have forbidden them to speak unless they succeeded in being actually elected to office. This probably brought the total number to something like 500, which Sulla no doubt felt was about right.

The age of entry to the Senate was now set at thirty, the youngest that one could be elected to the quaestorship. The quaestorship would confer senatorial status, there would be twenty quaestors every year, and candidates for the office must have completed some years of military service. It looks as if the earliest age for entering the army was seventeen, and the earlier proviso that a man should complete ten years before holding office was reduced to three years of cavalry service or six in the infantry.

There would now be eight praetors, minimum age thirty-eight, while the minimum for a consul was forty-two, though it might be possible to hold the office one year early if one were a patrician or had performed some act of valour (Gaius Julius Caesar would qualify on both counts). Sulla made no changes in the aedileship, but tribunes of the plebs were stripped of the right to stand for further office or to introduce bills before the assembly, and also lost their veto power. The one power left to them was that of *provocatio* – the right to protect Roman citizens from the arbitrary actions of magistrates (which some historians thought was their original purpose).

The changed size of the Senate, the murder of many senior members who had sided with Carbo and the creation of new jury courts meant that it would no longer be dominated by former magistrates, as had tended to be the case in earlier generations. Power resided with sitting magistrates, who now stayed in Rome during their years in office. They could effectively silence members who had not been elected, or, early in their careers, needed support from the more influential. Another result of Sulla's legislation – this one surely not unintentional – was that, with the small age differential between the praetorship and consulship, it was difficult for a person who lacked wealth to make a successful run for the highest office. Indeed, the only 'new man' who reached the consulship during the next three decades was Cicero, and that was under some quite exceptional circumstances. Most senators did not even have a shot at the praetorship, which may have reduced the restrictions on future office-holding for tribunes, who, as events will reveal, felt in no way silenced by the other constraints placed on their careers. The competitive pressure for praetorship increased the value of aedileship, via which lavish games could enhance both praetorian and consular campaigns and ratchet up the pressure to extract large sums of money from those unfortunate enough to be governed by any magistrate elected under the new regime.

The level of corruption in government during the next decade reached record levels, while senatorial juries were notorious for their unwillingness to find even the most egregiously corrupt individual guilty.

Sulla's impact on the land of Italy was even more decisive than his impact on its ruling class. He had twenty-seven legions under his command by the time Praeneste finally surrendered a few weeks after the battle of the Colline Gate (the younger Marius committed suicide before the surrender; afterwards, Sulla separated 'Samnite' prisoners from the rest and murdered them). As Sulla's legions were gradually demobilised, their men were settled in new colonies around Italy, most likely one for each legion. Areas regarded as especially Marian suffered worse than others. Samnium, the object of special Sullan antipathy, according to Strabo, was subjected to what would now be called 'ethnic cleansing'. Urban development was set back, and in the next century few Samnites were to be found in the ranks of the Roman aristocracy. Volterrae, which like Praeneste held out well into 81 BC, was deprived of citizenship and land, as was Arretium. There is a record of antipathy between the Sullan colonists and the original settlers long after the incomers arrived, as they seem to have regarded themselves as a conquering force set down among riffraff. They also had more money at their disposal, having been rewarded generously by their general. The primary areas of settlement, Etruria and Campania, would be places of significant unrest in the decades to come.

Instead of creating solid and secure lands filled with men who owed their prosperity to the stability he had created, Sulla created a landscape filled with the dispossessed. These were people who would pledge their loyalty to anyone who placed their interests first, whether that person was a charismatic ex-gladiator, a rogue aristocrat or a revolutionary general. In the next half century, hundreds of thousands of Italians would serve in armies whose primary purpose was not the defence of the state; they would fight for pay and privileges, often for a future on land that had been taken from someone else.

18

SULLA'S LEGACIES

Sulla retained his dictatorship until the end of 81 BC, at which point, having been elected consul for the coming year, he laid down the office. It was in the year of his consulship that it became clear that he was not in absolute control. Gnaeus Pompey had pursued Carbo through Sicily to North Africa, and defeated Carbo's few remaining followers, before capturing and killing him. He then wrote to Sulla demanding a triumph and took for himself the cognomen Magnus, 'the Great', clearly claiming to be the modern Alexander.

Sulla was not happy with this, but he went along with it. In the meantime, Quintus Sertorius, a pro-Cinna praetor in 84 BC, was initiating a series of campaigns that would threaten the central government's control of Spain during the next few years. In the east, Sulla's governor of Asia provoked a war with Mithridates, invaded Pontus, and was soundly beaten. On Lesbos, Mytilene rebelled, and fell only after a siege that lasted into the year 80 BC. With Lucullus in command of the army, the young Gaius Julius Caesar distinguished himself by being the first man over the city wall.

Caesar's survival signals one of the cracks that was opening in the Sullan façade. As Marius' nephew and Cinna's son-in-law, he was a prime candidate for immediate execution. In later life he would tell the story that, having offended Sulla by refusing to divorce his wife, he went into hiding, was tracked down by one of Sulla's most notorious henchmen, then brought before the dictator himself. Here, an alliance of Vestal Virgins with his relatives, the Aurelii Cottae (staunch Sullans), saved his life. Sulla grudgingly granted the request to spare him, observing that he perceived 'many Mariuses' in the young man (Suetonius, *Life of Caesar* 1.3).

Little of what Caesar would later relate about his early life is entirely believable. If he had in fact been run to ground as one of the proscribed, he would have been killed on the spot; if Sulla had really felt he was a threat to his new order, equally, he would have killed him. The truth was that, like many Romans, Caesar had a foot in both camps. The question as to where to draw the line between friends and enemies, while easy in theory, proved difficult in practice. It was also hard to keep everyone happy when allegiances were so ambivalent. Caesar's survival represents a concession on Sulla's part to a corner of his camp that was increasingly at odds with some of his most trusted advisers.

During his campaigns, Sulla had evolved an administrative structure bearing some similarities with the royal courts of the eastern Mediterranean. Such structures were important for the mobilisation of resources to support what would be, in effect, a privately funded army backed by the contracting community.

One of the characteristics of this new court system was the division of subordinates into members of the 'inner' and 'outer' circles, with status defined entirely in terms of service to the ruler and careers defined through state offices (the two could overlap); also, the ruler's house was to be used as an administrative centre . Another fundamental feature of the system was some form of mass ideological communication – encapsulated, in Sulla's case, in his legislation. But the creation of 'inner' and 'outer' circles introduced the potential for conflict between people who saw their position as primarily resting on office-holding or ancestry (the group that supported Caesar) and those whose power depended on their proximity to the ruler. In the summer of 80 BC, tensions between the two groups exploded in a scandalous legal action that literally and figuratively put Sulla's regime on trial.

The case involved one Sextus Roscius, who came from the Etruscan city of Ameria. His father, also Sextus, was very rich, owning thirteen farms worth one and a half million denarii. At some point in the late spring of 81 BC, the elder Sextus was murdered in Rome. The younger Sextus' enemies then asked Sulla's freedman Chrysogonus to place the elder man's name on the proscription list, even though the closing date for the list, 1 June, had passed. The addition of the deceased Roscius' name to the proscription list meant that his estate was confiscated and available to be purchased by Chrysogonus for a small sum. He handed the estate over to a pair of the elder Roscius' relatives to manage and had the younger Sextus charged with parricide – to the Roman mind the most heinous of all offences. Sextus fled to Rome, where he sought protection from the noble Metellus clan with whom his father had had connections. He ended up in the house of Caecilia Metella, a cousin of Sulla's wife and of the Caecilius Metellus who, having been one of Sulla's generals, would become Sulla's colleague as consul in 80 BC.

Given the seriousness of the charge, the case was sure to draw attention, and the clan Metellus provided some of its members to assist the lead lawyer for the defence. That lead lawyer was Cicero, who had successfully defended a man named Quinctius the previous year. Quinctius' problem had been that he had been associated with a diehard Cinnan, and his estate had been stolen by staunch supporters of the new regime. Cicero's success stemmed from his ability to appeal to people who, while supporting Sulla's 'cause of the nobles', were somewhat anxious about their own fates. They were people whose family members' credentials were not obviously pro-Sullan, or whose careers might have raised doubts in the minds of the doctrinaire.

Cicero's defence of Roscius would be different from his defence of Quinctius, because he was now representing a person who as supported by a core member of the noble faction which, plainly, bore a grievance against Chrysogonus, who, although he was a member of Sulla's inner circle, was a freed slave none the less. And if Roscius was acquitted, then Chrysogonus would be taken down several notches in front of a very large crowd.

Roscius was indeed acquitted, and, in a crucial part of his address, Cicero carefully distinguished between Sulla and his subordinate. He showed that Chrysogonus had prevented an embassy of dignitaries from Ameria, who had come to protest the framing of the younger Roscius, from seeing Sulla; and that he had also purchased the estate for a mere 500 denarii from the treasury and set Roscius' relatives up to manage it. But Sulla, he said, had no knowledge of all this. How could that be? It was not right, but it was par for the course:

> Even if Jupiter Optimus Maximus, by whose nod and will, heaven, the earth and the seas are ruled, often kills mortals, annihilates cities, or

ruins crops with fierce winds or massive storms, excessive heat or intol-
erable cold, we do not attribute these ills to the divine plan, but we
believe that they arise from the force and magnitude of nature itself.
On the other hand, the good things of which we avail ourselves, the
light by which we are nourished and the very breath that we draw,
are given and imparted to us by Jupiter. Thus, should we wonder,
gentlemen of the jury, if Lucius Sulla, when he alone ruled the state
and governed the world, and confirmed the majesty of the empire that
he had received through arms with laws, might miss something? Not
unless it should be amazing that the human mind should not have
achieved that which the divine force cannot achieve.

(Cicero, *On Behalf of Sextus Roscius of Ameria* 131)

Chrysogonus, Cicero continued, who had a house on the Palatine, an
estate near Rome crammed with the finest Greek artwork and the latest
in sophisticated cookware, as well as an army of slaves, was the real villain
of the piece. The jury should not think in terms of the power that Sulla
had granted him, but realise that he had *no* power. 'Did the distinguished
nobility recover the state by arms of steel, so that freedmen and little slaves
should, at will, be able to oppress the property of the nobles, our lives and
fortunes?' (Cicero, *On Behalf of Sextus Roscius of Ameria* 141). A judgment
for Roscius was not a judgment against Sulla, he concluded, but against
Chrysogonus.

The jury held for Roscius, and Sulla's power appeared to be waning.
His governor of Asia had suffered an embarrassing defeat at the hands
of Mithridates, having provoked a war without Sulla's permission, and
Pompey had celebrated a massive triumph over Sulla's muted objection.
Quite likely aware that his health was failing, Sulla retired to spend his last
months in a villa near the bay of Naples. There he composed his memoirs,
which remained incomplete when he died in the first half of 78 BC. They
were finished and published by Lucullus, who would remain one of the
men most loyal to his legacy.

Sulla's funeral was held at public expense, overriding the objections
made by one of the consuls of 78 BC. It was a massive, rain-soaked, affair.
The 10,000 freed slaves who had taken his nomen joined the funeral
procession, during which were burnt two life-size images of the former
dictator made of incense, thereby drenching the mourners in eau de Sulla.

Even before Sulla died, Cicero took off to Rhodes to enhance his education. That he should go east at this point in his career to study with Apollonius Molon, a famous rhetorician on the island – the same man in fact to whom Julius Caesar would also go for instruction – shows how important a cognisance of Greek culture was for the aspiring Roman leader.

Italy itself was changing, too. The amount of money flowing into private hands was staggering, even by the standards of the second century BC. Luxury villas (the plural is significant) became an important marker of status for some members of the higher echelons of the aristocracy. New building types began to appear, changing cityscapes. The most spectacular of these would be the stone amphitheatre, the venue for gladiatorial combat. The earliest was built at Pompeii in the early 70s BC, perhaps to advertise the attachment of the new settler-veterans to Roman ways.

Now, too, there is evidence that large-scale landholding – which Tiberius Gracchus had claimed was destroying Italy's agriculture in the second century – was genuinely on the upsurge. This was stimulated, at least in part, by the concentration of wealth in the hands of Sulla's backers, who gobbled up properties that had fallen to the treasury through Sulla's proscriptions and other confiscations. But rich though these people were, they cannot, on their own, account for the expansion of the economy. In rural areas like Umbria, though not directly affected by Sullan confiscations, the transformation was striking. People were now moving to urban centres, leaving behind the rural sanctuaries that had been so important for earlier forms of social organisation. Also, to judge from the increased survival of Latin inscriptions on non-perishable materials, Latin also now became more widespread as the language of official discourse in Italian cities.

The economic and cultural transition on the Italian peninsula did not occur against a background of peace and amity, however. The rain that had drenched Sulla's funeral pyre had barely ceased before his legacy was being fiercely challenged. The tribunes demanded the restoration of their full powers. The consul Aemilius Lepidus resisted their demands: he wanted to play tribune himself, moving bills to increase the supply of subsidised grain and to rescind Sullan settlements in parts of the Italian countryside where there were already signs of unrest. A revolt broke out that necessitated the dispatch of an armed force commanded by Catiline, who had already amply demonstrated his psychopathic tendencies by torturing Marius Gratidianus to death. Then there was a rebellion at Faesulae in

Etruria, where locals attacked a veteran settlement – the Sullans had constructed a fortified camp when they arrived, in an unambiguous sign that they were not expecting their presence to be welcome.

Before the summer ended Lepidus had himself appointed as commander of an army that would suppress the revolt in Etruria, which it duly did, but he then refused to return to Rome or dismiss the army: he would need it, he said, when he took up his command in southern France the following year. As soon as the new year dawned, however, he led that army on Rome. A later historian suggests that, in what was considered at the time an outrageous act, his main aim was to revise Sulla's settlement programme and to secure a second consulship for himself.

Lepidus reached Rome before encountering an army commanded by Lutatius Catulus, the other consul of 78 BC, and Gnaeus Pompey, who as far as we can tell had again raised an army at personal expense. Defeated outside the city walls, Lepidus withdrew through Etruria and embarked his army for Sardinia. When he died soon after arriving on the island, significant numbers of his men took ship for Spain, where they joined forces with Sertorius. Meanwhile, in Italy, another constitutional showdown followed as Pompey refused to lay down his command; it was finally agreed that he could take his men to Spain to fight Sertorius. An individual of no experience in civilian government, and still too young to hold even a quaestorship, Pompey understood that his own path to domination at home lay in retaining military commands abroad. It is a sign of his success that he would be the most powerful man *not* to declare war on the government of the Republic in the first half of the first century.

The story of Sertorius mirrors the fluid situation in the contemporary Mediterranean. After leaving Italy, well ahead of the final collapse of Carbo's cause, he had tried to establish himself in Spain. Having failed to make headway upon his arrival – indeed, having suffered a series of defeats – Sertorius involved himself in a coup against the king of Mauretania (roughly, modern Morocco). Sulla, who had links with that royal house dating back to his capture of Jugurtha in 106 BC, had sent a small army to support the king. But it arrived too late, and was taken over by Sertorius when its general was killed.

The former Sullan army formed the core of the new anti-Sullan revolt. Drawing strength from the leaders of tribes in Lusitania, in the year 80 BC Sertorius began what would be a much more successful campaign in Spain. Notable, and again evocative of the new world order, was his effort to integrate his local allies into his command structure, while providing their children with a good classical education in Latin and Greek. He trained some of his Spanish allies to fight like Romans, while retaining other units as skirmishers. By the end of the year, having defeated the governors of the provinces of both southern and northern Spain, he was deemed such a threat that Metellus himself was sent to deal with him.

Metellus was not successful. By the end of 79 BC he was bottled up by Sertorius in the south, and the governor in the north had been decisively defeated by an army commanded by one of Sertorius' lieutenants. With Sulla's death and the opening stages of Lepidus' coup now occupying centre stage in Rome, no aid was forthcoming to Metellus in 78 BC. In 77 BC, the survivors of Lepidus' cause, amounting to slightly more than five legions, were transported from Sardinia under the command of Marcus Perperna. After some confusion – Perperna was initially unwilling to serve as Sertorius' subordinate – the new troops joined Sertorius. Pompey was not far behind.

Pompey's arrival did not have the salutary impact he had expected. Sertorius kept Metellus in southern Spain and prevented Pompey from joining forces with him. The situation was complicated by the fact that the Roman state was once again in financial crisis. Although the moneyers of 79 BC had used over 600 obverse dies, there had been a steady drop-off, even with a separate mint working for Metellus and Pompey in Spain. Including the production of that mint, in 77 BC the Roman state used around 460 dies, which was not enough to pay the twenty-four or twenty-five legions then in the field. It is no wonder that Sallust, who could remember these times, would make shortages a theme of these years; that in 74 BC the Senate would take over the region of Cyrenaica, left to Rome twenty years earlier in the will of King Ptolemy Apion in the hope that it might generate taxes in excess of those needed to pay for its governance even after decades of unstable government; and that there was agitation for a change in administration, represented by the restoration of tribunician rights.

A contributing factor was the threat of 'piracy', which once again had become significant. When Sertorius landed in Morocco, he had been assisted by a considerable force of nautical free agents. The consul of 79 BC had been sent to southern Turkey with instructions to quash them there. He claimed a triumph, but the offenders, who appear to have belonged to an increasingly sophisticated network representing liminal communities around the Mediterranean, stayed very much in business.

It is again Sallust who evokes the sense of crisis, in speeches he fabricated for Marcus Aurelius Cotta, a consul of 75 BC, and Gnaeus Pompey when describing these years in the great history he wrote of the period after Sulla's death. According to Sallust, Pompey threatened to bring his army home from Spain if he did not receive proper support. His men had not been paid and Spain was so ravaged that governing it was costing a lot more than expected. He implored the Senate to recall that its interests and his were the same. This notion that a servant, loosely defined, of the state might have interests of his own was a legacy of Sulla's, and Pompey was certainly not the last person to harbour such a sentiment. Sallust's Cotta sums up the position in which the state found itself:

> Our commanders in Spain are calling for pay, soldiers, weapons, and food, circumstances compel them to do so since the defection of our allies, the flight of Sertorius through the mountains, prevents them from either engaging in battle or providing for their necessities. Armies are being maintained in the provinces of Asia and Cilicia because of the excessive strength of Mithridates. Macedonia is full of foes, and so are the coastal regions of Italy and the provinces. In the meantime, our revenues, made scanty and uncertain by war, barely suffice for a part of our expenditures ... Imperial power involves great anxiety, many heavy burdens; it is in vain for you to seek to avoid them and to look for peace and prosperity when all the provinces and kingdoms, all lands and seas are racked by hatred or exhausted by wars.
>
> (Sallust, *Histories* 2.44.6–7; Fr. 14 (McGushin))

This was the situation in the summer of 75 BC. Some people were already questioning the survivability of the Sullan system, especially as regards the tribunate. Indeed, Cotta, who had helped save Caesar and was, according to Sallust, 'from the centrist group', passed a law rescinding Sulla's ban on tribunes seeking higher office.

Bad as things were in 75 BC, they would soon get worse. Mithridates was again on the move, and this time he had friends to back him. He received ambassadors from Sertorius, asking for money in return for training the army, which he now began to raise. These ambassadors exploited the pirate connection in order to cross and recross the Mediterranean. At the same time, the health of Nicomedes IV of Bithynia, who was heavily dependent on Roman financiers, was plainly in decline. He had made a

THE ORIGIN OF EMPIRE

will disinheriting his son by Mithridates' daughter so as to make Rome heir to his kingdom. The Roman state, on the verge of annexing Cyrene, was not about to turn Bithynia's bequest down, and initiated preparations for the war against Mithridates which became inevitable when Nicomedes died as the year drew to a close.

As preparations for the war with Mithridates were getting under way, a new initiative was launched against the pirates. One of the praetors of 74 BC, Marcus Antonius, was granted a new form of command – 'unlimited *imperium*' – around the Mediterranean, which meant that he could order up from any province the anti-pirate resources he needed. Although for this year his actions were limited to the western Mediterranean, in 73 BC he would transfer his operations to Crete. In some ways, the command could be seen as a throwback to the older notion of *imperium* relating to a task rather than to a province, but previously there had been no question of allowing one magistrate to give orders in the *provincia* of another. Antonius' ability to do so may be seen as an offshoot of the notion of graded *imperium*, whereby one person's *imperium* was superior to another's, that appeared in the *lex Valeria* that had help create Sulla's dictatorship.

For the war with Mithridates, initial dispositions included Cotta being assigned a fleet to operate in Pontic waters, while his co-consul Lucullus was told to take over Cilicia when the governor of that province suddenly died. As Sulla's former quaestor and a man who had done extensive service in the east, Lucullus was an obvious appointment. He was aware that anti-Roman sentiment was running at an all-time high, as those Roman bankers who had lent the money that enabled provincial cities to pay Sulla were charging interest rates of up to 48 per cent. Some cities had managed through vigorous diplomacy to limit their exposure, but these were the exceptions. Others could tell stories of random acts of administrative brutality, such as the rape at Lampsacus of a distinguished citizen's daughter by a Roman official, as well as narratives of fiscal oppression.

The former governor of Asia had begun the takeover of Bithynia, so Cotta took his fleet to the sea of Marmara to support the Roman annexation, botched the operation, and ended up being besieged at Cyzicus by Mithridates' whole army. Lucullus gathered five legions from Cilicia and, as a thoroughly modern Roman general, demonstrated his grasp of the fact that one did not need to fight in order to win. Taking up a position from which he could cut off Mithridates' supplies, he soon reduced Cyzicus' besiegers to starvation. Mithridates' army withdrew into Pontus, with Lucullus, now in command of Cilicia, Asia and Pontus, in pursuit.

Lucullus spent the rest of the summer systematically capturing Pontic cities so as to deprive Mithridates of bases for future action. This operation was well under way when winter came, at which point Lucullus had to withdraw. But, his reputation in tatters, Mithridates could do nothing to retrieve the situation. What was less obvious at the time was the significance of Lucullus' massive command. He not only governed three provinces, but was also free to expand the war zone as he saw fit. To be able to exercise complete control over a vast swathe of territory set the gold standard to which others would successfully aspire during the next twenty years. It would also provide the foundation for the demolition of republican government.

In Spain, the war continued with alternating successes and defeats, though with the balance turning in favour of Pompey and Metellus. In Italy, however, things took a turn for the worse. At some point a group of gladiators who had allegedly been imprisoned in a training ground near Capua broke out and fled to Vesuvius. There they gathered with other malcontents and began to raid the area, where the local authorities proved incapable of dealing with them. The gladiators, led by one Spartacus, then moved on to raise the standard of revolt elsewhere.

In the modern world, Spartacus has attracted more attention than many who may at the time have seemed more deserving of a place in the pantheon of highly significant personages. Like another figure, Jesus of Nazareth, he is viewed as a champion of the downtrodden and a victim of imperial oppression. That crucifixion figures in the demise of both elicits, not unreasonably, sympathy from modern historians who regard that appalling form of execution as particularly Roman. In fact, it wasn't: like many of their most disturbing habits, the Romans imported this form of punishment from abroad, from places such as Carthage, Greece and Egypt. In part because of his profession as a gladiator, Spartacus is often now seen as a sort of proto-Marxist revolutionary, emerging from the most downtrodden and wretched circumstances via an inherent nobility of soul that enabled him to encourage others to stand up to oppression.

There is a good deal more fiction than fact in modern reconstructions of Spartacus' career. To begin with, Roman gladiators did not rate as poor or downtrodden. Although theirs was a dangerous trade, it was scarcely the only dangerous trade in the Roman entertainment industry. Many gladiators were free men who fought for substantial purses; slave gladiators were expensive, and hardly readily expendable. Furthermore, gladiators of all sorts could find ample employment outside the amphitheatre: they appear in the pages that follow as bodyguards for the rich and famous and as essential 'muscle' at times of political stress.

Spartacus' revolt was *not* a slave revolt. Spartacus' army was dangerous precisely because it could fight as an army. Our sources make clear that his people could engage toe to toe with Roman legionaries. It is undoubtedly true that a gladiator untrained in the deployment of large formations would scarcely have been able to build such an army from nothing. But, as was the case with a rural revolt a decade later, the men who followed Spartacus were already trained legionaries. Dispossessed by Sullan confiscations, embittered by the gross economic unfairness of the post-Sullan world, these were individuals whose lives had been undone by rapid change. Spartacus' revolt began as a run-of-the-mill protest and morphed into a peasant uprising. Spartacus himself must have been extraordinarily charismatic, but he was also cruel – he had an unwholesome taste for human sacrifice.

The revolt's initial success owed more than a little to the fact that Rome's best generals were abroad and its most experienced soldiers, if not joining the revolt, were retired. The first response was to dispatch two praetors at the head of hastily raised armies, whom Spartacus either eluded or defeated with alarming ease.

The war continued into the following year, with both consuls deployed in Italy. Spartacus' force had split in two and one section, led by a man named Crixus, was wiped out by the consul Gellius. However, Roman efforts to deal with Spartacus himself were dogged with failure. Moving from Campania, across the Apennines and into Picenum, Spartacus defeated the joint forces of the two consuls, then the garrison of Cisalpine Gaul. At that point, if he had indeed intended to escape with his army across the Alps, as was alleged, nothing could have been done to stop him. Instead, he turned south again, recrossing the Apennines and ravaging Campania, then moved into Lucania where he occupied the city of Thurii. At this point, command of the opposing forces was taken from the consuls and given to the praetor Marcus Licinius Crassus, who had recently been acquitted of the dubious charge of corrupting a Vestal Virgin.

A veteran commander with experience in the civil war, Crassus imposed

1. Archaeology constantly renews our understanding of antiquity. This is one of the rams from the floor of the sea off the Egadi Islands that has reshaped our understanding of naval conflict in the first war between Rome and Carthage (see p. 24).

2. A view of the very Greek Athena temple at Paestum from the very Roman-style Curia (Senate House) in the Roman-style Forum (p. 36).

3. A relief from Tarquinia showing a battle between local troops and Gauls. This image of third-century warriors underscores the community of interest that bound Etruscan states to Rome.

4. The goddess Roma observes the founding of Rome. The image of the city goddess looks out at the myth of Romulus and Remus and the augury that accompanied the city foundation. The coin seems to echo Ennius' account of the foundation of Rome (p 106).

5. This coin commemorates the passage of the lex Porcia of 199 BC by an ancestor of the official who minted this coin in 110/9 BC. The lex Porcia extended the right of appeal or provocatio to Roman citizens in the provinces. Here a soldier invokes the right of appeal against magistrate who stands to the left with his lictor on the right – the verb provoco 'I appeal' appears below the soldier's feet. Provocatio would be central to political discussions in the second to first centuries (p. 134, 196).

6. The theatre built by Statius Clarus at Pietrabondante (p. 152).

7. *The site of the temple of Fortuna Primigenia at Praeneste. The temple was incorporated into the Palazzo Colonna Barbarini, but the meeting area that was attached to the site is visible in this picture (p. 114).*

8. *The garden of the vast House of the Faun at Pompeii. A mosaic (now in the Museo Archeologico Nazionale di Napoli) depicting Alexander the Great was once located in the structure in the middle of this picture (p. 153).*

9. *The spacious interior of the House of Menander at Pompeii looking out towards the peristyle court and garden.*

10. Gnaeus Pompey.

11. Julius Caesar.

12. *A portion of relief depicting the Battle of Actium from a monument originally constructed at Avellino (p.294).*

13. *The gemma Augustea showing Augustus enthroned in the company of the gods on the top register (it is possible that Roma, who sits next to Augustus has the features of Livia). The lower register shows the erection of a trophy to celebrate a victory over northern peoples.*

14. The temple of Jupiter at the north end of the forum at Pompeii is emblematic of the transformation and homogenisation of urban space under Roman influence. Vesuvius lurks in the background (p. 153).

15. The amphitheatre at Pompeii, modelled on the Colosseum replaced an earlier amphitheatre (where Spartacus would have fought). It is modelled on the Colosseum and is characteristic of building projects in first-second centuries AD (p. 348).

16. *Germanicus Caesar, son of Drusus and Tiberius' nephew.*

17. *Bust of Augustus, who remains perpetually youthful in representations created throughout his reign.*

18. *Bust of Tiberius, who, like Augustus, remains perpetually youthful. Suetonius reports that, contrary to the image here, that Tiberius was completely bald.*

19. *Livia, wife of Augustus and a person of great influence in her own right.*

20. *The Villa Jovis at Capri was Tiberius' principal residence after his departure from Rome in 27 BC. The site's spectacular natural beauty cannot conceal the fact that the villa is far too small to house the bureaucracy needed to run an empire (p. 337).*

21. *The villa at Sperlonga was another of Tiberius' favorite places, but it too is far too small to house the government of the empire (compare the imperial reception area in Hadrian's palace at Tivoli, p. 383).*

22. *Two imperial princes, most likely Nero and Britannicus,*
from the Sebasteion at Aphrodisias (p. 351).

23. Cameo portrait of Claudius. The image echoes that of his brother, Germanicus.

24. *Agrippina the Younger, daughter of Germanicus, wife of Claudius and mother of Nero.*

25. *Nero, the image is distinctive, stressing his difference from Claudius.*

26. Vespasian. The stress on his maturity distinguishes him from Nero.

27. Domitian. Like Tiberius, his portraiture shows him with more hair than he possessed in his mature years. Juvenal referred to him as the 'bald Nero'. It also distinguishes him from his father and brother whose public images were virtually identical.

28. Vespasian began the rebuilding of the imperial palace on the Palatine on a much more generous scale, the scene here is of the stadium that was part of the palace.

29. *Scenes from Trajan's Column, depicting his campaigns in Dacia (p. 393). In addition to slaughtering Dacians, the column suggests the process of incorporating the new area within the empire through its stress on Roman building projects.*

30. *The Canopus, a part of Hadrian's palace at Tivoli named for a famous suburb of Alexandria on the western bank at the mouth of the westernmost branch of the Nile Delta (see p. 398).*

strict discipline upon his troops, but with an unpleasantly antiquarian touch, claiming that the practice of decimation – the execution of every tenth man in a defeated unit – was sanctioned by ancient tradition, and proceeded to inflict it upon sections of his own army. He then set about transforming the conflict with Spartacus to one of positional warfare, much as Lucullus had done in the east and Metellus and Pompey were doing in Spain. Spartacus responded by planning to evacuate his force to Sicily, aided by a fleet of Cilician pirates: a threat deemed sufficiently serious that the governor, Verres, was moved to take active steps to prevent the crossing. It might be that Verres' own connections with these same pirates facilitated a negotiation that ended their dealings with Spartacus.

The year 72 BC was not a bad one for the Roman state. Abroad things went well. Lucullus continued his successful operations in Pontus, forcing Mithridates to seek refuge with his son-in-law Tigranes of Armenia. In Spain, the war came to a sudden end. Perperna, who had never reconciled himself to his subordination, murdered Sertorius at a banquet. Then, discovering that he had minimal support, he surrendered to Pompey. Pompey had him summarily executed while making a show of not reading Sertorius' correspondence, turned over by Perperna and allegedly containing all manner of juicy treasonous material. Before returning to Italy in 71 BC, he incinerated the lot.

On arrival, Pompey found that Crassus had finally managed to crush Spartacus' army in a major battle at Senerchia. Spartacus is said to have died fighting. Crassus then crucified 6,000 captives along the Appian Way, in an act of brutality which, when considered alongside his harsh treatment of his own men, might have made his fellow Romans less willing to give him full credit for ending the war. That went to Pompey. He rounded up some of Spartacus' followers before returning to Rome to celebrate a massive triumph for his victories. Crassus was predictably furious.

But there were more pressing things to do. Both Pompey and Crassus were elected consuls. The first censors since 86 BC were also elected and moves were afoot to restore the rights of the tribunes and eliminate corruption in public life.

The rights of tribunes were restored early in 70 BC. Another focal point for complaints about wrongdoing was the Sullan jury system, which found itself on trial, along with Verres, the former governor of Sicily, when he was brought up before the court on charges of corruption and extortion.

12. This bust of Cicero, dating to around a century after his death, reflects the continuing Roman fascination with Cicero as a defining cultural figure of his era.

Cicero was the prosecutor, and the jury never had to vote in the case, for Verres was so obviously guilty that he fled into exile before the witnesses Cicero had assembled finished testifying. Still, in the published version of his speech, Cicero lambasted the old regime. He declared Verres' betrayal of Carbo reprehensible, called the proscriptions a national misfortune, and said of Sulla that:

> His power was so great that no one was able to retain property, homeland or life itself if he was unwilling; so great was his inclination to audacity that he said in a public meeting that when he sold the goods of Roman citizens he was selling his own plunder, we retain his acts today and even defend them with public authority for fear of worse things.
>
> (Cicero, *Verrines* 2, 3.81)

Cicero was not the only one calling for reform. Even as Verres' trial was unfolding, the consul's brother Marcus Aurelius Cotta, who was now a praetor, introduced legislation changing the composition of juries so that they would be impanelled from three groups: the Senate, the equestrian order and the *tribuni aerarii* – an *ordo*, like the equestrian, that formed part of the first census class. Even the censors got in on the act, expelling sixty-four men from the Senate, which is something of a statement about perceived levels of corruption within that august body. Included among the expellees was Lentulus Sura, who had been consul just a year before. Sulla may have thought that he was creating a better Rome by devising a system whereby magistrates with *imperium* would set the tone. What he had in fact created was a kleptocracy, whose inefficiencies now appalled even some of his own supporters, who sought to restore decency by reinstating checks on magisterial misconduct.

Although Crassus and Pompey both said they supported the restoration of tribunician authority, and Pompey, at least, went on the record complaining about senatorial corruption, they did little during their year in office to advance the tribunician cause. Mutual dislike stood in the way of united action until the point where Crassus staged a miracle: a man appeared in the forum claiming he had had a vision of Jupiter in which the god had announced that the consuls could not leave office until they were formally reconciled. They did as the god commanded, and neither man drew a province for the coming year, although this could quite possibly be because there was no reason to remove Lucullus from his command against Mithridates, as he continued his methodical reduction of Pontic cities and was now requesting ten commissioners be sent to confirm the arrangements he was making in conquered territory as the war drew to its close.

Despite Lucullus' request for commissioners, he was not winding the war down. He now moved into the kingdom of Tigranes of Armenia (where Mithridates was still to be found), crushing the son-in-law's army outside the city of Tigranocerta in northern Mesopotamia. His victory was a resounding one, but its circumstances should have alerted the authorities in Rome, for Lucullus had initiated a major war as a continuation of an existing one without consulting the Senate. Also, successful as he was, he seemed unable to finish what he had started. Despite their defeat, Mithridates and Tigranes were still at large. In 69 BC Lucullus defeated Tigranes once again, driving him from his kingdom, but still the war dragged on.

After further fighting in Pontus during 68 BC, Lucullus encamped at Nisibis (modern Nusabyn) on the Tigris. His army was growing restless, not helped by the fact that Lucullus appeared to be considering extending the campaign further by intervening in the affairs of neighbouring Parthia, where a civil war was brewing over the succession. Then there were the *publicani*, whose plundering of the provinces was persistently hampered by his presence. So it was that Lucullus' power no longer went unchallenged and a governor was sent to Asia to replace him at the start of the next year. At Nisibis it was becoming clear that the main army was exhausted. Further discontent was fuelled by the mutinous conduct of an obnoxious but extremely well connected young officer called Publius Clodius, a son of the Caecilia Metella whom we met at the beginning of this chapter. Finally, the legions that had come to the east under Flaccus and Fimbria over two decades previously refused to obey further orders.

When new governors were sent to Bithynia and Cilicia in 67 BC, Lucullus' tenure ceased. His command evaporated, and with it any sense of coherence in the Roman action against Mithridates. Moreover, there was still the piracy problem, exacerbated when some pirates kidnapped two praetors off the Campanian coast and held them to ransom. That one of the consuls for 67 BC was suspected of having engaged in extraordinarily lavish bribery in order to be elected did nothing to improve the situation. Indeed, failure and scandal caused a crisis in government. Two tribunes, Aulus Gabinius and Gaius Cornelius, introduced a mass of legislation aimed at saving the situation. Both men were former officers of Pompey's, so it was no surprise that one of the solutions involved his immediate return to public life to deal with the piracy.

A later historian, Cassius Dio, viewed the response to the pirate issue as the beginning of the end for republican government. This was something of an overstatement, for the major provisions of the bill that the tribune Gabinius presented in the summer of 67 BC (the *lex Gabinia*) drew upon elements of previous anti-piracy legislation. The main difference between Gabinius' proposals and earlier ones was the scale of the operation. According to Gabinius' proposal, the holder of the command against the pirates would be given a fleet of 200 ships, fifteen legates, a very large budget, and the authority for three years to give orders to governors whose provinces bordered the sea. The crucial aspect of the new law was the concept, borrowed from Antonius' earlier command, of *imperium infinitum*, 'unlimited *imperium*': this meant *imperium* not limited by a specific *provincia* but not an *imperium* that was 'greater', *maius*, than anyone else's. The right to select fifteen legates of any rank gave the holder

of this office enormous influence simply because he could dish out potentially lucrative commands. But what made the bill especially controversial
was the obvious fact that the intended holder was Pompey.

Only one senator supported the bill when it was introduced – Gaius
Julius Caesar. Lutatius Catulus, the leading representative of those who
wished to preserve Sulla's constitutional regime, lined up two tribunes
to veto the proposal. When one of them, Trebellius, attempted to do
so, Gabinius, taking a leaf from Tiberius Gracchus' book, introduced a
bill to remove a tribune from office for defying the will of the people. As
the votes began to come in overwhelmingly in Gabinius' favour, Trebellius withdrew his veto. When the law creating the command against the
pirates was passed, Gabinius brought in another bill, this one handing the
command to Pompey. The legates appointed under the first bill would
thereafter describe themselves as 'legates of Gnaeus Pompey imperator'
– the first time, as far as we know, that officials created by one law would
refer to themselves as subordinate to an official created under another.

The thrust of Cornelius' legislation was anti-corruption. He introduced a law forbidding loans from senators to emissaries from foreign
states because such loans tended to predispose the lenders to favour the
requests of emissaries in whom they had a financial interest. When that
failed, he proposed a new law controlling bribery in elections; then one
stating that only the people could grant legal exemptions, this having
become a senatorial prerogative; while another compelled praetors to
follow the prescriptions of the edicts they issued on the way they could
conduct legal business.

The first law failed, which prompted the consul Piso, who had himself
been suspected of corrupt practices, to draw up a law of his own on the
subject of bribery. Possibly in deference to his authority, the people passed
it. The failure of the Cornelian law on loans set the stage for another law
on the same topic from Gabinius, which was successful. The law on legal
exemptions passed, but in compromise form (there would have to be a
quorum of 200 at Senate meetings where exemptions were granted), as
did the law requiring praetors to follow their own edicts. Later that year
a third tribune, Roscius, introduced a bill restoring the earlier regulation
reserving the first fourteen rows of seats in the theatre for equestrians.
The point here was to make the theatre a place that gave the impression of
an ordered Roman society – which by this point may well have seemed a
thing of the past.

Several of the meetings Cornelius summoned were marred by violence, and a salient feature of this year is the extent to which he resorted to violence to support his legislative programme. When Piso introduced his bribery law, Cornelius encouraged the men who distributed the 'gifts' that candidates could make to fellow tribe members to break up the meeting. When he had proposed his earlier law on senatorial embassies he had recruited 'muscle' from ancient associations (*collegia*) that celebrated the traditional *Compitalia* in January of each year. Originally this festival had celebrated the spirits that inhabited crossroads, but by the first century its main focus was on drawing neighbourhoods together. In theory, the associations represented groups that had existed before Rome itself, such as 'the mountaineers of the Oppian Mount' or 'the villagers of the Janiculum'. These groups had once had aristocratic patrons – an inscription on the Capitoline associated with one of them features an equestrian – but they appear to have dropped away as the festivals grew rowdier and the 'leaders' (*magistri*) delighted in dressing up in aristocratic garb. Furthermore, the timing of the *Compitalia*, happening as it did at the start of the year, coincided exactly with the moment when a tribune might need to drum up voters for a new bill.

By the beginning of 66 BC, Sulla's vision of a reformed Republic had collapsed. As street gangs were being recruited to support laws challenging the integrity of the political system, novel commands that broke with the traditions of republican government were being created and recreated through the legislative process. Among those who must take greatest responsibility for this state of affairs were Lucullus and Pompey, who had been two of Sulla's most important supporters. The Sullan regime had been undone from within.

19

POLITICS IN A POST-SULLAN WORLD

❦

The political ascent of Gaius Julius Caesar, a minor player in the story so far, reflects above all Caesar's understanding of the political order. He had not made much of an impression in Rome. He had returned from the east in the early 70s BC to conduct a high-profile, though unsuccessful, prosecution of one of Sulla's leading lieutenants, and then a successful prosecution of another Sullan officer who had plundered Greek cities in the lead-up to his commander's invasion of Italy. Then Caesar had gone east again. But his star was plainly rising. The college of pontiffs accepted him into their number during the year 74 BC, at which point he returned home. Serving as a military tribune in 71 BC, he was a vocal supporter of the move to restore the rights of tribunes the following year.

A year later, when he was quaestor, his first wife Cornelia, Cinna's daughter, died. At her funeral, he celebrated her family. It is unlikely that anyone had dared celebrate Cinna in public in more than a decade. In the same year, when his aunt Julia died he pronounced a funeral oration for her in the forum. This time the procession would have focused on *his* family – which claimed descent from Aeneas – and Gaius Marius, the late Julia's husband, whose image was put on display. The following report of a passage from his oration for Julia is our first surviving public statement of Caesar's, in which he shows himself to be fully in tune with the delight taken by members of the aristocracy in mythological and historiographic fantasies:

The maternal family of my aunt Julia arose from kings, the paternal side is linked to the immortal gods. The Marcii Reges [her mother's family name] are from Ancus Marcius; the Julii, of which clan our family is a part, are from Venus. There is in our line the integrity of kings who had the greatest power amongst mortals and the sanctity of the gods, in whose power are kings.

(Suetonius, Life of Caesar, 6.1)

Caesar's advertisement of his Marian connections was perhaps not so radical and risky as it was made out to be by later writers. Cicero, whose views were scarcely radical, would often use Marius as a role model in his speeches and other published work. And just as important was Caesar's stress on the antiquity of his own line.

To recall what was good about Marius was also to recall what was bad about Sulla. Pompey himself was plainly a Sullan revisionist, and so Caesar could fit within the spectrum of Roman politics as being opposed to diehard Sullans without necessarily being seen as a revolutionary. Indeed, in the year that he came out in support of the *lex Gabinia*, he married Pompeia, the daughter of Pompeius Rufus and thus the granddaughter of Sulla himself. The marriage was, on a personal note, a failure. Caesar rapidly began an affair with Servilia, a woman who had once been married to Marcus Iunius Brutus, a supporter of Cinna whom Pompey had killed in 82 BC. She was also the sister of Marcus Porcius Cato (grandson of the censor), who was soon to begin a career notable for its vehement opposition to both Pompey and Caesar, although the two may not have been close.

Perhaps more significant than the rather murky details of his private life is the fact that Caesar's career was to some degree dependent on his connections with powerful women. His status was initially boosted by that of both his aunt and his first wife, who may have brought with her a substantial dowry. So, too, Pompeia is likely to have been quite well off, while Servilia's independence – ignored by her second husband, a man a few years older than her – was likewise supported by considerable wealth. Women, under Roman law, could own property, and the dowries they brought with them into a marriage remained their own in the event of divorce. The money could also be used to jump-start a career, as in the case of Cicero, whose wealthier wife Terentia helped fund not only his entrée into politics but also his somewhat spendthrift habits.

Politically powerful in their own right, aristocratic women were not simply chattels, to be married off as guarantors of the political deals that their fathers were striking. Despite the theory of *patria potestas* through which a Roman male controlled the fate of everyone in his household except his wife (most Roman women were married without passing into their husbands' *potestas*), Roman fathers usually deferred to their daughters' choice of marriage partner, or at least did not compel them to marry someone they considered odious. And divorces could be a problem for either partner. Pompey was appalled, he claimed, to discover that his second wife Mucia was an adulteress. He divorced her and wrecked his relationship with her family, who were not alone in feeling she had been mistreated. Pompey's love for Julia, Caesar's daughter, whom he married in 59 BC, stabilised an otherwise difficult partnership between the two men. A divorce initiated by a woman, which was allowed by law, could be financially ruinous for an overstretched husband.

For all that he had thought he was restoring some golden age of the mythic past, Sulla created yet more space for women of the nobility to exercise their influence. The proscriptions had strengthened them in that they had retained family property when their husbands' was confiscated. These same women whose marriage partners saw themselves as world rulers were not raised to be subordinate spouses. Indeed, they are increasingly visible in accounts of the period as conduits for potentially difficult conversations between husbands who could not deal directly with each other, or as independent voices whose wishes their spouses were expected to heed. Clodia, sister of Publius Clodius, acted as a channel for negotiations between Cicero and members of the aristocracy even after he had become her brother's bitter enemy, and it was said that if one wanted to obtain mercy from Sulla, the best thing to do was to talk to his wife Caecilia.

It was not just aristocratic women whose position was enhanced in the destabilised society of post-Sullan Italy. The second century had already seen an expansion of theatrical culture, and the pace quickened in the 60s BC as the financial situation began to improve. Men and women pursuing stage careers could do very well for themselves, occasionally achieving incomes that exceeded even those of senators. Their routines were not limited to traditional art forms; increasingly, musical acts on mythological themes, and what were essentially classical sit-coms, provided new roles. To judge from the way women are represented in paintings that may have derived from stage shows, there was a demand for actresses to shed a lot of their clothes while imitating heroines of mythology.

At the upper end of the spectrum, actors of both sexes mixed freely with the ruling classes – as did athletes of all sorts. At the lower levels, women might have acted as well-paid professional companions to young men in a cultural demi-monde of sexual exploitation. Before marriage (and well after it) Roman men with money would spend it on sex – and their sisters might well have been playing the same game. A female descendant of the Gracchi is described as:

> learned in Greek and Latin letters, and knowing how to sing and dance better than necessary for a respectable woman, and possessing many other qualities that are the tools of luxury; everything was more important to her than reputation or chastity, you could hardly tell if she was more sparing of money or reputation; her passion was such that she more often approached men than was approached by them.
>
> (Sallust, *Conspiracy of Catiline* 25.2–3)

This is not meant as approval, but it does indicate the impact of theatrical culture as people came to see themselves as acting out grand roles in their own lives. This was the society in which Caesar moved – his 'open relationship' with Pompeia might have scandalised Catulus, but it marked him out as a member of his generation's jet set.

Caesar was at present performing largely on an urban stage, though he had supported a failed bill to extend Roman citizenship to communities north of the Po river. Did he already sense that this was where his future might lie? It is impossible to know, but it is worth noting that northern Italian traders had a presence in Bithynia, where he too had connections. These were latecomers to the eastern bonanza, previously dominated by central Italians. Otherwise, Caesar's audience, and that of Cicero or Cato, would depend to varying degrees upon the aristocratic culture of Rome. The government had utterly failed to enhance urban amenities – for instance, no new aqueduct had been built since 125 BC – but the city's population had grown from around 400,000 to around 700,000 in the mid-60s BC. Many of these people were transients, far more men than women, who had moved there during their twenties and would later move away. Others were slaves, or freed slaves. For the vast majority, life was very hard – they probably had to pay about half their annual income, something like 250 denarii, in rent. The fact that the grain available for distribution at reduced prices was more than sufficient for one person suggests that men often lived together in the tenements that housed the bulk of the city's people.

The social world of the average Roman would be defined by his or her workplace – women worked when they were not either pregnant or looking after children. And if someone died, their companions tried to ensure that they received a decent burial. Otherwise, the body would be interred in one of the shallow mass graves just outside the city, where dogs scavenged the remains. In life, many rented rooms on the tenements' upper storeys on a day-to-day basis, while others lived in huts, or even tombs, outside the city gates; they slept on straw and had only the clothes on their backs. Mostly they ate at *tavernae*, and their diet was simple – bread, olive oil, wine, some meat, probably stewed – although this, too, was seen as a sign of the times and of a changing population. Allegedly there were no public bakers in Rome before the mid-second century BC; before then, women had baked what was needed at home. There was a tendency among the rich to associate smelly food with smelly people. The city itself stank; excrement was everywhere.

The streets weren't safe, there was no police force, and fires were extinguished either on the spot by those at risk of incineration, or by private contractors. Crassus was notorious for owning a personal fire brigade that would show up at burning buildings and demand that the owner sell the place at a knock-down price before it would get to work. Buildings were not well maintained by their owners, who saw them simply as sources of profit. Cicero would come to own a group of tenements in Puteoli which were, by his own admission, in dreadful shape.

The massive underplanned and underserved expansion of Rome's population had a significant impact on the practice of politics in ways that Sulla would have deplored – which is why he had tried to make sure tribunes could not introduce legislation to the *comitia tributa*. By this time, with legislative power restored to the tribunes, some 70,000 people could take part in the coming election, now routinely held on the Campus Martius rather than in the more cramped quarters of the forum. These swelling numbers demonstrate the expansion both of the city population and of the overall citizen body after the censorship of 86 BC. Gabinius' theatrics in 67 BC would have played to such an assemblage, where the poor could simply outvote the wealthy.

The laws restoring tribunician power and the changes in the composition of juries – the crucial reforms of 70 BC – were passed not through
the *comitia tributa* but through the *comitia centuriata*. Since the property
requirement for admission to the first census class had not changed
through the centuries, the *comitia centuriata* was no longer a particularly
plutocratic playground. In a book on the ideal Roman constitution that he
wrote in the late 50s BC, setting it as a dialogue between Scipio Aemilianus
and his friends, Cicero has Scipio observe that the wise lawmaker organises
elections so that 'the greatest number should not have the greatest power'
(Cicero, *The Republic* 2.39), but even Scipio envisages a system in which
the first census class does not consist only of the very rich. Indeed, when he
describes the first census class with a century of carpenters (useful people,
he says), he suggests that to be in the first class one did not need to be
especially well off. The amount of property that a person must possess
to be registered in the first census class was still only 6,250 denarii, the
equivalent of the 100,000 bronze asses that defined a member of the first
class in 241 BC.

In Caesar's day, the first census class would include, at one end, people
like the *tribuni aerarii*, whose fortunes cannot have been all that different
from the equestrians with whom they served on juries, or the people who
managed tenement blocks for men like Cicero. At the other end, it would
include shopkeepers, bakers, schoolteachers and the like, people who
could own property, but not a great deal. And then there were the soldiers,
whose presence could alter a consular election. The men sent by Caesar
from his army in Gaul for the consular election of 56 BC were serving
soldiers, but they could not have been in the lowest census classes if their
presence was to have any impact on the result. When defending the victor
in a consular election who was charged with corrupting the electorate,
Cicero would say that 'men of more modest means' (Cicero, *On Behalf of
Murena* 71) earned favours from senators by supporting them when they
stood for election, and that such men had only their vote to offer. Clearly
he thought that the votes of these *homines tenuiores*, as he called them,
carried some weight.

In summing up the 'good people' of Rome, Cicero would include equestrians, *tribuni aerarii*, businessmen, municipal worthies and freedmen. For
him, the good of the state depended upon the community of interest of
people who came from different social backgrounds but who had certain
things in common – they listened to speeches in the forum, they went to

the theatre and they voted. It was via the votes of those who had enough free time to hang around the forum and were not too proud to talk with the slaves from the houses of the mighty, who might reveal intimate secrets of their owners' lives, that elections would be decided. Cicero knew this, his brother Quintus knew it – he stresses the importance of being nice to one's slaves in a pamphlet he wrote for Marcus on how to be elected consul – and Caesar knew it. Caesar knew that the Roman people appreciated generosity and honoured a good war record, and he sensed that they would support someone willing to take on the most conservative members of the Sullan establishment, even though he was married to Sulla's granddaughter. For Caesar, Sullanism was not so much the issue as the need for efficiency, and the responsiveness of the state to the voting public.

Elections, being about personalities, could be shaped in public debate and often via legal actions, where the public images of prosecutors and defendants were set against each other on the stages offered by courts convening in the forum. If the poor were to be energised, it would be to support people they saw as their patrons. At the intermediate level the tribes and, when they were permitted, the *collegia* – whether of craftsmen or of communities such as the groups celebrating the *Compitalia* – were mobilised by leaders with whom they had long-term connections. Such groups probably lay behind the gangs mobilised by Cornelius, and they would re-emerge in the 50s BC as particularly influential forces behind long-established leaders like Clodius and his rival Titus Annius Milo.

Men who wished to be consul, however, knew that it was best to keep such people at arm's length. It might be necessary to be patrons of such groups early in one's career in order to gain office through the *comitia tributa*, but as time went on one should broaden one's reach to groups outside the city, to people who could be brought in, as needed, to reinforce support in the first census class. Cicero would speak of the importance of 'the little people' and of 'neighbourliness' (Cicero, *On Behalf of Plancius* 19), the quality that inspired people to come to Rome and support candidates who either were from their area or had done favours for it. In addition, to defend a man of slender means, Cicero remarked, was to gain a good reputation among the poor, whose views mattered. In this way elections to the higher magistracies gradually came to take on a broader Italian aspect.

One place to offer support, as Cicero's career shows, was the law courts, where the discourse could be highly specific and highly personal, if not always accurate. One had to be careful about which fights to pick, and with whom. It was a fine thing to be a 'new man', making one's way in the world through displays of hard work, integrity and devotion to the cause of the downtrodden and threatened. But one could go too far. Not every defendant would be as obliging as Verres in the late 70s BC, who slunk off before he could be tried properly. The prosecutor could be seen as an upstart, unaware of his proper station in life, a threat to public order, a friend of lying, cheating provincials. To some, Cicero might have seemed arrogant and acerbic. His enemies, however, tended to be murderers, thugs, perverts, drunks (and dancers) – all villains supported by the great wealth of their aristocratic ancestors. He knew that the response of the crowd listening to the advocates in the law courts could have a powerful impact on the verdict, and some of his courtroom techniques were overtly theatrical. A law court was a good place to shape public opinion.

No one was perfect. If one was smart, one would be open about a few well-chosen vices. So with Caesar it was sex, but he didn't drink, and he lived simply. Drink was a curse of the aristocracy, and Sulla was a major tippler. Lucullus, for all his glory, gave in to the temptation to spend what he had won in his wars even as he waited, year after year, to be allowed to celebrate his richly deserved triumph (which eventually happened in the late summer of 63 BC). But by then his massive villas and lavish parties had become an issue. Pompey stayed away from the law courts, the rough and tumble of which he was not equipped to handle, and rarely spoke at public meetings. This strategy made sense: the world's greatest man had to be above conventional politics.

If electoral politics were highly personal, then the great issues of the day, expressed through legislative programmes and debated before crowds at public meetings, were best wrapped in conventional abstractions. The reaction of the crowd was important; if favourable, the passage of a bill could become inevitable and if negative it would be withdrawn. But would the power of the people to determine the direction of the state be respected? Did the people truly possess the freedom (*libertas*) to which those who ruled the world were entitled? Would the magistrates abide by the concept of an ordered society, celebrating the shared interests of all (the *concordia ordinum*)? This was a virtue often asserted by new men and by members of the equestrian order, as was the quality of decency, *clementia*. But *clementia* could slip into softness and disorder, whereas what might be needed was severity, so long as it did not lapse into cruelty.

Sulla had been severe, not cruel, it could be said. Decent people advertised the strength of their friendships, stretching across social boundaries. Friendship (*amicitia*) was the glue that bound an ordered society together. Foreigners might be clients to Romans, but good Romans wanted other Romans to be their friends – to be called a 'client' was 'next to death' for a Roman. The opposite of the good man was the one who strove to deprive the people of their liberties through conspiracy and factionalism. 'These things [political alliances] are friendship amongst good men, faction amongst the evil,' said Sallust (*Jugurthine War* 31.15) – although no one self-identified as being evil, and party designations were flexible and inevitably in the eye of the beholder. Still, it could be agreed that enemies of the state connived as factions: just a few individuals – factions were always such – had the power to reduce the people to slavery (*servitium*), could establish *dominatio*, or worse yet *regnum*, a tyranny of the sort most recently witnessed in the debased kings of the east and recalled in the last Tarquin. Above all, it was wrong to use the power of the state against its citizens, to kill without trial – except, of course, when citizens had abandoned the responsibilities of citizenship to become themselves enemies of the state. It was now that the 'final decree' could be passed, enabling the magistrates to protect the state – that is, unless it could be shown after the fact that the final decree had been imposed by a faction or a tyrant.

Friendship and good order could be secured through legislation that would promote the public good, such as cheap grain and land distributions. But those could also be tools of domination in the hands of an unscrupulous faction. To be a *popularis* was to work in the interests of the people, protecting them from the domination of factions. But to be a 'good' (*bonus*) man or one of the 'best' (*optimus*) was to respect limits – anyone who valued an ordered society could be *optimus*. A good man was one whom a humble person could look up to without fear, and who took precedence without displaying contempt. The best people recognised false *populares* for what they were: spendthrifts whose projects served not the public good but their own interests.

The fractionalism of the political class circumscribed the terms used in the public discourse of politics. As an aspiring politician often moved from convenient alliance to convenient alliance, masking political expediency with the vocabulary of 'friendship', so the public positions that he adopted became increasingly conventional. Gaius Gracchus had enshrined in the public consciousness a discourse stressing the people's right to determine all policy, as well the notion of the corrupt brutality of the 'nobles'. The people had rights to land and to subsidised grain. They could secure those rights by taking control of the law courts to punish magistrates who defied their will, and they could compel adherence to the popular will through oath clauses in the laws that were passed. Although the number of martyrs to the cause of popular power grew over the decades, Tiberius and Gaius Gracchus remained the principal saints of popular culture. The stability of the Gracchi was perhaps connected to the fact that, although they had both been victims of violence, neither employed it. This was certainly not true of their ideological heirs, Saturninus, Glaucia and Sulpicius, whose use of violence played into the hands of the nobles. Their argument was increasingly that stability depended on the maintenance of the *mos maiorum* or 'the habits of the ancestors'. The ancestors had rewarded citizens who murdered aspiring tyrants, so it went, and had secured victory over Rome's enemies through their superior virtue, bringing peace and stability to the lives of all.

Particular groups would make claims to particular virtues. The aristocracy, in their own view, were the 'good' or the 'best'; they were also 'famous', 'blessed', 'ample', 'outstanding' or 'exalted'. This is what it meant to be 'nobles' or 'leading men'. But they could also be 'the few', 'the dominant', 'the arrogant' or 'the minders of fish ponds' (a term that seems to have become current when Lucullus was building his mansions). The equestrian order could be quite 'splendid' or 'eminent'; equestrians would have their own 'leading men' and their own 'dignity'. The plebs were either the *populus*, the sovereign body of state, or the 'rabble', the 'mob', the 'lowest' or the 'humble'. The predominance of negative terms reflects, no doubt, the overwhelming upper-class bias of our surviving sources.

In Caesar's view the wisest course was to build alliances across borders, to appeal to a broad spectrum of Roman society. He steered clear of the law courts and dined with his fellow *pontifices*, but he also sought to display the sort of public munificence that Cicero said voters expected. He sought to reconcile his alleged descent from Mars, Venus and the kings of Rome with the notion that he must be able to win the love of the Roman people. He was becoming famous for his good nature, his generosity, his eloquence, his intelligence and his service to friends. He was a man whom others thought was capable of great things. Some rejoiced at the prospect, others not so much.

20

63 BC

The year 63 BC was a momentous one for three of the individuals whose careers we have been tracing. For Gnaeus Pompey, it was the year in which he ended the Mithridatic war. For Cicero, it was the year in which he became consul. For Gaius Julius Caesar, it was the year in which he won two elections, establishing himself as a rising star in the political firmament. It was also the year of a botched effort by Catiline to overthrow the government.

Pompey had obtained the command against Mithridates in the wake of his spectacularly successful campaign against piracy in the latter half of 67 BC. It had taken him six months to do what none of his predecessors charged with the suppression of piracy across the Mediterranean had managed. And while it would be an exaggeration to claim, as Pompey did, that the threat had been eradicated, the wide-ranging illicit fleets of previous years were no more. Pompey possessed extremely well-developed administrative skills and, despite what his detractors might say (for example, that he had been a teenage assassin), he was not a mass murderer. Recognising that piracy was a lifestyle choice for people living in otherwise economically challenged circumstances in Crete and southern Turkey, he resettled former pirate communities in areas where they might be able to support themselves through agriculture, some of them a long way from home – ex-pirates have been detected in Cyrenaica and even in northern Italy. Aware they could get a deal from Pompey that was markedly better than taking their chances with his legates, Cretan communities sent peace-seeking envoys to him while he was in Cilicia.

While Pompey was dealing with the pirates, the Mithridatic war took a turn for the worse. Mithridates had returned to Pontus in 67 BC, and that autumn had defeated the Roman garrison, then crushed a force commanded by a legate of Lucullus named Triarius (the new governor, Glabrio, would not arrive until the end of the year). With his army on strike, there was nothing Lucullus could do; he was told to hand over part of his army to Glabrio when he arrived, to dismiss the mutinous Fimbrian legions, and to start on the return journey to Italy with those men whose retirement would become final when they reached home. He could not now challenge Mithridates in Pontus, and his replacement as governor of Cilicia, who had elected to intervene in Antioch where the vestigial Seleucid regime had collapsed into chaos, was in no position to do anything about the unravelling situation in the north.

When news of Triarius' defeat reached Rome, panic seems to have broken out, especially among those who had just taken out the contract for tax-collecting in Asia. No one thought, apparently, that Glabrio would be up to the task. Another solution was both needed, and to hand. On 11 December Manilius, a tribune, introduced a bill to transfer command of the war against 'the kings' – Tigranes as well as Mithridates – to Pompey, who, conveniently, was already in Cilicia. According to this bill Pompey would be given two provinces, Bithynia and Cilicia, and the additional right, formerly possessed by Lucullus, to decide who to fight; but any administrative arrangements would have to be made in conjunction with a board of ten selected by the Senate, and in the fullness of time confirmed by them. This time the law faced less opposition – Cicero, who would be praetor in 66 BC, made a speech supporting it, as did Caesar, while a number of ex-consuls jumped on the Pompeian bandwagon. The law was passed through the *comitia tributa* in early January.

Pompey was nothing if not efficient. After the anticipated failure of desultory negotiations with Mithridates, he moved his army into Pontus, where he confronted the king's force. He was quite happy now, as in Spain, to wage a positional war, avoiding a major battle until he could anticipate the demoralisation of an enemy force that was significantly smaller than his own. When the battle came, Mithridates' army collapsed. The victory was nearly bloodless from the Roman viewpoint; at least, that is what we know from the accounts, probably based on Pompey's own account or on those of his supporters.

Taking with him what remained of his treasury and his army, Mithridates fled through what is now Georgia, around the Black Sea to the Crimea, then ruled by one of his sons. Pompey pursued Mithridates as far as the southern end of Georgia, where he defeated an army assembled by local kings. Then he turned his attention south, to Tigranes, who remained at large. This would also mean dealing with the Parthians, but that was no great challenge as they had just been through a civil war and Phraates III, the new monarch, was eager to avoid conflict with a man who appeared to be living up to his claim to be the new Alexander the Great. Phraates went so far as to support the invasion of Armenia by columns of Roman soldiers under Pompey's legates Afranius, Metellus Celer and Flaccus (all men we will be hearing about again). Pompey himself struck a deal with Tigranes' son, then a refugee from his father at Phraates' court, promising him Tigranes' kingdom.

Pompey lied; he accepted Tigranes' surrender and threw his son in chains. He then had to decide on the limits of Tigranes' kingdom, so he sent an army south under Gabinius on an exploratory mission in the area near the modern city of Mosul. Phraates, who was content to allow Pompey to set up client kingdoms so long as they stayed away from his capital at Ctesiphon, near modern Baghdad, may have intervened so that Tigranes' kingdom was restricted to a region north of the Taurus mountains.

The important thing that Pompey recognised, as 66 BC became 65 BC, was that this was no part of the world for Romans. There were no urban centres of the sort they were comfortable dealing with, and it was already quite enough to have to construct a Roman province out of Mithridates' old kingdom of Pontus. This was a defensive measure to ensure that the king could never come home; and it involved the foundation of cities with self-congratulatory names – a local tradition since the time of Alexander himself. Two of Pompey's new foundations in Pontus – now, ironically, to be joined with Bithynia (Mithridates' dream in the first place) – were Nicopolis (Victoryville) and Pompeiopolis (Pompeyville).

The settlement of the kingdom of Armenia left Pompey with one further problem. What to do with Syria? The old centre of the Seleucid empire had been annexed by Tigranes, then freed by Lucullus, who restored as king a member of the Seleucid house, Antiochus XIII, a gentleman whose career suggests that generations of close kin marriage were having a deleterious effect on the royal household. There was some sort of problem with him in 67 BC, which explains the previous governor of Cilicia's presence there.

Pompey decided that enough was enough. The core of the old Seleucid realm contained several cities of the Greek sort that could be made into a province, and that is what he proposed to do. Leaving his legates to impose order in Armenia, he sent his quaestor, Aemilius Scaurus, into Syria, where chaos reigned as local dynasts strove to take over bits of the former Seleucid heartland – or, as in the case of the Jewish state centred on Jerusalem, were simply fighting each other. Pompey imposed peace and deposed Antiochus. He left Scaurus to figure out what a new province of Syria should look like, while he finalised arrangements for Pontus and the states of Cappadocia and Commagene, to be left under their own kings; and Galatia, the Celtic area of central Turkey, also to be left in the control of local dynasts. These new rulers would not be paying tribute to Rome, but it appears that they started borrowing from Roman financiers – some, possibly most, of whom had connections with Pompey. Most likely, any tax revenue would not have covered the costs of direct Roman administration, but the kings' needs enabled Pompey to collect large sums of interest.

While Pompey was bringing order to the east, Caesar and Cicero were advancing their careers in the west. Cicero was devoting much of his energy to gathering the support he would need to win the consular election of 64 BC for 63 BC, and Caesar was putting on a show of his own. As aedile in 65 BC, he had restored Marius' trophies for his victories over the Cimbrians and Teutons and promised an immensely lavish gladiatorial display. This so outraged those who were becoming suspicious of his apparent devotion to the status quo that they organised a senatorial decree banning the display, and took the blame for the disappointment of all those who had been looking forward to the event. This incident is the first of a number in which Caesar gave his opponents a choice of two unpalatable options – for while he did not actually put on the grand display, he still got the credit for trying.

He returned to the cause of the northern Italians, whom Crassus as censor in 65 BC was proposing to enrol as citizens, only to be thwarted by his colleague Lutatius Catulus. Catulus also prevented the passage of a bill annexing Egypt, which Ptolemy X had left to Rome in a will he composed while seeking Roman support for an attempt to retake the throne from which he had been driven in 88 BC. The disputes between Crassus and Catulus reached such a point that they laid down office without completing the census; the new censors, too – elected to complete the registration of citizens in 64 BC – resigned in the face of tribunician opposition.

The failure of the censors was not the only scandal of these years – the consuls elected for 65 BC, one of them Sulla's nephew, had both been convicted of bribery and were prevented from taking office. The year had opened against a background of threat and invention. Unfounded rumours were circulating that the convicted consuls would try to murder their successors, and the Temple of Capitoline Jupiter was struck by lightning. At a moment when the developing historiography of the Italian war was recalling all manner of signs of divine displeasure, such incidents could cause genuine stress – so much so that they were still recalled with dread some years later.

An observer of the political scene might also have found that the results of some major trials had been unpredictable (or just plain illogical). Thus, a coterie of Sulla's associates failed to convict Cornelius for treason as tribune in 67 BC, with Cicero appearing for the defence, while Manilius, who was prosecuted by a relatively unknown leading counsel, was convicted for his actions in bringing the bill that gave Pompey his command. Then there was the failure to convict Catiline for corruption when he was governor of Africa. It was said that the jury had been bribed, which did nothing to improve Catiline's already dubious reputation, and the trial cost him a chance to run for the consulship. Cicero thought briefly of running with him rather than against him, and even of appearing for his defence, but that task went to Clodius, freshly returned from his adventures in the east.

The consular election of 64 BC played out against the previous year's scandals and the restoration of Marius' trophies. The fact that Sulla's nephew had to resort to bribery is telling – if anyone should have been able to run on his name, it was him. The fact that he could not shows just how deep were the cracks in the Sullan establishment, and that the rules of conventional politics had changed to such an extent that extreme Sullanism had become a liability. But had the rules changed enough to enable a 'new man', the only one with no Roman magistrate among his ancestors, to win in a field of seven in which of the other six two were patricians, two had consular fathers and two had magisterial ancestors? If Cicero won, he would be the first 'new man' to hold the consulship in thirty years.

Cicero had been playing the same card ever since he began his legal career, arguing that the 'new man', having no ancestors to fall back on, had to be especially virtuous and competent. He had only once conducted a prosecution, in the case of Verres, whom everyone agreed was beyond the pale. Cicero was a defence lawyer through and through. Through his advocacy he had built up connections throughout the equestrian order and municipal Italy, hoping to build a rapport with people who might come to vote for him, not to mention all the individuals he had defended. Aside from money, the factors influencing people's voting decisions were the obligation to return a favour, the hope for better things, and personal affinity with a candidate. Cicero had travelled throughout Italy to drum up support, convincing Italians that as potential new men themselves they shared with him the values of decency, persistence and efficiency.

Catiline and Gaius Antonius, Cicero's leading opponents, made very different claims. Catiline was a patrician, although from a family that had not produced a consul since the fifth century and whose most distinguished recent ancestor had been praetor over a century earlier. Antonius was the son of the consul and famous orator Marcus Antonius, at whose feet Cicero had sat to learn his trade. Both, however, had nasty reputations. Antonius had been brought to trial by Julius Caesar for reprehensible conduct as a Sullan cavalry commander in Greece. He was acquitted, but that was in the era of senatorial juries and there was general agreement that he had behaved poorly. Catiline had not only behaved exceptionally brutally on Sulla's behalf, but it was widely held that he had bribed his way out of the charge of extortion brought against him by the people of Africa, and that he had been involved in the alleged plot against the consuls in 65 BC. Cicero would claim, when defending men charged with electoral corruption, that the plaintiffs (in his cases, always the defeated candidates) had admitted being behind in the battle for public support when they started mooting bribery. That line of defence was effective for Cicero. But in 64 BC he turned the tactic to his personal political advantage, delivering a blistering speech in the Senate in which he charged Antonius and Catiline with blatant attempts to corrupt the electorate. This time the charge served to activate memories of his opponents' legal problems. On election day Cicero triumphed. Antonius came second, allegedly because people remembered his father.

If the consular election was about personalities rather than issues, this did not mean that the political arena lacked serious subjects for discussion. Those would be dealt with through the *comitia tributa*, which had again become the primary agent of policy-making and the expression of popular will, even though there was no unified 'popular' view of the way the world should work. The primary question remained Sulla's legacy, and on this topic, despite his marriage connection, Caesar was notably active.

Caesar's main issue was the illegality of arbitrary death sentences. His position was that *provocatio*, the right of appeal to the judgment of the Roman people against the action of a magistrate, was the defining right of a Roman citizen. In the ever expanding historiography of early Rome arose a notion of an archaic 'struggle between the orders', which pitted patricians (who resembled contemporary *nobiles*) against plebeian tribunes, who pressed for *provocatio* and debt relief in the misty years of the fourth century BC. So in 64 BC, working for perhaps the only time in his life with Marcus Porcius Cato, Caesar challenged the immunity given to murderers under the Sullan dispensation, while others sought to restore civil rights to the children of the proscribed. As *iudex quaestionis*, the presiding judge for a standing court when a praetor was not available, Caesar had allowed charges to be brought against some of the more notorious characters who were still living off the proceeds of their corrupt behaviour – until Catiline was brought before him. Having some sort of connection with Catiline, Caesar dropped his action. But the point had been made.

As the new year approached, a number of proposals were put forward by the tribunes who were due to take up office on 10 December 64 BC. One, which may have seemed innocuous, advocated altering the system of choosing members for the board of *pontifices*. In 104 BC, when Marius had been on the ascendant, at the behest of the tribune Domitius Ahenobarbus the people had passed a law making the board elective. Sulla had tossed this law out, but now the tribune Titus Labienus, a known supporter of Gnaeus Pompey, proposed to return to the Domitian election system. At the same time another tribune, Rullus, introduced a bill to appoint a board of ten land commissioners who would have *imperium* and be allowed to distribute land in Italy as well as in the provinces for the foundation of new colonies, using public monies and war plunder. There was, too, a proposal to restore the civil rights of the sons of the proscribed – which balanced another proposal, supported by the incoming consul Antonius, to restore the civil rights of the consuls designate for 65 BC, which they had lost along with their office.

The proposal concerning the former consuls elect went nowhere, and Cicero devoted himself to convincing people that Rullus' bill was a bad idea. A true friend of the people looked not at handouts as a way of guaranteeing the welfare of Roman citizens, but rather at ways to enhance the stability of the state and its financial resources. Cicero found a tribune who would veto the bill, and Rullus did not force the issue.

Although Rullus' bill failed, its powerful land commission reflected what appears to have been a growing sense among members of the political classes that nothing worthwhile could ever get through the Senate. Effective action required officials unfettered by conventional office-holding. With Lucullus still waiting outside Rome for the Senate to approve the triumph his deeds merited, this was arguably a reasonable viewpoint. On the other hand, the fact that he was still sitting there could also be taken as a warning that Pompey might not get his way either. Rullus' bill had followed the example of Tiberius Gracchus by making the decisions of the land commissioners final, which was not in keeping with other strategies for making government accountable. Pompey would still have to submit his settlement in the east for senatorial approval when he returned from the seemingly inevitable victory.

The bill allowing the direct election of pontiffs turned out to be a great deal more significant than might have been expected. If it had not been passed, the college of pontiffs would simply have selected one of its members to take up residence in the 'State House', in the heart of the forum. Had this been the case when Metellus, *pontifex maximus* since 80 BC, died, it is likely that an old Sullan crony would have got the job. Servilius, well placed but ineffective against the Cilician pirates, was one possibility; another was Lutatius Catulus. Catulus might have been the favourite because he had taken charge of the reconstruction of the Temple of Capitoline Jupiter. But that was not to be. Julius Caesar declared himself a candidate when Metellus died, shortly after the bill passed, and was elected. To some it might have been a shocking result, but Caesar knew what a risk it was and sensed the response to his anti-Sullan acts of recent years. The man who had restored Marius' trophies was going to be a lot more popular than one who had complained about that restoration, as Catulus had done.

At the age of thirty-seven, Caesar had solidified his position among the most potent politicians of his age. His election also suggests that, when the right candidates were involved, voting could have an ideological tinge. Catulus represented old-school Sullanism; Caesar represented the idea that the mistakes of the past should be admitted.

The biggest mistake, in Caesar's view, was the perpetuation of the Senate's authority to suspend the right of *provocatio*; with Labienus' assistance, he now raised this issue again. In addition to moving his bill on the election of priests, Labienus, whose uncle had been killed with Saturninus, brought an action for high treason known as *perduellio*: a word defined not as the diminution of the majesty of the Roman people, for which there was a standing court under the Sullan system, but rather as treason of the sort that angered the gods and consequently threatened the very existence of the state. The procedure, probably invented for the occasion, involved prosecution before two judges (one of whom would be Caesar, while the other would be his cousin, one of the consuls of 64 BC). If the defendant was found guilty, he could appeal to the people in the tribal assembly, from which seventeen tribes would be drawn to cast their votes – a procedure that also featured in the Rullan bill and in the bill for electing *pontifices*. It could be taken as certain that the people would be summoned, as the mandatory penalty for *perduellio* was crucifixion.

In 63 BC Labienus, who publicised the trial by erecting a cross in the forum, brought the case against an elderly senator called Rabirius. Cicero spoke against the process, raising the point that the decree ordering magistrates to take whatever steps were needed to protect the state that had been used from Opimius' time onwards (now known as the *senatus consultum ultimum*, or 'final decree') was a necessary tool for the protection of the state. He was proud of his performance, for he would later publish the speech – although it was not that which saved Rabirius, but another's resort to ancient practice. The praetor, Metellus Celer, lowered the red flag that flew over the Janiculum hill, which in earlier times had signalled the approach of an enemy army and brought all public business to an end.

Caesar may not have minded. He had made his point; the case was not brought again. Besides, by the time summer rolled around, big news had arrived from the east.

Mithridates was dead. His son had driven him to suicide in the Crimea. Pompey, meanwhile, was still bogged down in the complex politics of Syria, trying to ensure that the Greek core of his new province would not be raided by the Arab tribes in southern Syria and Jordan who had been plundering the place in recent years. In addition, he was dragged into a nasty civil war between two brothers that was engulfing the Jewish Palestinian state. Pompey marched on Jerusalem, installed one of the brothers as high priest, arrested the other – and then found that supporters of the arrested brother had seized the Temple Mount in defiance. He then captured the heavily fortified temple, massacred the defenders, visited Yahweh and went on his way. He did, however, leave the temple treasury intact – he already had plenty of money and it was time to go home.

While Pompey made his way west, the elections for 62 BC took place. Caesar became a praetor, and Catiline lost another consular election. He began to plot a special revenge on those who had defeated him, while another vanquished candidate arraigned one of the victors for corruption. Cicero spoke for the defence. He admitted that there might have been some minor irregularities (in fact, blatant violations of statute), but the consul elect, Murena, had lived such an exemplary life – he was a military man, after all – that such little details did not matter. The thing was that people liked him. 'Military glory is better than anything else,' said the defence attorney, and the Roman people, after all, did love 'public munificence even as they despised private luxury' (Cicero, *On Behalf of Murena* 22; 76). Besides, the defeated candidate was a dull jurist and his co-counsel for the prosecution, Marcus Porcius Cato, was a dreadful bore, too, so attached to the tenets of the Greek philosophical sect of Stoicism that he could not function in the real world.

Murena was acquitted during a domestic crisis that would cast a long shadow over Cicero's career, for all his claims that he did what he had to do to save the state. The problem was Catiline. On 27 October a man named Manlius had raised the standard of revolt in Etruria, and there were rumours of incipient rebellion in a number of other places, too. Cicero had the Senate pass a decree authorising the magistrates to take whatever action was necessary for the defence of the Republic – the very decree whose legality had been questioned at Rabirius' trial.

The army Manlius was assembling was probably similar in make-up to the one that had followed Spartacus – primarily, dispossessed veterans who could supply their own weapons. Cicero would describe them as degenerates of all sorts; Sallust specified that many were former Sullan settlers – a comment that indicates the abiding unpopularity of Sullan colonists. Manlius possessed an eagle that had once been carried in Marius' army, an unlikely rallying point for Sullans. In Rome on the night of 6–7 November, Catiline sent one of his co-conspirators to murder Cicero at his house. The attempt failed and the next day Cicero summoned a senatorial meeting at which he denounced Catiline. Catiline's response was to cast aspersions on Cicero's parentage, calling him a 'transplant', before leaving in a huff (Sallust, *Conspiracy of Catiline* 31.7). That night he left the city; friends said he was heading into voluntary exile in Massalia (Marseille). It turned out he was heading to join Manlius.

The military response to Manlius was desultory at best, calling on troops waiting outside Rome to celebrate triumphs that the Senate had not got around to approving. Then, in early December, Catiline's remaining supporters in Rome did something stupid. Their leader's plan was apparently to take Manlius' army to southern France; wishing to help, his friends approached some ambassadors of the Allobroges, a powerful tribe in southern Gaul. But the Allobroges promptly notified Cicero, and Cicero arranged for a couple of praetors to arrest the ambassadors with incriminating documents in their possession. On 3 December Cicero produced the documents and denounced the Roman conspirators to the Senate, which ordered their detention. On 5 December, Cicero summoned another senatorial meeting, presenting a proposal under which the conspirators would be executed. The senators spoke in order of rank: an ex-consul was always designated to deliver his opinion first, except at the consular elections when the consuls designate would speak first, then ex-consuls, praetors elect, praetors and ex-praetors, and so forth.

Agreement with Cicero's position was unanimous until it was Caesar's turn to speak. He delivered an eloquent plea to spare the conspirators: they should be imprisoned for life, he said, expressing a view that accorded well with the criticisms he had already been making of what he claimed to be extraconstitutional butchery. His view looked like it might prevail until Cato, as tribune elect, got up and spoke in favour of execution. That view ultimately carried the day – a day when the political significance of oratorical skill was put on ample display.

Cicero led the condemned conspirators to the state prison in the forum and personally oversaw their strangulation. Sometime in the winter of 62 BC an army under the now ex-consul Antonius caught up with Catiline and destroyed his army in a hard-fought battle at Pistoria (Pistoia). Catiline died on the battlefield.

The events of 63 BC illustrate the malaise into which the post-Sullan state had sunk. Domestic politics were largely backward-looking – the central issue remained the validity of the Sullan dispensation for murder. How many of Sulla's laws and decrees could be retained? For all that he claimed to have saved the state from Catiline, Cicero could at no point profess to have furthered the betterment of the Roman people. His great claim to fame was that he had unified people against Catiline at the end of a year when his most noteworthy acts had been preventing things from happening and successfully defending people who were guilty of the crimes with which they had been charged. The Senate was largely incapable of making decisions, while the *comitia tributa* was unusable except by those strong enough to overrule potential tribunician vetoes.

The contrast with events in the east is striking. Pompey laid the foundation of a frontier system based on the integration of 'friendly' kings with provincial structures, an arrangement that would last for more than a century. Indeed, over 150 years later the rules he had laid down for the administration of the new province of Bithynia–Pontus were still in effect. Just as important was the empire-wide presence that he developed. While Rome might still count family or regional ties as determinants of office – such that Catiline could think to score points by sneering at Cicero's ancestry – Pompey was employing a Spanish gentleman alongside one from Turkey as his senior lieutenants. They did not hold formal office, but anyone who wanted to get things done knew they had to go through them. Pompey's staff provided a model for later imperial administration. Like Caesar, he was appealing, consciously or unconsciously, to those qualities that had made Rome successful in the past.

When Catiline died, the Sullan republic had thirteen years left to live.

21

LAW AND DISORDER

❦

The growth of court-like institutions based on independent fiscal–
military networks in the decade after Catiline's death fractured the
existing structures of the Roman state. One was linked to the victorious
Pompey. After 58 BC it was joined by a network developed to support
Julius Caesar's campaigns in France. The development of these organisa-
tions around Caesar and Pompey does not mean that other Romans saw
themselves as individuals of secondary value. The internal politics of these
years resound with the efforts of men like Cicero, Cato, Clodius, Crassus
and Gabinius to assert their prominence through traditional institutions.
The tension between supporters of quasi-monarchies in Gaul and Spain
and those seeking power through older structures, snapped when a faction
in Rome attacked the power that had emerged in Gaul, violated the laws
that had been passed to create it and started a civil war.

The development of the state from its quasi-democratic form to some
sort of quasi-monarchy was not unforeseen. In the second half of the 50s
BC, Cicero envisaged an improved version of the Roman Republic as having
a moderator and imagined Gnaeus Pompey in that role. Allowing that 'by
the judgement of all men [Pompey] is by far the first man [*princeps*] of the
state' (Cicero, *Concerning His House* 66), Cicero none the less thought
the great man could not go it alone. Like Scipio Aemilianus, whom he has
proposing this idea in his dialogue on the Republic, Pompey would need
wise friends. Cicero was always available.

Pompey lacked the patience necessary for domestic political success.

From the perspective of those fond of the republican system, his lack of political skill was particularly unfortunate. For Pompey the traditional Republic provided the theatre in which he could strut his own magnificence. His problem in realising this ambition was that he had made many enemies, chief among them Lucullus, who knew how to disrupt the machinery of state. The result was that he depended upon more politically astute individuals to get his way. This dependency would soon deliver him into Caesar's hands.

Pompey arrived at Brundisium in December 62 BC; eight months later he spent two days celebrating his triumph over the pirates Mithridates and Tigranes, beginning on 28 September 61 BC, his birthday. In January 59 BC he was still waiting for the Senate to approve all the measures he had taken in the east. This delay was partly his fault in that, unlike Lucullus, whose arrangements, made with the requisite committee of ten senatorial legates, he had torn up, Pompey had not bothered to ask for the appointment of legates. Lucullus insisted that the Senate review each of his actions, and, while it had approved all the measures to do with the establishment of provinces, raising the state's revenues from 50,000,000 to 85,000,000 denarii a year, it had not dealt with the arrangements he had made with the eastern kings. Lucullus and others would have seen that Pompey, not the state, would be the chief beneficiary of those dispositions. Being the world's most famous and powerful man required a great deal of money, and for Pompey that necessitated accessing the wealth of the eastern dynasts.

Aside from straightforward obstruction, led by Cato and backed by various members of the older generation, a heady cocktail of scandal mixed with impending crisis distracted people from the business of government. On 5 December 62 BC, Clodius had been found at a 'women only' gathering at Caesar's house. The event, which brought the Vestal Virgins together with various women of standing, was the celebration of the Good Goddess (Bona Dea). Clodius was allegedly there to consummate a relationship with Pompeia. Caesar promptly divorced her, saying that his wife must be above suspicion – which must have seemed like a bad joke given his own extramarital career which had led Sulla's former lieutenant Curio to snipe that he was 'every man's wife and every woman's husband' (Suetonius, *Life of Caesar* 52.3). Caesar had then left town to become governor of Farther Spain.

Cicero would have been well advised to follow Caesar's example and avoid having anything to do with the Bona Dea scandal. But he could not. When Clodius asked him to provide an alibi, he refused and gave testimony against him at the trial. Clodius was found not guilty, allegedly because members of the jury received generous financial inducements. He then declared himself Cicero's mortal enemy.

Cicero, in the meantime, complained that the alliance he had constructed to defeat Catiline was being pulled apart by both the failure to act on Pompey's business plans and the refusal to adjust the sum owed by the corporation that had taken out the contract to collect taxes from Asia, but which had massively overbid for it. Cato stood in the way, giving endless speeches in the Senate, while Cicero now complained that he seemed to be 'living in Plato's Republic rather than Romulus' cesspit' (Cicero, *Letters to Atticus* 2.1.8). But there was nothing to be done here, and equally, nothing to be done about the very real problems that were brewing in France.

The Allobroges of southern Gaul had rebelled in 62 BC, but to no great effect. Then, in 61 BC, the Sequani, a tribe whose lands lay between the Rhône and the Rhine, inflicted a massive defeat on the Aedui, Rome's most important ally north of the provincial boundary in the Rhône valley. The Sequani had imported Ariovistus, a mercenary captain from across the Rhine, who had given them the advantage. The Aedui appealed for aid from Rome, but, despite some sympathetic gestures (an embassy and the assignment of the Gallic provinces to the consuls of 60 BC), no meaningful help was forthcoming.

With gridlock in the Senate and tensions building concerning the situation in Gaul, Caesar returned from Spain, where he had made a substantial amount of money by attacking tribes in Lusitania. He claimed a triumph, and announced that he would run for the consulship. Those who disliked him delayed a vote on the triumph, hoping to leave him stranded outside the city gates, since he would have to give up his *imperium* (and hence the right to a triumph) in order to declare his candidature. Caesar decided to do without the triumph, and came in at the head of the poll.

When he took up office on 1 January 59 BC, his consular colleague was Marcus Calpurnius Bibulus, who hated him. That did not matter. Bibulus was not the brightest of men, and his bad temper would play into Caesar's hands. In the month before he took up office, Caesar approached Pompey, offering to support the ratification of his achievements in the east; he then invited Cicero to join in what would result, effectively, in a legislative coup d'état. Cicero refused. He also approached Crassus, who did not. For Caesar, there was no single path forward – he was willing to mix, match and negotiate until he got his way. His primary goal was to gain a better province than the one he could look forward to – 'Italian hills and dales' – which would have left him policing the countryside. Domination of the Roman state would come later.

Caesar's consulship initiated a decade of law-making unparalleled in its diversity and implications. Although leaving the essential structure of elected magistracies unchanged in terms of function and of those who tended to be elected – nobles only, for the consulship – these legislative programmes created new regulations, new boards of officials and new provinces. Among the more noteworthy events in these years would be a major military disaster initiating a conflict with Parthia, unauthorised by the Senate; an invasion of Egypt (also unauthorised); and, in an initiative that was justified after the fact, the bringing of the whole of Gaul, which had previously been divided into three parts, under the nominal control of the Roman state.

One thing that all the legislative programmes of the 50s BC had in common was that they were introduced by Gnaeus Pompey, on behalf of Gnaeus Pompey, or by people who acted with Gnaeus Pompey's tacit support. This principate of Pompey was born of his perception, shared with some others, that true power lay in the hands of those who could access provincial or regal resources away from the bustle of conventional senatorial politics.

In keeping with the balance of power – Pompey had more of it than he did – Caesar opened his year in office by announcing in the Senate that records of its proceedings would now be made public. He would propose a bill confirming all of Pompey's outstanding acts; then a bill distributing land in Italy, with a very large board of commissioners (which included Pompey and Crassus) that would purchase land from individuals for inclusion in the distributions; and another bill reducing by a third the tax assessment for the public contractors (*publicani*) of Asia. When Cato threatened a day-long filibuster, Caesar had him arrested and hauled off to prison. As many senators chose to walk out and join him, the Roman populace was given a good view of who was opposed to the legislation that they, by and large, favoured.

Caesar then took the matter to the people. He began with his bill on land distributions, speaking from the *rostra* in front of the Senate House with Pompey and Crassus by his side. In February, control of the agenda passed to the tribune Vatinius, as it was Bibulus' turn to run senatorial meetings. It was Vatinius who moved the bills confirming Pompey's eastern arrangements. In March Caesar introduced more bills, including one to change the bid on the taxes of Asia and another (for which he received a very large payment) confirming Ptolemy XII as king of Egypt.

At the beginning of May Caesar proposed a second land bill that particularly upset Cicero because it made land that Rome had confiscated from Capua in the Second Punic War available for distribution. Cicero had opposed this vigorously when it had appeared in Rullus' land bill of 63 BC, claiming that Rome could not afford to give up the rental income. Caesar's point may have been that, with all the new money Pompey was bringing in, Rome did not need the Campanian rents.

He may also have had a sense of local opinion. He had a villa outside Baiae, a fashionable resort on the north side of the bay of Naples, and kept his gladiators at Capua; his new father-in-law, Calpurnius Piso, had a magnificent villa at Herculaneum, at the foot of Mount Vesuvius.

The events surrounding the passage of the second land bill, which took place in May, would have long-range consequences. When the bill was introduced, Caesar's co-consul Bibulus spoke against it. He probably did not anticipate that he would be greeted with a bucketful of faeces. Covered in the stuff, Bibulus went home, where he stayed for the rest of the year, claiming that he was watching the heavens for a sign that no public business could be conducted. For good measure, he posted insulting things about Caesar on his front door.

Given that Romans did not ordinarily carry buckets of excrement into the forum, it is most likely that Caesar set the incident up with a view to making Bibulus look foolish – which, of course, he did. It may well have been amusing for people who had no high opinion of the man, but it pleased Caesar even more: with no consular colleague to thwart him, he could run all the Senate meetings on his own. On the other hand, convenient as this was, it might allow questions to be raised about the legality of another, crucial piece of legislation: the law brought in by Vatinius conferring upon Caesar a province consisting of Cisalpine Gaul (the area between the Alps and the Rubicon river, just north of modern Rimini) and Illyria (a rather amorphous area to the east of Cisalpine Gaul). This command was for five years, with the added provision that its end date would be 1 March 54 BC.

Cicero, who had turned down another offer – a post on the first land commission – that would get him out of Rome and provide him with protection from prosecution, had a good deal to say about Caesar's domestic legislation, none of it good. But his surviving letters of the year make no reference to Vatinius' bill, whose importance he would later come to appreciate, or to a subsequent bill adding Transalpine Gaul to Caesar's command when its governor died in June. Perhaps no one thought that Caesar could accomplish much with four legions, and it may even have seemed that the situation in Gaul was cooling. Probably in February, the Senate, with Bibulus in the chair, had voted to name Ariovistus, the Sequani's mercenary chief, a 'friend and ally' of the Roman people. The granting of Transalpine Gaul to Caesar was not part of any grand plan to settle the distressing situation in the Rhône valley on Caesar's part or anyone else's.

Towards the end of the summer, Cicero convinced himself that the power of the 'three-headed monster', as he called the Pompey–Crassus–Caesar clique, was weakening. When he gave an especially ill-advised speech attacking them, any interest that Caesar might have had in protecting him evaporated. Caesar and Pompey oversaw the process whereby Clodius was transitioned from the patrician to the plebeian order so that he could run for the tribunate of the plebs.

Cicero would regret some of his decisions, but what is most striking is just how wrong he was about what was happening. The consular elections returned Caesar's father-in-law Piso, and Gabinius, the author of the bill creating Pompey's command against the pirates. That two men with such obvious connections with the 'three-headed monster' should come in at the top of the poll suggests rather strongly that members of the highest census classes did not disapprove of what Caesar had done. Members of the *comitia tributa*, who voted to make the recently plebiscised Clodius a tribune for the coming year, also seem to have been pleased with the way things turned out.

Clodius was deemed deeply suspect in many quarters. Cicero was just one among many who thought that he should have been convicted of impiety; Lucullus hated him; and there were those who recalled that he had defended Catiline at his trial in 65 BC, in which corruption seemed to have played an undue part. On the other hand, Clodius was ambitious, so Caesar had forgiven him his indiscretions. Also, he was somewhat pliable: in return for not standing in the way of his vendetta against Cicero, Caesar and Pompey would benefit from the raft of legislation that Clodius promised to bring forward. One bill would make conduct such as Bibulus' observation of the heavens illegal in order to head off any claim that all legislation passed after the fracas in May was illegal, since the business of government could not be legitimately conducted if a consul was watching the heavens.

The structure of Clodius' plan reveals a fair amount of forethought. One of the first bills he introduced restored the *Compitalia*, banned since 64 BC as a threat to public order. Piso, as presiding consul from 1 January 58 BC, even allowed the festival to be celebrated that day, presumably because he thought the bill that Clodius had introduced on 10 December would pass. Another bill, introduced at the same time, changed the subsidised grain system to direct hand-outs. This was financed by accepting the legitimacy of the will that King Ptolemy Alexander I had made in which he had left his kingdom to Rome – although what exactly this meant was open to debate. Hitherto, it had been interpreted as Egypt, and there had been some discussion of annexation when Rullus had introduced his land bill in 63 BC. But given that Ptolemy XII had just been recognised as Egypt's king, if Rome was going to accept the will of Ptolemy Alexander, then the kingdom in question would have to be Cyprus, which the latter was ruling when he died.

Cato was appointed to oversee the process. At the same time Clodius introduced a bill swapping the provinces around, giving Piso Macedonia and Gabinius Syria – both areas that promised military action. Foreign policy was being flexed to accommodate political ambitions.

In March 58 BC many Romans may have been stunned by a bill that would exile any man who had put a Roman citizen to death without trial – there was only one man to whom it applied, and that was Cicero. This was followed by a bill exiling Cicero by name, once he had fled the city. At the same time, Caesar was receiving reports from Gaul that he would use to declare a national emergency that could only be solved if he led his army north of Transalpine Gaul.

As Caesar proceeded towards the conquest of Gaul (a matter to which we will shortly return), the next year saw other legislative moments. One, not unrelated to the fact that Clodius had managed to annoy Pompey on several fronts, was the recall of Cicero from exile. He returned to a great fanfare, and Pompey's supporters took advantage of the influx of anti-Clodians who turned up to vote for Cicero's return to pass a bill creating a new job for their man. Backed by fifteen legates, he was to take charge of the grain supply, with *imperium* equal to that of any provincial governor anywhere in the empire. Given that Rome either did not control or had not developed the lands that would later provide the bulk of the city's grain – they were in North Africa and Egypt – and that the result of Clodius' bill had been an upsurge in claimants on the grain rolls (people had freed many of their slaves so that the state could feed them), this was a necessary step; and one that demonstrated the fact that the Senate had no way of solving a structural problem other than by creating an ad hoc commission.

Pompey's ability to deal with the grain supply, and certainly his overall standing in Rome, took a turn for the worse at about the time the new commission was created. The occasion was the arrival of King Ptolemy. Ousted from his throne by subjects angered by the Roman annexation of Cyprus, he presented himself at Pompey's massive villa in the Alban hills with a view to getting his host to reclaim his throne for him. He brought with him his daughter Cleopatra, who was to begin her education in the ways of the Romans.

Sadly for Ptolemy, his conduct gave rise to scandal, as well as to two of the most memorable pieces of Latin invective from this or any other period of Roman history. The first was the speech that Cicero gave defending his young friend Caelius Rufus on a charge of attempting to poison Clodius' sister. The case was complicated by the suggestion that Caelius had been involved in the murder of ambassadors from Alexandria on a mission to ask Rome not to allow Ptolemy to return home. The other is an extraordinarily pornographic poem by Valerius Catullus, the greatest poet of his age and coincidentally another former lover of Clodius' sister, in which he transformed a Greek panegyric on an earlier Egyptian queen into a study of incestuous rape. The notion these works helped foster, that Ptolemy was a murderous sexual deviant, mirrored some portion of educated Roman opinion.

Pompey was unable to control the reputational damage an association with Ptolemy inflicted. Consequently, the desultory debate about whether and how someone should restore the king to his kingdom, and who that someone should be, continued for the better part of a year. The matter was further complicated when a member of the College of Fifteen for Making Sacrifices, whose duty was to protect the newly assembled collection of Sibylline Oracles, released an oracle stating that Egypt's king could not be restored 'with a multitude' (meaning 'an army') (Cicero, *Letters to His*

Friends 1.7.4). Ptolemy gave up, and had left Rome by the end of 56 BC, looking for a new person to bribe. He found that person in Gabinius, who, ignoring the senatorial ban on military intervention, restored him to his throne in 55 BC.

Pompey's weakness in the face of the Egyptian business encouraged his enemies to hope that something could be done to change the political balance of power, which could involve replacing Caesar in his provinces. Caesar and Pompey held an emergency meeting at Lucca in the spring of 56 BC, at which it was agreed that Pompey would run for the consulship, with Crassus again as his partner. The two were duly elected, and a tribune named Trebonius passed a law declaring Spain, where allegedly there had been some trouble recently, and Syria, as the provinces for the consuls of 55 BC. The governors were given a five-year term, and permission to take whatever actions they deemed necessary against neighbouring peoples. Pompey and Crassus then carried a law extending Caesar's command in Gaul for what they may well have thought was five years. But this law, which was exceptionally badly worded, appears to have stated that Caesar's command would be extended for a *quinquennium ex hac lege* ('for five years through this law'), which left open its interpretation to mean from the point at which the law was passed rather than from the end of Caesar's command under the *lex Vatinia*. Both readings would be extant in just a few years' time.

Pompey was content to stay in Rome after 55 BC, governing Spain through legates. As a matter of convenience he had a house near what is now Vatican City, to avoid staying in his downtown Roman residence (off limits while he held *imperium* as a provincial governor). He also dedicated Rome's first permanent theatre in the Campus Martius, which had space for meetings of the Senate outside the *pomerium* that he was therefore allowed to attend. Crassus, however, left as soon as he could to relieve Gabinius of his command and carry on the war with the Parthians that the latter had started.

Caesar's command in Gaul set the standard of independence to which Crassus aspired. Caesar's narrative of those years reveals both the practical and the political limitations of senatorial control, as well as structural issues in managing an empire without any permanent bureaucratic staff. One political limitation was that tribunician legislation had deprived the Senate of oversight, so that in significant cases it no longer controlled appointments under Gaius Gracchus' old law on consular provinces (still technically on the books). The very opening of Caesar's campaigns reveals the extent of the structural difficulties. Without a permanent staff, no one was responsible for gathering intelligence. Information from underdeveloped areas was still filtered through a governor's office to the Senate, or was transmitted by ambassadors. But what happened when there were no ambassadors and no governor? The situation that erupted on the border of Transalpine Gaul in the spring of 58 BC, as Caesar was sitting outside Rome waiting for Cicero to go into exile, is a case in point.

With the death of the governor, probably in April 59 BC, the administration of Transalpine Gaul had fallen to the quaestor. This official – his name has not survived in the record – seems not to have been informed of developments. These developments included negotiations between factions within the Aeduan and Sequanian leaderships with a faction within the Helvetian leadership to move a large number of Helvetians into Aeduan territory, thereby providing the additional force needed to get rid of Rome's 'friend and ally' Ariovistus. To make this move, the Helvetians would ideally need to travel through Roman territory on the south bank of the Rhône. Caesar was surprised to be told that the Helvetians had shown up at Geneva on 28 March BC, asking for passage. On that day three of his legions were over 400 miles away, in Aquileia in north-eastern Italy.

Surprised though he was, the appearance of the Helvetians gave Caesar the opportunity for the campaign of his dreams. But he was seriously unprepared. He would have to move his army north of the Alps with all speed without knowing whether it would be big enough – he had at his disposal about 20,000 men. As he raced to Geneva from Rome, covering something like ninety miles a day, he took advantage of the right of a governor to raise new troops in an emergency. He would be personally responsible for paying the men, which suggests that he really did regard the situation as urgent.

As the reports back to the Senate that inform the opening chapters of his *Gallic Wars* reveal, the emergency needed be couched, for domestic consumption, in terms evocative of dreaded moments of the past: even if Caesar had no clear plan of what to do when the Helvetians arrived, he rapidly concluded that any move he made must be of more than local significance. The threats he faced would inevitably be threats to 'all Gaul'.

He did everything he could to expand upon the dangers the Helvetians posed. They had turned up in massive numbers, their skills as warriors were legendary, they were a menace on a par with the Cimbrians and Teutons, and their migratory habits evoked memories of the distant movements of other peoples across the Alps, the very peoples who had sacked Rome in 390 BC. There was a personal angle, too: nearly fifty years earlier, his wife's grandfather had been killed during a disastrous encounter between the army in which he was serving and a Helvetian subtribe. This was enough to justify Caesar's taking his army across the border in pursuit of the Helvetians – who, truth be told, were not actually threatening the province. The subsequent campaign evoked Marius' struggles with the Cimbrians. Just as Marius had done in 102 BC, Caesar first defeated an enemy subtribe while crossing a river – the very people whose ancestors had killed his wife's grandfather! A few days later, a huge phalanx (Caesar uses the Greek word here) of the remaining barbarians attacked uphill and, just like the Cimbrians at Aquae Sextiae, they were smashed by volleys of *pila* and driven back. Having surrendered, the few survivors were sent home. Caesar could later document the slaughter from Helvetian census records (written in Greek). Only 110,000 people were left alive out of an initial migratory group of 362,000.

The numbers Caesar gives for the Helvetians are obviously false, but his claims of their use of Greek may not be. Mediterranean culture had long been mediated through Massalia, founded by Greek settlers in the sixth century BC. Coincidental accuracy could help obscure deliberate fabrication, which would become ever more creative as Caesar continued his narrative of the summer of 58 BC. In mid to late May, when chieftains representing 'all Gaul' came to congratulate Caesar on his victory, some admitted in secret conclave that Ariovistus was not a pleasant person (perish the thought!). He was cruel, tyrannical and treacherous, and he was oppressing friends and allies of long standing, the Aedui. It soon emerged that he did not understand that his acceptance as a 'friend and ally' meant that he had to do what Rome told him. He was even unaware that, thanks to the victory of Fabius Maximus and Gnaeus Domitius Ahenobarbus in 121 BC, all Gaul was a Roman province. It just had not been occupied – something which required rectification if Rome were to remain safe.

Caesar reminded the Gauls (and his readers) that just two years earlier the Senate had instructed the governor of Gaul to make sure that no harm came to the province – which was as relevant now as it was then. They should be aware that Ariovistus was in contact with some people in Rome who wanted him, Caesar, dead, and that he was bringing new Germans across the Rhine. He had even tried to murder Caesar during a negotiating session, so Caesar had no choice but to destroy him. (Which he did, at Vesontio, before the summer's end.) It seemed best, when he returned to fulfil his judicial functions south of the Alps, to leave the legions encamped along the Rhine.

Caesar presented himself as a staunch traditionalist, for all that he never used the traditional phrase to describe the Roman state, '*Senatus populusque Romanus*' ('Senate and people of Rome'), in his account of the Gallic wars. He was there simply to represent 'the Roman people'. His deeds would be worthy of them. His enemies included conniving Gallic aristocrats who exploited their domestic clients and plotted to achieve extraconstitutional domination of their peoples, who were keen on torture, were utterly faithless, and worshipped gods who routinely demanded human sacrifice. The behaviour of his enemies evoked memories of the most appalling events of the past; the potential for disaster was obvious to all.

In 57 BC the Belgae, the confederation of Gallic states in what is now Belgium and north-western France, conspired to attack the Remi, who had made a *deditio in fidem* (just like the Mamertines in 264 BC) and thus had to be defended. In 56 BC the seafaring Veneti imprisoned a number of Roman ambassadors somewhere along the English Channel, and were punished by Caesar's army; in 55 BC, Germanic tribes crossed the Rhine and negotiated with him in bad faith – or so he said – which therefore called for their annihilation. They were clearly vagrants, the worst sort of barbarian, and Caesar's readers would know from earlier accounts that they were primitive nature-worshippers, incapable of farming or a settled life. After he defeated these Germans, Caesar had to cross the Rhine, building a bridge worthy of both his dignity and that of the Roman people. Later that year, even Britain, home to a people who persistently stirred up trouble in Gaul, got a visit.

When he read Caesar's reports from the front, Catullus, who was not always a fan, remained unimpressed. He had bitter things to say about him, saying that he did not give a damn who he was – words that may have been as hurtful as his claims that Caesar took his chief of staff Mamurra, whom Catullus called 'Mr Prick', to bed with him. Catullus also complained vociferously about Mamurra's new wealth. Caesar would later call on Catullus' father and then have Catullus himself to lunch. What transpired goes unrecorded, but shortly afterwards the latter wrote a poem in which he envisaged crossing the Alps to see 'the monuments of great Caesar, the Gallic Rhine, the dread Ocean and the farthest Britons' (Catullus 11.9–12). That was far more on message.

By now Caesar could present himself as having extended the empire to the world's western limits, as Pompey had extended them to the east. Cicero, now publicly reconciled with Caesar, would praise his achievements in a debate over the assignment of consular provinces in March 55 BC. Previous generals, he said, had freed the state from the immediate fear of the inhabitants of Gaul; the great Marius, with his 'divine and outstanding virtue', had checked the flow of northerners into Italy. But Caesar had conquered the people who previously could only be checked. He had defeated not only the Germans and the Helvetians, men famed for their warlike prowess, but even peoples no one had ever heard of; in no more than two years, 'through fear, hope, penalty, reward, arms or laws, he was able to bind all Gaul with eternal bonds' (Cicero, *Concerning Consular Provinces* 34). He therefore fully deserved the year or two more in charge of Gaul that he needed to finalise the conquest. Caesar was no longer to be seen as a mere radical politician, but as the saviour of Rome.

This was the message Caesar wanted the people to receive. Cicero's brother joined Caesar's staff, as did one of his young protégés, Trebatius.

While publicising his new-found admiration for Caesar, Cicero took the opportunity to pinpoint the need to recall Gabinius and Piso from their provinces. Piso had not done much in Macedonia; but in Syria, Gabinius' gubernatorial freelancing was in many ways more disturbing than Caesar's. For while Caesar could justify his actions in terms both of past crises and of his own success, Gabinius was even now garnering support for a war with Parthia and thereby revealing the Senate's unwillingness – or inability – to rein in an aggressive governor.

Gabinius did not doubt his own worth. In the preamble to a law he proposed as consul, granting the island of Delos immunity from taxation, he announced: 'The pirates, who [laid waste] the world for many [years], and pillaged the sanctuaries, shrines and images of the gods and the most sacred sites ... have been defeated and eradicated by the *lex Gabinia*' (*RS* n. 22). As governor of Syria he altered the tax-collection systems without reference to the Senate, and early in the year 55 BC he took it upon himself to use his army to restore Ptolemy to the Egyptian throne. Gabinius left a substantial body of men behind in Egypt to keep Ptolemy on the throne, and the king employed another Rabirius – a financier, and the son of the man over whose trial for *perduellio* Caesar had presided in 63 BC (this was surely a family that didn't bear grudges) – to collect the money he still owed Pompey and Caesar, as well as what he now owed Gabinius. The education in Roman politics of King Ptolemy's daughter Cleopatra took another step forward; she also seems to have chatted briefly with Marcus Antonius, one of Gabinius' young officers.

The Egyptian expedition interrupted Gabinius' interventions in Parthia, which had begun a year earlier. In 57 BC King Phraates III, the victim of Pompey's bullying back in the 60s BC, was murdered. The killers were his sons Orodes and Mithridates, who were now fighting each other for control of the kingdom. Orodes, who had visions of restoring the ancient Persian empire which had extended from Afghanistan to Greece, soon gained the upper hand. Mithridates, now king of Media Atropatene in north-western Iran, appealed to Gabinius for help. But before he could respond, Ptolemy turned up. Given the choice of which king to restore first, Gabinius chose Ptolemy. By the time he returned from Egypt, Mithridates' situation had deteriorated and he had fled to Roman territory.

Gabinius supported Mithridates when the latter invaded Parthia, but could do no more. Given that Roman opinion took the Parthians no more seriously than it took Tigranes' Armenians, the prospect of bashing the Parthians was too good an opportunity for Gabinius to miss. But he would not be given the chance. As a result of his Egyptian adventure and constant complaints about his behaviour from the *publicani* of Syria, he was profoundly unpopular among the political classes of Rome. Upon his return to the city in the summer of 54 BC, he was charged with treason (*maiestas*, in this case) for his actions in Egypt. It is said that Pompey's influence and money bought him acquittal. But this would not work later in the year, when he was tried for extortion. Cicero was dragooned into defending him, but to no avail. Gabinius went into exile.

Although the Senate had not officially declared war on Parthia, and some senators objected very strongly to the prospect of his doing whatever he liked, Crassus was assembling a large army for the invasion of Parthia. Part of his army would have been the regular garrison minus the men who had stayed with Ptolemy in Egypt, and state money would have been available to make up the number of legions to the previously assigned total; also, Crassus was allowed to raise troops in Italy. Later dispositions suggest that the state-funded contingent was two legions. But when he invaded Parthia, Crassus had seven under his command, which suggests a very heavy commitment of cash on his part – possibly enough for five legions. The need to recoup this investment may help explain why he acted as he did – this was war not for strategic purpose but as private enterprise. It was noticed at the time that he was particularly worried about money.

Crassus spent the latter part of 54 BC establishing a bridgehead into the northern Mesopotamian kingdom of Osrhoene, making contact with Artavasdes, the king of Armenia, who was at war with Orodes, and possibly preparing to aid Mithridates, who was now being besieged in Seleucia. A city at the heart of the Parthian kingdom and located just opposite the capital Ctesiphon, Seleucia – whose citizens remembered their privileged position under the Seleucids – tended to be hostile to the Parthians. The Seleucians had not, however, been able to hold out against Surenas, Orodes' leading general, and had surrendered while Crassus was in northern Mesopotamia. Now, in the spring of 53 BC, Crassus launched a full-scale, if belated, invasion in the direction of Seleucia. This meant ignoring Artavasdes, who had offered him assistance if he would fight in northern Mesopotamia. Crassus also alienated Abgar, the king of Osrhoene, who became an agent for the Parthians.

Crassus did not get very far on his march to Seleucia. On 9 June, the day after he left Carrhae, his army was intercepted by a Parthian army commanded by Surenas in the valley of the Balissus river. Unable to deal with the strong force of Parthian horse archers and heavy cavalry, the Roman army was stopped in its tracks. After a day of substantial losses, Crassus ordered a retreat to Carrhae, at which point his army fell apart. Some (at least a legion) escaped under the command of his quaestor Gaius Cassius. Others surrendered after Crassus, trying – or so he thought – to negotiate a treaty, was murdered when the Parthians attempted to kidnap him.

Rome now had a real war on its hands, though fortunately Parthian politics prevented an invasion. What to do? The answer was nothing. Cassius stayed in command for more than a year while a domestic political crisis almost swallowed the Roman constitution.

The problem was Clodius. On 19 January 52 BC he had been murdered by Titus Annius Milo, a long-standing political rival of his who was close to Cicero. His servants brought his body to his house on the Palatine that night, where his wife Fulvia and supporters (including Sulla's grandson, brother of Caesar's ex-wife) displayed it. The next morning, having assembled a huge crowd in the forum to view the body, one of Clodius' trusted henchmen carried the corpse into the Senate House, which the crowd then set fire to. The Basilica Porcia, which abutted the Senate House, went up in flames, too. Mobs wandered the city, finally taking the fasces – the emblem of official authority usually stored for use in public funerals at the Lucus Libitinae (the grove of the goddess of funerals) on the Esquiline – to Pompey's garden near what is now Rome's Villa Borghese, asking that he be named either consul or dictator.

The situation was complicated by the fact that there were no consuls in place. Despite the crisis in the east, political squabbling had forced the elections to be postponed into the new year. This quarrel followed a horrendous electoral scandal in 54 BC, which had caused the consuls of 53 BC not to take office until July. The issue in 54 BC was not the fact that the two candidates had offered a huge financial inducement plus the pick of the provinces to the incumbent consuls if they would rig the election, but that one of them had been stupid enough to reveal the deal at a Senate meeting. By the time the consuls of 53 BC took office, the violently contested elections for 52 BC, in which Milo was standing for consul and Clodius for praetor, were already well under way and chaos reigned in the streets.

The violence continued in the weeks after Clodius' funeral. After mobs had prevented successive *interreges* (interim kings) from naming new consuls for a whole month, the Senate convened on 18 February to pass a version of the 'ultimate decree', asking Pompey, the tribunes and the sitting magistrates to take whatever action was needed to bring order to the city. Pompey responded by calling in the troops, while legal actions were brought against Milo for murder and against various Clodian supporters, including Fulvia, for promoting disorder. Still there was no final decision, and no consul either. The reason was that Ravenna, where Caesar was currently based, was a long way from Rome, and nothing was going to happen until Caesar and Pompey reached agreement. Cicero was one of the intermediaries.

It would not be until mid-March that the solution was found: Pompey would be sole consul and would introduce laws to end the political chaos of the last few years, while protecting the interests of Caesar, who announced that he would stand for election to the consulship of 48 BC. The first of these bills was brought by the whole board of tribunes, stating that Caesar could stand for election without giving up his *imperium* (granting, in this instance, the *ratio absentis*, or 'right [of standing for election] in absentia').

Another bill fundamentally altered the way provinces would be assigned. Adapting a proposal first put forward in response to the scandal of 54 BC, but never acted upon, the new 'Pompeian Law on the provinces' replaced the old *lex Sempronia*, stating that no one could proceed directly from a consulship or praetorship to a province, and stipulating that for the next five years the provincial governors would be selected from among former magistrates who had not previously taken up provincial commands. In a curious loophole, this bill also allowed that a tribune could veto a provincial appointment (something the *lex Sempronia* forbade). Moreover, it made the point that government service was to be just that – service, not an opportunity for self-enrichment. Other bills included one to control gang violence of the sort just witnessed, and a second which would restrict electoral corruption – in both cases with heavier penalties and new provisions to shorten trials; a third would lay down that people who wanted to stand for office had to show up in person to declare their candidacy (although it is alleged that once the bill was passed, Pompey went to the public record office and inscribed a further clause exempting Caesar from its requirements).

Caesar did not stay in Ravenna to observe the whole of Pompey's performance, which might explain why a legislative programme that began so favourably with the law of the ten tribunes veered off course. But Caesar had little choice: the situation in Gaul was spinning out of control. Indeed, things had been difficult for a while as the leaders of the Gallic tribes adjusted to his administration with varying degrees of acceptance. There were some who found the opportunity of service with Caesar beneficial and who considered collaboration with Rome the fastest route to political success at home, while there were others who were deeply resentful. Early in 54 BC, while preparing a second invasion of Britain, Caesar had assassinated a major chief of the Aedui with whom relations had long been souring. In the autumn, because of the poor harvest and the need to feed his troops throughout the winter, he had scattered his legions across northern Gaul rather than concentrating them in a single camp. This had provided the opportunity for a local leader, Ambiorix, to trick a garrison out of its camp with rumours of a conspiracy, then ambush the column and annihilate it. Revolt spread among the Belgae, but was quelled when Caesar arrived in person.

Caesar had spent the rest of 53 BC dealing with the aftermath of the rebellion and other indications of discontent, but his execution of another major Gallic leader had created considerable antipathy. While he was detained in Italy, a serious new revolt began in central Gaul as local tribesmen massacred members of the Roman contractor community that had evolved to support the occupation. The violence spread and found an able leader in one Vercingetorix. He was forced to surrender at Alesia by the end of the summer, but the campaign had been hard fought and Caesar suffered a defeat in person when an assault on the Gallic town of Gergovia went awry. He would spend the year 51 BC restoring his control of Gaul.

To make up for the troops he had lost to Ambiorix in 53 BC, Caesar had borrowed a legion from Pompey (presumably from the garrison in Spain) and assembled two more of his own. In the summer of 50 BC, the Senate urged both Caesar and Pompey to contribute a legion each from their state-funded forces to the defence of Syria (presumably replacing the state-funded forces lost at Carrhae). Pompey asked Caesar to return the legion he had lent him: thus the whole contribution in response to the Senate's request came from Caesar's force.

This was not the first sign that relations between the two had cooled since the death of Julia, Pompey's wife and Caesar's daughter, of a miscarriage in 54 BC. Even before her death Caesar had discreetly begun to assert his architectural presence in the heart of the city. As time passed the new forum that he was building, centred on a temple of Venus the Ancestor, may have become more offensive and appeared to challenge the centrality Pompey had asserted through the construction of his theatre. In 52 BC, Pompey married again, this time the daughter of Metellus Scipio, whom he had made consul with himself in the second half of 52 BC and who disliked Caesar intensely. Tension mounted the next year when another of Caesar's enemies, Marcellus, who was now a consul, flogged a man who had been a magistrate at Novum Comum. This man was a Roman citizen and so should have been immune from such treatment, but Marcellus claimed that people settled at Comum under a *lex Vatinia* of 59 – which was illegitimate in his view – were not citizens. Cicero and others like him thought this was an extreme viewpoint, but there were now plenty of extremists who wanted Caesar out of Gaul. There were arguments in the Senate about what the *lex Pompeia Licinia* meant (was the end date of Caesar's command 28 February 50 BC or 49 BC?). But Pompey, who presumably knew what he meant when he drafted the law, was temporising as early as October 51 BC, putting off any debate about Caesar's succession before 1 March of the year 50 BC.

That summer of 50 BC, having assured his friends that he had but to stamp his foot and armies would spring up from the soil of Italy, Pompey fell seriously ill. By the end of the year the question was clear enough: when he stood in the consular election of 49 BC, using his legal right to stand for office in absentia, would Caesar still have his army?

After a decade in which legislation had generated anomaly after anomaly, it is fitting that the formal issue leading to civil war would be framed as an argument over the wording of a law.

22

POMPEY AND CAESAR

The consular elections came and went in the summer of 50 BC, with no resolution to the problem of Caesar's command and two diehard anti-Caesarians elected for the coming year. Caesar's people claimed that the result must be fraudulent, because voters had been happy to turn out for Marcus Antonius, Caesar's quaestor, who had handily defeated Lucius Domitius Ahenobarbus, the anti-Caesarian consul of 54 BC (and Cato's brother-in-law), in that summer's election for the augurate. The people of Italy would have preferred as consul a man known to be close to Caesar, or so Aulus Hirtius, one of his most trusted lieutenants, recalled.

Aulus Hirtius' input is of great importance. At the time he was writing, Caesar was already dead and Hirtius was looking forward to taking up the consulship on 1 January 43 BC, with the prospect of fighting a war against the very same Marcus Antonius for whom, he was saying, Caesar had had such great affection. He was reminding the late Caesar's now fractious supporters of what they had all stood for just a few years before. He recalled Caesar's enemies as consisting of 'a few men' (Hirtius, *Gallic War* 8.52.3) who had perverted a political process in which all of Italy had a say, just as all of Italy would have a role to play after 1 January 43 BC. That Hirtius writes as he does about the importance of opinion outside Rome for Roman politics shows just how much political society had expanded in the generation that had grown to maturity after Sulla's death. A further reminder of that change was that one of Hirtius' colleagues on Caesar's staff in 50 BC was Publius Ventidius, who in 88 BC had been led as a child in the triumphal procession of Pompeius Strabo, his father having been a leader of the revolutionary cause.

In Hirtius' account there is no doubt that 50 BC was meant to be the last full year of Caesar's term. That would not have been a problem, had the electoral and legislative organs of the state been allowed to function in accord with popular will. Hirtius' stress on this point obscures the extent to which his memory had been clouded by a need to conceal how ready Caesar was to invade Italy if things did not go his way. Caesar had left four legions encamped with the Belgae and four with the Aedui, Hirtius said, and had only one legion with him at Ravenna, the Thirteenth, which replaced the one he had dispatched for the Parthian war. This was a lie.

In January 49 BC Cicero arrived in the suburbs of Rome; he would not enter the city itself because he was expecting to celebrate a triumph – a miscalculation on his part, as it turned out – for some minor military successes in Cilicia. He had played no direct role in the debates about Caesar's command, so had not grasped the levels of anxiety on both sides. On 12 January he wrote to his immediate family, explaining that he had walked into a mess:

> When I arrived at the city on 4 January, nothing could have been more flattering than the reception I received. But I have fallen into the very flame of civil discord, or, rather, of war. When I attempted to remedy the situation, as I think I can, the desires of certain people were an impediment (there are those on both sides who want to fight). In short, this is what happened. Caesar, our friend, sent a menacing and harsh letter to the Senate, and is still shamelessly insistent on retaining his army and province against the will of the Senate. My friend Curio eggs him on. Our friends Antonius and Quintus Cassius, expelled (with no violence), have set out for Caesar with Curio. Then the Senate called upon the consuls, praetors, tribunes of the plebs and those of us who are proconsuls to see to it that the state should come to no harm. Never was the state in more danger, never have bad citizens had a better prepared leader. Everything on this side is prepared with great diligence. It is done through the authority and zeal of our friend Pompey, who has lately come to fear Caesar.
>
> (Cicero, *Letters to His Friends* 16.11.2–3)

At the meeting on 7 January that Cicero is reporting on, the Senate declared a state of emergency as Caesar's three supporters made their way north. What the Senate did not do was declare Caesar an official enemy of the state. There was still hope in some quarters that a negotiated settlement would be possible. It was not. On the evening of 10 January Caesar addressed the men of the Thirteenth Legion, urging them to protect his dignity and reputation and to defend the rights of the tribunes and of the Roman people themselves. On gaining their assent, he led them across the Rubicon and occupied Ariminum the next morning.

Caesar does not mention his passage of the Rubicon in his own account of the civil war, but others would embellish it with stories of divine intervention and recall his exclamation, '*alea iacta est*' ('The die has been cast!'), at the crossing (Suetonius, *Life of Caesar* 32). Neither does he record the extent of his preparation. He had clearly predicted the response to his letter, read out to the Senate on 1 January, and had already set in motion five legions, two veteran and three newly raised, in addition to the Thirteenth. When, hot on the heels of Pompey, he reached Brundisium in early March, he would have had those six legions with him and would have added another three at Corfinium, where he had compelled Lucius Domitius Ahenobarbus to surrender. Ahenobarbus' father had amassed huge estates through his service to Sulla, so those three legions were raised from among Ahenobarbus' tenants at Ahenobarbus' expense.

Pompey had predicted Caesar's movements with great accuracy, which is why he left Rome as soon as news came of the crossing of the Rubicon, and headed for Brundisium. He had asked Ahenobarbus to join him there, but Ahenobarbus refused. A letter survives from Pompey to Ahenobarbus telling him what would happen if he did not follow orders:

> I think you are acting with great spirit and courage in this matter, but we must take great care that we are not divided since we cannot be equal to our adversary, for he has great forces at his disposal and will soon have greater. You do not owe it to your foresight to consider this alone: how many cohorts Caesar has with him against you now, but rather what great forces of infantry and cavalry he will muster in a short time. The letter that Bussenius sent me, in which he confirmed what others had written, states that Caesar has gathered the forces that were raised in Umbria and Etruria and marches to join Curio. If these forces are gathered in one place, with part of the army sent

to Alba, and part advancing on you, he will not attack you, but he will repel you from his positions. You will be in a trap, for, with the forces you have, you will not be able to gather supplies against his multitude.

(Cicero, *Letters to Atticus*, 8.12c)

Things happened pretty much as Pompey predicted. Ahenobarbus became trapped in Corfinium. When he received another letter from Pompey explaining that under no circumstances would he be coming to his aid, Ahenobarbus behaved oddly, and his men negotiated their surrender to Caesar. What neither Pompey nor anyone else had predicted was what happened next: Caesar mustered the rank and file of Ahenobarbus' army into his own army while letting the large assemblage of senators and other dignitaries whom Ahenobarbus had with him go free.

Caesar's act of mercy resonated throughout Italy. He was not another Sulla.

Pompey's summary of the situation for Ahenobarbus, even if he could neither predict nor understand Caesar's clemency, reveals how much Caesar and Pompey tended to think along similar lines. The retreat to Brundisium was planned even before Titus Labienus, Caesar's right-hand man for the last nine years, changed sides after the crossing of the Rubicon, and confirmed that Pompey had accurate information about the strength of Caesar's army. He knew he could not fight in Italy because Caesar had more veterans at his disposal. But Pompey did have an army in Spain, and he knew that before Caesar could move east he would need the rest of his veteran legions for that conflict, and could only have them if he beat his, Pompey's, Spanish army.

By the time Pompey left Italy, Caesar's men were on the move into Spain. In order to support an army that he could use to invade Italy, Pompey was counting on the fact that the eastern Mediterranean had greater economic resources than the west, and on his own networks throughout the east. As he somewhat unfortunately remarked: 'Sulla could do it, why can't I?' (*Sulla potuit, ego non potero*) (Cicero, *Letters to Atticus* 9.10.2).

For the next eighteen months, two great masters of warfare would be engaged in a duel with a very small margin of error. Aside from his veteran troops, Caesar's great advantage was that he was supported by staff who wanted him to become the world's leader. Pompey's great disadvantage was that on his staff were people like Ahenobarbus, Cato and Bibulus, who wanted to restore the status quo. They ultimately forced Pompey to fight the battle he wanted to avoid, and probably could have.

The decisive encounter came at Pharsalus in Thessaly on 9 August 48 BC. Caesar had compelled Pompey's Spanish army to surrender before summer's end in 49 BC, forcing it out of a well-defended position around the northern city of Ilerda, then cutting it off from supplies. The commanders, Afranius (consul of 60 BC) and Petreius (who had been in functional command of the army that killed Catiline), and who were both long-time supporters of Pompey, were sent back to join his staff. Terentius Varro, governor of southern Spain and the greatest scholar of his generation, was forgiven his trespasses and subsequently found employment advising Caesar. In the winter of 48 BC, Caesar, now elected consul, took advantage of the mismanagement of Pompey's fleet by Bibulus and landed his army, albeit not without mishap, near the city of Dyrrachium (modern Durrës in Albania), which Pompey was building up as a base for his invasion of Italy. Pompey found himself under seige, but this did him no harm as he was better supplied than Caesar and could pick his moment to attack in a way that would nullify the superior fighting qualities of Caesar's troops. In April, he broke through his opponent's siege lines. Caesar admitted later that, had he been bolder, Pompey might have been able to end the war then and there.

Pharsalus was another matter. This would be a set battle, and the side with the better infantry would have a great advantage. Pompey was only fighting because the strife between him and his staff had intensified: people were accusing him of prolonging the war for his own ends and preventing them from reaping the rewards of victory – talk of proscription was in the air. Cicero, who had resisted Caesar's overtures to remain in Italy because of his personal loyalty to Pompey, was disgusted. He headed for home immediately after Pharsalus, even though as the senior surviving ex-consul in the camp he could have become titular head of the anti-Caesarian cause.

Both leaders understood that if Caesar's superior infantry could overcome Pompey's men, the day would go swiftly to Caesar. To this end, Pompey did the only thing he could: try to outflank Caesar with his superior cavalry. Caesar saw what he was doing and so withdrew six cohorts to form a special reserve that would attack Pompey's cavalry when it outdid his. Pompey held his infantry back to give his cavalry more time; seeing that they were rapidly advancing over twice the usual distance, Caesar's infantry halted to catch their breath before resuming their advance. As they did so, his reserve troops routed Pompey's cavalry – it is said that Caesar told his men to aim at the faces of the rich young men who would be in the front ranks. When Pompey saw his cavalry collapse, he knew he had lost. Not waiting for the end of the infantry action, he withdrew to his tent and removed his general's cloak. Then, when he heard Caesar's men approaching, he fled.

Reaching the coast ahead of pursuit, Pompey took a ship for Mytilene on the island of Lesbos, home city of his good friend Theophanes, where he had left his wife Cornelia. They then travelled to Egypt, seeking refuge with Ptolemy XIII, the son of Ptolemy XII Auletes. But the younger Ptolemy thought to gain favour with Caesar by murdering Pompey. He was stabbed to death and decapitated on a beach near Alexandria on 28 September. Cornelia would recover his body and inter his ashes in the great tomb, possibly still extant, that stood by his country estate near Bovillae.

Pompey was beaten, but not the Pompeians. In the summer of 49 BC, King Juba of Numidia had proclaimed his loyalty to Pompey and wiped out a Caesarian force sent to occupy Africa. Now men who had escaped the rout at Pharsalus began to gather in North Africa, and there would soon be stirrings of trouble in Spain. Nor was all well in Italy. The invasion had caused a massive debt crisis and the short-term credit market had evaporated – Pompey might well have had this in mind when he left for the east. The economic situation Caesar would be confronting was not dissimilar to the one Cinna had faced in the 80s BC. But Caesar was not Cinna. Before invading Italy he used silver taken in the Gallic campaigns to mint the largest single issue of denarius coinage in Rome's history to ensure his troops would be paid no matter what went wrong in the civilian economy. Before leaving for the east he had had the praetor Marcus Aemilius Lepidus (we will be hearing more about him soon) pass a law appointing him dictator. Eleven days after returning from Spain he enacted debt-relief measures to relieve the currency shortage; introduced a law restoring the civil rights of people other than Milo who had been exiled in 52 BC, plus a few others (Gabinius, for one); and another law restoring the rights of the sons of the proscribed.

Still the regime in Italy had not stabilised, and while the campaign was unfolding in Greece, Caelius – praetor and former lover of Clodius' sister Clodia – tried to upset Caesar's debt-relief scheme. Then, when that failed, he introduced radical measures eliminating rent payment for a year and cancelling debts. He also aligned himself with Milo, who had returned to Italy uninvited and had had some thugs try to evict the young woman occupying his old house on the Palatine (they failed). This woman's husband was with Pompey's army, and her own ability to stay on reflects the Caesarian regime's exceptional tolerance for anyone willing not to rock the boat. In the end Caelius was driven from Rome to join forces with Milo, who was now fomenting a revolt in Campania, where they were both killed.

The deaths of Caelius and Milo did not end Italy's troubles, as troops returning from Greece demanded their discharge, and Caesar had vanished. He had pursued Pompey to Egypt, arriving a couple of days after his death, and delivered to Ptolemy XIII a bill for the money Ptolemy XII still owed him. He professed to be horrified by Pompey's treatment, and made the acquaintance of Cleopatra, whose co-rulership with her brother had collapsed into a welter of discontent. At the moment of Caesar's arrival, she was advancing on Alexandria at the head of a mercenary army from Syria. One result of their rapidly evolving friendship was a child, born on 23 June 47 BC, indicating that their liaison had begun almost as soon as Caesar had got off the boat. This may also explain why Caesar almost immediately found himself embroiled in the Egyptian civil war and under siege in Alexandria.

Before coming to Egypt, Caesar had arranged for several legions, former Pompeians, to be sent from Asia Minor to join him. When they arrived he promptly eliminated Ptolemy XIII, placed Cleopatra on the throne, took a boat trip up the Nile with her, and learned that Pharnaces, son of Mithridates, was trying to regain his father's kingdom. Leaving Egypt before the birth of Cleopatra's child in the summer, he caught up with Pharnaces at Zela in Pontus and made short work of his army. The famous crisp message perfectly sums it up: *veni, vidi, vici* – 'I came, I saw, I conquered' (Suetonius, *Life of Caesar* 37.2). He had now to deal with the problems of Italy and the emergent Pompeian threat from Africa.

Caesar's eastern tour had a point. This was Pompey's country, and he needed to introduce himself to people who owed their positions to his late rival. He also had to feed Rome, and it is quite likely that his intervention in the war of the Egyptian succession ensured that there would be a regime willing to send its surplus grain to his home city.

Caesar's eastern tour may have been necessary, but the problems in Italy remained, and they remained largely because of Caesar's own style of leadership. His subordinates found him intimidating. Those who knew him thought him the smartest individual they had ever met and were afraid to act on their own initiative. Hence the regime in Italy had sought to do nothing more than maintain the status quo, despite growing concern about an invasion from Africa. By July the regime fell to fighting about debt relief in the face of fresh rioting in Rome, and was failing to manage a serious mutiny. All nine veteran legions that had returned from the wars in Spain and Greece had been quarrelling with the people in the cities where they had been billeted, and were now demanding the pay they were owed as well as release from service.

When he returned to Italy, Caesar was again made dictator. The first thing on his agenda was to clean up the mess that had developed while he was away, starting with the mutiny. The second was to admit that his conservative debt-relief measures of 49 BC were inadequate. Back in Rome in September, Caesar introduced more radical debt-relief measures and cancelled rent payments for a year. He also ordered subordinates who had bought estates belonging to prominent Pompeians (most notably Pompey himself) to pay the treasury their assessed pre-war value. He was short of hard currency, and currency was what was needed to end the mutiny. Despite later claims that Caesar quelled it with a single word, 'citizens' in place of 'fellow soldiers' – thereby indicating that he was dismissing his men from service – the mutiny does not seem to have ended until four legions had been discharged and the remaining five had been paid substantial bonuses to continue fighting.

One effect of the chaos was that towards the year's end Caesar had to embark for North Africa with untried troops, only regaining what remained of his veteran army in the spring. When he finally reached full strength he sought a decisive battle, crushing the Pompeian forces at Thapsus. Again, Caesar asked his men to spare the surrendering enemy, but they did not; ordinary soldiers were much less keen on Caesar's *clementia* than were the aristocrats. Soldiers saw it as prolonging the war, and at least one key Pompeian was executed; others, having escaped the slaughter on the battle-field, committed suicide – one of these was Cato. The survivors fled to Spain.

The year 46 BC was the longest in Roman history. Literally. It had 445 days, thanks to the fact that Caesar introduced a new calendar on 1

January 45 BC. This was in the air when, as consul for the year, he returned to Rome to celebrate triumphs for his victories in Gaul, Egypt, Pontus and North Africa and to accept the post of dictator for a ten-year term. The quadruple triumph stressed victories over foreign peoples rather than in civil war, but paintings of suicidal Pompeians, displayed in the North Africa triumph, proved a public relations fiasco.

Caesar's point was that these men were serving Juba, but many people saw it differently – as celebrating a triumph over other Romans. Caesar then compounded the problem by publishing a vitriolic attack on the memory of Cato. Here, his point was that membership of the Roman state involved acceptance of his authority. It was not that people could not criticise him – he allowed his soldiers to sing rude songs about him at his triumphs, promoted authors of works about Cato that attacked his own writings, and sat through theatrical events at which he was openly chastised – but it did mean that people must recognise that the ultimate authority resided with him. As dictator, he was not a Ciceronian moderator of the state, he was the state's ultimate authority.

The driving principles behind the reforms Caesar initiated after his return in 46 BC were that Rome should function as an imperial capital, that it should look like an imperial capital, and that provincial society should be integrated with Italian society. He owed his victory in the civil war not just to his legions' loyalty, but also to the firm support of, and the contribution made by, the areas from which they had been recruited – northern Italy and Gaul. One point that Hirtius was at pains to make was that by the summer of 50 BC the Gallic tribes were united behind Caesar. Roman armies were no longer entirely Italian. In 48 BC the Pompeian armies had been heavily recruited from provincial communities; Pompey's Spanish armies had 'gone native', Caesar suggested.

One way to better integrate the provinces with Italy was to settle more Italians abroad. Caesar was stymied when it came to finding land for his legions – there was just not enough left in Italy for large-scale veteran settlements, and he was unwilling to repeat the Sullan exercise of widespread expropriation. Only 15,000 of Caesar's Gallic veterans had received Italian land. Also about this time, he attempted to address the living standards in Rome. Two new officials were appointed to take charge of the city's grain distributions, and the rolls of grain recipients were revised, lowering the number of those eligible for free grain from 320,000 to 150,000. This measure was accompanied by new public expenditure as work continued on Caesar's new forum.

Eighty thousand people were selected to settle across about thirty new colonies, including at Carthage and at Corinth. The foundations planned for these two might have had significant meaning for some members of the ruling class. It was widely regarded among the intelligentsia that Rome's problems began with the influx of wealth after the sack of Carthage, which had removed the fear of a real rival, or, in an alternative version, from the conquest of the east. The refoundation of these two cities, a hundred years after their destruction, could be seen as declaring an end to an era of self-indulgent corruption. More practically, the two foundations might well elicit some gratitude towards Caesar in parts of the empire that had previously had stronger connections with Pompey.

Pompey and Sulla can be detected in the background of other reforms: one eliminated the *tribuni aerarii* from the juries, another expanded the Senate to 900, bringing in many new men from northern Italy and southern Gaul, thereby making the Senate less central Italian, more imperial. Given the number of Senate members either in exile or recently killed in battle, Caesar's newly appointed senators may have made up about half the order – though for many the title may have been more honorific than functional if they had no permanent residence in Rome.

Also, Caesar modified Pompey's administrative arrangements by eliminating the five-year waiting period for provincial governors, as well as reducing the terms of praetorian governors to one year and of consuls to two. This could be announced as not only a measure to limit corruption, but as a sign of Caesar's continued devotion to the idea of honest provincial government as enunciated in his law of 59 BC. A new development, however, was that he was given the right to designate candidates for office, to which they would be elected without competition, and to fix the election of magistrates, including consuls, several years in advance.

The officials charged with ensuring that all these initiatives were carried through were members of Caesar's inner circle, of whom the three most important were Balbus and two other equestrians, Oppius and Matius. These were the people who would deal with, for instance, the drawing-up of charters for the new settlements. And when Cicero had a technical question, he wrote to Balbus for an answer. This sort of thing would have been discussed in the Senate in past years, as would issues such as the rights of temples in Asia Minor (now decided by Caesar himself). It was almost as if being a magistrate did not matter all that much, now that the real business of government was in the hands of professional administrators

13. The remains of the podium of the temple of Venus Genetrix.
The temple was the centrepiece of Caesar's new forum.

working directly for Caesar. Caesar's notion of elected magistrates having a somewhat secondary role was particularly evident when Fabius Maximus died on 31 December 45 BC, with one day left in his consulship: Caesar appointed Caninius Rebilus to the post, allotting him a term of exactly one day. As members of the equestrian order, Oppius and company were not as offensive to upper-class sensibilities as Chrysogonus had been back in 80 BC, but the tension that had existed in Sulla's time between inner and outer court circles was becoming evident as the year 45 BC ended.

The way Caesar's inner circle was functioning made two of his other projects symbolically problematic, even if they had a clear practical value. These were the reform of the calendar and a plan to found a public library.

Badly out of alignment with the seasons by 49 BC, the calendar year, which previously had lasted for 354 days but was brought back into alignment through the inclusion of a twenty-two-day intercalary month every two years (omitted in the political chaos of recent years), was now even more awry. Instead of resorting to the traditional fix of adding an intercalary month (or in this case, nearly three), Caesar came up with a brand-new calendar year of 365 days, based on the most advanced astronomical scholarship. The Julian calendar, as it became known, remained the norm in some areas of the world well into the twentieth century – its last significant use ended when the Eastern Orthodox Church adopted the Gregorian calendar, as instituted in 1582 by Pope Gregory XIII, in 1924. As for the library, Caesar had invited Terentius Varro to work on it, but it never came to fruition in his lifetime. He had obviously been inspired by his contacts with eastern realms, which had their own calendars and whose kings had engaged in competitive library foundation. The best of these was at Alexandria, or had been – there is some question as to whether it was seriously damaged during Caesar's war with Ptolemy XIII – and the scholarship that lay behind the new calendar was also Alexandrian.

In the course of 45 BC, Cleopatra came to Rome. Caesar kept her in a villa south of the Tiber with their son Caesarion on display, while busying himself with placing a golden statue of Venus, rendered in her likeness, in his new Temple of Venus Genetrix ('the Ancestress'), which was aligned with the Senate House he was building, in a new location to make the sight line work, to replace the one that had been destroyed in 52 BC.

Two events impeded the continuing development of the Caesarian regime. One was a renewed bout of civil war, in Spain this time. The other was Caesar's assassination. The war in Spain, led by Labienus along with Pompey's two sons, stemmed not only from a long-standing loyalty to Pompey in those regions but from incompetence on the part of Caesar's local officials. In the winter of 46 BC, Caesar realised that he would have to go to Spain himself, taking with him one of his few young male relatives, his grand-nephew Gaius Octavius, who so impressed him that Caesar decided to adopt him in his will.

What followed was a short, brutal campaign which ended at the battle of Munda on 17 March 45 BC. The final battle was a close-run thing, as Caesar was forced to attack uphill against Labienus' army. But, on his return to Rome in the summer, he celebrated a triumph. This was not universally well received: it was perceived in some quarters as a triumph over Roman citizens. The trouble was that in Caesar's view, people who opposed him were *not* Roman citizens.

This phase of the war over, Caesar returned to his reform agenda, allowed himself to be made dictator for life and issued coins with his image on them. This smacked of royal prerogative, which raised, probably not for the first time, the question of whether he would restore kingship to Rome. The question was perhaps all the more significant given that Pompey's younger son Sextus, who had survived Munda, was now styling himself Magnus Pius (essentially, 'Dutiful Son'). There could also have been a suspicion that Faustus Sulla had been killed after Thapsus because he was Sulla's son. A sense of dynasty was in the air and, with Cleopatra in the wings, some people were becoming very suspicious indeed.

But Caesar did not need to be king of Rome. He already dressed, in public, as the king of Alba Longa, a sartorial fantasy that derived from his family's alleged connection with the ancient city of Alba from which Rome had been founded. However, this did not end the speculation or the questions about the other institutions that might spring up around him. One of the first of these was the establishment of a state cult of Caesar, which was very much in the air as 45 BC turned into 44 BC. The granting of divine honours to mortals was common in the eastern Mediterranean. It was a way of thanking civic benefactors; and in Ptolemaic lands, as it had once been in Seleucid lands, it was also a way of directing public opinion. Indeed, Caesar was already the recipient of divine honours in several Greek cities – also true of a number of other senators at this point – and had been honoured as a god by some individuals in Italy. He had received honours typical of a ruler cult – although without the apparatus of a cult – following his victorious return from Thapsus and Munda.

Caesar knew perfectly well that he was mortal – he had been discussing the best way to die the night before he was assassinated – although he does appear to have been working towards some sort of personal state cult, quite possibly based on the Ptolemaic model. In late February or early March the Senate, apparently, voted to create such a cult – perhaps in support of Caesar's plan to invade Parthia. The campaign would give him the opportunity to put down deeper roots in the eastern provinces, where Pompey's memory was still powerful, while a state cult would provide a mechanism of communication with provincial groups through routine celebrations that offered a chance to spread good news about the regime. Caesar had plainly decided that the way the Roman state had run its empire needed some profound changes, and reforms verging on the regal were just that – tried and trusted administrative forms adopted from other states to improve Rome's efficiency.

Caesar appears to have been thoroughly convinced both of the correctness of his views and of the notion that people would realise that, although they were not happy with him, the alternative was a return to civil war, which could only be worse. He recognised that he was disliked. When he came to dinner at his house, Cicero says, he arrived with an armed guard looking as if forewarned of a plot; Caesar himself said, after keeping Cicero waiting on one occasion, that he understood why he angered some people. But he could never have imagined a conspiracy of over sixty men, some of them his former lieutenants furious that he had not rewarded them sufficiently – some of them, even, men whom he had spared. A few may have believed that in killing the 'tyrant' they would save the world. Their leaders were Marcus Brutus, the son of Caesar's old flame Servilia, and Gaius Cassius, who had taken over the defence of Syria in 53 BC. Used as he was to rumours of assassination, Caesar took minimal precautions, even though tensions were running high as the date of his departure approached.

On 15 March 44 BC, at the last meeting of the Senate before he left for Parthia, the conspirators stabbed him. The meeting had been scheduled to take place in the Theatre of Pompey. Caesar fell dead at the feet of a statue of his old rival.

23

CAESARIANS AND
POMPEIANS

The vision of government taking shape before 15 March 44 BC involved Caesar acting as chief executive of a state staffed by administrators, ideally senators, at least in the traditional roles such as the oversight of the financial system, running the city of Rome, governing the provinces and commanding the armies. With elections under Caesar's control, traditional politics no longer had a place, and with no need to buy office via the electoral process, administrators would not have to fleece their subjects.

Likewise, since Caesar could put on a spectacle like no one else, there was no point in trying to compete. Conventional politics would end – and end with the overwhelming support of the Roman people, who preferred Caesarian proficiency to the incompetencies of the previous regime. Caesar had fixed the problems in the fiscal system that his invasion of Italy had sparked, and settled veterans without deranging civilian society. Members of the established governing class, those who deplored institutional dysfunction, were supporters of the new efficiency. Efficiency was also the vision of government to which the inner core of Caesar's administration was attached – people like Oppius, Balbus, Matius and Hirtius.

But what of the Senate? Did it have a part to play in the new regime, or didn't it? This issue was still unresolved on 15 March and was dividing Caesar's own supporters – as with Sulla, there was no single definition of what it meant to be a partisan. One of the charges that the assassins brought to justify their action was that Caesar had failed to stand when greeting a deputation from the Senate informing him of decrees that had been passed in his honour. He had not previously agreed to accept all extraordinary honours he had been voted, and there was some tension here. The power to honour Caesar was the power to cast judgement upon him. He had to acquiesce.

Cicero had his own ways of questioning Caesar's power. When he delivered a speech asking him to allow Marcus Claudius Marcellus, consul of 51 BC, to return from exile, he was asking Caesar to live up to his own message of *clementia* by offering a vision of a 'restored Republic' in which traditional institutions would continue to function; he pointed out at the same time that there were people who hated him. On another occasion, Cicero told Caesar bluntly that holding a trial in his own house was grossly irregular, even as he was speaking for a defendant in Caesar's presence. The dictator had to agree to allow Marcellus back, and he freed Cicero's client, an eastern potentate named Deiotaurus, whom we will meet again in the next chapter. Cicero could get away with his carefully worded challenges, in part because Caesar liked him, but also because he had to allow the most senior consul a voice. Still, there are signs that Caesar was becoming more autocratic with the passage of time, and it is notable that the complaints the assassins used to justify their action all had to do with events after Caesar's return from Munda.

Another individual whose relationship with Caesar illustrates the increasing complexity of the regime was Marcus Antonius, whom Caesar had chastised for his conduct during the debt crisis. He had designated him co-consul in 44 BC even though temperamentally the two were poles apart: now the husband of Clodius' widow Fulvia, Antonius was a heavy drinker who cavorted with actresses. Arguably, he had embarrassed Caesar by offering him a crown at the Lupercalia, probably Rome's most boisterous and popular festival. It featured semi-clad priests running through the streets striking topless women with strips of goat skin in order to enhance their fertility. Antonius was one of the priests and the event could not have been more public. Caesar had turned the crown down as he sensed that accepting it would be profoundly unpopular.

When Caesar laid down his consulship in 44 BC, which he had expected to do as he set out for the Parthian war, it would be taken up by Cornelius Dolabella (as 'suffect', or substitute consul). Dolabella had been Antonius' primary antagonist during the debt crisis. Caesar was not personally close to either man; so appointing these two to the consulships could have been his attempt to help leaders of various groups work out their differences. And the selection of Marcus Aemilius Lepidus, son of the rebellious consul of 77 BC, to be his deputy as dictator, his 'master of horse', also appears to have been political. Lepidus had been useful in the past, but he was not a man of scintillating intellect.

Traditional aristocrats complained that there were too many 'new men' around Caesar. With an Antonius, a Cornelius and an Aemilius in the governing group for 44 BC, others may have thought there were too many *nobiles*.

The divisions between the different groups of Caesarians would prove to be even more significant than the division between the Caesarians and Caesar's killers. One group of Caesarians, in fact, joined the assassins; others felt it expedient to negotiate with them; yet others thought that they should be killed. These various stances, along with an almost immediate break between Antonius and the inner circle, laid the groundwork for the most extraordinary coup d'état in Mediterranean history. By the end of 44 BC the assassins would be assembling armies in the east, while Antonius would be on the brink of being declared a public enemy. At centre stage in Rome would be the young man whom Caesar had adopted in his will. Born Gaius Octavius, the 19-year-old Gaius Julius, son of Gaius, Caesar – henceforth Caesar Jr – would be working with members of the inner circle (and the acquiescence of others) with a view, in the opinion of some, to preserving the Republic, and of others, to preserving Caesar's legacy. In truth Caesar Jr was taking the first steps towards establishing a new form of monarchy.

The split in the Caesarian camp emerged within days of the assassination. On the night of 15 March, Antonius had gone to Caesar's house, relieving his widow Calpurnia of his papers and a massive sum of money (the beginning of a process via which he transferred cash from Caesar's coffers to his own). At a meeting the next day, he agreed with Hirtius – and against Balbus – to make a deal with the assassins, who were holed up on the Capitoline. On 17 March Antonius convened a meeting of the Senate, at which it was agreed that Caesar was not a tyrant and so his acts (even the unpublished ones, now in Antonius' possession) would be valid, but that his killers would be granted an amnesty. That evening Lepidus and Marcus Antonius dined with Brutus and Cassius.

The situation changed drastically, however, when Caesar's will was made public, just before, if not at, the funeral on 19 March. In the will it was revealed that not only had Caesar adopted Gaius Octavius but that he had named him as his principal heir and as recipient of three-quarters of his estate. Caesar had included Antonius among heirs of the second class (who would receive legacies only if the primary heirs turned their inheritances down). In addition to the bequests to individuals, Caesar left a very generous gift to all male citizens of Rome.

The funeral itself was an extraordinary spectacle, including a chorus singing a hymn to Caesar, a pop-up wax statue of the deceased displaying his wounds, and a stunning speech by Antonius, after which the crowd rioted, burnt Caesar's body in the forum and laid siege to the houses of the assassins, who left town within days.

It was now that Antonius broke with the inner circle. He began to use his control of Caesar's unpublished acts to make gifts that people in the know knew Caesar had not intended: it was their work that Antonius was perverting. Then there was the problem of the false Marius, who had appeared before Caesar's death. Caesar had banished him, but now he was back promoting popular commemoration of the late dictator. Antonius' violent suppression of Marius damaged his previously high standing with the Roman people. At the same time, a massive eruption of Mount Etna so altered atmospheric conditions even as far north as Rome that the summer of 44 BC proved to be one of the coldest on record. Then, during the games held in honour of Caesar's goddess Victoria in July, a comet appeared. This was interpreted as Caesar's genius – the divine spark that animated all people – entering the heavens to join the gods. For those inclined to take such signs seriously, as many were, it proved that the gods were appalled by the murder.

Gaius Octavius needed all the help he could get, divine or otherwise, when he arrived in Rome in April. At first Antonius tried to ignore him, then he tried to invent legal roadblocks to the adoption. That, too, was a mistake. Oppius, Balbus and Matius welcomed the young man with open arms, while Cicero found him interesting. In July, when Antonius and other senators wished to prevent the celebration of games dedicated to the Victory of Caesar, the inner circle made sure that the games went on and that Caesar Jr had a major role to play in them.

By the end of July, Antonius was in trouble. Brutus and Cassius were still in Italy agitating for the 'restoration of traditional government', while anger was growing among Caesar's strongest supporters and veterans. Seeking a unified front, they demanded a public reconciliation between Antonius and Caesar Jr. The relationship between the two sides continued to degenerate until, on 1 August, Caesar's father-in-law Piso, the consul of 58 BC, attacked Antonius in the Senate. The next month, again in the Senate, Cicero showed considerable courage by trading insults with Antonius, albeit at alternating sessions so as to avoid personal confrontation. In September, deciding that he needed more muscle, Antonius summoned four legions from Macedonia.

The first three legions arrived in Rome in mid-October, by which point both the young Caesar and Antonius had raised units from among Julius Caesar's veterans. The former also had agents leafleting Antonius' Macedonian legions when they landed. Antonius quelled the incipient mutiny with a series of executions, then began to march north. In mid-November he returned to Rome, with the intention of occupying the city with his troops, but soon left in a huff. News came to him that two of the legions had mutinied. Now on full civil war footing, Antonius began raising new legions and joined his remaining army to the fourth Macedonian legion. He then marched on Cisalpine Gaul, making the valid point that in June its governorship for 43 BC had been transferred to him. The sitting governor was Decimus Brutus, one of the assassins. He was not about to hand anything over to Antonius. As the new year opened, war threatened.

Having reached the end of his pro-Antonian account of the year 50 BC, Hirtius recognised that reconciliation was impossible. He wrote to Balbus that he had taken the story to the end of Caesar's life, but had made no mention of the civil dissension 'to which we see no end in sight' (Hirtius, *Gallic War* 8, praef. 2). He would do his duty. Envoys sent from the Senate to Antonius in January failed to convince him to stand down and, as the situation worsened, efforts were made to draw in two Caesarian armies north of the Alps, commanded by Lepidus and Munatius Plancus, who despite professing loyalty to the state showed little evidence of it. In February armies were sent north under the consuls and Caesar Jr, who was awarded a praetorship.

As the year 43 BC began, news came that Brutus had seized the province of Macedonia and Cassius had acquired Syria, where a Caesarian general, one Staius Murcius, had been trying to eliminate a man called Bassus who had murdered a previous governor and taken the province for himself. When Cassius arrived, Murcius declared his loyalty to the assassins; he would play a major role as their admiral in the following years. There was news, too, of a remarkably brutal civil war in western Turkey, where Dolabella, who was supposed to be governing Syria, had attacked one of the assassins, then governor of Asia, and tortured the man to death. His disappearance facilitated Cassius' takeover.

By late March, Caesarian armies in southern France were standing on the sidelines of a war that two Caesarian consuls, in the company of Caesar's heir, were about to fight against a Caesarian ex-consul in order to rescue an army commanded by an assassin. At the same time, at a meeting attended by Piso and several former Caesarian consuls, the Senate voted to recognise the legitimacy of the coup by means of which Brutus had seized Macedonia; in April, it also legitimised Cassius' seizure of Syria, while condemning Dolabella for his repellent behaviour. Overtures were made to the great Pompey's son, Sextus Pompeius Magnus Pius, who with seven legions was waiting in Marseille, unbothered by the Caesarian armies around him. These meetings epitomised the nadir of aristocratic politics and the tradition they represented, whereby all that mattered were the interests of the governing class – interests about to be thrust aside as forces driven by loyalty to Caesar's memory compelled obedience to their wishes.

The prelude to the military revolt was enacted outside the *colonia* of Mutina, when Hirtius and his fellow consul, Pansa, defeated Antonius in two battles, compelling him to raise the siege of the city and withdraw towards the Alps. Hirtius and Pansa both died in the fighting – some said that Caesar Jr helped them on their way, although that may just be a nasty story. Antonius' escape was aided by the lack of coordination between the consular army, now commanded by Caesar Jr, and Brutus' force. Even though ordered by the Senate to subordinate himself to Brutus, Caesar Jr refused. He would not speak to the assassin. In the meantime, Antonius crossed the Alps. The surviving extensive correspondence between Cicero, Plancus and Brutus is an ample chronicle of delusion and duplicity on the part of all three men. In the end, when Antonius entered southern France, the armies of Lepidus and Plancus compelled their generals to make a deal with him. The troops could not understand why they should fight each other while in the east the strength of the assassins was growing. The combined armies moved south. Brutus' position became untenable and he fled into the night, later to be killed by a Gallic chieftain.

Caesar Jr withdrew in the face of the superior forces now pouring over the Alps. He demanded a consulship to enhance his status. The Senate, which had granted Cassius command of 'the war in Syria' and an official position to Magnus in the wake of Mutina, demurred. A deputation of Caesar Jr's centurions pointed out that the Senate really had no choice in the matter. There was then an election, which Caesar Jr won, along with a man named Pedius. As part of the deal that made him consul, Pedius introduced a bill ordering that Caesar's killers be tried. The amnesty of 17 March was thereby rescinded. All the trials took place on one day, and the assassins were found guilty. The prosecution of Cassius was entrusted to a young man called Marcus Vipsanius Agrippa.

The armies of Antonius and Caesar Jr now met at Bononia (modern-day Bologna), where the soldiers insisted that the generals deal with each other face to face. It was agreed that Caesar Jr would lay down the consulship (to be given to Publius Ventidius), and would join Antonius and Lepidus to form a board of three for setting the state in order (*tresviri rei publicae constituendae*). Granted essentially dictatorial power, the board was appointed for a five-year term. The young Caesar cemented his alliance with Antonius by agreeing to become betrothed to Fulvia's daughter, Clodia. Lepidus' inclusion in the group was crucial for defusing the antipathy between the other two principals. On 7 November the tribune Titius brought the bill creating the board to a vote. The triumvirs promptly ordered the deaths of thirty-seven individuals, then on 23 November issued an edict ordering a new round of proscriptions. The order and form of the names in this edict reflect the compromise that had brought the board into being: Lepidus, Antonius, Octavius Caesar. That Lepidus' name comes first indicates his importance to the settlement; that Caesar Jr should appear as 'Octavius Caesar' indicates a further concession on his part – that he was Caesar's heir, not Caesar himself.

Cicero was one of the first victims of the proscription. He was murdered on 7 December 43 BC. The list of those proscribed grew until it contained some 2,000 people, who were all sentenced to instant death, their property confiscated. Terror gripped Italy as soldiers hunted down their victims, though it seems that they were not all that efficient about it. In most cases, they really did not care. What the triumvirs needed was money to fund the coming war against Brutus and Cassius. The party of Caesar, still disjointed at the top, had been restored by military men devoted to the memory of an individual whom average Romans saw as putting their interests first.

*14. Marcus Aemilius Lepidus, seen here on a denarius issued in
42 BC. Born in 89 or 88 he was the oldest of the triumvirs.*

The *lex Pedia* and the proscription edict transformed the struggle gripping the Roman state from an internal senatorial dispute over Caesar's legacy to a military referendum on the result of the previous civil war. On the one side were the murderers and Magnus, who had taken advantage of his brief commission as admiral of the Republic to establish a base in Sicily. Magnus was now himself proscribed, and his camp became a haven for others on the list who had been able to escape. On the other side were the triumvirs, who had at their disposal the not inconsiderable military might of western Europe (around forty legions). Moreover, on 1 January 42 BC, the Senate recognised Julius Caesar as a god. The triumvirs were fighting for the memory of the most extraordinary man of the age, but this did not confer extra authority on Caesar Jr. Perhaps indicating an awareness of his diminishing authority, he now called himself 'the son of a god', which he was indeed entitled to do. He also grew a beard and swore off sex for the sake of his health and mental capacity (or so he said).

The triumvirs had to take the offensive – the funding for their enormous enterprise was to be achieved by pillaging the estates of the proscribed, and those resources were finite. Brutus and Cassius raised more than twenty legions of their own, funded largely through Cassius' plundering of the cities of Asia. They did not have the resources to invade Italy, but could hope that the sense of general unrest would destabilise the regime. Concerted naval action by their forces and those of Magnus kept the triumviral army bottled up in Italy until September when, aided by a fleet from Cleopatra, it finally made the crossing. Lepidus remained

15. Caesar Jr., the portrait here is on the reverse of the coin bearing Lepidus' portrait in 42 BC. The beard that he sports signifies his continued mourning for Julius Caesar.

behind in Rome, where he bullied civilians and continued to oversee the proscriptions.

The assassins drew up their army at Philippi, hoping that a shortage of supplies would disable the much larger army that the triumvirs had at their disposal. This might have worked, had not Antonius' principal quality as a general been his exceptional boldness. He compelled Cassius to give battle, and in a complicated day's fighting crushed his opponent's army, while Brutus' forces overwhelmed those of Caesar Jr (who, claiming to have been ill, escaped his camp's capture allegedly via divine intervention). Cassius killed himself, reportedly by mistake. Brutus' turn would come next. A few weeks after the first battle, on 23 October 43 BC, Antonius forced him to fight again, and beat him badly. Brutus' suicide was not a mistake.

The triumvirs were now faced with the prospect of demobilising an army they could not pay. A subtle administrative shift left Caesar Jr in control of Italy, Africa, Sicily and Sardinia. Lepidus, suspected of some sort of devious conduct, now entered a temporary political limbo. Antonius, on a tour of the eastern provinces, imposed fresh fines on the cities of the region, while making it clear that his personal favour might lighten the individual burden. He was beginning to build his own administrative structures, and for that purpose needed his own people.

The demobilisation of the troops in Italy resulted in chaos and civil strife. The young Caesar resorted to Sullan-style mass confiscations: eighteen cities had been selected at the meeting in Bononia to suffer large-scale expropriation to make way for veteran settlements. People were appalled. Leaders from central Italy, where most of the targets lay, came to Rome to protest. Caesar Jr suggested deals that would favour large landholders; Lucius Antonius, Antonius' brother (and consul for 41 BC), spurred them on, declaring that he was interested in restoring the traditional government of the Republic – a somewhat self-serving claim because under his scheme Lucius would still be consul and Caesar Jr would be out of a job. What his claims to be supporting civilian government were also about was setting the Italian gentry against the military. Class solidarity drove the soldiers, initially sceptical of Caesar Jr, into his arms. Then Magnus and his allies, survivors from the assassins' fleet commanded by Gnaeus Domitius Ahenobarbus and Staius Murcus, intercepted some grain shipments. The triumvirs now had no fleet with which to contest the seas. As the violence escalated, Lepidus fled, leaving Caesar Jr to deal with Lucius.

Open war broke out in the summer, Lucius Antonius counting on aid from three associates of his brother – Asinius Pollio, Publius Ventidius and Munatius Plancus – who had armies in northern Italy. But Lucius was cut off, and Marcus Vipsanius Agrippa now assumed the leading role among Caesar Jr's commanders. He besieged Lucius at Perugia, where he had taken refuge. The expected support did not materialise: Pollio and Plancus hated each other, and Plancus had insulted Ventidius. Lack of coordination in Lucius' camp and Agrippa's superior planning led the potential relieving force to withdraw twice. Lucius was then allowed to surrender and leave Italy with Fulvia. Perugia was sacked. A poet, native to the region, would later write:

> Tullus, you ask about my family and where I am from, for friendship's sake. If the Perugian graves of the fatherland are known to you, and the ruin of Italy in dark times, when Roman discord drove its people on (you are an especial grief to me, Etruscan dust, for you allow the cast out limbs of my friend to be abandoned, you touch the poor man's bones with no earth), neighbouring Umbria, a land rich in fields, bore me on the plain below.
>
> (Propertius, *Poems* 1.22)

Another poet (from Mantua) – a friend of Pollio and of Maecenas, another of Caesar Jr's close friends – soon wrote a poem to publicise an improvement in Caesar Jr's dealings with people, in which he imagined a man who had lost his farm but had had it restored when he came to Rome, his benefactor (Caesar) being like a god to him.

Antonius was less happy. Interrupting an affair that he had begun having with Cleopatra in Egypt, he stormed west in alliance with Magnus. War threatened as he landed with an army at Brundisium, but again the troops intervened. A new settlement was imposed to bind the two commanders together. Lepidus was stripped of almost all his power and shipped off to Africa. In September, since Fulvia had by this time died, Antonius agreed to marry Octavia, the recently widowed sister of Caesar Jr, who in turn agreed to marry Scribonia, a somewhat older woman whose niece was Magnus' wife.

The inclusion of Magnus in the peace negotiations at Brundisium had important consequences. It opened up space for further conversations between the triumviral side and various individuals associated with Magnus. It appears that Plancus met with Gnaeus Domitius Ahenobarbus, whose fleet had been dominating the Adriatic. He negotiated a settlement whereby Ahenobarbus was forgiven his service with the assassins and joined Antonius. Another associate of the Antonian triumvirate that failed to relieve Perugia was Pollio, who was now consul, and a patron of promising artists. The treaty of Brundisium promised that his consulship might be remembered as the beginning of a new era of peace. The same poet – Virgil – who had celebrated Caesar Jr's generosity performed a poem drawing on the themes of prophetic poetry from the east, announcing the birth of a new golden age in conjunction with Pollio's consulship and the birth of Pollio's son. The prophecy proved premature – but given that the next round of fighting between the triumvirs and Magnus would have ended in 36 BC, it was realised when Virgil completed the cycle of ten poems that would constitute his *Eclogues*.

Ahenobarbus' decision to join the triumvirs was the proximate cause for yet more conflict. Lepidus, it seems, stayed in North Africa, while Antonius remained in Italy, joining Caesar Jr in Rome. Magnus, by controlling the harbours of Sicily, Sardinia and Corsica, could launch raids against the Italian coast and interrupt grain shipments to Rome with impunity, effectively wrecking all efforts to celebrate the victory over Caesar's murderers. Even without the disruption of agriculture caused by the colonisation schemes, the city was dependent on imported grain, which typically came from Sicily and, by now, North Africa. To the food shortage was added an ongoing financial crunch as the oversized armies of Italy needed to be paid, leading to both the imposition of new taxes and the continuation of revenue-generating schemes (other than proscription) that had previously been imposed to pay for the war with the assassins. In the midst of all this, Caesar Jr discovered that one of his closest associates had tried to betray him. He was executed.

While the triumvirs faced riots in Rome, Magnus had new problems of his own. Staius Murcus began negotiating with the triumvirs. Magnus executed him, but it was plain that he was now facing more pressure to end the fighting. He reached a deal with the triumvirs in the spring of 39 BC, according to which: he would be recognised as governor of Sicily, Sardinia, Corsica and other islands, as well as the southern Peloponnese (an addition to his previous areas of operation); those who had survived the proscriptions would be allowed to return home (although those convicted under the *lex Pedia* were excluded from the amnesty); his soldiers would have the same privileges as those of the triumvirs; and he would be made consul in 35 BC. The treaty was confirmed with massive celebrations at Misenum on the bay of Naples. One of the dinners that finalised the treaty was held on Magnus' flagship. Menophilus, one of his officers, allegedly suggested that he might just sail off with Antonius and Caesar Jr as his prisoners (without Lepidus). That would be dishonourable, Magnus replied.

While Antonius was in the west, the Parthians, emboldened by Rome's difficulties, had launched a major invasion. One wing of the Parthian force, led by the son of the Labienus who had served, then betrayed, Caesar, reached western Asia Minor; another defeated Roman clients in Syria and Palestine. Antonius, still busy with Italian politics, would get no further than Athens. But he sent Publius Ventidius, plainly now forgiven for his lacklustre support of Lucius, ahead with troops from the western invasion force. In 38 BC Ventidius crushed two Parthian armies, killing many senior officials. This was too much for Antonius, and off he went east. Meanwhile, Ventidius returned home to celebrate his triumph.

Antonius worked tirelessly on reorganising the eastern provinces. Caesar Jr, meanwhile, performed an extraordinary volte-face and entered a life-and-death struggle with Magnus. The treaty of Misenum broke down within about six months. Antonius never made good on his promise to deliver the Peloponnese, or its tax revenues, to Magnus; then the tensions on his staff re-emerged. Magnus' governor of Sardinia and Corsica, Menodorus, delivered those islands, his ships and three legions to the young Caesar, who was by now styling himself Imperator Caesar, son of the divinity, taking what was once just the title of a victorious general and using it as his first name, just as Magnus had done with his father's old cognomen. When Imperator Caesar declared Magnus to be a pirate, Magnus responded by again interrupting grain supplies and raiding the west coast of Italy. His enemies, who may have been genuinely surprised by Menodorus' offer of service, lacked the ships to defend their coasts. The fleets they finally launched in the summer of 38 BC were shattered by a combination of Magnus' superior forces and a storm, which left Imperator Caesar shipwrecked and stranded on the shore of Calabria.

His reputation in tatters, assaulted by angry mobs, and rumours spreading about his participation in a sacrilegious feast, Imperator Caesar did not help himself by becoming embroiled in a scandal in his personal life – he divorced Scribonia in order to marry Livia, the wife of Tiberius Claudius Nero, formerly a vigorous partisan of Lucius Antonius. Claudius had fled to Greece with Livia, and their small son, but had returned with his family after the conference at Brundisium. When Imperator Caesar met Livia, pregnant with the unhappy couple's second son, he fell hopelessly in love. Although, according to standard practice, Livia could not divorce and remarry while carrying her first husband's child, Imperator Caesar convinced the *pontifices* to issue an exception in this case. It was a genuine love match. Livia would remain his wife until his death.

By the end of 37 BC it was clear that Imperator Caesar would have to earn his new name and find a way to outwit Magnus, or his career would be over. This was sufficiently obvious for Lepidus to stir himself and bring an army to Sicily for the summer of 36 BC, ostensibly in the cause of the triumvirate, but quite likely with a view to joining whichever side prevailed in the naval war. Renewal of this war was made possible partly by Antonius, who went briefly to Tarentum, leaving there a substantial number of warships in return for a promise of legions to support the invasion of Parthia. At the same time, the two triumvirs agreed to renew their positions for another five years (backdated to 1 January) and to annul Magnus' future consulship.

Antonius' ships joined a new fleet that Agrippa had assembled in the bay of Naples, and had equipped with a new technology. A student of warfare, he was probably familiar with the story that Gaius Duillius had defeated the Carthaginians in 260 BC by using grappling tactics that he had devised to offset the superior Carthaginian seamanship. Agrippa's

16. The young Caesar's dynastic claim to power comes through clearly on this coin, issued in the context of the final campaign against Sextus. On the obverse Caesar is shown still with his beard of mourning for Caesar, the reverse shows the temple of the Divine Julius which was still under construction on the site of Caesar's funeral pyre in the Forum.

plan was to equip ships with grappling hooks that could be fired from war machines, thus turning the sea battle into a land battle.

Despite setbacks at the beginning of the summer, when the fleet encountered a storm and Imperator Caesar botched a landing on Sicily (he fled, leaving his troops behind), Agrippa persisted. In late summer, he won two victories, one at Mylae – the very location of Duillius' triumph – and the other at Naulochus, destroying Magnus' fleet. Meanwhile, Imperator Caesar crossed at Messana with massive new forces, and Lepidus, having decided which side to back, advanced with a large army from the south. Magnus fled east, where after various adventures he was killed by one of Antonius' lieutenants. With Magnus Pompeius died the last vestiges of resistance to the cause of Julius Caesar.

Imperator Caesar now turned his attention to Lepidus, whom neither he nor Antonius trusted. In a move somewhat reminiscent of Antonius' subversion of Lepidus' army in 43 BC – and one no doubt set up through extensive advance negotiation with unit-level officers – Imperator Caesar rode into Lepidus' camp and convinced the army to desert its general. Stripped of his power, though not of the post of *pontifex maximus* that he had claimed after Caesar's murder, Lepidus was sent into what proved to be a lengthy retirement at his villa near Circeii (now Monte Circeo) on the Italian coast.

Imperator, son of the god Caesar, had emerged.

PART V

MONARCHY
(36 BC–AD138)

24

IMPERATOR CAESAR AUGUSTUS

The problems Antonius confronted in the wake of Brundisium and Misenum, although at first less personally threatening than those faced by Imperator Caesar, were none the less severe. Antonius' plan after Philippi had been to pay his army by means of yet another massive fine imposed on the cities of Asia. Now he needed to do something more – reset the Roman frontier system and avenge the Parthian invasion. He had to become the new Gnaeus Pompey, using the east to construct a base from which to rule the empire. Any failure to do so would have dramatic consequences.

Julius Caesar's organisation of the eastern provinces had depended upon Gnaeus Pompey's. That should not be altogether surprising, as both men appear to have taken the view that regional security depended on the alliance between local leadership and imperial governors. Caesar, for instance, had been content to allow Lycia, formerly famous as a nest of pirates, to remain independent, and he had retained Pompey's client kings even though he had good reason to suspect the loyalty of one of them, Deiotaurus, a district ruler (tetrarch) of Galatia in central Turkey. Deiotaurus' own grandson had charged him with plotting to assassinate Caesar during his brief appearance there, but Cicero had successfully defended Deiotaurus during his trial, held at Caesar's house. Elsewhere, Caesar had left in place the rulers he had found, even though they, like Deiotaurus,

17. Portraits of Antonius and Cleopatra on a silver tetradrachm issued in Syria in 36 BC. The coins reflects the integration of the two regimes in the context of the Parthian war. Antony is described as imperator and triumvir, Cleopatra as the 'younger goddess.'

had sent men to fight on Pompey's side – or, as Cicero might have put it, had valued their friendship with Pompey ahead of their friendship with Caesar. Caesar's handling of Deiotaurus was indicative of his desire, at least until he had time to take stock, to maintain the status quo – he probably would have agreed with Cicero that his own achievements had not outshone those of Pompey.

Brutus and Cassius had upset the status quo. They had terrorised the rulers and cities of the east, slaughtering the Lycians and sacking the city of Rhodes, among other indecencies. Although Antonius had been aware of the stress the system had been under when he arrived after Philippi, he could accomplish little of substance. Again, the case of Deiotaurus is telling. He had sent troops to the aid of Brutus and Cassius, but had previously sent Antonius a large gift to secure his throne – which Antonius had retained because the troops, commanded by his secretary Amyntas, had deserted on the eve of Philippi. Also, in what was little more than a year between his arrival and his departure for Brundisium, he had met Cleopatra. After the spectacular encounter in southern Turkey he had accompanied her to Alexandria. She was pregnant with twins by the time he left.

Antonius' failure to establish a coherent relationship with the other dynasts of the east may explain why rulers whose theoretical function was to protect the tax-paying urbanised zones of the west offered no resistance to Labienus.

Antonius would now be more proactive, and he had quite likely laid plans for restructuring the eastern frontier before he returned from Italy. There is evidence that the Senate was rubber-stamping decisions he had made concerning people and places in the east around the time of the treaty of Misenum. When Deiotaurus died, his kingdom went to Amyntas, and Antonius began to rearrange the states of southern Anatolia, delivering them to men who had proved their loyalty during Labienus' invasion. These included Polemo of Laodicea, a respectable public intellectual, and Cleon and Antipater, both said to have been brigands. In the north, in assembling a new kingdom of Pontus for Darius, grandson of Mithridates, he cut loose territory from the eastern edge of the province of Bithynia–Pontus. Cappadocia, occupying a strategic position south of the Armenian highlands stretching west from the Euphrates, had lost its king to Cassius and offered no resistance to the Parthians. Antonius now gave the realm to the deceased king's son Ariarathes, who had once sought Julius Caesar's patronage. In Commagene, at the eastern end of the Anatolian plateau, King Antiochus was accused by Publius Ventidius (probably for good reason) of aiding and abetting the Parthians. But Ventidius, who may well have taken a large bribe from Antiochus, once a client of Pompey's, pursued his removal with less than his usual vigour. Antonius, who certainly received a substantial payment, left Antiochus in place.

Antonius did more than re-establish links with local dynasts: he began the deaccession of territories that were insufficiently urbanised to support a standard Roman administration. Thus Cilicia, once the strategic key to the Roman east as the link between Syria and Asia, vanished. In northern Anatolia, where Darius had died, the Pontic kingdom went to Polemo of Laodicea. Lycia was once again left independent, while Cleon and Antipater were awarded Lycaonia on the northern slopes of the Taurus mountains. Cleopatra received Cyprus and portions of Palestine, the rest of which went to Herod, who, along with his brother, had been appointed as tetrarch to support the Hasmonean high priest Hyrcanus. A Parthian column had eliminated Hyrcanus and Herod's brother while supporting a Hasmonean pretender to the high priesthood in Jerusalem. When the Parthians were driven back, Herod was the only one left. The area to the east of the Jordan river remained under the control of the king of the Nabataeans, based at Petra.

Antonius' arrangements reveal a strategy to provide cost-effective security through a cordon of client kings. Syria, drawing support for any military adventure from these same kings, would remain a forward Roman base against Parthia. The gifts to Cleopatra, which restored previous Ptolemaic territory, were part of the grand plan to reduce the Roman footprint in marginal lands, and might be seen as recompense to Cleopatra for her services against the assassins. Also, she was rich, and Antonius needed her money for his proposed invasion of Parthia; he could no longer rely on extortionate demands for cash if he wished to secure the loyalty of the eastern provinces while continuing to pay his very large army. It was in the planning stage of the Parthian war that the partnership between the two was solidified. Cleopatra became, in effect, the paymaster of the Roman army. Octavia, with whom Antonius had two children, remained in Athens with their offspring as well as the children from both her and Antonius' previous marriages.

In this era of widespread marital infidelity, Antonius' conduct towards Octavia was not seen as especially remarkable. Critics would later stress, not his infidelity, but his penchant for drunken parties and self-display that echoed that of eastern dynasts. More serious than infidelity was the charge that his love life was affecting his judgement. It was rumoured that Archelaus, who replaced Ariarathes as king of Commagene in 36 BC, received the kingdom only because Antonius had had an affair with Glaphyra, his mother. In Rome, reports of Antonius' behaviour might recall Cicero's accounts of his debauchery, especially in the *Second Philippic*, his creative denunciation of Antonius' earlier life that had circulated in the late summer of 44 BC.

Antonius needed now to show that he was still at the top of his game. So in the summer of 36 BC he was at last ready to launch his expedition against Parthia, where yet again there was administrative unrest. The current king, Phraates, had murdered his father Orodes (ruler when Carrhae was fought) and his brother two years earlier. Antonius sent four legions into Armenia to secure the loyalty of its king, Artavasdes, while he assembled a vast army in Syria and demanded that Phraates return the surviving prisoners from Carrhae as well as the standards taken in the battle, plus some lost to Labienus. This was the first time that legionary standards had become such important symbols. Julius Caesar never mentions the need to recover the one his legates lost in the winter of 54 BC, nor does anyone mention lost standards in the more neutral – from Caesar's viewpoint – account of the

Helvetian victory over the Romans in a previous generation. The recovery of standards from the Cimbrians and the Teutons was a non-factor for Marius; and there were peoples such as the Scordisci in the Balkans whose occasional victories over the Romans must have left them with quite a stockpile. In his virulent attack on Piso, Cicero, who was not one to refrain from retailing the embarrassments of those he disliked, never mentions the loss of a military standard that was recovered with some fanfare in 30 BC.

Critics would later write that Antonius botched the Parthian invasion because his infatuation with Cleopatra clouded his judgement. That was not the problem. The problem was that Antonius was careless. Although he could be charming and courageous, he could also be delusional. Seeing himself as somewhat larger than life, he was prone to mistake theatrical grandiosity for careful planning; he could be bad with detail and incapable of seeing the world from any perspective other than his own. So it was in the hope of achieving something great without much effort that he allowed himself to be drawn into protracted negotiations with a brother of Phraates, who had briefly deserted during the spring of 36 BC. Then, when he found the Parthian army massed across his path, he had to turn north to gather his full force in Armenia. Arriving at the end of the summer, he should have stayed put; but he did not, instead resolving to advance through the highlands of Armenia into Media Atropatene (the modern Iranian province of East Azerbaijan).

Antonius proceeded down the valley of the river Ar before turning south to lake Urmia; and then from the valley of the river Barandouz that empties into the lake from the south he turned east to the royal city of Phraaspa, leaving his siege train to play catch-up. But Phraates destroyed the siege train and the force guarding it (while adding to the Parthian collection of Roman standards), which made the siege itself impossible. Antonius was left to fight his way back to Armenia, his army suffering the effects of both the winter weather and a lack of food. It was now that his positive qualities came to the fore, as he inspired his men and in so doing preserved about two-thirds of his original force.

After several months of moping about on the Syrian coast, and having received a serious injection of cash from Cleopatra, Antonius claimed that the campaign's failure was in fact Artavasdes' fault, because the outnumbered Armenian cavalry had not saved the siege train. Now allied with the king of Media (also called Artavasdes), Antonius pursued his Armenia vendetta over the next two summers. During the campaigning season of

34 BC, he finally took Artavasdes the Armenian as prisoner and in 32 BC he received back from Artavasdes the Mede the standards lost when his baggage train was destroyed two years before.

The capture of Artavasdes the Armenian was the occasion for a triumphal procession in Alexandria, at which Antonius announced the reorganisation of the eastern provinces, the upshot of which was essentially that Cleopatra would receive more territory. He also announced his forthcoming divorce from Octavia and his marriage to Cleopatra, and that Caesarion was Julius Caesar's biological child (which he was). He allegedly stated, too, that his three children by Cleopatra, twin boys and a girl, would have kingdoms of their own in the future. For two of them (a son and the daughter) these kingdoms would be carved out of territory that was currently Roman, while the other son, now betrothed to the daughter of Artavasdes of Media, would receive a vast realm constructed from Parthian territory. Or so it was said.

If the story of the future dispositions is true, it would appear that Antonius had a new vision of the world, involving a permanent division of territory between himself and Imperator Caesar, as well as a new understanding of what it meant to be a Roman magistrate (who hitherto had had no authority to give away chunks of the empire). Antonius may have had his blind spots, but he was fully aware that any dispositions he made were subject to approval by the Senate, and the next summer he would need a sympathetic audience in Rome – which makes the story about the announcement of new kingdoms look, at best, an inaccurate exaggeration.

In reality, the administrative structures of Cleopatra's realm were becoming inextricably linked with Antonius' command. Not only had she made significant contributions to the eastern war effort but she was offering generous grants to some of Antonius' generals from her royal estates; and Antonius had broken off relations with Octavia, who had been stranded in Athens since the summer of 35 BC when she had come east with fresh troops for her husband. The acknowledgment of Caesarion's paternity was a direct attack on Imperator Caesar's claim to be Julius' sole heir, and might have been connected with the anticipation of some new division of territory, as triumviral power was due to expire on 1 January 32 BC.

For his part, Imperator Caesar had not been idle. He had campaigned in the Balkans, fighting successful campaigns in the Alps; and in what is now Croatia he had quashed a major military mutiny, finished some building projects and generally tried to make himself agreeable to an

Italian audience as he prepared his coup d'état. He knew that two associates of Antonius were scheduled to be consuls in 32 BC, and that Antonius could, in theory, set a senatorial agenda through them. But their ability to do so was being rapidly undermined. Talk of new kingdoms for Antonius' children was so appalling to Roman opinion that his supporters in Rome tried to prevent Imperator Caesar from disseminating the news – which, in all probability, Imperator Caesar had invented anyway. It was his avowed opinion that Antonius was totally enthralled by Cleopatra, had ceased to be Roman, and had descended into a life of debauchery that corrupted the true Roman virtues. There were, for instance, tales of one of Antonius' entourage, the former consul Plancus, stripping off his clothes, painting himself blue and attaching a fish tail to his naked behind to play the role of a sea god at dinner parties!

The technical issue on which Imperator Caesar would base his claim to power was that his *imperium* as triumvir would not lapse with the office (one thing that he and Antonius could agree upon), so long as he did not cross the *pomerium*. He did not attend the Senate meeting at which the new consul, Gnaeus Domitius Ahenobarbus (formerly Brutus', Cassius' and Magnus' admiral), presided, for that was within the *pomerium*. But the next meeting was not, and Imperator Caesar entered at the head of an armed guard to seat himself between the consuls – through which symbolic act he asserted his superior authority – and read out a denunciation of Antonius' relationship with Cleopatra as 'conduct unbecoming to a Roman magistrate'. The consuls were allowed to leave for Alexandria, as were other senators who felt personal loyalty to Antonius. Several hundred seem to have made the trek.

As the summer progressed, Imperator Caesar launched ever more strident attacks on Antonius, even claiming that he had received a copy of his will from the Vestal Virgins in which Antonius again announced his desire to reside in Alexandria and be buried with the queen. Seeing that war was inevitable, Antonius began to muster a massive army and navy for the invasion of Italy. Cleopatra, who again provided many of the ships and much of the money for the expedition, insisted on accompanying Antonius as he made his very deliberate way towards Actium on Greece's west coast. At some point, possibly as the fleet approached Athens, Antonius sent Octavia a formal notice of divorce, and she returned to Rome.

Imperator Caesar claimed that 'all Italy' swore an oath to support him and asked him to be leader in the war – declared (technically, against

Cleopatra) towards the end of the year. The campaign that followed, in 31 BC, was something of an anticlimax. Antonius had once again botched the logistics, leaving his army stranded at the end of an over-long supply line. Agrippa and Imperator Caesar crossed the Adriatic in the spring with forces to match those of Antonius. There followed a series of engagements in which Agrippa gradually cut off Antonius' communications, and senior members of Antonius' staff, including Plancus and Domitius, deserted.

On 2 September Antonius resolved to fight his way clear from the bay of Actium. We cannot be certain what happened next, but the best evidence is perhaps a remarkable monument from Avellino in Campania depicting the battle as a hard-fought affair, an image corresponding to one version of the story in literary accounts. It is also the impression to be gleaned from a monument that Imperator Caesar later erected in the city, appropriately named Nicopolis (Victoryville), that he founded to commemorate the victory at nearby Actium. That monument contains the prows of ships captured in the engagement. The battle may even have been well-nigh lost when Cleopatra hoisted sail and led an Egyptian squadron in flight from the mêlée, followed by Antonius' flagship. The land army surrendered the next day and was incorporated into Imperator Caesar's army.

Perhaps conscious that future resistance would be deemed futile, Imperator Caesar took his time pursuing Antonius. He first had to quell a mutiny staged by the troops who had been returned to Sicily and Italy after the battle and now wanted to be demobilised; and then to establish his own government of the eastern provinces. On his way to Alexandria, he received the submission of the various kings Antonius had installed; then, at last, nearly a year after Actium, he gathered his massive forces on Egypt's border.

Antonius now endured a series of betrayals as, one after another, his supporters went over to Caesar. Indeed, the higher the rank, the faster the betrayal, so that beyond the Egyptian border the most noteworthy Antonian loyalists were seemingly a bunch of gladiators fighting their way from western Turkey to Alexandria. Once in the capital, Antonius made vain efforts at negotiation. Then, in a final betrayal, Cleopatra herself opened talks with Imperator Caesar behind his back.

But there was no deal to be made: Imperator Caesar, who really wanted both Antonius and Caesarion dead, had already made too much of Cleopatra's corrupting influence, and he had other agents at work. So it was that, when his forces approached Alexandria, after some desultory fighting Antonius' troops surrendered. Hearing that Cleopatra had committed suicide, Antonius stabbed himself, then learned that she had merely betaken herself to her tomb, whence he had himself brought to die in her arms. What happened next is not known, except that Cleopatra died. It was allegedly suicide, brought about by a spectacular failure of security when the guards posted outside her tomb failed to notice the asps being transported into her quarters.

The kingdom of Egypt was the great prize of the war. Still wealthy and producing a surplus of grain, it was to be treated with care. Imperator Caesar determined that it should not pass from his direct control. No senatorial governor was to be appointed – rather, he would appoint an equestrian who would report directly to himself as its ruler. The first governor was Cornelius Gallus, a capable soldier and famous poet, friend to both Propertius and Virgil as well as lover of one of Antonius' old flames, an actress called Volumnia.

With victory secure, Imperator Caesar could begin the gradual restructuring and repurposing of the Roman army. This meant reducing the number of legions from something like eighty to a more manageable and affordable twenty-six, twelve of them units that had long been in his service (and in some cases, his father's), the rest taken over from Lepidus and now from Antonius. Antonian veterans demobilised at this point were settled in provincial colonies; Caesar's, many of whom may have served for no more than a year or two, may simply have gone back home and received a cash bonus and a land grant to thank them for their participation. New soldiers would be expected to serve for sixteen years, the theoretical maximum in previous generations. The legions themselves were located in potential hotspots such as Spain and Gaul, as well as Syria and Egypt. Two legions were assigned to Africa, and some to the Balkans.

Even as the reorganisation of the army was in train, answers to the question of what the new political order would look like were beginning to surface. When news of Alexandria's capture reached Rome, the Senate had voted that a triumphal arch be erected in the forum along with many other marks of distinction. At the beginning of 29 BC it had voted that the gates to the Temple of Janus be closed, symbolising that the state had now won the peace: a little optimistic, since there were still a few wars raging in the provinces. Imperator Caesar was also awarded various attributes of tribunician power. Since 36 BC he had been deemed 'sacrosanct' (inviolable), a status recognised as more honorific than practical; now he was granted the right to bring aid to citizens (the tribunician *ius auxilii*) across the whole empire; and if there was a tied verdict in any jury trial, anywhere, his vote would be counted as being for acquittal.

The new arrangements in the eastern provinces occupied Imperator Caesar for the better part of a year. They included the development of provincial cults honouring him – perhaps the sort of thing that Caesar had imagined for himself before his death, though these would not be accompanied by any public cult in Rome. The need to make new connections meant a long, slow trip; Imperator Caesar only returned to Rome to celebrate a triple triumph on 13–15 August 29 BC for his victories in Dalmatia, at Actium and at Alexandria. Other features of this special event were generous distributions of cash to citizens and soldiers, and quite astonishing spectacles – beast hunts involving rare animals, among them the first ever rhino in Rome, gladiatorial contests and theatrical events. All could join in celebrating the dawn of the new era.

Victory won, Imperator Caesar needed to decide his own political future.

Antonius was not alone in his predilection for evoking images associated with eastern potentates. In the previous few years Imperator Caesar had adopted increasingly regal and divine forms of display before settling on a patron divinity, Apollo, about the time that he had defeated Magnus. Apollo was something of a novelty in this role. Sulla, Pompey and Caesar had all stressed the guardianship of Venus, as a goddess of fortune; Antonius claimed Hercules as an ancestor. Apollo, god of prophecy and culture, was the antithesis of Dionysus, whom Antonius often invoked along with Hercules, and was renowned as a destroyer of barbarians. It was, then, altogether appropriate that, as the war with Cleopatra got under way, the crowd would be able to look up from the chariot races in the Circus Maximus to see a new Temple of Apollo arising alongside Imperator Caesar's residence on the Palatine. The temple would be formally dedicated on 9 October 28 BC.

This was but one of a number of projects to commemorate the role of the Caesars, father and son, in perpetuating Rome's greatness. The Temple of the Divine Julius, begun in 42 BC on the spot in the forum where Julius Caesar's body had been burned during his funeral, was dedicated thirteen years later; it would receive spoils from the triumphs, as would the Temple of Capitoline Jupiter (usually the home for war booty).

Imperator Caesar may have fallen nearly as far short of his father's intellectual ability as he did of his physical courage, but that was actually an advantage. Unlike Julius, he knew he had to work with others and that those individuals deserved public recognition. Statilius Taurus, who, like Agrippa, lacking any senatorial ancestors, had commanded the land forces at Actium and had already been allowed to build Rome's first permanent amphitheatre in his own name, on the Campus Martius. Plancus (the former exotic dancer, soldier and consul) had repaired the Temple of Saturn. Pollio built a massive shrine to the goddess Libertas to which he attached a public library, while Quintus Cornificius, an important commander in the fight against Magnus, fixed up the Temple of Diana on the Aventine and Marcius Philippus repaired the ancient Temple of Hercules and the Muses.

Imperator Caesar encouraged men who had celebrated triumphs to contribute funds to urban beautification – as peace came, the leaders of Roman society collectively improved the city and, beyond that, Italy's road system. Agrippa was everywhere, and Maecenas, who had managed Imperator Caesar's interests while the war with Cleopatra ran its course, was likewise highly visible. In a further piece of political theatre Marcus Licinius Crassus, grandson of Caesar's old partner, claimed both a triumph and the *spolia opima* for victories in the Balkans, the first person to make such a claim since Marcus Claudius Marcellus in 222 BC. But, Imperator Caesar explained, this was not possible since Crassus had been operating as a proconsul and thus with inferior *imperium*. It was an important point, because Imperator Caesar was now attempting to bring order to the somewhat chaotic understanding of *imperium* so as to ensure that he could run the empire by virtue of his own *imperium* as a consul.

Crassus agreed not to claim the *spolia*, thereby consolidating Imperator Caesar's constitutional claims. In so doing he was following the current fashion, set by Agrippa, of egotistical self-secondment to the spirit of the harmonious new age. Crassus also celebrated a triumph in the summer of 27 BC, and his deeds would subsequently be trumpeted by historians friendly to the Augustan regime. He, along with the others celebrating triumphs in 27 and 28 BC, represented a governing class reunited after the era of civil war, delighting in the construction of a new Rome on a bed of barbarian corpses.

The ideology of shared victory was linked with one of shared propriety, especially among members of the upper classes. One of the tasks that

Agrippa undertook with Imperator Caesar was the censorship, which the two of them held in 28 BC. Reform of the Senate was on that year's agenda as well. Nearly 200 men were removed from its rolls – fifty who had taken the hint and resigned voluntarily and 140 who found their names posted on a list. The purge may not have been unconnected with rumblings of discontent in previous years, not least concerning an alleged conspiracy led by the son of Lepidus, who had committed suicide when the plot was uncovered.

In purging the Senate, the censors also sought to display their concern for ancestral institutions by increasing the number of patricians on the grounds that more were needed for the continuation of (largely religious) traditional practices. Senators as a group were forbidden to leave Italy without permission, and urged to attend meetings regularly. At the same time the censors announced the astonishing result of their efforts at counting the population: there were now more than 4 million Romans! It is not entirely clear how this demographic miracle was achieved (the censors of 70 BC had counted around 900,000 souls). Quite possibly this number represents not just the males, but also the women and children, who would usually figure in the censuses conducted at various times in the provinces.

Demographically curious though Caesar's census might have been, it did have both ideological and practical significance. The increased population mirrored the health of Roman society. So it was that, learning that the 'Republic was restored' (*Laudatio Turiae*, col. 2.25–8), an aristocratic couple who had lived through hard times apparently celebrated the glad event with enthusiastic fornicating. But the child they hoped for never arrived to enjoy the blessings of the new age.

At the time he dedicated the Temple of Palatine Apollo, Imperator Caesar was himself undergoing a painless, if scarcely superficial, transformation. Governing now as consul (he had held the office every year from 31 BC onwards), he finally gave up his power as triumvir and, as he would later put it, 'restored the state from his control to the determination of the senate and people of Rome' (*RGDA*, 34.1). A coin minted in the year 29 BC displays an image of him sitting on his magistrate's chair holding out what is most likely the text of an edict through which 'he restored laws and statutes'. He would say later that he undid everything unjust that had been done during the triumviral period. An echo of the language of this decree is preserved by Cassius Dio, now our best source for these matters. He writes of the 'very many illegal and unjust regulations during the factional strife and the wars, especially in the period of [Imperator Caesar's] joint rule with Antonius and Lepidus' (Dio 53.2.5). That was now long in the past. The triumviral era may have ended, too, but what now lay in store?

On 13 January 27 BC, Imperator Caesar announced that elections would now be open competitions; the Senate thanked him and awarded him a new cognomen, Augustus. Henceforth he would be known as Imperator Caesar, son of the divinity, Augustus (we will call him Augustus from here on in). He thanked the Senate and agreed, upon their urging, to take up the management of numerous provinces, largely ones with armies, for a ten-year term, as consul or proconsul. As a Greek contemporary put it:

> When his fatherland bestowed upon him the principal position of leadership, and made him lord of war and peace for life, he divided the whole realm into two parts and assigned one to himself and one to the people. To himself he assigned as many as had need of military garrisons (that is to say, the part that was barbarian or near to unsubdued barbarians or was poor or difficult to farm, so that, while unprovided in everything else, they were well provided with strongholds and prone to rebellion), to the people he gave the rest in so far as they were peaceful and easy to govern.
>
> (Strabo, *Geography*, 17.3.25)

In theory, Augustus would be a normal consul with a few extra honours such as tribunician powers, and a multi-provincial command, larger indeed than those of Lucullus, Pompey or Caesar, but still conferred in the tradition of pre-triumviral Rome. It is striking that in our contemporary's view the power to rule those provinces not assigned to Augustus was that of the people, and that Augustus himself was the creation of the 'fatherland'. It is indicative of the symbolic importance to Roman life of voting that the restoration of regular elections for the consulship mirrored the restoration of consensus in public life, which was the essence of traditional government restored.

Elections might now be 'open', but the consular list indicates the power of the victorious faction. Augustus had shared the consulship of 29 BC with his nephew Sextus Appuleius. Agrippa was consul with him in 28 and 27 BC, then Statilius Taurus in 26 BC; in 25 BC it was Junius Silanus, whose life epitomised the crises of the previous decades. In his youth he had been one of Julius Caesar's legates; hated by Lepidus, he was proscribed; rescued by Magnus, he returned after the peace of Misenum and took service with Antonius; hated by Cleopatra (so the story goes), he changed sides before Actium. Augustus' consular colleague in 24 BC was Gaius Norbanus Flaccus, whose father had played a significant role on the winning side at Philippi; and for 23 BC it was Varro Murena, who had a family connection with Maecenas and had recently served with Augustus in Spain.

The Spanish campaign had begun in 26 BC, the primary event in a three-year absence from Italy planned to drive home the significance of Augustus' grand governorship. The war itself, however, may have been something of an accident. Augustus had been aiming for Britain, people were told. But competition with his father's deeds would have to be postponed, he realised, when trouble broke out in northern Spain. Augustus went in person, which seems not to have been a good idea. The Spanish tribes in the foothills of the Pyrenees and in the western reaches of the peninsula were a tough bunch. He became ill, as he was wont to do when danger reared its head, and withdrew to Tarraco (today's Tarragona), whence he could offer 'strategic advice' while his generals won a few battles. By the end of 24 BC he felt that enough had been achieved to declare victory, return home and shut the gates of the Temple of Janus yet again.

Two things emerged from this campaign. The first was a new Spanish city, Augusta Emerita (modern Merida), where a large group of veterans were settled; use of provincial locations, founded or refounded as Roman colonies, for veteran settlement would hereafter become standard. The other was Augustus' realisation that he was not cut out for soldiering. He would never again take direct command in battle.

While Augustus was away, Agrippa had continued the process of transforming the Roman cityscape with new victory monuments and the architecturally adventuresome temple to 'all the gods', the Pantheon, which stands today in the heart of Rome. He also redesigned the voting area on the Campus Martius, building fancy new 'pens' in which voters would stand while waiting to cast their ballots. Voting in 'the restored Republic' was meant to be orderly.

At about this time Augustus himself appears to have completed a new building on the Campus Martius, close to the banks of the Tiber: a massive mausoleum, also still standing, for himself and his family. It was a statement: in the restored Republic Augustus' family would be *a* dynastic family, as the Scipios had been, but not necessarily *the* dynastic family. Unfortunately for Augustus, in the summer of 23 BC the mausoleum received its first occupant. This was his nephew Gaius Claudius Marcellus, husband of his daughter Julia and the man believed to be next in line for Augustus' *statio*, his position in the state. He had died of a nasty illness that had spread even among the rich; indeed, Augustus himself had very nearly died of it that same summer.

Illness and the Spanish campaigns raised questions about the stability of the regime. So did an expedition to Yemen commanded by the prefect of Egypt. The aim was to seize control of an important outpost in the lucrative spice trade between the Indian Ocean and the Mediterranean. The expedition had not been a total success and was presented now as a 'recognisance in force'. This offered a stark contrast to campaigns that had ended in the triumphs celebrated by Crassus, Messalla, Carrinas and Autronius, and indeed to campaigns waged subsequently by Appuleius in Spain, by Marcus Vinicius against the Germans and by Lucius Antistius in Spain during Augustus' illness. Nor did it help Augustus' overall reputation that there was a crisis in Macedonia, where the governor Marcus Primus was charged with having waged an illegal war. He was tried for treason, offering as his defence that either Marcellus or Augustus had authorised his action. The defence was weak, but Augustus' refusal to provide an alibi angered a son of Licinius Murena, the consul in 62 BC, who had served as Primus' lead defender.

Before the end of 22 BC, the Murena who had been Primus' advocate constructed a plot to murder Augustus. Clearly, for all that his popularity with the Roman people remained intact, and even after he had formally changed his state function during the summer of 23 BC, annoyance was surfacing among the aristocracy. The likely cause was that while he was ill he had handed his seal ring to Agrippa, thereby implying that Agrippa would continue in a similar position to him; but there was no way within the traditional structure of the state for him to do that.

Two new constitutional status markers were created to define the stations of Augustus' chief men. These were tribunician powers, and *maius imperium* over multiple provinces, probably defined as '*maius imperium* in any province into which [the holder] should come', which was in addition to Augustus' *imperium* as a proconsul in those provinces that were under his direct rule. The new powers could co-exist for extended periods; hence, after he laid down his consulship in 23 BC, the Senate voted Augustus both tribunician power and *maius imperium* for a term of five years. It awarded a similar honour to Agrippa, who was now married to Julia, while his own daughter Vipsania had married Tiberius, the oldest of Livia's boys by her previous marriage.

Tacitus, who wrote a brilliant history of post-Augustan Rome from AD 14 to 96, would later refer to tribunician power as the 'term for the highest position' (Tacitus, *Annals* 3.56.2), which indeed it would become, though it took a while for this to become apparent. It gave its holder the power to summon senatorial meetings, to introduce legislation and call voting assemblies, to veto motions in the Senate, and to bring aid to a Roman citizen anywhere in the empire. Tribunician power would be held only by members of the immediate imperial family.

The settlement of 23 BC created the terms under which imperial power would be exercised for centuries. When at the year's end a rumour spread of an imminent grain shortage, a riot broke out. To solve the crisis, people demanded that Augustus be made dictator – a demand that surely demonstrates the popular misconception of just how much power he possessed. Augustus refused the dictatorship, which had never been reinstituted after its formal abolition in 44 BC. He did, however, accept the old Pompeian post of director of the city's grain supply for five years. At that point he left town for a while for, although he remained popular with the mass of Rome's people, his military failures needed to be removed from the governing class's view, lest further questions be raised about his fitness to be the state's commander-in-chief – and then, possibly, the regime's ideology could be subtly shifted to play down the persistently militaristic tone.

The proximate cause of Augustus' departure was a potential crisis on the eastern frontier, a situation that would give rise to a claim that he was trying to rectify old failures. About the time when the conflict between Augustus and Antonius was winding down, a civil war had been raging in Parthia, and once again the loser had taken refuge in Syria. Also, Augustus had received one of Phraates' sons as a hostage, which, given the fratricidal habits of the Parthian royal house, was a way for Phraates to ensure his son's survival. In 23 BC Phraates had asked that his former rival Tiridates and his own son be handed over. The first of these requests Augustus denied, but agreed to the second if Phraates would return both the standards taken from Crassus and any captives still alive. This Phraates is said to have acquiesced to, but by 22 BC he had done nothing. His failure to keep his promises gave Augustus the excuse to head east.

The expedition would last four years and was more of a grand tour than a military operation. Phraates was not interested in fighting, and Augustus was not keen to force the issue. Much of the time he spent in Athens or on the island of Samos. He never reached the Euphrates frontier; the standards and the surviving prisoners were received back by Tiberius, who was by now a potential heir apparent. When the Armenian king Artaxias, son of the Artavasdes whom Cleopatra had killed, was assassinated in the year 20 BC, Tiberius was charged with ensuring the succession of his brother Tigranes. The arrangement seems to have been thoroughly agreeable to the Armenian nobility even though the change of regime meant a tilting of allegiances away from Parthia and towards Rome.

Regarding the new Roman alliance as protection against his domestic foes, Phraates delivered even more of his children to Augustus. So it was that, by exploiting Phraates' domestic troubles, Augustus secured the northern wing of the eastern frontier. Pompey's plan for that frontier was at long last confirmed. And how appropriate, since Augustus' remit, stemming from the vast extraconstitutional powers granted him by statute, for fixed terms, had itself evolved from the positions Gabinius and Manilius had created for Pompey in the 60s BC. Augustus knew that to govern he had to function within and alongside the traditional institutions of the Republic, not above them, which had been the version of autocracy favoured by Sulla and Caesar. The end of the civil war represented a compromise between Caesar's politics and Pompey's vision.

25

THE AUGUSTAN EMPIRE

n 19 BC Augustus returned to Rome in a blaze of glory. Standards had been recovered, kings installed, royal hostages taken – and all without significant loss of life. The Senate decreed that the consul Quintus Lucretius, accompanied by some of the praetors and tribunes, should go all the way to Campania to greet him on his return to Italy. That was an unprecedented celebration.

Rome had not been exactly peaceful while he had been away. There was considerable popular unrest and unease at the thought that Augustus would not be consul. In 22 BC, the voters had elected only one consul and, when he returned, Augustus had to order an election of the second (which was marred by corruption). The censors elected for the year fell to quarrelling and failed to complete their task. Agrippa had returned from the eastern expedition in 21 BC (a sign that significant combat had not been anticipated) but was forced to head off to Gaul and Spain, where there was some serious fighting. The result was further tension in Rome and, in 19 BC, there was again only one consul. The problem this time was that a man named Egnatius Rufus was trying to make the (illegal) jump from aedile to consul based on the popularity he had gained from organising a fire brigade the year before. The driving force behind these electoral spats appears to have been the desire of voters in the first census classes for guaranteed order – which was why a man like Egnatius Rufus, who put fires out, could be a serious candidate even though Augustus did not like him. While Augustus was on his way home, it was discovered that Egnatius had formed a cabal to assassinate him. It is not clear that the case ever came to trial but Egnatius did not survive even to Augustus' formal return.

The combination of a general desire for effective administration and the continuing unease about the future underlies the next great transition in Augustus' vision of government. This was a vision based not so much upon public law and the creation of new offices as upon tradition and marital bliss (which, it transpired, was something to be legislated). To take the lead in this programme, Augustus had to bury his own past very deeply. It was not just that his marriage to Livia was scandalous – that was long ago in the past, and people were getting used to the increasingly public role that the sons she had had by her first marriage were coming into play. It was the fact that Antonius could produce an ample list of women with whom Augustus might have been sleeping when not with her. His lecherous inclinations were sufficiently well known that his associates had to claim that he was only sleeping around to learn the secrets of his enemies. Then there was the boyfriend. At a party in Alexandria, a friend of Antonius had put Cleopatra's nose a bit out of joint when he complained about the bad wine, speculating that Sarmentus, Augustus' *paidiskos* ('boy toy'), would be drinking better. If the Roman world was to be reformed, serial fornication would have to go. Sexual predation was the act of a tyrant, as everyone steeped in the traditions of classical thought would have known. Augustus was not a tyrant. To know that, all one had to do was ask him.

No sooner had Augustus returned from the east than the process of moral reform began in earnest. The operative principle for Augustus was the same as that which lay behind Sulla's reform. This was the idea that a good constitution shaped people who behaved well within it. Augustus, too, was aiming to create the best possible aristocrats to help run the state.

In 19 BC the Senate had granted Augustus the right to exercise consular authority within the *pomerium* (a measure designed to calm disquiet at his not being consul) and the title of 'guardian of customs and laws' (*cura morum et legum*), which granted him the power of a censor to reshape the domestic order. With Agrippa at his side, he initiated the thorough reorganisation of the senatorial and equestrian orders that would continue for the better part of the decade.

In the Senate's case, there were two principles at work, one of which was that 'respectability' in the eyes of fellow senators was a necessary qualification for rank, the other being personal wealth. The aim was to produce a functional body consisting of the respectable rich. To evict people, Augustus invented a process whereby a select group of thirty of the 'best men' would each select five men who would be guaranteed membership in the Senate, then one man from each group of five would be selected to choose another five men. At this point the whole thing seems to have become too complicated, there were claims that some people were protecting unworthy friends, and Augustus declared that since the Senate had failed to police itself, he would do the job himself (probably his intention from the start). He posted a list of 600 men, and imposed a new census qualification for membership. To be a senator one now had to have property valued at 250,000 denarii; previously the minimum requirement had been 100,000, which was what was still required to be entered on the list of the equestrians. Senators had already been forbidden some 'disreputable professions' (e.g. acting), and were now forbidden from marrying women who were too far 'beneath' them – such as their freedwomen or the actresses and courtesans with whom they had been consorting for decades.

At about the same time that he introduced the new requirement for membership of the Senate, Augustus reinvented the old ritual of public inspection for the equestrian order. This 'approval of the equestrians' (*probatio equitum*) had been a traditional feature of the censorship, when membership of the equestrian order had been based upon membership of the eighteen centuries of equites 'with the public horse'. But those traditions had fallen by the wayside, and a *probatio equitum* had certainly not been seen in Rome for more than forty years after Pompeius had presented himself to the censors of 70 BC. It may only have been resurrected for the censorship of 28 BC, but now it became something quite different: an annual 'review of the equestrians' (*transvectio equitum*) which was linked with an 'examination of the equestrians' (*recognitio equitum*) by a board of three senators who approved the moral fitness of the members of that order. The equestrian order, now reinforced by hundreds of men who had been expelled from the Senate, was no longer to be the Senate's judge and jury, or even identified as the mouthpiece of the contractor class. Its purpose was to support the Senate and offer an example of ideal conduct for the lower classes. At a separate ceremony, 14-year-old boys from families with the property necessary to support a senatorial career were reviewed, it seems by Augustus himself. If they passed inspection, they received the 'broad stripe' (*latus clavus*), a purple band that was sewn on to their togas signifying their eligibility to stand for senatorial positions when they reached their twenties. In the meantime, they were to attend Senate meetings so that they could become accustomed to appropriate senatorial behaviour.

The 'purification' of the Senate occupied the latter part of the year 19 BC, and the ceremonial enhancement of the equestrian order may have fallen in the same year or a year later. It was certainly in 17 BC that the most radical measures were put into action as a way of celebrating the dawn of a new era, or *saeculum*. Unlike for the previous two (or three) celebrations of the secular games, Rome was at peace. The new *saeculum*, the seventh of Rome's existence (so it was now determined), would be the best ever. Records of the year, inscribed on a massive stone stele, have survived revealing a series of nighttime processions and sacrifices presided over by Augustus and Agrippa, with the assistance of the members of the College of Fifteen for Making Sacrifices. There were to be six sacrifices, three at night, three in daytime, between the evening of 31 May and the afternoon of 3 June. Theatrical performances and chariot races would follow the daytime sacrifices, and then there would be seven more days of the same once the sacrifices had been concluded. Augustus was present at every sacrifice and, on the last day, a hymn composed by the famous poet Horace was sung by a chorus of twenty-seven boys and twenty-seven girls whose mothers and fathers were still alive. On opening night, Augustus himself had offered the following prayer, mingling archaic-sounding sentiments (and using the ancient term for Romans, the Quirites, to refer to both subordinate Latins and the people of Rome) with utterly contemporary references to himself:

O Fates! As it has been prescribed for you in those books – and by virtue of those things may every good fortune come to the Roman people, the Quirites – let sacrifice be made to you with nine ewes and nine female goats. I beseech and pray to you, just as you have increased the empire and majesty of the Roman people, the Quirites, in war and in peace, so may the Latins ever be obedient; grant everlasting safety, victory, and health to the Roman people, the Quirites; protect the Roman people, the Quirites, and the legions of the Roman people, the Quirites, and keep safe and increase the state of the Roman people, the Quirites; be favourable and propitious to the Roman people, the Quirites, to the College of the Fifteen Men, to me, to my house and

my household; and be accepting of this sacrifice of nine ewes and nine
female goats, perfect for sacrificing ...

(*Commentarium Ludorum Saecularium Quintum* 92–8)

Horace's poem had done the same, invoking the memory of Rome's
foundation while also praising the new law governing marriage, which,
continuing a theme emerging from the annual inspections of the equestrian order and the 'cleansing' of the Senate, extended the reach of the state
into the private lives of Roman citizens. Roman women were now encouraged to have three children. Men whose wives had the requisite number
of children could hold office before the legal minimum age; those who
had no children would be cut out of wills. And spouses were supposed
to be faithful. Adultery was declared a public crime, to be prosecuted
before a new standing court. Given the personal lives of the Roman upper
class in the previous half century, this was a major change. But family life
was now public life. It was in this spirit that Augustus had uttered the
opening prayers of the secular games before 110 married women and why
the children who sang Horace's hymn had to have living parents.

The new model family was that of Augustus. Reorganised after the
tragedy of 23 BC, when Marcellus had died, it had Augustus and Agrippa
representing the hope of current prosperity, Tiberius and his brother
Drusus representing the hope of the next generation, and Julia – who was
now having a lot of children – appearing to guarantee the more distant
future. It was an ideal family, dedicated to the service of the state, taking
pride in ancestral offices and winning ever more victories over barbarian
peoples. It was a family that needed to be seen in the context of the greater
and longer history of Rome. To help reinforce the message, Augustus
could rely upon the efforts of sundry men of letters.

Horace is the only person named in the record of the secular games
who was not a sitting magistrate or a member of the College of Fifteen.
That surely reflects both his own prominence and the prominence cus-
tomarily attributed to successful public intellectuals. A generation before,
Cicero had, in defending Archias, a Greek poet whose claim to citizenship
was questioned after he had written an epic poem (in Greek) to honour
Lucullus, described huge crowds that had turned up to listen to his recitations (also in Greek). Horace's more standard appearances would have
included the performance of poems in various metres adapted from the
Greek, on themes ranging from love and the good life to the evils of civil

war, the demise of Cleopatra and advice to various public figures such as his special friend Maecenas, as well as Plancus, Pollio and Sallustius Crispus, the adopted son of the historian Sallust, who was now employed by Augustus for confidential assignments.

Agrippa seems not to have liked Horace, who rarely mentions him. But Horace thrived, none the less. Other poets, too – Propertius, for instance, who had lamented so memorably the ruin of Perugia and celebrated the joys of love (and of the charming Cynthia) as opposed to war – found time to compose on other themes that Augustus favoured. Propertius devoted attention to some of the ancient myths of Rome and the battle of Actium. Pride of place, however, went to Virgil.

Shortly after Augustus' return from the east, however, Virgil dropped dead in his villa near the bay of Naples. This was a tragedy, if for no other reason than that his greatest poem, the *Aeneid*, which was by now well known through public recitations, lay unfinished. The villa had been a gift from Livia, moved to tears by a vision of Marcellus in the underworld at the end of a procession of spirits heading for reanimation as Rome's greatest heroes. The great Pompey had been there as well, as had Caesar, who was briefly admonished for starting the civil war. That was more than Pollio had ventured, whose history of the civil wars would have appeared during these years. Horace knew that Pollio set the beginning of the conflict at the alliance between Caesar, Pompey and Crassus in 60 BC. More than that, though, in the *Aeneid* Virgil had shown Rome's founder himself to be human, a man who could be led astray, uncertain of the future, and deeply in need of divine guidance. Yet Aeneas accomplished the great feat of bringing the Trojan survivors to Italy to join with the Latins and beget the line that would found Rome itself.

Mingled with predictions of limitless imperial glory and visions of civilisation's gods amassing to drive off the monstrous divinities of Egypt at Actium are Aeneas' grief at breaking off his affair with Queen Dido of Carthage – deeply unhappy, cursing him as he sails off – and his rage when he sees Turnus, leader of the Latins, wearing a belt ripped from one of his men. It is this rage that prompts him to kill Turnus. Only then can peace be made, and the Trojans unite with the Latins. Augustus asked two well-known poets who were friends of Virgil to edit a final version of the *Aeneid*, the one we have now.

In composing the epic poem, Virgil had drawn not only upon the traditions of Italian history and mythology, but also, as was true of every significant Latin author since Naevius, on the traditions of Greek poetry from Homer onwards. Knowledge of Greek theory was important for prose writers, too, but Cicero gave it a particularly Italian spin, and now the conventions of the two languages were beginning to exercise a reciprocal influence on each other. Cicero had drawn on the style of 'Attic' orators of the fourth century BC – especially Demosthenes, whose attacks on Philip II of Macedon had provided the title for Cicero's oeuvre against Antonius, the *Philippics* – but also on the more florid traditions current among contemporaries in western Turkey. Augustan tastes, generally, turned far more pointedly in the direction of Demosthenes, creating the school of Attic oratory that was now shaping contemporary expression in Greek.

A high priest of the new style was Dionysius, from Halicarnassus in western Turkey. In addition to works on rhetoric addressed to important Romans, he compiled a voluminous account of Roman antiquities which proved that the Romans were really Greek. It was now important for both Greeks and Romans to be able to integrate the history of Rome into that of the wider world.

Even before 'Atticism' invaded the eastern Mediterranean, there had been historians of the Polybian sort who had written contemporary history offering a local take on Roman affairs. Posidonius, whose description of the pro-Mithridatic faction at Athens we found sharing the political tendencies of Sullan narrative, was a case in point. He was later asked by Cicero to produce a Greek history of the events of 63 BC; he refused, saying that he could not match Cicero's deathless Atticising prose. Pompey's powerful assistant Theophanes of Mytilene had written a history of the great man's doings, and in the next generation Timagenes of Alexandria wrote a history in which various Romans appeared in less than flattering portrayals. Such works mirrored the politicised contemporary histories, along with the memoirs of Sulla, Caesar and now Augustus himself, who wrote an autobiography offering the Roman public his perspective on events from Caesar's assassination into the 20s BC.

Sallust's history – with its anti-Sullan, though not obviously anti-Pompeian, slant – was the previous generation's best-known history, but he was reacting to an extensive history of the social and civil wars by Cornelius Sisenna, a man of decidedly right-wing views who had defended Verres against Cicero. Sallust said that Sisenna was not nearly as critical of Sulla as he might have been, but this was not an issue with the work of Licinius

Macer, an anti-establishment tribune of the 70s BC who was elected to the praetorship in the early 60s BC. Licinius may not, however, have got all that far – he fell down dead on the day he learned that he had been convicted of extortion during his governorship of Africa, at a trial over which Cicero, as praetor, presided. Then there was Lucceius, a failed consular candidate aligned with Caesar in the year 60 BC, who wrote a long history of the same period as Sisenna and, like Posidonius, turned down the opportunity to write a special account of the key year 63 BC, even though Cicero offered him his notes.

Cicero's interest in being the object of a special history reveals the importance accorded to historical writing in aristocratic circles. Even when deeply partisan, it stood for the idea of truth. This much Cicero allowed when he said that the first rule of historical writing was that the author should not lie; Pollio claimed to have corrected errors in Caesar's writings. Of course, the narrative should also be entertaining. Some writers of the previous generation had attempted to move beyond contemporary events to cover the whole of Roman history – a case in point being Valerius Antias, probably writing in the 70s and 60s BC, who was notable for the wildly exaggerated numbers he attributed to enemy casualty lists. His rough contemporary, Claudius Quadrigarius, eschewed the earliest history of Rome as fantasy and began with the Gallic sack. Skipping rapidly over the years between 390 BC and the tribunate of Tiberius Gracchus, his history none the less grew exponentially.

But whatever their perspective on events, what all could agree on was that Roman history had changed course in the later second century BC. It had become very nasty indeed. The question for historians of the Augustan age was this: would it change course again? Livy was the man to answer that question.

Livy, like Virgil, became famous well in advance of the completion of his work – which in fact would not be until after Augustus' death. The story goes that one man came all the way from Spain just so that he could say he had seen him. Another Spaniard, Lucius Annaeus Seneca, an aficionado of rhetorical training also known as the Elder Seneca (we will meet the Younger Seneca in a couple of chapters' time), offers insights into the literary world of the time through a remarkable work in which he recollects all the best rhetorical exercises of his era. He was aware, of course, of Livy's glory, but also of Pollio's belief that he himself was the foremost man of letters of these years. Pollio was powerful enough to tell Augustus off when the emperor complained later that he didn't take proper account of his grandson's demise – Pollio accused him of having conducted business in public very soon after the death of his own son – and took umbrage when Messalla suggested that Cicero was still the greatest man of letters in the Latin language. Pollio had pointed out that Cicero could be obnoxious; in a similar vein he had said that Livy was at heart a small-town boy (although the same could have been said of Pollio).

Still, Augustus liked Livy. He also called him a 'Pompeian' – a term that meant something very different in his mouth from when his adoptive father used it. And this is key to Augustus' programme of reshaping the public memory of his era.

A 'Pompeian', in Augustan terms, was not a supporter of Gnaeus Pompey, and certainly not of his dreadful son Magnus, now to be remembered as a pirate. It would have been meaningless as an ideological designation while Pompey was alive – as Cicero said, in private, there was no difference between what he wanted and what Caesar wanted. It was also likely to mean nothing to Pollio, which might explain why he found Livy so irritating. Nor did it mean that one disapproved of Caesar, exactly. Livy sang Caesar's praises at enormous length, we are told in a summary of his books that has survived intact from the second century AD. What emerges from this is that the Italian war was for him, as for other historians of his time, the decisive moment in Roman history, the point at which everything changed.

But why did it change?

In Livy's view, it changed because of the irresponsible conduct of the tribunes of the plebs. Tiberius Gracchus was dreadful, and Gaius was no better; Saturninus was a nightmare, as was Livius Drusus, who had single-handedly triggered the Italian revolt. About the only thing the tribunes did right in the late Republic was to propose Pompey's great commands. Livy did not need to poke about in the archives to come up with his view of tribunician disorder. He appears to have shared some false ideas about Tiberius' programme with Cicero, who saw the latter as a catastrophe whose agenda violated the agreements made with the Italians.

Cicero was generally back in vogue. Seneca, who reproduces various discussions about the man – in which only Pollio stresses the negative points – notes that his own teacher, Cestius Pius, said that if only Caesar and Pompey had listened to Cicero there would have been no civil war. There is a story that when Augustus found his grandson Gaius trying to hide a book of Cicero's from him, he assured the young man that Cicero had been a great Roman. His murder was Antonius' fault, after all. This is something Livy made crystal clear – his Cicero had warts, but 'in weighing his faults against his virtues, he was a great and memorable man, and to sing his praises one would need Cicero himself as the eulogist' (Seneca, *Advisory Rhetorical Exercises* 6.22).

The pleasing fantasies in which Livy enveloped the earlier history of Rome are preserved for us because they interested senators of the fourth century AD, who prepared the editions from which the surviving manuscripts derive. Tribunes and the like held no appeal for them: they wanted ripping yarns about kings and conquerors, not detailed accounts of the political struggles of the late Republic, which was the key point for Livy; and Livy's Pompey supported tribunes who knew their place, who were therefore ideal for the Augustan age now that there was a *statio*, as Augustus called his position, that prescribed properly exercised tribunician power.

In laying out his history 'from the foundation of the city', Livy benefitted from Augustus' notion of its foundation date, calculated by Terentius Varro. Roman history was not simply a series of edifying tales; it also had to place the Roman experience in the broader context of meaningful accounts of the past. To do this, lists that could be reconciled with other lists were drawn up. It had begun to happen in Pompey's lifetime. The first man to reconcile the Greek system of dating according to the four-year Olympic cycles (Olympiads) with a list of consuls was Castor of Rhodes; then Romans took up the challenge, including Cornelius Nepos, a friend of the great poet Catullus. By aligning Olympiad dates with consular lists he produced synchronisms between great events in earlier Roman history and equivalents in the history of Greece.

The project was taken up by Cicero's great friend Atticus, who wrote his own chronicle of world history. Nepos' and Atticus' chronicles, like Castor's, have not survived, but we can gain some impression of what they achieved through the work of Diodorus Siculus, whose *Library of History* has offered us crucial information about the outbreak of the First Punic War, slave revolts in second-century Sicily and the outbreak of the Social War. He also commented on the Egyptian reverence for cats and on Caesar's deification.

List-making was very important to Augustus – he requested a list of the greatest Romans of all time so that he could include their images in a portico he planned to build alongside the massive Temple of Mars the Avenger in the new forum that was under construction to the north of Julius' Temple of Venus. The display of illustrious Romans would bear inscriptions describing each man's service to the state. A second portico would contain images of his own family members, including Romulus and Aeneas, the progenitors of the Julian clan. These two porticos together made Rome's heroes a matter of public memory and community history. All the heroes of the past could perhaps be seen as equivalent to the Julii.

In the old forum, where the Senate had voted to erect a triumphal arch in honour of the battle of Actium and to expand it to commemorate the triumph over Parthia, would be inscribed a list of all Romans who had celebrated triumphs, beginning with Romulus. These included the names of those they had defeated and, according to the Varronian dating system, in what year after Rome's foundation. Augustus also had a list of consuls inscribed on the walls of the Regia. Again, the aim was to codify a record of Rome's greatness as a community achievement.

The inscriptions in the forum set a fashion for the rest of Italy, where inscribed calendars (*fasti*) begin to appear, bringing Roman time and Roman history into the heart of the urban environment, sometimes employing prominent intellectuals such as Verrius Flaccus, an expert on Roman antiquities, to do so. Quite often these displays consisted of a calendar with inscriptions explaining important dates and with space to allow for updating. Important men began to post texts listing their offices in ways that were plainly influenced by the texts in Augustus' gallery of heroes.

The interest in chronology was but one feature of a new Augustan impulse for measurement. The gradual transformation of Roman government in the next few decades was not so much a matter of deliberate policy, though some changes – such as altering the position of legion chief-of-staff (*praefectus fabrum*) from one held by senators to one held by equestrians – were certainly deliberate. When given the choice between creating new systems and practices, or not, Augustus tended to go for it.

In the fifteen years after Actium his two most significant changes were the formation of a professional long-service army based in the provinces and the creation of a relatively coherent tax system. Instead of basing provincial taxes on the best bid that a corporation of *publicani* could offer, they would now be based on regularly held, thoroughgoing provincial

18. The enormous Temple of Mars the Avenger (Mars Ultor) was completed in 2 BC as the centrepiece of Augustus' new forum.

censuses. The amounts imposed would vary from province to province according to local custom, but the state could predict income and expenditure with some degree of accuracy, even while it continued to depend, quite often, on subsidies from Augustus' personal fortune. When Luke the evangelist wrote that Jesus of Nazareth was born when 'Cyrenius was governor of Syria' and that a decree had gone forth from Caesar Augustus that all the world should be taxed, he was reflecting a provincial perspective on Roman government. Luke's 'Cyrenius' was in fact Publius Sulpicius Quirinius, governor of Syria in the year we now call AD 6; he held a provincial census in the year of his governorship.

The transformation of the army was no more sudden than was the transformation of the tax system. In 13 BC, however, Augustus may have faced an unusual problem, in that the men who had been recruited immediately after Actium were due for retirement, so it was proving difficult to find new land in which to settle them. The turnover among the military rank and file gave Augustus, in consultation with the Senate, an opportunity

19. It was once believed that the person honoured on this inscription, found at Tivoli, was Sulpicius Quirinius and the last line 'as pro-praetorian legate of the divine Augustus for a second time, he obtained the province of Syria and Phoenicia' was mistranslated to imply that he had been governor of Syria twice, the only way of preserving the integrity of Gospel accounts of the birth of Jesus which combine Quirinius with Herod.

to alter the terms of service for the new recruits: they were told to expect generous cash payments at the completion of their sixteen years, rather than the land grants of earlier eras. Augustus had spent a lot of his personal wealth on land for veteran settlements the year before. He may have introduced a new regulation forbidding serving soldiers to marry – a regulation that was largely ignored, but which made an ideological statement about how Roman citizens in the legions should remain separate from the provincials among whom they were now living for prolonged periods.

Even as the new army was being raised, new campaigns were being launched both in Gaul and against some Alpine tribes who were stubbornly maintaining their independence. The Gallic campaigns, which opened along the Rhine in 16 BC following German raids and the loss of a standard, were serious enough to require Augustus' presence to support the operations from a safe distance to the rear. The leadership of the Alpine campaigns had been assigned to Tiberius and to Drusus, his younger brother, to demonstrate their readiness to step up if something should happen to Augustus or Agrippa.

The campaigns along the Rhine proved successful; so, too, the Alpine campaigns. And the publicity back in Rome succeeded in promoting a positive image. On the domestic front, the long-overdue death of Lepidus permitted Augustus to hold an election for a new *pontifex maximus* – himself. Great crowds, Augustus said later, came from all over Italy to elect him to the post. To commemorate the event, he inaugurated a new altar of peace near his family tomb on the Campus Martius. The processions that visitors can still see decorating the altar may recall his assumption of the priestly office.

Then it all started to go wrong. Agrippa died in the year 12 BC. A part of the oration that Augustus delivered at his funeral has survived, stressing the important role that Agrippa had played as his associate:

> The tribunician power was given to you for a term of five years in the consulship of the Lentuli, and once again for another five years in the consulship of Tiberius Nero and Quinctilius Varus, your sons-in-law, and into whatever province the affairs of the Roman people should call you, it was ensured by a law that no one in those provinces would have greater powers than yours.
>
> (*GC* n. 294)

Here Agrippa appears as another Augustus, so it was appropriate that his body be buried in Augustus' family tomb, where he was shortly to be joined by Octavia, Augustus' sister and Antonius' widow. Three years later, Drusus, too, would be buried there. The author of a long poem offering consolation to Livia on her son Drusus' death notes the griefs of recent years:

> We have seen him [Augustus] mourning for the offspring of his sister, torn away; that grief, as in Drusus' case, was public; he placed Agrippa in your tomb, Marcellus, and already the tomb held his two sons-in-law, and scarcely had the door of the tomb been closed, with Agrippa laid to rest, then, behold! His sister receives the last rites. Behold! Three times already have the rites been given, now, with the latest funeral, Drusus is the fourth to have tears from great Caesar.
>
> (Ovid, *Consolation for Livia* 65–72)

While Drusus' death was a family tragedy, his achievements were set in a traditional context, for his ancestors would receive him, we are told, decked out in the glories of consular command and bearing the standards taken from the Germans.

Drusus had proved to be an able soldier, campaigning during the years 12–9 BC and laying the foundation for a new province between the Rhine and the Elbe, in western Germany The campaigns had not been uneventful – at some point tribes had ambushed him on the march, and one year he had experienced difficulties getting his fleet home. Tiberius, meantime, had campaigned in southern Germany and in the Balkans, leading columns from the Adriatic north towards the Danube in the region then known as Pannonia (now southern Hungary). In the east the Parthian king Phraates, worried about the well-being of his family in the brutal world of Parthian politics, dispatched four of his sons to be raised under Roman protection.

Tiberius could be difficult and was somewhat less popular than his brother, for all that both were quite able in the performance of their duties. The poem about Drusus' death mentions Tiberius' carefully contrived facial expression (*vultus*), which would become something of an issue as his effort to exhibit utter impassivity in public was taken as a sign that he was given to deceit. But Tiberius was the eldest and, in the Augustan scheme, the most eligible successor.

But what *was* Augustus now? There was still no definition of his role, other than that he was the most important man in the world. He spoke of his *statio*, but this was still an ad hoc collection of positions that required renewal. The way to become *like* Augustus, as the example of Agrippa showed, was to hold similar positions: the way to assemble an appropriate curriculum vitae to build a *statio* like Augustus' was via traditional offices. That much is abundantly clear in the poem quoted above, where Livia is told how happy she should be that, even as the gods joined mortals in mourning his death, her son had been consul, and that both her sons had proved their worth by fighting beyond the boundaries of the empire.

With Drusus gone, the succession was once more a work in progress; given the family mortality rate, it was plainly necessary to prepare several members for the role. Tiberius, though promoted and sent back to the Rhine in the year 8 BC, was not the only show in town, and his frequent absences left space for younger family members to attract public attention.

One issue, as far as Tiberius was concerned, was his relationship with Julia, whom Augustus had compelled him to marry when Agrippa died (forcing him to divorce Agrippa's daughter, whom he genuinely loved). The truth was that they hated each other. Julia's two elder sons by Agrippa, Gaius and Lucius, were growing up, and the former was replacing the absent Tiberius on some public occasions. In 6 BC Gaius was elected consul, by popular acclaim, for 1 BC; Augustus complained that he was too young, worrying publicly that all this attention would impinge on the modesty he desired in the young man. Tiberius was no fool: he could tell that Julia's children, Augustus' biological progeny, were being groomed to take leading positions. Would there be room for three men at the top? Triumvirates tended to lose their third members rather quickly.

Rome was where the action was. But Tiberius kept being sent on campaigns – first to the Danube; then, in 6 BC, as instability threatened Roman influence to Armenia. Although he was granted tribunician power Tiberius decided that he had had enough. He refused to do what Augustus told him to. He retired to Rhodes where he wished to live as a private citizen, he said.

Tiberius' departure left Augustus with a problem: the wars had to continue to be waged and Gaius was too young to take command. There were senior members of the Senate who would readily accept the opportunity to win military glory in the service of the state. That being so, how important was Augustus, really? He was in his early sixties now and not getting any younger – of that he was painfully aware. Was his approach to the succession perhaps a little blinkered? Were there others who might step forward? It was crucial that Gaius get a chance to prove himself. He would go east to deal with the Armenian situation even before taking up his consulship in 1 BC; at the same time, in a carefully crafted piece of political theatre, Augustus tearfully accepted, on the commendation of the Senate, the title of 'Father of the Country' from the Roman people. Cicero had once been named Father of the Country by senatorial decree, for having quashed Catiline's conspiracy. It is perhaps ironic that Augustus himself would suddenly be embroiled in controversy and conspiracy.

Shortly after Gaius left town with great fanfare, his mother was arrested and exiled. She was charged with having violated her father's adultery laws with an impressive assortment of middle-aged members of Rome's elite, including Iullus Antonius, Antonius' son by Octavia, who had been consul himself a few years earlier. Iullus committed suicide. Julia was exiled to Pandateria off Italy's west coast. Augustus was mortified.

There was worse to come. His adopted son Lucius, dispatched to Spain in AD 2, expired in Marseille. Gaius was still in the east, where he had benefitted from regime change in Parthia: Phraates IV had succumbed to a conspiracy launched by his son, who now took the throne as Phraates V. Even though Gaius covered himself in glory for his successful negotiations with the Parthians on the banks of the Euphrates, the succession now hung by a narrow thread, unless Tiberius returned from Rhodes. Tiberius was duly summoned, and it may be that friends of his in Rome forced Augustus' hand, for he does not seem to have been overjoyed to see him. He was asked to remain out of public sight, which he did, until word came that Gaius had died suddenly of an illness, on 21 February AD 4.

An inscription recording the honours voted in his memory at the city of Pisa mirrors the way Gaius was imagined at the time and how deeply embedded in the traditions of previous generations the expressions of power still were. Like Agrippa and Drusus before him, he can be seen as a super-magistrate somewhat in the tradition of Pompey:

> Since on 2 April news was brought that Gaius Caesar, son of Augustus, father of the country, *pontifex maximus*, guardian of the Roman Empire and of the whole world, grandson of the Divinity, after his consulship, which he bore successfully, waging war beyond the farthest boundaries of the Roman people, doing well by the State, conquering and receiving into *fides* the most warlike and powerful nations, he, having received wounds on behalf of the State, was torn by the cruel fates from the Roman people, being a man already designated as a *princeps*, as being most just and most like his father in his virtues.
>
> (*ILS* 140: 7–12)

It was only now, as Tiberius re-emerged from internal exile, that Augustus, possibly with the younger man's assistance, began to see that change was inevitable. Government needed to become less personal, more bureaucratic. As Livy, reimagining the past, by now would have been working his way through the era of the civil wars, Augustus was coming to imagine a new future.

26

ECCENTRICITY AND
BUREAUCRACY

The year AD 6 was notable for nativities. One of these, in Palestine, was that of Jesus of Nazareth. The date of his birth was later erroneously set in the consulship of Gaius Caesar and Lucius Aemilius Paullus (our I BC), but our AD 6 was the year Publius Sulpicius Quirinius held that census in Syria with which the Gospel of Luke connects the birth. That census came about as Quirinius reduced a part of the former kingdom of Herod, who died in 4 BC, to the status of a dependency of the province of Syria, to be governed by an equestrian official or a prefect. This decision was taken because Herod's appallingly badly behaved son Archelaus had massively upset his subjects, who had asked Augustus to intervene on their behalf. Augustus banished him to Vienne in the Rhône valley.

The other birth is figurative and took place in Rome, where Augustus set up the structures necessary to ensure the long-term administration of the city and the empire. These included a regular police and fire department for Rome, and a new method of guaranteeing the retirement bonuses for soldiers, stabilising their terms of service in what was now recognised as a long-term army, permanently based in the provinces. Within the next year or two a new arrangement for ensuring Rome's grain supply would be up and running. All three systems would still be functioning in the fourth century AD.

Bureaucracy is a cure for eccentricity. It may be dull, but it creates systems that function even when executive power is operating with marginal efficacy. The development of a bureaucratic, as opposed to a political, Senate, which could fulfil the responsibility of running an empire, had begun after 19 BC. The crucial features of Augustus' programme were: senators must appear regularly for work; the number of assignments available to men between magistracies must be increased; a special advisory council, on which senators rotated in six-month terms, should be developed; changes in electoral procedures and in the criteria for office (chiefly as relating to personal behaviour and census qualifications) should be introduced.

Some of these changes were responses to difficulties such as an unwillingness to stand for the aedileship, which required holders to sponsor expensive games that were no longer of value in furthering their political careers; or to stand for the tribunate of the plebs, now considered somewhat déclassé because activist tribunes were blamed for past troubles. Other changes, especially those concerning elections, may have derived from demands that the process become less risky as the potential rewards diminished. One might still be consul, but no one could imagine himself occupying an equivalent *statio* to Augustus and his family members. At the same time, since holding traditional offices of state came to define a princely career, it was important for those offices to appear desirable. Indeed, office-holding as a state service had to become a status marker in its own right. The creation of new posts was an administrative default setting when problems arose, while rules governing attendance, personal behaviour and census qualifications were designed to enhance the overall dignity of the order.

Augustus' advisory council probably came into existence in 18 BC, at a time when he was intending to be more regularly resident in Rome and was dealing with the fall-out from his second 'purification' of the Senate. The council's primary function, other than giving magistrates a chance to get to know Augustus (and vice versa), was the drafting of legislation; and now, it appears, some *senatus consulta*, largely on administrative issues, obtained the force of law. The convention whereby the *comitia centuriata* passed laws conferring important political appointments was retained – it was through this process that grants of *imperium* were conferred on Augustus and family members – and the *comitia* also dealt with laws such as those governing marriage.

But on other issues, such as corruption and some matters of public morality – for instance, whether men and women of the senatorial and equestrian orders could fight as gladiators or appear on stage as actors – a *senatus consultum* had the authority of a *lex*. It may have been in the Senate in AD 8 that Augustus established that the state could force the sale of slaves who might be tortured for evidence against their masters. This was an extension of earlier invasions of matters domestic: Augustus had already allowed slaves to testify against their owners in adultery cases and to expose criminal conduct with respect to the grain supply. In 4 BC Augustus advertised the fact that his council had drawn up a new procedure for hearing extortion cases that was more fair to provincials, and in AD 13 his council was given legislative authority because it was now difficult for him to attend Senate meetings.

The restoration of 'free' elections had symbolised the restoration of the Republic in 28 and 27 BC. For Augustus, elections represented the stability of the political order and the friendship of the gods towards the Roman state, so it was important that they be orderly and inclusive. To this end Agrippa had built some elaborate new voting booths on the Campus Martius, and Augustus made provision for civic magistrates throughout Italy to send in their votes. This last may have happened earlier, when 'all Italy' was probably invited to swear an oath of loyalty and, as he put it, 'asked him to be the leader in the war' against Antonius. It was also symbolic of the link between elections and the Augustan *statio* that in AD 5 a law was passed adding ten new voting centuries to the first census class, in honour of Gaius and Lucius Caesar.

Thanks to the details on an inscription recording the new regulations, we have a glimpse of the ceremonial world of Augustan elections: on the day when the senators and knights shall be present to cast their votes, we are told, the presiding magistrate, with the praetors and tribunes of the plebs sitting beside him, will put out ten large wicker baskets

> in order that the voting tablets may be placed in them, and he shall order that as many wax tablets as he thinks necessary will be set out next to the baskets; and he shall have a care that the white boards with the names of the candidates written on them shall be placed where they can be most easily read, and then, in the sight of all the magistrates and of those who are about to cast votes, sitting on benches ...
>
> (*RS* 37–8:19–22)

The magistrate would then order that thirty-three balls, one for each tribe (excluding the two in which no senators or equestrians were registered), be placed in a rotating urn

> and that the allotment be announced and then carried out to determine which senators and which equestrians ought to cast a vote and into which basket.
>
> (*RS* 37–8: 24)

The theory here was that the random assignment of the upper classes into centuries that would vote first would show who the gods favoured – and, now that the gods were so closely involved, minimise the opportunity for anyone to rig the results. For Augustus it mattered that corruption should still be considered a potential problem, so that it could be seen to have been successfully guarded against, even if the results would rarely have been in doubt. He had gradually been given the right to 'nominate' his preferred candidates for the consulship, and most for the praetorship, even being able to 'commend' some individuals who would run unopposed. He would not name preferred candidates for *all* the praetorships, and in the end this caused stress, because people wanted the assurance that they would win if they stood.

Despite the importance that Augustus attached to office-holding, finding the people to fill those offices was becoming problematic. The census qualification – possessing 250,000 denarii – appears to have been a genuinely high bar. In 13 BC, when there were not enough candidates for the tribunate, men who had been quaestors were allowed to run for the office even though they were below the minimum age (probably thirty at this point). Augustus also compelled some equestrians who possessed the census qualification to become senators. This was not a popular move, however, so when there were too few candidates the next year, he allowed equestrians of the appropriate census rating to be tribunes without being quaestors first.

Being a senator could be a drag if one was after a life of leisure, for there were now so many new posts – to do with the treasury, road inspections and other public services – that senators were expected to volunteer for if they wished to advance. But even if they were ambitious, most would still not rise beyond the level of praetor because even with what became the regular appointment of two sets of consuls every year – the 'ordinary consuls' who opened the year in office and gave it its name, and the 'suffects', who held office from July onwards – there were only four annual vacancies (or fewer, if Augustus or a member of his family wanted the position) and usually sixteen ex-praetors. Indeed, one reason some post-praetorian careers were expanding may well have been because it was hard to find people who saw any point in continuing their political lives after that point, making it harder to fill ever more administrative positions. Also relevant is that in 13 BC Augustus had reduced the number of pre-senatorial positions, usually held by young men aspiring to senatorial office, from twenty-six – the number during the Republic – to twenty. In AD 5 he allowed the consuls for the year to issue a 'note' changing the minimum ages of thirty and thirty-five for the quaestorship and the praetorship that had been enshrined in his marriage laws of 18 BC to twenty-five and thirty respectively.

Just as the Senate was a work in progress, so, too, was the administration of the city of Rome. The two big moves of AD 6 came at the end of long periods of experimentation. Fighting fires had always been a problem – in previous generations it had largely been a matter of private enterprise, as we saw earlier (Caesar's partner Crassus was notorious for the way he used his personal fire brigade to help increase his property holding at knock-down prices). In 26 BC, Augustus had ordered the aediles to take over fire protection (with no extra funding); four years later he assigned 600 public slaves to work for them, but that, too, turned out less than satisfactorily. In 7 BC, he had divided Rome into fourteen regions and transferred fire-fighting duties within them to local magistrates; then when that did not work, he organised 3,500 men into seven cohorts of *vigiles* ('watchmen'), protecting two districts each, and placed them under the command of 'the prefect of the watchmen,' (*praefectus vigilum*) who would report directly to the palace. This was one of the big changes of AD 6.

Food was another major problem. In 18 BC, Augustus had entrusted oversight of the grain supply (the *annona*), under his personal control since the year 22 BC, to four former praetors. This system seems to have broken down over the years, and in AD 6 he appointed two consuls to the task; a year later an equestrian prefect, the 'prefect to the grain supply' (*praefectus annonae*), took over. The prefect to the grain supply and the prefect of the watchmen joined the equestrian prefect of Egypt and the prefects (usually two) to the imperial guard (*praefecti praetorio*), all serving at Augustus' pleasure as the state's senior equestrian officials. Even if the creation of this group was the gradual response to earlier failures rather than part of some master plan, it none the less represented a radical shift. There had been no equestrian officials holding offices of such significance in the previous 700 years of Roman history.

The major equestrian offices at Rome were associated with the palace, where a much wider ranging bureaucracy was evolving. Augustus needed not only to manage the spectacles that were becoming an ever more central part of his brief, all of which required a staff, but also to ensure that the appurtenances of his properties were kept up to scratch, that good food was on the table when guests arrived, and that the people in his service were properly dressed. Although most of his staff were slaves, he insisted that some basic tasks be shared with the family – for instance, he expected that the women of the household spend their time weaving. Then, there was a corps of people who handled his correspondence, the key figures being the secretaries 'for Latin letters' and 'for Greek letters', who often drafted responses for Augustus' approval. As many matters that came his way involved the law, he also developed a legal staff. Jurisprudence as an intellectual discipline had become increasingly important in previous generations, so that professional jurists, usually equestrians, sometimes senators, were employed at the palace.

The palace network extended far into the provinces where Augustus had vast estates, and his financial managers assumed administrative roles as representatives of the state as well as of Augustus personally. A fascinating document from around 15 BC reveals the interplay between communities, the palace and one of his local representatives, a procurator (manager) in the province of Asia and the governor who, as a proconsul, was not Augustus' direct appointee, and who writes:

> Gaius Norbanus Flaccus, the proconsul to the magistrates, city council and citizens of Aizanoi, greetings. Menecles, Hierax and Zeno, your ambassadors, presented me with the letter of Augustus Caesar, in which he wrote that the procurator, Ofilius Ornatus, had allowed you to hold a meeting concerning freedom from taxation for a priest because of the sacrificial ceremonies, but he did not allow the city to contribute to the other expenses. Wishing, for my part, to enhance the benefits your city enjoys, I permit, in accord with what was authorised by Caesar ...
>
> (*AE* 2011 n. 1303)

Flaccus' good manners here disguise the fact that the people of Aizanoi had gone behind his back, through the procurator, to Augustus himself seeking permission to give one of their fellow citizens a tax break. They had also hoped that the man might be given some further privileges. Ornatus, who may have smelled a rat, suspecting that a person of wealth was trying to wangle greater benefits from his office, limited the city's response to the tax break. Having noted that Augustus appeared to be open to offering enhanced benefits, our text breaks off at the point where the governor looks like he is going to overrule the procurator. What emerges from all this is that the emperor had, via his financial officials, built up a network that ran parallel to that of the state. Moreover, a governor who wanted to overrule a procurator could do so by pointing to the fact that he was acting in the spirit of Augustus' earlier ruling.

Augustus had financial interests throughout the empire, but his resources were not infinite, and as the army expanded – reaching twenty-eight legions – he had to shift the expenditure from his own budget to that of the state. So it was that in AD 6 he set up a state treasury to pay soldiers retirement bonuses. The mass demobilisations from the post-Actian army in 13 BC had led to retirement benefits being calculated in cash only (see p. 295), but in 2 AD (another year of mass retirements) Augustus had been short of the cash needed. Consequently, he ordered that men be held in service under 'emergency' conditions for four more years. But now their payment had come due and the soldiers were openly mutinous, so he offered a one-time grant to create a new treasury that would subsequently be funded with tax revenues. When he asked the Senate to propose an amount, its members – who would be the ones paying it – could not come up with one. Augustus then proposed a 5 per cent tax on inheritances and created a board of three ex-praetors to oversee its levying. Terms of service were also reset, so that twenty years became the norm for legionaries and sixteen for the imperial (praetorian) guard, whose members would also receive substantially more money than the fellows on the frontier.

The theory that lay behind this law – that wealthy people should pay for a government service rather than be paid for it – constituted a fundamental shift away from the practices of the fiscal–military state of the pre-civil war era.

Just before he died, Augustus advised that the empire be kept within the limits defined by the river Euphrates in the east, the Danube in central Europe, and the Rhine and the Elbe in the west. Exactly when he determined these limits is not known, but they were certainly defined by AD 6 when Tiberius headed off to the Balkans to ratchet up the subjugation of the suddenly restive peoples of the region. Cities were being built north of the Rhine, and three recently raised legions were assigned to a base close to the Elbe. Drusus had established that armies could be floated from the mouth of the Rhine and into central Germany.

Strategic decisions were made in Rome, but the process through which they were made involved considerable communication between Augustus and his subordinates. It is via the suddenly enhanced documentary record of the period that we glimpse how this was achieved: provincial communities, invariably the source of documents reflecting Roman rule, were making ever more extensive records, on non-perishable materials, of their dealings with the central government. Two items in particular reveal the mechanisms through which information passed back and forth. The first is the record of a settlement with a Spanish tribe in 15 BC; the second, a remarkable legal inscription from Cnidus in the province of Asia in 6 BC. The first reads as follows:

> Imperator Caesar, son of the Divinity, Augustus, in the eighth year of his tribunician power, and proconsul, said:
>
> I have learned from all my legates, who were in charge of the province of Transduriana, that the *castellani* Paemeiobrigenses of the nation of the Susarri remained dutiful when all others were deserting. Therefore, I give all of them perpetual immunity, and I order that they hold those lands, within those borders, which they possessed when my legate, Lucius Sestius Quirinalis, held the province, without controversy.
>
> In place of the *castellani* Paemeiobrigenses, of the nation of the Susarri, to whom previously I have granted immunity in all matters, I restore in their place the *castellani* Aiiobrigiaecini, and I order the *castellani* Aiiobrigiaecini to perform all duties with the Susarri ...
>
> (*AE* 2000 n. 760)

The province of Transduriana was a short-lived administrative entity in northern Spain where there had obviously been a revolt in which one subgroup of a local tribe, the Susarri, did not participate. The governor, Augustus' legate, has decided to grant this subgroup, the *castellani* Paemeiobrigenses, privileges for their loyalty, and to adjust the boundaries of the area to include a new subgroup that would contribute to the tasks assigned to the Susarri – largely, we may assume, the payment of taxes. Although the matter is presented as Augustus' decision, it was the governors who possessed the local knowledge needed to make these arrangements, and it looks as if Lucius Sestius Quirinalis or his successor (or both) decided what should be done and got Augustus' approval for it. The *castellani* Paemeiobrigenses, delighted by what happened, recorded the decision on the bronze tablet that has survived to this day.

As a method of government, this procedure can be observed via Caesar's account of his conquest of Gaul, as he spent his winters in northern Italy and left the army to his legates. In 54 BC he had been sorely disappointed by his legates Sabinus and Cotta, who, he felt, should have written to him for advice about threats from the people with whom they were quartered – when they went to leave camp, their men were massacred – whereas he praised his legate Quintus Cicero for staying put and keeping him informed. Caesar implies that his legates should have been aware of the way he would respond. Similarly, in this case, it is unlikely that the legates would have acted as they did if they had not thought Augustus would approve. Indeed, it is likely that before they left Rome they had received general instructions (*mandata*) outlining the policy as well as on how to apply the *mandata*. It is also very likely that, before issuing the *mandata*, Augustus would have consulted people with direct knowledge of the area in question – in a letter to Tiberius he mentions playing dice with Silius Nerva and Marcus Vinicius, a pair of ex-consuls who had recently commanded armies in the Balkans.

The Cnidus case resembles the Aizanoi one, in that the protagonists bypassed the governor to access Augustus directly. In making his decision, Augustus was acting both on information that had reached him directly from a local source and on what he felt to be the principle on which government should be based. He wrote:

> Your ambassadors, Dionysius II and Dionysius II the sons of Dionysius, came to me in Rome and gave me the decree accusing Eubulus son of Anaxandrides, now deceased, and Tryphera, his wife, present here, of the murder of Eubulus the son of Chrysippus. I ordered my friend Asinius Gallus to interrogate those of the household slaves who were involved in the case under torture, learning that Philinus the son of Chrysippus attacked the house of Eubulus and Tryphera for three

nights in a row, by force and in the manner of a siege, that he brought
his brother Eubulus with him on the third night, that Eubulus and
Tryphera, the owners of the house, neither by negotiating with Philinus
nor by building barricades were able to be safe from his attacks in their
own house, assigning one of their slaves not to kill them, as one might
be inclined to do out of justifiable anger, but to drive them off, by scat-
tering the household excrement on them. The slave assigned the task,
whether willingly or unwillingly – he denied it steadfastly – let go of
the chamber pot and Eubulus fell under it although it would have been
more just for him to be spared than his brother. I have sent you the
records of the interrogations.

(GC n. 6)

Given the document from Aizanoi, dating to a few years before this
one, it should not surprise us that Augustus says he 'ordered' the senatorial governor Asinius Gallus (Pollio's son) to conduct the investigation.
Augustus became aware of the case because the victims had fled to Rome
to complain of their treatment, and it looks like the initial embassy from
Cnidus turned up because Augustus had demanded to know if he was
being told the truth. Augustus saw his job as protecting the 'common
safety of all', so he was appalled to find out what had happened, and that
the aggressors had not been charged.

One reason why this procedure was so important for provincial government was that it made clear who was responsible for a disaster that struck
in AD 9. At that point, the bulk of the army, commanded by Tiberius,
was completing the reconquest and reorganisation of Balkan lands that
had risen in revolt. At the same time, in Germany the governor Quinctilius Varus, who as Agrippa's son-in-law was very close to the imperial
family, received warning that a revolt was brewing in the lands separat-
ing his camp near modern-day Minden in west central Germany from
the garrison cities on the Rhine, near the modern cities of Nijmegen in
the Netherlands and Xanten in Germany. Although he was an experienced official, having previously governed Syria successfully, he must have
consulted Augustus before deciding, that autumn, to withdraw the three
legions under his command to the Rhine.

But, leaving his base, Varus marched straight into a trap laid by Julius
Arminius, the chieftain of the Cherusci, an important tribe in the area, who
had earned Roman citizenship through his service in earlier campaigns.

*20. In 1987 Major Tony Clunn, a British army officer, began uncovering large
numbers of coins with a metal detector this area near Osnabruck in Germany.
It has subsequently been identified as the (or a part of the) area where Varus'
legions were destroyed. The area in the centre shows the reconstruction of the field
fortifications from which the Germans launched their attacks on the Romans.*

The battle lasted for several days until Varus' army was annihilated. When
he received the news, Augustus is said to have roamed the palace exclaim-
ing, 'Quinctilius Varus, give me back my legions!' (Suetonius, *Life of
Augustus* 23), thereby planting the blame for the defeat squarely on the
general's shoulders. Others in Rome accepted his view and subjected
Varus' son to public shaming. But this could not change the fact that the
decision to pull the legions back to the Rhine was Augustus', or that after
the Balkan war there was no money for new troops. Tiberius was sent with
troops from the Balkans to retrieve the situation.

Despite Tiberius' victory in the Balkans, Varus' defeat came at a
difficult time for Augustus. In AD 5, popular unrest compelled him to
allow his daughter Julia, who remained popular despite the scandals of 2
BC, to return to Italy and take up residence in Reggio. In AD 9 he gave in
to pressure to allow major reforms to his marriage legislation through the
lex Papia Poppaea, a measure brought before the Senate by the consuls of
that year. His willingness to do so may not be unconnected with the fact
that the year before there had been another domestic scandal. Augustus'
granddaughter, also called Julia, was found to be pregnant, but not by her

husband Aemilius Paullus, who refused to acknowledge that she was an adulteress. Both were exiled and the baby, a boy, was killed – although their surviving daughter Aemilia was adopted by her uncle, who was an ally of Tiberius, and would go on to play her own role in the domestic politics of the era.

Additionally, there was a suggestion that Augustus' surviving grandson, Agrippa Postumus, who had been under house arrest since he was ousted from the line of succession for erratic conduct in AD 6, was conspiring against Augustus (a charge possibly connected with the ongoing outbursts of unrest). He was now sent into exile on the island of Pandateria, off the coast of Naples, while at least one other perceived enemy of public order was shipped off to Tomis (today's Constanța) on the Black Sea. This person was the poet Ovid, who would remain there until his death in AD 17, having created a substantial collection of poetry in which he asked to be allowed to return home. It becomes clear in these poems that after AD 9 he saw Tiberius as the guiding force in Roman politics, but when he found he was getting nowhere with him he began to address himself to Tiberius' nephew and adopted son Germanicus, who had taken over command on the Rhine from Tiberius.

In AD 13 Tiberius was formally given powers equal to Augustus' in all the provinces. In the summer of the next year Augustus, now aged seventy-six, showed signs of terminal illness. Livia took him to the family villa near Naples and summoned Tiberius to his bedside. Tiberius, who was en route to the Balkans, hastened to see him. It is unknown if he arrived in time. Rumours of all sorts abounded as to his accession – people who did not like Tiberius, of which there were plenty, suggesting that Augustus might try to restore Agrippa Postumus to public life. No one knew what to expect when the dominant force in Roman politics – albeit more symbolical than actual in his declining years – would no longer be present. On 19 August AD 14 it was announced that Augustus had died at his villa at Nola, in the room in which his father had also died.

Cornelius Tacitus, began his *Annals* with the accession of Tiberius, thinking that the successful transition of power marked a crucial turning point in Roman history. He was right, but Augustus may not have been fully aware of what his legacy would be. A few years before his death he had written to Tiberius, who was something of a workaholic, to say that if he and Livia should hear that he had become ill, they might themselves die and the 'Roman people would be shaken with respect to the most important aspects of its empire' (Suetonius, *Life of Tiberius* 21.7). Such language reveals that while Augustus believed he had created a unique *statio*, he had no idea that he had built such a stable framework for government that it would last for 1,800 years, the last person claiming to hold an office descended from his *statio*, the last Holy Roman Emperor, only abdicating on 6 August 1806. It is ironic that his abdication was forced by the emperor Napoleon, who took his inspiration from Roman history: whose armies marched behind eagles; who had studied Caesar's commentaries; and who claimed to be the 'best of the race of the Caesars'.

By now, public funerals for members of the imperial house were well-practised events, and Augustus was cremated on the Campus Martius after Tiberius had delivered a eulogy in the forum. His ashes were placed in the great mausoleum by the banks of the Tiber, where the record of his deeds that he had composed in the months before his death would soon be inscribed on two bronze tablets by the tomb's entrance, quoting decrees in his honour and listing his many accomplishments.

The funeral's aftermath was considerably more interesting than the event itself. One senator swore that he saw the genius of Augustus, the divine spark that was within him, ascending to the heavens to join the gods. The Senate would duly vote for the creation of a new state cult in his honour. At the meeting that followed, Tiberius delivered an address and had Augustus' will read out, along with his final memorandum listing the assets of the state and offering advice for the future – namely, that wars of expansion should cease. The Senate clamoured for more, in response to which Tiberius delivered a truly awful speech that left everyone confused as to his intentions. Would he or would he not accept Augustus' *statio*? He agreed to do so. The Senate then passed a bill that appears to have conferred upon him powers that were neither part of his tribunician authority nor the granting of authority equal to Augustus' in all the provinces. Some of these have survived in a document composed in AD 70 listing the powers of the emperor Vespasian, who took office that year.

The outcome of this meeting was that there was now, for the first time, a document spelling out the job of the person who could now be called *princeps*.

Tiberius' son Drusus by Agrippa's daughter and his adoptive son, his biological nephew Germanicus, were next in line for the office. Drusus was a few years younger, so Germanicus was regarded as the immediate heir apparent and received the most important command, avenging what

21. The Temple of Rome and Augustus in Ancyra, Turkey. The best, most extensively preserved text of Augustus' account of his life – the 'Deeds of the Divine Augustus' – is inscribed on the inner wall of this temple (photo courtesy of Professor C. Ratté).

was now called the 'deceitful slaughter of an army of the Roman people' in Germany (*RS* 37: 14–15). Drusus, in Italy when Augustus died, was dispatched to the Balkans. Both of Tiberius' sons now faced mutinies in armies that saw themselves as being very much Augustus' men – not unreasonably, since their late leader had called them 'my armies' when compiling the record of his deeds. In the Balkans, the troops were protesting against the poor conditions of service and the fact that they were being kept in the military beyond even the extended term Augustus had imposed in AD 6 – some of those rebelling in AD 14 would have been recruited into legions newly formed for the invasion of the Balkans more than a quarter of a century previously.

On the Rhine, the mutiny appears to have been caused by the news of regime change. There is no reason to think that Tiberius was especially unpopular in either place, and some local mismanagement may have contributed to the trouble. In the end, Drusus managed to suppress the Balkan mutiny with minimal bloodshed. Germanicus had more difficulty and, after considerable internecine violence, led a large-scale raid into southern Germany to restore morale.

This year also saw the shifting of elections for minor magistrates away from the *comitia tributa* to the Senate (although the *comitia centuriata* continued to function as it had under Augustus), plus several salutary assassinations, eradicating sources of the earlier opposition to Tiberius' accession. Agrippa Postumus was killed before Augustus' funeral. His mother, Julia, died sometime before the end of the year; one of her alleged lovers, a descendant of the Gracchi who had written letters critical of Tiberius, was killed in his place of exile on an island off the coast of Africa.

At first, the main problem facing Tiberius was what to do about Germany. Augustus had favoured the recovery of all that had been lost by Varus, but this was not practical. After a couple of years during which Germanicus led armies deep into German territory, suffering some heavy casualties without winning a decisive result, Tiberius decided to declare victory and abandon the effort. Germanicus celebrated a triumph: it was announced that he had defeated the Germans, removed them from Gaul and recovered lost standards. He did manage to recover two standards, but there was never any question of having to remove the Germans from Gaul, as they had never invaded in the first place.

As the German campaign ended, disorder threatened the east. The king of Armenia had died and Tiberius, who was not the forgiving sort, wished to settle a grudge with the king of Cappadocia, who had offended him during his years on Rhodes. There was an extra complication in that before Augustus' death the Parthian nobility had asked for the return of Vonones, son of Phraates IV, to be their king (Phraates V having died). But they soon found Vonones to be 'too Roman' and replaced him with Artabanus, a distant relative. Vonones fled to Armenia, where he took the vacant throne, but was unable to retain it in the face of threats from Artabanus. He was now in Syria.

Germanicus was sent off to settle the issue of the Armenian succession without starting a war. He was accompanied by Gnaeus Calpurnius Piso, consul in AD 8 and a close friend of Tiberius. Unfortunately, Piso and Germanicus loathed each other: Piso evidently claimed that, while Germanicus might have *maius imperium* with respect to senatorial governors, he could not override *mandata* received from Tiberius. Piso gave Germanicus minimal support, instead expressing support for Vonones. That was not part of Germanicus' plan. He made Polemo, grandson of the Antonian dynast of that name, king of Armenia; then he met up with Artabanus and went on a grand tour of the eastern provinces, reaching as far south as Egypt, where he took a trip up the Nile. Piso, in the meantime, supported a botched coup that aimed to put Vonones back on the Armenian throne. This was more than Germanicus could tolerate. Returning to Syria, he dismissed Piso for gross insubordination. But then he fell ill, and died on 10 October AD 19; the suspicion was that he had been poisoned.

Germanicus' death unleashed a crisis. Piso, claiming that he had been wrongly dismissed, tried to retake the governorship of Syria by force of arms, failed, and was arrested. There were massive outpourings of grief in Rome, where Germanicus was a crowd favourite. In trying to express his grief Tiberius said, rather unfortunately, something along the lines of 'I will not dissimulate my sorrow' (RS 37 col. II, 16), which led some people to think that he was in fact hiding his joy at Germanicus' demise. Piso's show trial in May AD 20 ended with the defendant's suicide and the publication of a massive decree at the end of the year explaining his 'crimes' and declaring that order was now restored. Among Piso's alleged crimes were that he had raised the spectre of civil war, which had been 'buried' by Augustus and Tiberius, and had corrupted the military discipline that Augustus had instituted. The decree concluded with a list of the various virtues that members of the imperial family had displayed for the edification of the Roman people. Then the Senate and the equestrians were thanked for quelling the anger of the plebs with their supportive acclamations, as were the soldiers who had displayed loyalty to those officers who showed the greatest loyalty to the 'Augustan house'.

Despite Tiberius' efforts to maintain that he was simply the caretaker and educator of the state, much uncertainty remained, and the frequency with which treason charges were now being brought was deeply disturbing. Everyone agreed that Piso was guilty, and that Scribonius Libo Drusus – who had also committed suicide, while on trial for attempting to kill many aristocrats through black magic – was dangerously deranged, but in other cases the guilt was less obvious. Tiberius had tried to prevent the charge being used as an add-on to more conventional charges; he found it embarrassing to be present at such cases, which were inevitably tried in the Senate, but had limited success in restraining prosecutorial zeal because such prosecutions provided career opportunities for those who wanted to advance at the expense of their rivals.

Tiberius was now sixty. Germanicus' death heightened concern for the future; but Drusus was still alive, with a young son, and had adopted Germanicus' older children, who began their public careers in AD 22. The next year things took a turn for the worse, when Drusus suddenly fell ill and died. Now the empire was to be ruled by an ageing emperor who was becoming increasingly uninterested in his role, and his adoptive grandchildren.

Bureaucratic government came a step closer. Aelius Sejanus, who was now sole praetorian prefect, started taking on more and more responsibility for the daily management of the empire. Despite having no military reputation, his control of the emperor's appointment calendar gave him control of the whole political scene, through which he hoped to be Tiberius' Agrippa. His hand was further strengthened in AD 27 when Tiberius left for Capri, where he consorted with academics, ate a vegetarian diet and was (falsely) rumoured to have engaged in large-scale child molestation. He would never return to Rome. A modern visitor to his favoured residence, the Villa Jovis on Capri, will be struck both by the extraordinary natural beauty of the site and the relatively small size of the establishment. It is nothing like large enough to house the number of people needed to run an empire. That was being done by bureaucrats who were now stationed around the bay of Naples.

Sejanus exploited the limited access to Tiberius by causing rifts between the emperor and Germanicus' family, which led to the imprisonment of the latter's widow Agrippina and his two eldest sons. By AD 31 the only possible heirs to Tiberius were Gaius, better known by his nickname Caligula – or 'little boots', taken from the footwear he wore when he accompanied his father Germanicus on campaign – and Drusus' son Gemellus. Caligula was a teenager, Gemellus was not yet in his teens. This is when ambition got the better of Sejanus. He began an affair with Julia Livilla, Drusus' widow, then hatched a plot to kill Caligula – which failed. The elimination of a young 'imperial' would have had an unwelcome impact on the people in his or her household, who would suddenly have found themselves out of work, demoted and/or reassigned. Sejanus would not have been popular, either, with the palace staff, whose friends were suffering in the wake of the many arrests. And other households, too, would have been ruined, while he concentrated on managing the Senate via more strategic prosecutions and control of the somewhat limited opportunities for advancement.

Her staff would certainly have noticed Sejanus' relationship with

Livilla and would have had their own networks independent of those he controlled. Courtiers were aware they were fighting for their own survival, which made it possible for Antonia, Germanicus' mother, to get two of her freed persons to contact people around Tiberius on Capri and expose Sejanus' plan to murder Gaius. Both of her agents, Antonia Caenis and Antonius Pallas, would go on to positions of exceptional influence, easily equivalent to that of the most powerful senators.

Tiberius had retained more control of the bureaucracy than Sejanus realised, and he knew where the praetorian prefect's enemies could be found. In October, at the end of a long letter to the Senate about Sejanus, Tiberius instructed Sutorius Macro, the prefect of the *vigiles*, to arrest and execute the man. Job done, Macro immediately took Sejanus' place at the head of the bureaucracy and set about conducting the business of state – collecting taxes, appointing governors, defending frontiers. He stood aside as senators, while professing hostility to Sejanus, got on with the business of promoting their own careers via cases that now tended to end with the death sentence and the confiscation of estates (some of which would go to successful prosecutors). Tiberius had no interest in putting his foot down.

But none of the prosecutions in the Senate, while profoundly upsetting to the imperial elite, would prove as important, in the long run, as one that took place in the distant province of Judaea. Occasional revolts (p. 364) may have made imperial officials particularly prone to hear cases against people accused of threatening the public order. Here, the imperial official was a long-serving prefect, one Pontius Pilate. Pilate did not generally see eye to eye with the priestly authorities in Jerusalem, but at Passover in the year AD 30 he agreed with them on one thing: there could be no doubt that the radical preacher Jesus of Nazareth was a dangerous man who should be executed.

Within a few years, Jesus' death inspired powerful fantasies among his followers, not least that the world would soon end and that Jesus had risen from the dead. It is appropriate that it should have been a representative of the new bureaucratic class who was unwittingly responsible for the single most significant event of Tiberius' reign.

27

THREE MURDERS AND
THE EMERGENCE OF AN
IMPERIAL SOCIETY

The events referred to in the title to this chapter involve two Roman emperors and an empress. Possibly, a fourth assassination should be added, but to do so would be to accept as true the story that Tiberius was smothered in his sleep by Macro, now the praetorian prefect. We do not know whether that is what happened, or if it was a story made up later to justify Macro's own execution. Crucially, the obvious instability of which these events are symptomatic had minimal impact on the empire's development.

Despite bouts of volatility and some unpleasantness, the emergent bureaucracy proved capable of running the empire day to day. This, and the general peace in the central Mediterranean, facilitated the smooth incorporation of local aristocracies within the Roman system, the protection of their interests, and a rise in overall prosperity. The spread of Roman power, largely unsupervised by the palace, can be attributed to bureaucrats whose self-interest guaranteed orderly solutions to problems at the local level. Theft, plunder and militarism were no longer paths to political power.

In addition to permitting provincials access to its administrative structures, the imperial system meshed regional economies into a network that allowed for some redistribution of resources via the mechanisms created to ensure Rome's food supply and the nurturing of frontier armies. Regional economies in more settled areas deployed the surplus stemming from greater security into urban development, while the frontier zones, which were the recipients of tax surpluses from other regions, developed their own forms of economic and cultural power. Tribal Europe now entered a Mediterranean world where the emergence of homogeneous patterns of urban settlement promoted economic success and intercultural communication.

Tiberius' great contribution to the development of the Roman Empire was to have shown that an emperor did not need a war to justify his existence. There were no major campaigns after the end of the German war in AD 16. Not even the Armenian succession crisis that broke out in AD 35 required the deployment of troops to the Syrian garrison – because, as usual, there was great instability among the Parthians. When the Parthian king demanded the return of the ancestral lands of the Achaemenid monarchs whom Alexander the Great had dispossessed – that is, the entire eastern part of the empire – leaders of the Parthian aristocracy asked for the return of one of the Parthian princes whom Phraates IV had deposited in Roman custody for safe-keeping. The reason this candidate (also named Phraates) died shortly after taking the throne was allegedly because his luxurious Roman lifestyle had left him unfit for the rugged existence of a Parthian king.

Still, the Roman governor Lucius Vitellius managed quite well to keep the Parthians at each other's throats, thereby maintaining peace on the Roman side of the border. Vitellius would also dismiss Pontius Pilate for egregious brutality in dealing with a religious demonstration in Samaria. We do not know whether Vitellius ever heard what had happened to Jesus of Nazareth a few years earlier. Despite fictions concocted by his later followers, it may be taken as read that Tiberius had never heard of the man.

By the spring of AD 36 Tiberius was faced with a problem. He was dying and he did not like Caligula, his obvious successor. The other possible, Drusus' son Gemellus, was still too young. Tiberius, as was his wont, sought a solution through astrology, at which he believed himself adept. He could find none. A powerful faction was forming around Caligula, led by Macro. Then, on 16 March AD 37, Tiberius Caesar breathed his last.

In Rome, widespread rejoicing greeted the news of Tiberius' demise. This was not to be wondered at. Tiberius had always lacked the popular touch, and no one had seen him in the city for a decade. A massive fire had recently ravaged the Aventine but he had shown no interest in alleviating the people's suffering. The city's grain supply was functioning well, but Tiberius had not spent lavishly on public spectacle, and it was common knowledge that senior senators were being arrested on charges of treason. But despite Tiberius' unpopularity, there was unanimity among the Senate leadership, the court and the people of Rome that the position of *princeps* be continued. In order to do so efficiently, the Senate voted that Tiberius' will, which named Caligula and Gemellus as co-heirs, be set aside because the emperor had not been of sound mind.

Caligula had a good deal going for him – not least the fact that very few people outside the immediate palace circle knew him, and so were unaware of his unstable temperament. An excellent orator, he could charm an audience in a way Tiberius never could; people saw him as the reincarnation of his father Germanicus, and Caligula had a sense of theatre that Tiberius lacked. He arranged a massive public funeral for his adoptive father, whose ashes were placed in Augustus' mausoleum; he then had the ashes of his mother and brothers re-interred, placing them alongside Tiberius' in the family tomb. He sponsored three months of games, and paid the legacies that had been left in Tiberius' will to the imperial guard and the people of Rome – even though they were not technically owed anything, the will having been invalidated. Caligula took credit for this act of generosity.

Caligula wanted to be seen as the 'anti-Tiberius'. To that end, he announced that the *comitia tributa* would elect its traditional officials and that he would try no senator for treason. He also recalled men who had been exiled under Tiberius and sought to restore the works of literary figures that had been banned from public libraries when their authors had been condemned for treason. One of these, Cremutius Cordus, was a sympathetic figure who had been tried for sedition because he had praised Brutus and Cassius in his histories (he had also been rather rude about Cicero). This had not bothered Augustus, but Cordus had offended Sejanus, which was why the charge had been brought. Two others, whose condemnation under Augustus for sedition had supplied the precedent for Cordus' trial, were Cassius Severus and Titus Labienus, son of the pro-Parthian operative of the civil war years. These were less sympathetic figures.

The initial enthusiasm for Caligula soon cooled. After an illness allegedly connected with too much high living, his conduct became increasingly erratic. He executed Gemellus, quarrelled with Macro and then had him executed, too. Macro's execution was the proximate cause of trouble with the establishment. People found Caligula disturbingly erratic and peculiarly interested in his own divinity. At one point, he built a bridge of boats over three and a half miles long from Baiae, where he had a villa, to the mole at the entrance of Puteoli harbour, west of Naples.

Writing in the 120s or a bit earlier, Suetonius, who was the author of a set of influential biographies called *The Twelve Caesars*, said that it had been heard from senior courtiers that he did this to disprove a prophecy from Thrasyllus, Tiberius' highly regarded astrologer, who had predicted that he would no more be ruler than he would cross the bay of Baiae on horseback. In this Suetonius employed language that would have been unthinkable under Augustus, for he used the Latin verb *impero*, 'to rule' (Suetonius, *Life of Caligula* 19.3), in stark contrast to the Augustan/Tiberian notion that the emperor's duty was to 'care for' the state. And in a decree summarising the role of the Syrian garrison in 'suppressing' Piso back in AD 20 the Senate had thanked the soldiers for their 'faith and devotion to the Augustan house, and hoped that it would continue to show that devotion forever, since they know that the safety of our empire is placed in the guardianship of that house' (*SCP* 161–3). It was rumoured that Caligula had been taking advice on autocracy from the children of eastern dynasts whom he had met while he was on Capri.

Caligula's behaviour grew ever more controversial as he began to display a penchant for matrimonial gymnastics and watching people die. When he had initially taken the throne, he had been married to Junia Silana, whose immensely influential family boasted a direct link with Augustus through his great-granddaughter Aemilia Lepida. That marriage collapsed, and now Caligula charged his former father-in-law with treason, despite having promised to steer clear of such excesses. There was also some suggestion that he was sleeping with the oldest of his three sisters, Drusilla; others said he was sleeping with all of them. His extraordinary display of grief when Drusilla died in AD 38 only strengthened the rumours. He was also easily bored, temperamental in public, and soon had cash-flow problems as he made his way through the large reserve that Tiberius had left in his personal account, known now as *fiscus Caesaris*.

In AD 39 it seemed a good idea for Caligula to get out of town and head for Gaul in order to let things cool down. His conduct in Gaul did little, however, to set minds at ease. He detected a conspiracy involving Lentulus Gaetulicus, who for some years had had a controlling interest in the two provinces known as Upper and Lower Germany. Gaetulicus owed his position to his friendship with Sejanus, and had retained it only because Tiberius had been afraid that if he tried to remove him there would be a civil war. The governor of Upper Germany was Gaetulicus' son-in-law, and together they controlled a third of the empire's armed forces.

That year, Caligula would not only have Gaetulicus killed but also order the execution of one of his own close companions, Marcus Aemilius Lepidus, the widower of his sister Drusilla and great-grand-nephew of the triumvir. Caligula had once declared that Lepidus was his obvious successor, but it appears that Lepidus had joined in the conspiracy against him with Gaetulicus. Caligula also exiled his surviving sisters, Livilla and Agrippina, for their links with Lepidus (whom Agrippina had taken as a lover). After some desultory campaigning along the Rhine and a feeble attempt to organise an invasion of Britain, Caligula went home to celebrate a triumph.

The events in Germany reveal several interesting features about the imperial system. First, the increasingly obvious incompetence of the emperor and his closest associates was still not calling into question the perceived need for a *princeps*; second, in the absence of sons, connections with women linked with Augustus' bloodline were regarded as sufficient qualification for succession. The fact that Caligula had had a minimal public career before becoming *princeps* clearly shows that the requirement that an emperor possess an impressive record before taking the throne no longer applied. This notion had died with Tiberius' son Drusus. But no one yet imagined that Germanicus' brother Claudius, who had a club foot and other disabilities, might be considered a candidate. Augustus had regarded him as an embarrassment, while Tiberius just ignored him; Caligula made him consul, then humiliated him. With the wisdom of hindsight, Tacitus would comment on the 'folly of human designs in all matters' when he contemplated Claudius' early career (Tacitus, *Annals* 3.18.3–4), for he knew that the man of whom no one expected anything would become emperor.

The plot that was to make Claudius emperor was hatched soon after Caligula returned to Rome at the end of the year 40. The imperial guard and the palace hierarchy had had enough of their master's eccentricity. We get a sense of what they had to tolerate from the account of envoys sent to Caligula by Jewish dignitaries from Alexandria, who wished to remonstrate with him about the appalling treatment to which they had been subjected by the prefect of Egypt, not to mention a threat to install a statue of Caligula in the temple at Jerusalem. But the *princeps* was not interested:

> Beginning to speak and inform him, he, having got a taste of what we were saying and realising that it was by no means to be despised, cut off our earlier points before we could bring our stronger ones, and dashed into a big room of the house and, walking around it, ordered the windows ... to be restored with transparent stones, which, in the same way as glass, do not obstruct the light but keep the wind and hot sun away. Then he approached again, at a moderate clip, and said, 'What are you saying?' and when we came to the next points in our argument, he ran into another room and ordered the original pictures to be reinstalled.
>
> (Philo, *Embassy to Gaius* 364–5)

Caligula's final response, that their persecutors did not seem like such bad chaps, left the terrified ambassadors feeling lucky to have escaped with their lives.

The conspiracy comprised members of the praetorian guard, recruited by one Cassius Chaerea, a palace administrator disgusted at being forced to assume the role of Caligula's personal torturer; some powerful palace freedmen, specifically Julius Callistus, who was close to Claudius; and some members of the Senate. The planned assassination was coordinated with a raid by the praetorian guard to secure the person of Claudius.

On 24 January AD 41 Chaerea and a small band of companions murdered Caligula as he left a theatrical performance on the Palatine. Claudius, who had left just ahead of him, was fetched from the palace and taken to the praetorian camp, where the guard swore an oath of loyalty to him.

Senators who had not been privy to the plot summoned a meeting on the Capitoline to discuss the restoration of traditional, *princeps*-free government. Protesting crowds gathered in the forum, fearing the chaos somehow recalled from the age before Augustus. A dynast from Judaea and friend of Claudius, Herod Agrippa, engaged in some careful negotiations to calm things down so that the Senate could declare its loyalty to Claudius – which it did, after a tense couple of days. The Senate then passed a resolution, as it had for Tiberius and Caligula, conferring the necessary traditional powers of a *princeps* on Claudius. *Imperium* would be conferred by the *comitia centuriata*, and tribunician power by the *comitia tributa*, as the conventions of the distant past melded with the realities of a system where court and praetorian guard reigned supreme.

Claudius recognised that he was not in a strong position, though he retained the loyalty of the most powerful palace freedmen and of the guard. An attempted rebellion by the governor of Dalmatia within months of his accession helped convince him that he needed to win military glory of his own. Fascinated by Julius Caesar, some of whose unfinished domestic projects he set out to complete, Claudius chose Britain as a suitable venue to display his martial talents and started to collect the necessary transports. To command the expedition Claudius appointed Aulus Plautius, a loyal general with no obvious connections to the old nobility and therefore not likely to claim the throne in the event of extraordinary success.

Plautius was an excellent choice. A talented general, he was supported by some outstanding subordinates including one named Vespasian, the son of an equestrian auctioneer who, along with his brother, had become a senator. Like Plautius, Vespasian was the sort of 'new man' from the Italian backwoods who was willing to take advantage of the senatorial fast track to show his mettle. And just as the commanders were new men, so, too, would this be the first major offensive undertaken by the new model Roman army, drawn primarily from northern Spain and the Rhineland. So, ironically, it would be an army of largely Celtic descent that would invade Celtic Britain.

The initial invasion went smoothly enough as Plautius' army, which had some support from rulers in southern Britain, fought its way across the Thames and into the London area, where Vespasian distinguished himself. Claudius left Rome in September AD 43 and spent two weeks on the island (accompanied by some war elephants) before withdrawing to spend the winter in the more salubrious region of Lyons. He returned to Rome in the spring of AD 44 to celebrate a triumph.

The triumph was all well and good as a celebration, but it indicated that Claudius had no intention of withdrawing his troops from Britain – which, as a policy, was not such a good plan. The shaky finances of the post-Caligulan age meant that the army still consisted of twenty-five legions, of which no more than three could be spared for the conquest. That was simply not enough for the job – even with the addition of a substantial force of auxiliaries, largely drawn from the same areas as the legions. Plautius was therefore left to impose a whole new political order on the island with roughly 30,000 men.

Military conquest being impossible, what was needed was diplomacy and gentle persuasion – the more attractive aspects of urban culture. Thanks to the fact that people tended to write on erasable wood-backed wax tablets, which the ample bogs of Britain preserved, we can decipher evidence of continental culture as settlements came into being and pens scratched through the wax to leave us traces of correspondence. Colchester was founded as a colony for retired veterans, while London grew rapidly as a major port. It is from London that several tablets from these years have survived, one offering important evidence for the spread of soft power:

> They are boasting through the whole forum that you have lent them money; therefore, I ask you, in your own interest, not to appear disreputable ... you will not thus favour your own affairs.
>
> (*WT* 30, tr. Tomlin (adapted))

Here, within a few years of the initial conquest, is a town with a business centre that can be called a forum, and – appropriately enough for the heart of London – a banker whose manager fears he may not be conducting himself in a suitably decorous fashion. We cannot know exactly where these people came from, but it is more likely that they were from the Rhine settlements than from Italy itself. The people boasting they had borrowed money would have been locals; that they had acquired the loans proves they were trusted by the new establishment. That would become a controversial position.

Augustan expansion stopped because Rome lacked the resources to make up for the losses in Germany and Claudian expansion stalled for much the same reason. At this point it should be admitted that, although one of the main arguments of this book is that the empire succeeded because of its ability to integrate diverse peoples into its system of governance (and we will be seeing some very good examples of that process before the end of this chapter), the initial period of occupation could be brutal for those who were not able to make immediate profits.

The basic tools of Roman provincialisation, collaboration and census taking, were inherently disruptive. Even in a place with a tradition of bureaucratic government like Syria, the arrival of the Roman census takers, who were also there to set basic rates of taxation, was profoundly annoying. One reason the governorship of Sulpicius Quirinius was so memorable was that in AD 6 his imposition of a census in Syria caused a revolt. Census takers did not sit idly by while people lied to them about their goods and chattels. They snooped and pried, looking for ways to enhance the government's revenue. For people living at subsistence levels and without powerful friends to protect them, the added burden could be bitter.

It was not just in Syria that a revolt broke out. Difficulties with Roman tax assessment were also a primary cause of the revolt that began in the Balkans and were also a factor behind Arminius' uprising. But that was only part of the story of what was an almost perfect storm of Roman provincialisation, including the imposition of a Roman-style judicial system, economic change and interference in local politics. It is Velleius Paterculus, the author of a short history dedicated to the consul of AD 30, who tells us that Varus spent the summer before his death trying to 'soften by law those whom he could not defeat in battle' (Velleius Paterculus, *Short History* 2.117.3). Softening was not always what people thought of when confronting Roman law. One reason for Vercingetorix' revolt against Caesar was Caesar's imposition of a Roman-style penalty of brutal flogging ahead of decapitation on a tribal chieftain, and a Greek notable was once publicly thanked for saving one of his fellow citizens from a 'Roman death'. The development of a Roman-style city at Waldgirmes, in west central Germany, at roughly the same time was a sign that Rome was encouraging new forms of economic activity among people whom Caesar had once said he could not be bothered to conquer because they were insufficiently agricultural. Also, somewhat before Varus' term began, Lucius Domitius Ahenobarbus (son of the Gnaeus Domitius Ahenobarbus whom we encountered in the era of the civil wars) had been interfering in the movements of peoples through the region. It is Tacitus who gives us details about the politics of the Chatti, Arminius' tribe, where the two leaders were Arminius himself and his father-in-law, Segestes, 'each one notable, one for good faith, the other for treachery' (*Annals* 1.55.2). Segestes had even tried to warn Varus that danger threatened on the eve of the uprising. Arminius' brother would serve with Germanicus, while

Segestes' son sided with Arminius. Arminius himself would fall to an assassin at some point after Germanicus' death in AD 19.

In Numidia, during Tiberius' reign, there was a seven-year struggle between the Roman authorities and the tribes that traversed the rim of the Sahara who had found a leader in a man named Tacfarinas, who, like Arminius, had served in the Roman army. Quite possibly Roman administrators were interfering with traditional movements as they had in Germany. In AD 28, as Tiberius was losing interest in the government, the Frisians, who lived at the mouth of the Rhine, rebelled rather than pay Roman taxes they could not afford. Tiberius decided that they were not worth reconquering.

The Frisians were not the only people Rome could not afford to govern. The system really did require cities and collaborators if it was going to work, and there were areas within the empire that were also rated too annoying to administer closely. The highlands of the Taurus mountains in southern Turkey were one such region – they would be famous for brigandage for centuries and the image of the country-dwelling brigand entered the Roman consciousness as the ultimate domestic terrorist. On the other hand, the fact that the crowd in the Gospel account of Jesus' execution wished to save the brigand Barabbas is a sign that in some quarters brigands were seen rather differently.

In the empire's more urbanised and longer-occupied zones, things were quite different. Throughout the empire, people were constructing and adapting buildings to create distinctive cities that fitted their needs. In Italy, the forums that had combined religious and commercial space in the later Republic were now becoming more obviously public, with new temples dedicated to the worship of both the imperial family and local divinities. Additionally, there were triumphal arches, new market buildings, improved water-distribution systems and other public spaces modelled on Roman prototypes. Further improvements included modernised public baths (and more of them), stone amphitheatres (at least thirty-eight towns added these during the first century AD) and even more theatres – a total of 175 are known to have been built between the mid-first century BC and Claudius' reign. Changes were seen, too, in the style of private urban houses among the better off, incorporating miniaturised aspects of the large suburban villas.

In Spain, Gaul and North Africa, where the concept of Italian-influenced urban settlement was relatively new at the time Augustus defeated Antonius, change was patchier. In Spain and Gaul the first sign of a Roman-style city in the making would be a planned grid adapted to accommodate a forum and temples, public baths and theatres within the city walls. These grids were influenced either by the rectilinear style long popularised in the eastern Mediterranean, the work of the fifth-century BC urban planner Hippodamus, or, where there had been military establishments, by the basic plan of a Roman camp, which had two main streets dividing a city into quarters. A visitor to these regions might have noted that amphitheatres remained rarities, and there was less interest generally in buildings evocative of Roman triumphal architecture.

In North Africa, where in Carthaginian times there had been a number of important cities, urban space would be transformed with the addition of walls around a new grid centred on a forum, typically bounded by a temple on one side, a basilica opposite, and commercial buildings on the other two sides. Temples other than those in the forum would tend to skirt the main street plan, though bathhouses would be incorporated into the domestic zones. Other regional variations were that North African cities were less likely to have an elaborate bathhouse than an amphitheatre, and Spanish cities might have a circus, in keeping with local traditions of superior equestrian husbandry.

Cities in western Europe might be built over Celtic settlements, which would be largely obliterated. In south-east Europe, where there was already a well-established tradition of urban settlement, things were very different. Greek cities tended already to have a well-articulated grid plan and their own architectural forms for their public buildings, which included temples, council houses and theatres. During the first century AD the main avenues of many of these cities were enhanced with colonnades that offered space for shops and the display of statues honouring prominent citizens. What there were not were building types associated with specifically Italian developments – bathhouses, amphitheatres and circuses. Indeed, the only two bathhouses in this region known in the first half of the first century were one donated to the city of Cyme in Turkey by a Roman magistrate and one built by an imperial freedman in a small town in the Turkish countryside.

Greek city leaders were no more interested in adopting Latin in their public or private lives than they were in filling their urban spaces with Italian-style buildings, so Italian settlers learned to communicate in Greek. The linguistic divide, which would remain throughout the rest of

Roman history, began on the coast of the Adriatic around Dyrrachium. From here, Greek would be the dominant language in a broad semicircle of territory ending in the region of Cyrene in North Africa (now part of Libya). North of Dyrrachium, in Illyria and in regions extending to the Danube, Latin would dominate until, following the Danube south to the area north of Thrace, Greek would begin to take over.

In the west, although the Roman government was willing to allow people to address their magistrates in Celtic and Punic languages, the pressure of soft power, the urge to be able to participate in the urban culture of the ruling power, tended to draw people towards adopting Latin for public expression and as a written language, even if they continued to speak to each other in their traditional tongues.

In what is now modern Greece, Greek would be spoken by pretty much everyone. In what is now Turkey, Greek would be the first language of the cities, as it had been for centuries, but other languages, such as Lycian, Carian and Lycaonian (Luke remarks at one point that people in Lystra in southern Turkey greeted Paul in Lycaonian), were spoken. In traditionally Semitic lands and in Egypt, native languages continued to be used alongside Greek for both written and verbal communication. Traditional expression in these languages had been a feature not simply of convenience, but also of identity politics in the face of the often overtly racist policies of the Greek kingdoms of the Hellenistic era. One of the curiosities of Roman rule in Semitic lands was that, even though there were ever more sophisticated literatures written in the native dialects, the use of Greek increased in daily life. The ability to function in Greek as well as Aramaic gave citizens access to positions within the imperial hierarchy.

With their own cultural traditions intact – and to some degree promoted by Roman officials who enjoyed the notion that their subjects were peoples with impressive pasts – eastern city leaders found many ways in which to express their links with the imperial regime. At Ephesus, the chief city of the province of Asia, the marketplace in the city's heart now had a triumphal entryway on its north side, constructed by two of Augustus' freedmen, Mazeus and Mithridates. At Aphrodisias, Gaius Julius Zoilus, a freedman of Julius Caesar's who had become enormously wealthy, had built a new theatre with a portico celebrating his rise from slavery to riches. Others had begun constructing a massive temple to pay homage to Augustus, fronted by a wonderful portico decorated with images evoking Augustus' victories and depicting members of the imperial

22. The Sebasteion at Aphrodisias [Photo: courtesy New York University Excavations at Aphrodisias (G. Petruccioli)].

house in the local representational idiom. Aphrodisias, named for the Greek counterpart of Venus, progenitor of the house of Julius Caesar, and a city possessed of significant marble quarries, found itself linked with Rome through its community of sculptors while enjoying technical independence from Roman government as a 'free city.'

Cities were either free, like Aphrodisias, or stipendiary, meaning they paid taxes to Rome; rural districts were either controlled by the cities or they were the personal property of the emperor, their revenues contributing to his private wealth, or *fiscus*, and governed by procurators such as Ofilius Ornatus, whom we met in the previous chapter.

Among stipendiary cities some were more equal than others, having been selected as *conventus* centres, meaning that they were effectively district capitals, places where governors would show up once a year to hold court. Another way that a city could achieve status ahead of others was to be recognised as a centre for the provincial worship of the imperial house. All cities might have shrines to the emperor – this was as true of Italy as elsewhere – but outside of Italy provinces were organised around imperially recognised centres where the local assembly gathered to pay homage to the emperor. The regional organisation of ruler cults had significant precedents under the Ptolemies and the Seleucids, but now that organisation was strengthened as provincial assemblies negotiated with imperial magistrates the form of provincial cult they were to adopt. In this way the cult came to have great practical value, since recognition as a high priest of a provincial cult marked a man out as of great importance, and was usually a stepping stone that a family aspiring to a place in the imperial governing hierarchy was eager to cross.

Although well established by AD 14, provincial cults were as slow to proliferate as any other aspect of the Augustan regime. It was Drusus, possibly inspired by Augustus' election as *pontifex maximus*, who initiated a cult at Lyons in 12 BC. Discontent began to stir as he was taking a census of the three provinces encompassing the three Gallic regions that Caesar had identified in his account of his conquests: Belgica in the north; Aquitania in the south-west; and Gaul proper between the Rhône valley and the Atlantic. On 1 August 12 BC, possibly taking advantage of one of the regular meetings of notables that had been happening since Caesar's time, if not before, Drusus established an altar at the confluence of the Saône and Rhône rivers, to be the centrepiece of an annual festival conducted by a high priest chosen from the Gallic leadership. The first of these, identified by Livy – who regarded it as an important development – was an Aeduan called Gaius Julius Vercondaridubnus.

Three years later, Paullus Fabius Maximus, governor of Asia, wrote to the province's assembly instructing it on the proper way to worship Augustus. In a document redolent of the ideology of the imperial regime, he stressed that the development of the ruler cult was a dialectical process between local groups and representatives of the imperial government, rather than some grand design that had emerged from the brain of Augustus himself. In a key section of a very long dossier, Fabius wrote:

> Whether the birthday of the most godlike Caesar is more a matter of joy or blessing, it is rightly held to be the beginning of all things, and he has restored to use if not its natural state every form that had fallen into disarray and misfortune, and he has given a different appearance to the entire world, which would readily have fallen into destruction, if Caesar had not been born to the common benefit of all men ... And since no one could find a more auspicious day either for themselves as

individuals or in public upon which to begin something than his day, which has been fortunate for everyone, and since just about every city in Asia uses this day as the day upon which new magistrates take up office ... and since it is difficult to render appropriate thanks for each and every one of his generous deeds unless in each case we should find some new form of devotion, people should celebrate his birthday with greater pleasure as a holiday common to all as if some special advantage came to them through his government.

(*RDGE* 65)

Therefore, Fabius continued, the new year should begin on 23 September, Augustus' birthday. The provincial assembly established in the wake of Actium already observed a cult for Rome and Augustus at Smyrna and Pergamum, and since most places were already using Augustus' birthday as the first day of the new year – an observation deriving from an earlier cult offered to Greek kings – it made sense for the whole province to observe 23 September as New Year's Day. The assembly then passed resolutions accepting the governor's recommendation. Behind the egregious rhetoric was this practical administrative point, and a few years later, in AD 11, Transalpine Gaul, the province from which Caesar had begun his career of conquest, adopted the same practice.

Keen to create institutions that would bring peace to Britain, Claudius set up a provincial cult for himself at Colchester. As something imposed rather than developing organically, it would prove less than successful. None the less, looking back over Claudius' reign, Tacitus later recognised the cultural growth that had taken place. In AD 48, at the end of a term in which he had held the censorship with the same Lucius Vitellius whom we met as governor of Syria at the beginning of this chapter, Claudius urged the Senate to allow men who had gained citizenship by virtue of having held office in Gallic cities that were Roman municipalities to be eligible for Senate membership. Some senators, fearing they would lose their status to richer men, objected to Gauls being admitted because, they said, they were descendants of Rome's ancestral enemies. Claudius rejected their complaint, quoting various instances from history – some of it history that he himself had written in his long years of political obscurity, other bits from Livy. Tacitus took his speech and transformed it into a statement of the way Rome had grown from a Latin to a Mediterranean community. 'I am not ignorant,' he has Claudius say, that the Julii came from Alba, the Coruncanii from Cameria, the Porcii from Tusculum, and, lest we just look at ancient history, that Etruria, Lucania and all Italy are incorporated into the Senate, and finally that Italy itself was extended to the Alps, and so that not only individuals, but lands and nations could come together as Romans ... all that we now believe to have been most ancient, plebeian magistrates in place of patricians, then Latins after the plebeians, then, after the Latins, magistrates from all the other peoples of Italy; some day what we hold to be novel will be old, and what today we defend with arguments from the past will be amongst the examples people use.

(Tacitus, *Annals* 11.24–5)

Claudius did have history on his side, but at the point he held the censorship he was also having some personal problems. When he took the throne, he was married to one Valeria Messalina with whom he had two children: a daughter Octavia and a son who was given the name Britannicus to commemorate the British war. Unfortunately for both parties, the marriage was in dire shape by the year 48. Claudius had mistresses, Messalina had lovers and was also reputed to be at the centre of a palace ring that peddled Roman citizenship to wealthy provincials. Even if the story that she won a contest with a leading prostitute to see how many men they could each have intercourse with in a single evening is false, she was looking for a way out of the marriage, and the root of her difficulty may have been that she had fallen out with the freedmen who, along with Vitellius, dominated the counsels of her husband.

That autumn she took up with the next year's prospective consul, Silius, moved into his house and conducted a mock wedding ceremony. Parties at which people mocked the institutions of Roman life (especially aristocratic wedding ceremonies) and had a lot of sex were scarcely unknown – Augustan puritanism was well and truly a thing of the past – but this threatened to make the emperor, who was in Ostia at the time, look foolish. His freedmen arranged for Messalina's speedy execution and arrested a number of her lovers, who were executed for treason.

But a wifeless Claudius was not safe, in the view of his closest associates. And at this point members of the palace establishment, including Antonius Pallas who had helped bring down Sejanus, Callistus who had done the same for Caligula, and Narcissus whom Claudius had freed from slavery, argued about who his new wife should be. Pallas came down hard in favour of Julia Agrippina, daughter of Germanicus, former lover of Marcus Aemilius Lepidus and Claudius' niece. She had a son by her first husband, Gnaeus Domitius Ahenobarbus (grandson of the admiral of the triumviral era), who was four years older than Britannicus; had been on bad terms with Messalina; and was in very good physical shape (she liked to swim). Vitellius agreed with Pallas, Claudius was smitten, and the Senate passed a decree permitting what was by any standards an incestuous union. The two were married early in AD 49, and Claudius adopted Agrippina's son, henceforth known as Nero, a name characteristic of the Claudian family. (Britannicus, though only ten at the time, recognised the threat and persisted in calling his new brother Domitius.)

Agrippina moved in with style and efficiency. By AD 51 she had replaced the prefects of the praetorian guard, accused of having been too close to Messalina, with her own man, Afranius Burrus; she had recalled Seneca, the well-known intellectual of somewhat dubious personal reputation, from exile to be Nero's tutor; and had a colony founded at the city of her birth in the valley of the Rhine. The place, once known as the Altar of the Ubii, would henceforth be known as *colonia Agrippensis*; it is now called Cologne. At Rome, she accelerated Nero's declaration as senior heir apparent and arranged his betrothal to the 10-year-old Octavia (no matter that they were technically brother and sister). She cut a splendid public figure; people would remember her golden dress at the mock naval battle that Claudius staged to celebrate his draining of the Fucine lake in AD 52, and her presence at the massive military celebration held in AD 50 to celebrate the capture of Caratacus, the leader of the resistance to the Roman forces in Britain. The event was compared to the great victories of Scipio Africanus over the Carthaginians and of Aemilius Paullus over Macedonia.

In AD 53, the ground was laid for a change of regime. Nero was taking on ever more public roles, and, with Seneca providing the material, was impressing people with his oratorical style. Narcissus, who had never liked Agrippina, kept trying to find a way to prevent Nero's accession and to protect Britannicus, which was somewhat worrying to Agrippina as he had Claudius' ear and Claudius was showing signs of favouring Britannicus while his own health declined. The emperor's growing frailty had one consequence whose significance was underappreciated at the time: Roman officials in the eastern provinces, lacking instructions from the emperor, did not intervene in the recurring trouble in Armenia. The problem would intensify, and soon require the creation of an extraordinary command. But that would have to wait.

On the evening of 13 October AD 54, Claudius suffered a fit. It is said that he collapsed at a dinner party for priests, but this appears to have been a story spread about to cover up the truth, which was that Agrippina, who had recently been consulting a professional poisoner, fed him a poisoned mushroom. When he was safely dead and the necessary funerary preparations had been made, on 14 October the palace doors opened and Nero was taken to the camp of the praetorian guards, who swore an oath of loyalty to him. The Senate then passed the customary laws conferring on him the powers of an emperor. It is said that the watchword Nero issued to his guards that day was 'best mother'. Claudius was given an elaborate funeral and declared a god; his remains were placed in Augustus' mausoleum.

Nero, who was seventeen when he became emperor, had little interest in the role. The same cannot be said of Agrippina, who had a few axes to grind. Narcissus died just before Claudius' funeral, and she sent assassins to deal with Marcus Junius Silanus, the governor of Asia. Silanus' mother was Aemilia Lepida, Augustus' great-granddaughter, and Agrippina had feared that Silanus would be preferred to Nero because he had a blood relationship, was older, and had experience of public life. Tacitus claims that Burrus and Seneca stepped in at this point to prevent a massacre of others Agrippina did not like. Nero himself pursued a vendetta against Britannicus, who succumbed to poison at a dinner party early the following year. People are said to have remarked that this was not such a bad thing, as power cannot be shared. One of the people at that party was Titus, Vespasian's eldest son, who would one day need to think about such issues himself.

As dowager empress, Agrippina's role was to stay out of the limelight, but she found this difficult. She was barely restrained from receiving an embassy herself on the festering issues in Armenia. Still, even though she did stay behind the scenes – quite literally, hidden by a curtain when the envoys were presented to Nero – it is unlikely that she had no say in what happened.

The choice of Domitius Corbulo to assume command of an enhanced army in Syria is a case in point. As a second-generation senator whose father had never been a consul, he would not be an obvious rival to Nero; but he was also, like Vespasian, Plautius and a third individual, Suetonius Paulinus, very able.

While Corbulo campaigned in the east, gradually reasserting Roman

23. Poppaea Sabina from a coin struck in 62/3 AD at Seleucia in Syria

control over Armenia, developments in Rome raised questions about whether Nero was in fact fit to rule, or could rule without his mother. The relationship between the two deteriorated rapidly. Nero, among other things, appears to have played down the significance of his adoption. Seneca, meanwhile, produced a work making fun of Claudius' deification, and progress on the building of a temple in his memory slowed to a halt.

Nero did not like his wife Octavia either, and was soon having an affair with Acte, a freedwoman. Agrippina was appalled, and made it clear that she disapproved. Then he began an affair with Poppaea Sabina, granddaughter of one of Tiberius' most trusted subordinates, who was also keen to be empress. Agrippina feared her son was forgetting that his claim to the throne was through Claudius; she had worked in the palace all her life, and understood only too well that without the crucial blood relationship the family had little going for it. She insisted that he remain married, no matter who else he was sleeping with. Nero did not care. So as to facilitate his relationship with Poppaea he had her enter a bogus marriage with his friend Otho, who had instructed him in the practice of erotic foot-perfuming. But it did not work out. In the spring of AD 59 Nero was thoroughly frustrated. He decided to murder his mother.

The assassination was supposed to look like an accident. Nero invited Agrippina to join him at Baiae, telling her that he wanted to repair their relationship. He then dispatched her for a cruise in the bay of Naples. But the boat had been rigged so that the stern, where she was sitting, would fall off once she was well out to sea. Which it did. The outcome, however, was not what Nero had intended. Agrippina was still a powerful athlete and smart enough to know when someone was trying to kill her. She swam ashore, where she was taken in by the staff of a villa she owned in the area, and sent a message to her son saying that she had survived an accident. In a panic, Nero sent a detachment of guards to murder her while putting out the story that she had tried to assassinate *him*. This time he succeeded.

Agrippina was given a private funeral; her servants retained her ashes and, once Nero was overthrown, erected a monument to her memory. Tacitus reports that it was something of a tourist attraction in his own day.

2 8

DYNASTIES COME AND GO

Agrippina's assassination would ultimately prove fatal for her son, too. She had recognised that imperial power needed to be exercised through an alliance between a competent palace staff and activist elements in the Senate, largely consisting of new families who owed their prominence to the regime. Older families were dangerous because they might claim that their ancestors had done as much or more than the Julii, the Claudii or the Domitii to gain the empire. The problem that Nero would never be able to solve was that competent people expected some level of competence from their superiors.

He became as tired of the officials with whom Agrippina had surrounded him, able and excessively loyal though they were – they had played along with his lies about his mother – as he had been of her. But if he got rid of Seneca and Burrus, who would replace them? Nero's personal predilections – drinking, sex, chariot-racing and the performing arts – did not lend themselves to daily association with people who excelled at running a complicated bureaucracy, or, since they had attained their positions by catering to the emperor's whims, at keeping a tight rein on him.

The year 62 would see radical change. Burrus died, Seneca had retired, and Pallas, whose dismissal in AD 55 had been a warning that Nero was unhappy with his role as puppet, died, too. People thought he had been poisoned. Chief among those who now moved up a step or two was Ofonius Tigellinus, whose background was in sexual servicing and chariot horses. He advanced from being prefect of the *vigiles* (a position awarded by Agrippina, who had shared his attractions with her first spouse) to the praetorian prefecture. It was clear that Octavia's future was in peril, but with the scandal of his mother's murder fresh in people's minds Nero did not dare move against her, no matter how badly Poppaea wanted him to marry her.

Tigellinus brought with him a range of allies, including two senators, his father-in-law Cossutianus Capito and Eprius Marcellus, who was famed for his oratorical talents. Within the palace Capito and Marcellus were aligned with freedmen who had recently come to prominence, such as Epaphroditus from the secretariat and Polyclitus and Helius from the fiscal service, the latter having committed a political murder for Agrippina while he was administering imperial territory in Asia.

As Nero's inner circle changed, the first of the crises that would undermine his control took place in Britain. The proximate cause, if Tacitus has the story right, was misconduct by an administrator working for the *fiscus*, the emperor's private account. Since Tacitus' future father-in-law was serving with the British garrison at the time, it is more than likely that Tacitus *is* right, that this was the proximate cause. There were, however, other factors of the sort that we discussed in the last chapter. There were deep divisions within British society between those who had benefitted from the Romans' arrival and those who had not. There was also a fundamental lack of respect on the part of Roman administrators for local power structures.

The divisions and unrest within the province may not have greatly interested the governor at the time, Suetonius Paulinus. Suetonius (no relation to the biographer) saw himself as Domitius Corbulo's rival for the title of 'great general of the age'. Both men took to writing memoirs, something that had not been seen since the age of Cicero, and which demonstrated a subtle shift in aristocratic culture from the attribution of all victory to the emperor to a climate in which senators could expect recognition of their personal achievements as servants of the state rather than as competitors to the *princeps*. For the British, the presence of a governor who would have been at home in the pre-Augustan era was an aggravating factor.

Suetonius' aim was to complete the conquest of Wales, where religiously motivated opponents of Roman rule had gathered, basing themselves on the island of Mona. Druids, who were the religious supervisors of the Celtic world, had a long history of antagonism towards the Roman state, whose interest was not in religious conformity – a preposterous notion in a world where local identity was so closely attached to local cults – but who took a dim view of cults it perceived as socially destabilising. The suppression of the Bacchic cult on the grounds of immorality in 186 BC had been a case in point; more recently, the Senate had banned 'Egyptian rites' during the struggles with Cleopatra.

Egyptian rites, notably the cults of Isis and Serapis, had returned to Italy after Actium as Rome's now cosmopolitan population brought their own forms of worship with them. Tiberius had banned the cult of Serapis again and had exiled its practitioners, along with some of the city's Jewish community, to Sardinia with instructions to suppress brigandage. This was in AD 19, when there were concerns about public morality involving women of the senatorial order: one had openly registered as a prostitute and another had been deceived by a man posing as an Egyptian god (what involvement the Jewish community had in this we do not know). The bans had not been very effective, and there were again substantial Jewish and Egyptian communities in Italy. Indeed, the European Jewish community had early contact with the followers of Jesus of Nazareth.

Given Rome's usually limited interest in quelling religious groups, the state's attitude towards Druids was striking. Claudius had banned Druidism, apparently because Druids engaged in human sacrifice, which Rome abhorred. Caesar had written that they burnt people in wicker cages, and there is archaeological evidence for ritual drowning in Celtic religious contexts. With most of his army advancing on Mona, it was now Suetonius' intention to wipe out the Druids.

As he was launching his attack, however, Decianus Catus, the administrator of the *fiscus* who was operating out of Colchester, committed an atrocity. The chief of the Iceni tribe had died, leaving his kingdom to Rome. When his widow, Boudicca, protested at the savagery of Catus' men in taking her husband's property, she was flogged and her daughters raped. The abuse of a distinguished person might not ordinarily have sparked a revolt, but it could only intensify the festering resentment of the Colchester settlers and the economic unrest stemming from the activities of people like the banker we encountered in the last chapter.

Boudicca, who was a charismatic leader, set out to eliminate all traces of Roman culture. While Catus fled to Gaul, her forces destroyed Colchester, ambushed a column sent to defend the city, inflicting severe casualties, and incinerated the emerging Roman settlement at London. The intensity of the fires her forces set is still evident in the archaeological record, but she did not have many followers beyond her homeland, so Suetonius had no difficulty in destroying her army with a relatively small force. His barbarous treatment of her people the following winter, however, led to his replacement, after a new procurator, Julius Classicianus (himself of British ancestry), had complained to the court.

Boudicca's revolt began in AD 60 and continued on into AD 61. By then Corbulo had dealt with the Armenian succession and imposed a new king, another Tiridates, sent from Rome. Corbulo's tactics had been no less savage than Suetonius', and the brutality of both their operations cannot be unconnected with the emerging military culture in the provinces.

The army was distinguishing itself as a privileged class. The soldiers were relatively well paid, and the Augustan ban on marriage had not prevented large-scale interaction with local populations. But, their presence underpinned by the notion that they represented a distant power, the soldiers belonged to a closed community. Natives of different parts of the empire, they were commanded by officers who, from the rank of centurion upwards, came from the urban aristocracies of longer-established provinces. The gap between officers and enlisted men was rarely bridged, which reinforced the self-reliant aspect of legionary society.

The auxiliary cohorts were an increasingly important component of the military. Between the legions and the auxiliaries, who usually served in areas close to home and under men who would have been local community leaders in peacetime, a tangible rivalry was developing. The auxiliaries were just as competent as the legionaries, but they were not Roman citizens; also, they had to serve for twenty-five rather than twenty years, and at a lower pay grade. And while they saw themselves as representing an imperial value system, their links with the local population enabled them to act as a bridge between their own communities and the empire as a whole.

The slaughter in Britain and victories in Armenia may have encouraged Nero to do what he had been wanting to do for years: divorce Octavia. With Burrus dead and Seneca forced into retirement (there was some suggestion that his money-lending habits had contributed to the disaster in Britain), she had no allies at court. Charged with adultery, she was sent into exile and murdered, but Nero had somewhat misread the situation: riots broke out, protesting at what seemed to the people of Rome a manifest injustice. Nero married Poppaea anyway, and her former husband was sent to govern Lusitania. The emperor's parties became ever more lavish and, despite being married to a woman he seemingly loved, he started performing sexual experiments in public, such as going through a mock wedding ceremony with one of his freedmen. He also encouraged the upper classes to flout other conventions – some would follow Nero on to the stage, others would sign up to fight as gladiators.

While Nero partied, the situation in the east took a sudden turn for the worse. Nero's appointee to assist Corbulo, Caesennius Paetus, botched an operation in Armenia, which had come under sudden heavy attack from a Parthian army. Paetus' army surrendered before Corbulo could relieve him, and Parthia now controlled the Armenian throne. Corbulo was then granted a command over all the eastern provinces described as 'equal to that of Pompey Magnus' (Tacitus, *Annals* 15.25.3). In AD 64 he used his new power to negotiate a settlement whereby the Parthian candidate for Armenia's throne would be crowned by Nero in Rome. By the time his embassy reached Rome two years later, Nero's regime had been shaken to the core.

A massive fire in late summer that year destroyed much of Rome, and even if Nero did not, as some claimed, greet the catastrophe by singing a poem about the destruction of Troy, his credibility came into serious question. Fake news can become real news, and people believed he started the fire. Nero's decision to build a gigantic new residence for himself, the Golden House, on the slopes of the Palatine, Caelian and Esquiline hills, announced loud and clear that he was going to profit from the disaster. Progress on the new construction was astonishingly rapid. Meanwhile, Nero was confronted with a badly organised coup attempt, led by a senior member of the Senate, Gaius Calpurnius Piso, grandson of the Piso who had quarrelled with Germanicus half a century earlier. Piso did not have the connections he needed within the palace, and the exposure of the plot gave Nero's supporters an opportunity to rid themselves of numerous adversaries. Seneca was ordered to commit suicide; likewise his nephew, the famous poet Lucan, of whom Nero was jealous.

Piso's conspiracy unsettled Nero. Further forced suicides – the preferred method of disposing of aristocrats – followed during the next year, including that of Gaius Petronius, who had advised on the important issue of parties at the palace after a senatorial career that had included distinguished service as governor of Syria. Thrasea Paetus' was another: he had specialised in irritating Nero and many senatorial colleagues by insisting that the Senate devote careful attention to what many regarded as trivial matters, then withdrew from public life in protest at Agrippina's assassination. His ostentatiously virtuous lifestyle and his claim to be imitating the conduct of Nero's ancestor the younger Cato, about whom he had written a book, held up an unforgiving mirror to Nero's openly anti-traditionalist behaviour. Could a man who so obviously refused to honour Augustus' traditions legitimately claim the position Augustus had created?

There was now no question but that the imperial system was not that of the traditional Republic, whose modus operandi was associated in some circles with *libertas*, freedom. To some, *libertas* meant no imperial court; to others the new system was a necessary improvement on the fractious past. Figures like the younger Cato or Pompey could become moral exemplars for members of the new order, and people could argue that Caesar deserved to be killed. But even when such opinions found support in the palace, the question arose as to whether *libertas* could figure in a world where the court was constantly covering up acts of indecency.

Nero's mental stability had come into further question when he killed Poppaea. She was pregnant with their child when he had physically assaulted her, causing the miscarriage from which she died. He displayed extreme remorse, allegedly stinking out the city of Rome with the vast quantities of incense that he burnt at her funeral.

But could he be trusted, even by his own staff? At the end of AD 66 he set out on a tour of Greece so as to participate in the great artistic and athletic festivals of Olympia, Delphi, Isthmia and Nemea, all of which were rescheduled to accommodate him. On the way he summoned Corbulo, now relieved of his command, to meet him at Corinth. When he arrived, Nero had him assassinated. This was the last straw. People were about to learn the big secret of empire, as Tacitus would put it: it was possible 'for an emperor to be made somewhere other than Rome' (Tacitus, *Histories* 1.4.2).

While Nero was heading for Greece, rebellion erupted in Judaea. The rebellion is yet another illustration of the difficulty Rome was having with a highly traditional society which did not operate according to the rules of the urban culture promoted by the imperial system. In this case Roman administrators had done nothing to solve long-standing regional tensions between the non-Jewish and Jewish populations, the latter a community whose splintered nature facilitated the rise of a radical faction. The absence of a governing group outside the court of King Herod Agrippa, who ruled part of the region, exacerbated the situation. There was no one with the clout to negotiate effectively either within Judaea or for competent government from Rome. So it was that, after months of increasingly bitter fighting, a radical group that had seized power in Jerusalem convinced the temple priests to stop offering sacrifices on behalf of Nero and Rome. This was tantamount to a declaration of war. The situation deteriorated further in November AD 66, when Cestius Gallus was thoroughly defeated at Beth Horon on the outskirts of Jerusalem.

With Corbulo dead and Gallus obviously incompetent, Nero's advisers looked for a new general to resume the Jewish war and for a new governor for Syria. They chose Vespasian to take command of the war and Licinius Mucianus to replace Gallus in Syria. The two were thought not to like each other. Vespasian, who had not been in the field for fifteen years, might not have been an obvious choice, not least because he had allegedly slept through one of Nero's artistic performances, but he did have connections at court. His brother Flavius Sabinus was well trusted in the palace and his companion of many years was Antonia Caenis, who had helped expose Sejanus' conspiracy.

And Vespasian was no one's fool. He had been around the court long enough to realise that winning a war was dangerous – he might have reflected that Suetonius Paulinus was retired and Corbulo had been murdered. Even as he led his army into Galilee for the campaign of AD 67, Vespasian was in contact with others who wanted to remove Nero from power. The conspiracy, which included Nero's supposed friend Otho as well as Galba, the elderly, childless governor of northern Spain, would be well under way by the end of AD 67.

Helius, who, although only a freedman, was running the palace in Rome, got wind of what was happening and wrote to Nero advising his immediate return to Italy. But he was ignored and Nero stayed in Greece into the autumn. In March AD 68 Julius Vindex, governor of Aquitania, declared his loyalty to the Senate and people of Rome, thereby denouncing Nero. Vespasian stopped campaigning immediately, so he must have known what was brewing. There were signs of trouble in Rome, where the junior praetorian prefect Nymphidius Sabinus had links with the conspirators; meanwhile, Tigellinus became suddenly inactive, allowing offensive edicts from Vindex to circulate in the city. There was a brief hiccup when the governor of Upper Germany, Verginius Rufus, lost control of his men outside the city of Vesontio (today's Besançon), where he had engaged with

Vindex. Vindex's men were slaughtered and the man himself committed suicide. The army offered Verginius Rufus the position of *princeps*, but he turned it down, declaring himself devoted to the cause of Galba.

On 9 June AD 68, correctly believing that he had been betrayed, Nero fled the imperial palace to the house of a freedman. This may have been a trap. Hearing sounds of pursuit and fearing humiliation, Nero took his own life. With Nymphidius Sabinus' encouragement, the praetorian guard proclaimed Galba emperor. The Senate followed suit. Nero was buried in the family tomb of the Domitii Ahenobarbi, in symbolic exile from the Augustan dynasty.

Galba's lack of children was important, for it allowed him to negotiate finding a successor. Various factions provided candidates. One was Nymphidius, who, claiming to be Caligula's illegitimate son, set up shop as interim emperor. When it became plain that he was not going to get the permanent job, he tried to launch a coup d'état in the praetorian camp. The guards, suffering a touch of buyer's remorse, killed him.

Someone else who thought he should get the job was Otho, who could bring with him support from within the palace. Another appears to have been Titus, Vespasian's older son, who was dispatched to Rome where his uncle Flavius Sabinus was manipulating opinion in his favour. Galba, who was a social snob, was repelled by the notion that he should choose an heir whose family could not be traced as far back as his. He could also be short-sighted. The empire's most powerful armies were those of Upper and Lower Germany, fully eight legions, and here Galba introduced confusion by changing the commanders of both. He removed Verginius Rufus from Upper Germany (alleging that this was for the betrayal of Nero rather than a sign that he did not fully trust him) and replaced him with an elderly non-entity. He then acquiesced in the murder of the governor of Lower Germany, who was alleged to be conspiring against him. In the place of the deceased governor he appointed Lucius Vitellius, son of Claudius' old friend. In so doing he was replacing an alleged conspirator with an actual conspirator.

Vitellius knew that to capture the throne he would need the support of the neighbouring army. Working through the legates Caecina and Valens, who bore grudges against Galba, taking advantage of the weak governor in Upper Germany, and soliciting troops who felt they had been inadequately rewarded for their desertion of Nero, Vitellius made his preparations. Assuming that ancestry still mattered, he could claim that his famous father, three times consul and censor, gave him the status that a man like Verginius lacked.

The revolt would begin when the legions of Upper Germany refused to take the oath of loyalty to Galba on 1 January AD 69, swearing instead their fealty to the Roman Senate and people, thus guaranteeing that Vitellius would not be facing a regional civil war before he could march on Italy. Vitellius himself did not claim at this point to be *princeps*, but rather that he was the representative of Rome. A supporter gave him a sword that had once been used by Julius Caesar himself (!) and had been stored in the Temple of Mars at Cologne.

Everything went according to plan, and by mid-January preparations were under way for the invasion of Italy. By then Galba would be dead, and Vitellius would be facing Otho instead.

Galba, refusing all advice, had selected a Piso as his adoptive son. This man, recently returned from exile, was not from the wing of the family represented by the conspirator of AD 65. He was the great-grandson of the consul of 58 BC, Caesar's father-in-law. Tacitus reports a speech Galba gave – like other Tacitean speeches, this would have offered the gist of what was said rather than the actual words spoken – in which he delighted in linking two old families, declaring that adoption gave him a chance to find the best man to be his heir and that the state would no longer be passed on as if it were the personal possession of the Julii and the Claudii. Tacitus had a deep sense of irony, for whereas he might here represent the ideology of imperial adoption as it stood in his own day, it would have been obvious to him that a man of such minimal experience was utterly inappropriate in a crisis. The adoption decision was confirmed within hours of the news of Vitellius' rebellion arriving at Rome.

Otho had promptly organised a group within the guard, using men he could trust to recruit others. On 15 January his plot came to fruition. Hearing that the guard had proclaimed someone else emperor, Galba dithered, then had himself taken down to the forum where Otho's men intercepted his litter and decapitated him. Piso was killed shortly thereafter. In summing up Galba's career, Tacitus noted that 'in the view of all men he was capable of ruling, if only he hadn't done so [*capax imperii nisi imperasset*]' (Tacitus, *Histories* 1.49.4).

Events moved rapidly. Vitellius, whose reputation as an idle gourmand was the consequence of civil war propaganda (more fake news), managed in early April AD 69 to get a significant strike force of around 20,000 men across the Alps, commanded by Caecina and Valens, as Otho assembled a scratch force around Rome. After some skirmishing in the Po valley, the rival armies encountered each other, somewhat by accident. Otho's men, worn out by their long march, and then defeated after a hard fight, fled to the nearby town of Bedriacum. It was scarcely a decisive defeat, and reinforcements were coming Otho's way from the Balkan garrisons, some from Moesia (a region now occupied by parts of Serbia, Romania and Bulgaria) having already arrived in northern Italy. But Otho's will was broken. After meeting with his senior officials, he killed himself. Tacitus observed that he was the first man 'to bring imperial power to a new family' (Tacitus, *Histories* 2.48).

The way was open for Vitellius to claim power for himself, which he would do with a display of respect for constitutional norms. He did not advertise himself as emperor until May, when the imperial powers were conferred upon him by statute. But well before then he had dealt his regime a fatal blow. He had not yet reached Italy when news of the debacle at Bedriacum arrived. At a victory celebration held in Lyons he forgave Otho's generals, who publicly confessed to having betrayed their emperor through poor handling of their men. He also spared Otho's brother but ordered the execution of the most strongly pro-Othonian centurions in the Moesian legions. How he would have known who those were, or if the charges were true, is unclear, and the difference between his treatment of junior and senior officials was lost on no one. Similarly, his decision to cashier the Othonian praetorian guard and replace it with men drafted from the northern legions, while a sensible precaution, gave the impression that men were suffering in inverse relation to their importance. In trying to advertise a new 'unity government' he sowed the seeds of his own destruction.

The executions alienated the Danubian forces, and elements of the three legions that had reached northern Italy put on a brief anti-Vitellius demonstration before returning to their camps to listen to another claimant. This was Vespasian, who had arranged his own acclamations, first in Alexandria on 1 July, where the prefect of Egypt took the lead. Then two days later the legions in Palestine acclaimed him, and the garrison of Syria was on board by the end of the week.

Vespasian had been laying the groundwork for a coup for several months. His brother Flavius Sabinus had been prefect of Rome under Galba, and in the months after Galba's assassination Vespasian had come to an understanding with Mucianus in Syria that they would act together. He now began to spread stories of miraculous events. It mattered to him that he be seen as the choice of the gods, and to that end he released from custody a Jewish leader, Josephus, whom he had captured the year before in Galilee. Josephus, who would become a major historian of the Jewish community, had predicted that Vespasian would be emperor. The same had been prophesied at an ancient shrine to Aphrodite at Paphos on Cyprus, and there had been another prophetic moment at a sacrifice on Mount Carmel in Syria. When Vespasian moved on to Alexandria after his proclamation, 'many miracles occurred' (Tacitus, *Histories* 4.81.1) as Vespasian healed the sick, Tacitus says.

Vespasian was expecting more trouble than actually materialised. He was in Alexandria, so he could control the departure of grain ships to Rome in the event of a long struggle. Titus was left to deal with the revolt in Palestine and Mucianus was sent with a substantial force from the Syrian army to invade Italy. Vespasian sent letters to leaders of the auxiliary units on the Rhine, urging them to rebel – it is somewhat ironic that, given he was technically in charge of an operation to quash a nationalist revolt, he should attempt to spark one in another part of the empire. All of this proved to be overkill: he had underestimated the Danubian garrisons' irritation with Vitellius and the deep mutual antipathy between Vitellius' chief generals, Valens and Caecina.

In early August commanders of the Balkan legions met at Poetovio (now Ptuj in Slovenia) to discuss letters that had arrived from Vespasian. The provincial governors, elderly appointees of Otho's, allowed Antonius Primus, a man with a somewhat disreputable past, and Cornelius Fuscus, an imperial procurator, to drive the agenda. The two secured general support for Vespasian, and at Primus' urging prepared to invade Italy without waiting for the rapidly advancing Mucianus. Primus wanted to get there before Vitellius could gather reinforcements from the German legions, and because his men had recently been in Italy he was aware of groups there that feared reprisals for having supported Otho.

When news that the Balkan legions were on the march reached Vitellius just after his birthday on 7 September, the defence of Italy began to disintegrate. Caecina, jealous of Valens, contacted Primus; on 12 October one of Rome's two major fleets, the one at Ravenna – the other was based at Misenum – declared its loyalty to Vespasian. On 18 October, Caecina tried to make his two legions follow suit, but was arrested and placed in custody at Cremona. Six days later, Primus' troops encountered Caecina's former army very close to where it had defeated Otho's a few months earlier. After a desperate night-long struggle, the Vitellian forces were defeated. Caecina negotiated their surrender at Cremona, which Primus occupied, then sacked. On hearing the news, Valens took flight. He would later be captured and executed. Caecina survived, and thrived for some time in Vespasian's court.

Primus halted for a while so that Mucianus could catch up. At the end of November their combined forces moved on Rome. There was nothing Vitellius could do to stop them. When the fleet at Misenum also changed sides, he was left with only the praetorian guard, who had nothing to lose by fighting on and could count on a swift departure from service when Vitellius fell – indeed, they were the driving force behind Vitellius' last days. Negotiating with Flavius Sabinus, who was still in Rome with Vespasian's younger son Domitian, Vitellius arranged to abdicate on 18 December. The guard refused to go along with this and, with his nephew and a handful of men, Sabinus seized the Capitoline. They held out for a day until the guard stormed the defences, burning the great temple as they did so. Sabinus was killed and Domitian went into hiding.

On 20 December, Vespasian's forces fought their way into Rome and Vitellius was killed by a mob. Vespasian was the fourth emperor of the year AD 69.

29

REIMAGINING ROME

Vespasian had a dream in which he and his sons were placed in scales opposite Claudius and Nero. It was a perfect balance. Suetonius, his biographer, thought it remarkable that Vespasian's dynasty would endure as long as the reigns of Claudius and Nero put together – twenty-six years.

Originally, the dream was interpreted somewhat differently. Vespasian revealed it to the Senate to 'prove' that the gods had determined both his future and that of his sons. That was useful to him, but for us the vision is interesting because it tells us something about the way he thought about recent history. Nero and Claudius still mattered, Augustus and Tiberius were distant figures, and it was perhaps best just to forget about Caligula. That was certainly something Vespasian would have been happy to do, as his early senatorial career had been notable for his abject flattery of the man. For now, however, the issue was whether he could cope with the bureaucratic monarchy that had replaced the Augustan and Tiberian visions of a managed Republic. Vespasian saw Claudius as the originator of that monarchy, and much of his efforts were directed towards renewing Claudius' projects while undoing Nero's.

Before Vespasian could renew anything, however, there was a great deal of other work to be done. The Jewish revolt had to be dealt with, and his attempts to destabilise Vitellius' support in the Rhineland had provoked a bizarre revolt that gathered steam even as Mucianus was marching on Rome.

The political situation in the Rhine estuary had been unstable even before Vitellius marched south. The area south of the river was home to the Batavians, a tribe that prided itself on its militarism and, along with tribes to their immediate south, had provided numerous auxiliary units to the Roman army. The contacts made between these groups' leaders during the British campaigns probably facilitated the development of the network that Vespasian would have to deal with – one of the revolt's leaders, Julius Classicus, figures on a writing tablet from London as commanding an auxiliary unit around that settlement in the immediate aftermath of Boudicca's revolt. Unrest in the area was smouldering before the rebellion against Nero, for Fonteius Capito, governor of Lower Germany, had sent a Batavian aristocrat, one Julius Civilis, to Nero on a charge of conspiracy. Galba released him, Capito was murdered by his men, and all might have been well had not Civilis aroused Vitellius' suspicions. The problem was that Civilis and Antonius Primus were friends, and in August or September he received letters from Primus urging him to lead a rebellion against Vitellius.

Civilis was a well-connected individual and, unlike the leaders of the Jewish revolt, who had minimal connection with the Roman power structure, the leadership of the revolt that was now taking shape derived essentially from the Roman administration. Civilis, who had one eye, was fond of comparing himself with Hannibal and Sertorius. Julius Sabinus, another rebel leader, claimed to be descended from a bastard fathered by Julius Caesar, and the burning of the Temple of Capitoline Jupiter was taken as a sign that Roman rule might be fated to end. The revolt, which led to Classicus proclaiming the 'Empire of the Gauls', would be not so much anti-Roman as alternative Roman. Civilis' evident hope, in the chaos of the civil war, was to establish an independent enclave straddling the mouth of the Rhine that he could rule on his own; and that seems largely to have been Classicus' notion as well.

Civilis was helped by Hordeonius Flaccus, governor of Lower Germany, once Vitellius' reluctant supporter and now an aspiring ally of Vespasian. Since Hordeonius' men remained loyal to those comrades who had gone south with Vitellius, his way of aiding Vespasian was to allow Civilis to build up his strength without interruption. This Civilis did and linked units of his fellow Batavians with people from north of the border – a move facilitated by his alliance with a holy woman named Veleda, who was thought to be good at predicting the future. The situation was complicated further when news came of Cremona, at which point Hordeonius tried to have his men swear an oath of loyalty to Vespasian. Instead, they killed him.

Hordeonius' assassination gave Civilis the excuse to continue to attack the legions, scoring a couple of notable successes. He captured Vetera (modern Xanten in North Rhine-Westphalia), which had been defended by two depleted legions: having sworn an oath of loyalty to the 'Empire of the Gauls', they were massacred anyway. Classicus, who dressed as a Roman emperor, took over three more legions – the garrison of Upper Germany – after their Vitellian commander had been assassinated. By springtime the rebels controlled a fair portion of the Rhine frontier.

Vespasian had no idea what was going on, and Mucianus, who had taken charge in Rome, was trying to build a government, which meant dealing with people he did not much trust. Domitian was young and, some said, obnoxious. The Senate was asserting itself forcefully under the leadership of the urban praetor Helvidius Priscus and, while it did pass a law granting power to Vespasian, Priscus made a point of the fact that it had been the Senate's decision to do so. Antonius Primus, who had been altogether too heroic, was blamed for pretty much everything that had gone wrong, including the destruction of Cremona, and was urged into gentle retirement in southern France. The surviving praetorian prefect was demoted; the surviving members of the guard, Vitellians to a man, were cashiered. An old family friend of Vespasian's was made praetorian prefect, but his closeness to Domitian led to friction with Mucianus.

The sheer number of troops in Italy was a problem, too, and if trouble was to be averted they had to be sent back to the provinces. Since Mucianus was stuck in Italy, the only person who could be trusted, politically, was Vespasian's son-in-law Petilius Cerealis, governor-designate of Britain. Except for his connection with Vespasian, Petilius would not have been an obvious choice for a major command. He was noted for his rashness, manifested when a column he had sent to relieve Colchester during Boudicca's revolt had been ambushed and suffered heavy losses; in the recent fighting he had advanced too eagerly on Rome at the head of a cavalry detachment, which had also lost many men.

Nevertheless, Petilius was sent north with a large force, combining troops from Vitellius' army with Primus' Balkan legions and a legion from Spain. Taking advantage of his superior numbers and displaying some diplomatic skill, he recovered the garrison of Upper Germany, and by the end of the summer had pretty much restored the situation on the

Rhine. Mucianus, accompanied by Domitian, went off to Gaul, where he organised the shifting of legions between the Balkan and Rhine armies so as to rebuild the latter and remove Vitellians from their home bases. Henceforth it became standard practice to deploy auxiliary units anywhere but in their home provinces. Of the leaders of the revolt, Classicus was killed, while Civilis and Veleda made off into the German forests.

Vespasian's older son Titus had been left to command Judaea in AD 69, and began the siege of Jerusalem in March AD 70. The city's sturdy walls and defendable features within them, the most important being the great temple, enabled its dogged defenders to hold on in parts of the city until the end of August, when Titus' forces finally burst into the temple. This they thoroughly sacked, removing its greatest treasures for display in the triumph to be celebrated in Rome that November. Resistance would continue in parts of Judaea for another four years until, just as the Romans were breaking through their fortifications, the defenders of Masada committed suicide rather than surrender.

Vespasian arrived in Rome in the autumn of AD 70 and would not leave Italy again. Concentrating his energies on restoring the state finances, ruined by Nero and the subsequent wars, he would also oversee some massive construction projects in Rome and the restructuring of the imperial defences. He would be long remembered for his creative approach to revenue enhancement (including a urinal tax), and for generally being a good ruler. According to Tacitus, who knew about his behaviour under Caligula, he was the one individual whose conduct actually improved after becoming emperor. Tacitus stressed the importance of his personal style for dissuading senators from ostentatious expenditure, and appreciated the fact that Vespasian promoted the rise of new families to the upper echelons of power. Tacitus had a link with the palace through his father-in-law Julius Agricola, who accompanied Cerealis on the Rhine and to Britain, where he would later serve an extended term trying to bring order to its northern reaches.

Personal connections mattered a great deal. On his return from Judaea, Titus took up the post of praetorian prefect, a highly unusual move as no senator had previously ever held the post, but he used the position to function as his father's deputy. In the east, Marcus Ulpius Traianus (father of the later emperor Trajan) assumed a role like Corbulo's in overseeing a radical reorganisation of the Persian frontier, once the revolt in Judaea was over.

Josephus, former rebel, later Roman spokesperson and personal prophet
to Vespasian, moved to Rome when the war in Judaea ended. There he
composed works denying that he was a traitor to his people. These works
include his surviving history of the Jewish war, which presents the conflict
as a civil war into which Rome had been drawn to defend public order. The
Jews had been led astray by radicals, he said, as had he when he assumed
command of Galilee. He then composed a nineteen-book history of his
people from earliest times through to the outbreak of the revolt; an autobiography refuting the charge (levelled by another Jew) that he had lied
about his role as an instigator of the revolt; and a defence of Judaism in
response to a violently anti-Semitic tract by Apion, a Greek grammarian
and sophist. The *Antiquities*, *Life* and *Apion* were all completed after the
deaths of Vespasian (in AD 79) and Titus (in AD 81) under the patronage of
Domitian (who would rule from AD 81 to 96) and the powerful freedman
Epaphroditus.

Josephus was not the only one to thrive via connections made at headquarters during the Jewish revolt. Titus had fallen deeply in love with
Berenice, wife of the Judaean king Herod Agrippa. He was compelled to
leave her in Judaea when he returned to Rome, but after a few years he
brought her to the city as his companion, where she remained until his
death. Another survivor was Caecina, whose treason in AD 69 was amply
rewarded; also powerful was Eprius Marcellus, the old friend of Tigellinus and, we may suspect, of Vespasian. Eprius was famous for a response
he had given to an attack on his character in the Senate during January
AD 70. Tacitus recalled him as reminding his colleagues that 'we long for
good emperors and live with what we get' (Tacitus, *Histories* 4.8.2). In AD
75, though, both men fell foul of Titus. Caecina was summarily executed;
Eprius committed suicide after a show trial for treason.

The initiator of the attack on Eprius in AD 70 was Helvidius Priscus, son-
in-law of the Thrasea Paetus who had annoyed Nero (Eprius was one of
those who had brought about Paetus' forced suicide). Priscus seems to
have resented the fact that people he regarded as Neronian toadies were
continuing to flourish under Vespasian, but his outspokenness led first to
his exile, and then, on Titus' orders, to his execution. The cult of Cato
that Paetus and Priscus had promoted was a feature of the rethinking of
traditional narratives that was characteristic of this age. Valerius Flaccus, a
poet writing towards the end of Vespasian's reign, composed an extensive

reinterpretation of the myth of Jason and the Argonauts that added a civil war to the goings-on in the mythical kingdom of Colchis, peopled with images of the tribes that Rome was finding increasingly troublesome in the lands of the Danube. The retelling of myth could thus be used to point up eternal verities, such as the fact that civil war was a bad idea.

One of the greatest poets of the era, Papinius Statius, who admired Lucan's unfinished poem on the civil war between Caesar and Pompey, wrote his own civil war poem in retelling the myth of the Seven against Thebes, the tale of how the great Greek heroes in the generation before the war at Troy tried to restore Polynices to the throne from which his brother had driven him. Turning to modern themes, he composed an epic about wars that Domitian fought in Germany, as well as numerous shorter poems honouring various of his contemporaries. Another senator, Silius Italicus, one of the last two consuls of Nero's reign, offered a massive poetic reinterpretation of the war with Hannibal in which he not only rewrote large parts of Livy in the Virgilian style, but contributed to the canonisation of the Senate of the Hannibalic era as a bunch of virtuous primitives.

Silius' vision of the Senate links thematically with one of the most remarkable compositions of Vespasian's reign, the 37-book *Natural History* by the elder Pliny. He had previously written a major history of the German wars and a history of the later Julio-Claudians. In the *Natural History*, Pliny's central concerns are man's perversion of nature for his own pleasure, and the dangerous effects of luxury on personal morality. He was a close associate of Vespasian and the work is dedicated to Titus, under whom he served as commander of the fleet at Misenum. Pliny despised Sulla as a mass murderer but had a more positive view of Marius, whose victories over the Cimbrians and Teutons he admired. He was deeply interested in the life of Scipio Africanus, thought highly of the elder Cato, and honoured the memory of other heroes of the distant past like Manlius Dentatus and Appius Claudius the Blind. He reports many things about the Julio-Claudians, ranging from their taste in wine and Tiberius' habit of wearing laurel to avoid incineration in thunderstorms, to miraculous events allegedly connected with their rise and fall. He seems not to have rated Agrippina very highly – he liked Claudius, whose poisoning appalled him – and felt that Nero was an offence against nature, as was Caligula.

These recollections show that the discourse of members of the imperial inner circle was not uncritical of individual emperors, even if it supported the imperial regime. Emperors were meant to be measured against other emperors – a major shift in thinking from the Augustan era – which meant that the good had to be taken with the bad. In the law granting Vespasian his imperial powers, only three previous emperors – Augustus, Tiberius and Claudius – are mentioned as worthy precedents.

The vibrant literary and intellectual environment of the Flavian era was not limited to Rome. One visitor to the city in Domitian's time was Plutarch of Chaeronea, who went home to compose his parallel lives of famous Greeks and Romans as well as a collection of lives of the Caesars, beginning with Augustus and running through to the year AD 69. He also left a large collection of works on topics ranging from ideal personal behaviour and the good marriage – in his view, women should be thoroughly subordinate to their husbands – to literary criticism, religion and politics. His two guidebooks for politicians deprecate activities that might draw the attention of the imperial authorities. People who competed for popular favour, putting on shows and games, should remember that there was always a higher authority. This is no different from the view that Josephus expressed: it was possible for the Jewish community to retain its integrity so long as its leaders acknowledged their place within the Roman system; and so, too, Greek city leaders, who could celebrate their cultural traditions *and* be members of the imperial community. In turn, imperial administrators saw themselves as providing the expertise that their local counterparts lacked. They were, ideally, mentors for the advancement of local culture as well as for the maintenance of law and order.

Plutarch stood at one end of a spectrum of responses to Rome. Loyalty and success were represented by interest in the shared urban culture, but that culture was still not for everyone. Jews, at least in some eastern provinces, felt left out, and the rabid anti-Semitism of people like Apion suggests that they continued to face violent hostility in some areas – chiefly Egypt, Cyrene and the Palestinian homeland. Elsewhere things could be different, as at Sardis, for instance, where the elegant synagogue located near the gymnasium represents both the openness of the local Jewish community to its neighbours and their integration within the community.

In Asia Minor the dialogue between the different communities led to a growing interest in the concept of a highest god, whose image seems to have been shaped by the concept of Yahweh in Jewish scripture. On the fringe of the Jewish community, linking Jew and non-Jew, was the developing Christian movement. Notable for its hostility to what its members perceived as the hypocrisy of a world where goodness and wealth were readily equated, this community was now generating its own literature. The Gospels of Matthew, Mark, Luke and John, as well as the Acts of the Apostles, are all products of the Flavian era, as is the Apocalypse of John (the Book of Revelation), which blends the history of Rome into a vision of the end of the world which Christians believed was imminent. Thus wrote John:

> And I stood upon the sand of the sea, and saw a beast rise out of the sea, having seven heads and ten horns, and upon his horns ten crowns, and upon his heads the name of blasphemy. And the beast which I saw was like unto a leopard, and his feet were as the feet of a bear, and his mouth as the mouth of a lion: and the dragon gave him his power, and his seat, and great authority ... And I beheld another beast coming up out of the earth; and he had two horns like a lamb, and he spoke as a dragon ... And he exerciseth all the power of the first beast before him, and causeth the earth and them which dwell therein to worship the first beast, whose deadly wound was healed. And he doeth great wonders ... Here is wisdom. Let him that hath understanding count the number of the beast: for it is the number of a man; and his number is 666.
>
> (Revelation 13 (King James translation, marginally adapted))

The beast of the number 666 is Nero, whose name written in Aramaic can be valued at 666 and whose appearance here indicates the Flavian promotion of Nero as the ultimate anti-emperor.

One of the earliest indications we get of the interaction between Christians and their neighbours, and of the separation of communities, comes in the correspondence between Pliny the Younger, the nephew of the Pliny we have already met, and the emperor Trajan (who reigned AD 98–117). These letters, written when he governed the province of Bithynia in AD 111–12, offer numerous exchanges about fixing messes that the locals had made. Ones touching directly on Roman interests required a direct Roman response, as did issues that could reflect on the greater glory of the emperor; others were plainly regarded as items not requiring the full attention of the imperial authorities. In the case of the Christians – two of whose leaders, both women, Pliny had tortured for information – Trajan decided that, even though their faith was not to be encouraged, no governor should waste his time trying to round them up.

24. Trajan, emperor AD 98–117, the portrait is intended to portray a personal style very different from Domitian's and project a youthfulness missing in Nerva's brief reign.

Turning to more practical matters, Pliny found, for instance, that the city of Sinope needed an extra water supply, which he thought could be sourced from a spring sixteen miles away. Trajan agreed: this was the sort of engineering that the Roman state was good at. Then, although the property of people who died without heirs normally went to the imperial *fiscus*, Pliny discovered that the people of Nicaea (modern Iznik) claimed that Augustus had allowed them to take possession themselves. Trajan ordered him to consult his provincial procurators, who would presumably have better records.

In another case Pliny encountered Dio Cocceianus, a distinguished intellectual, who wanted to transfer some building projects he had begun to his home city of Prusa (Bursa in modern-day Turkey), thereby saddling it with an expense that he had originally promised to pay. Members of Prusa's town council objected, adding that Dio had placed a statue of Trajan in his family tomb –which counted as treason and black magic, since he was associating the emperor with the deceased. Pliny investigated and found that Trajan's statue was in a library rather than a tomb, but wondered how to tackle what was clearly a local political spat. Trajan told him to drop the investigation into treason and follow the money – the emperor did not wish 'to gain respect' for his name 'through the fear and apprehension of the public' (Pliny, *Letters* 10.82), and nor did he want to have an imperial official tied up in what he saw as his subjects' personal problems.

Proper management of civic expenses was a technical matter an official could usually deal with. The trouble that Dio was having in Prusa stemmed from basic public finance issues common to all cities whose emoluments derived from public–private partnerships. At Nicaea, Pliny had found that a theatre being built with public money was badly engineered, subject to massive cost overruns and was already falling apart – which prevented the contractors from carrying through the promised additions to the building. He also found that the city was overspending on a new gymnasium, and that the people of Claudiopolis (modern Bolu) were overbuilding a bathhouse in a bad location. When Pliny asked Trajan for an architect to look things over, the emperor's response was that there must be a local who could do the job. By contrast, when he discovered an unfinished canal near the important city of Nicomedia (now Izmet) that would allow easier transport to the sea and asked if he should finish it, this, as with the Sinope case, was deemed a big enough job to merit sending out a Roman architect.

That government was for the big things was a feature of Vespasian's thinking. His building projects in Rome were all on a generous scale, beginning with a new temple for Capitoline Jupiter, with Vespasian himself taking a hand in removing the rubble of the old temple. Other projects included the completion of a large temple to the Divine Claudius (the failure to finish which had reflected badly on Nero), a huge Temple of Peace in its own forum near the Forum of Augustus, some public baths and, most spectacular of all, a new amphitheatre. The site chosen for the ampitheatre was that of an artificial pond in the grounds of Nero's Golden House and next to a colossal statue of the sun god Sol: originally with Nero's features, this was given a more traditional look by Vespasian.

The new Flavian amphitheatre, financed by plunder from the sack of Jerusalem, would ultimately take its name from the colossal statue of the sun god and become known as the Colosseum. It was unfinished when Vespasian died, so it was up to Titus to complete it and then open it, which he did with a hundred days of spectacular games. Domitian would add a gigantic palace whose remains now occupy the northern end of the

Palatine, divided between official state chambers with banqueting and reception halls, a stadium and the emperor's private quarters. The new palace offered a vision of professional government radically different from the houses of Augustus, Livia and Tiberius, whose style reflected the aristocratic sensibilities of an earlier age, and its remains survive to this day at the southern end of the hill.

Although his vision of government was grandiose, Vespasian's view of how an emperor should behave was anything but. He was hard-working, rising at dawn to deal with his correspondence – much of it letters from cities and individuals appealing for his intervention – and meeting with close advisers, one of whom was the elder Pliny. He even dressed himself – unusual for an emperor – which was a way of demonstrating that he would only take advice in public. When the morning's work was done, he would go for a drive, have a modest lunch and then, after Antonia Caenis died, enjoy some afternoon sex with one of his young women. He would bath, then have dinner, also accompanied. He sought to limit what he saw as the extreme indulgence of earlier eras, and his tastes were ostentatiously simple. The keynotes of his administration were civility, approachability and publicity. Partly, he was making a point about Nero's style, and even Claudius' tendency to work behind closed doors. An emperor was, in his view, what an emperor did.

When Vespasian died in AD 79 at the age of sixty-nine, Titus stepped easily into his shoes. Domitian, who was several years younger, had never been treated as an equal by Vespasian and had held just an ordinary consulship in a year when his father and brother were both censors. Upon their father's death, Titus brought Domitian somewhat more into the limelight, as he had no son. But he remained front and centre during the great games and then, after October, when the eruption of Vesuvius buried Pompeii and other cities, in bringing relief to the victims. The elder Pliny died sailing with the fleet from Misenum to bring assistance to those in danger. The younger Pliny, who was only seventeen at the time of the eruption and was with him in Misenum, stayed at home reading Livy, but has left us a stunning description of the event, written at Tacitus' instigation.

The opening of the Colosseum and the eruption of Vesuvius have bequeathed to the modern world two of the most memorable monuments of ancient times, falling in the same year in the reign of one of Rome's most short-lived emperors. Titus died on 13 September AD 81 after a reign of two years, two months and twenty days. His brother succeeded him.

Domitian was a difficult man. If one were to take at face value much of what the younger Pliny says – and he was quick to spread stories about the dire days of Domitian throughout the first nine books of his letters – he was an arrogant, self-righteous, somewhat paranoid individual prone to lecture people on their habits while routinely conspiring with a few toadies against honourable men. Pliny even claimed that he would have been killed by Domitian if Domitian had not been killed first (this was unlikely – Pliny had done well under Domitian). Tacitus, whose biography of his father-in-law Julius Agricola takes as its theme the difficulties of being a good man under a bad emperor, saw Domitian as deeply jealous of able subordinates who had proved their worth. This is one reason why, when Agricola had campaigned throughout Scotland and brought peace to Britain, Domitian abandoned the Scottish territories and refused to re-employ him.

Tacitus allows that he was personally 'promoted a long way' (Tacitus, *Histories* 1.1.3) by Domitian: he earned a reputation as a leading orator, was given a significant priesthood by AD 88 and was awarded a consulship for AD 97. Furthermore, he expresses dislike for people who deliberately provoked the emperor's bad temper. The poet Statius was a fan of Domitian; Martial, another excellent poet of the era, apparently wrote pretty much whatever he wanted, as did Quintilian, a great rhetorician and author of a book on oratory. Juvenal, however, the most brilliant satirist of the age, described Domitian as a 'bald Nero' who wrecked the world (*Satires* 4.38). Suetonius produced a series of nasty stories about him and is not alone in asserting that Domitian liked torturing flies. It is fair to say that people's reactions to the man were probably conditioned by the ways in which they had to interact with him, but also by the fact that he eschewed the public civility of his father. He was a man of the palace rather than of the people.

More important than Domitian's personality, though, were the changes taking place beyond Rome's frontiers and his reaction to them. On the positive side, although there was periodic tension with Persia – which was hardly news – it required no mounting of a major campaign even when the Parthian king asserted that a man claiming to be Nero was the real thing (this was in the 80s, almost twenty years after his death). Despite Tacitus' insistence that Scotland could have become a permanent part of Britain, it is hard to know whether this was a practical proposition. The German frontier, where Domitian went personally, appears to have been

25. *The honorific inscription for Tiberius Plautius Silvanus Aelianus is on his large tomb on the outskirts of Tivoli.*

reasonably stable, and his military presence there was largely to make up for his lack of military reputation.

The real problem was in the Balkans. The frontier Domitian inherited was essentially that of the Augustan era, based on the three provinces of Dalmatia, Moesia and Pannonia, whose garrisons played such an important role in the civil war of AD 69. The extent of the pressure on the region emerges from a speech Vespasian gave to honour his friend Tiberius Plautius Silvanus Aelianus, who had been governor of Moesia for an extended stint from AD 60 to AD 67:

> When [Tiberius Plautius Silvanus Aelianus] was serving as governor of Moesia he brought more than 100,000 of the Transdanubian

peoples with their wives, children, leaders and kings to pay tribute, he quashed a threatened invasion by the Sarmatians even though he had sent the greater part of his army to the campaign in Armenia; he brought kings who were hitherto unknown or hostile to the Roman people to pay their respects to the Roman standards on the bank that he protected, he restored to the kings of the Bastarnae and the Rhoxolani their children, and their brothers to the Dacians, who had been captured and taken away by enemies, from some of them he took hostages through whom he strengthened and extended the peace of the province, and, rescuing the king of the Scythians from the peninsula that is beyond the Borysthenes from siege, he was the first man to support the grain supply for the Roman people with a great deal of grain from that region.

(*ILS* 986)

The Borysthenes was the area around the mouth of Russia's Dnieper river, while the other peoples mentioned above lived in what are now Romania (the Dacians) and Bulgaria. In Plautius' time the dominant people north of the border were the Sarmatians. During Vespasian's time the balance of power swung in the direction of the Dacians under their new king Decebelus, who united the warring peoples north of the border and began raiding Roman territory, destroying one Roman army in AD 85 and another in AD 86, the latter commanded by Cornelius Fuscus who had helped Vespasian take the throne twenty-five years earlier. One Julianus, who may have been an ageing member of the same group as Fuscus, proved a better general, defeating the Dacians at Tapae, near Sarmizegetusa in Romania, in AD 88, thereby setting up an opportunity for Domitian to take the field a year later, after which he celebrated a triumph.

The two defeats, though, damaged Domitian's prestige, and his tendency to rely on a small clique of aged advisers prevented him from developing a broader network of friends. Also, there had been scandals that had left a bad taste in people's mouths. In AD 83 he had prosecuted a case involving three Vestals, who were accused on good evidence of being no longer virginal. They were executed. Then, following a botched effort at a military uprising by the governor of Upper Germany, came another Vestal scandal, involving the head of the order. There was no question of her guilt, apparently, but it begs credulity that these were the first sexually active Vestals in two centuries.

Domitian's interest in prosecuting such cases was perhaps not unconnected with his military disasters and an outbreak of plague, accompanied by rumours of a sort unheard of since the years after the defeat of Antiochus III – that people were engaged in widespread poisoning (in this case, using poisoned needles). Nor did it help that he was on terrible terms with his wife, while rumoured to be on all too good terms with his niece Julia. In AD 92 he was badly defeated, again by Decebelus, then negotiated a peace settlement that he tried to present as a triumph. The false triumph may have damaged his prestige quite as much as the defeat: defeats could be survived; blatant lies were less forgivable.

Domitian felt his grasp on power weakening, and his lack of a son was raising questions about the future. In AD 93 he struck out against his 'enemies', including supporters of Thrasea Paetus. The list of senior senators who fell victim to his suspicions reached the twenties, and people feared even their own slaves would become informers. Domitian increasingly cut himself off in his Alban villa; the elaborate spectacles that he put on for the people may have been marred by his excessive displays of partisanship, and his effort to change the basic structure of chariot-racing to accommodate two new 'factions' (teams) in addition to the traditional four was not enthusiastically welcomed. Quite possibly people felt that the new factions were too close to the palace; and they resented the fact that Domitian ended performances with pantomimes.

Pantomime, which had become very popular under Augustus, was a form of theatre in which a man danced to a myth-based libretto set to music. Fights between the fans of different dancers were commonplace, but the point of the spectacle was to give ordinary citizens some sense of control, a conduit for expressing their opinions. Because of the violence connected with these performances there had been cancellations in the past, but these were usually very short-term, unlike under Domitian. All in all, his general meddling and incompetence were causing ever greater societal stress; in the language of the time, Domitian was slipping from *principatus* (emperorship) into *dominatio* (tyranny).

The tensions reached breaking point with two executions. First, the emperor targeted one of his cousins, Flavius Clemens, whose sons he had adopted, on a charge of atheism. Then, in AD 95, he executed Epaphroditus, the freedman who had once worked for Nero. His staff had had enough. Both praetorian prefects joined with his wife, the chief chamberlain Parthenius and other staff members to find a senator who was willing to take Domitian's place. This proved difficult as the senators moved in different circles and some felt they were being set up. Finally, Cocceius Nerva, an elderly and childless senator originally from Umbria, agreed to take the position. He was assured that his horoscope indicated that he could become emperor. He therefore had nothing to lose.

Domitian's assassins, all members of the palace staff, ambushed him in his private quarters on 28 September AD 96. Then Nerva was proclaimed emperor.

30

THE VIEW FROM TIVOLI

Nerva was a survivor. He had been close to Nero, but also to Vespasian, with whom he had shared the consulship in AD 71. He knew that the most interesting thing he would ever do was name a successor and so he took his time, surrounding himself with men of his own generation, including Verginius Rufus – still famous for having turned down the job of *princeps* in AD 68 – and Julius Frontinus, who had been governor of Britain. Frontinus was also the author of two books that survive, one on stratagems, the other on aqueducts, the latter composed in this year, AD 96, when Nerva put him in charge of the city's water supply. Nerva also lowered taxes for the rich and cut public expenditure – both moves were political code for 'my predecessor was a spendthrift, a crook and a poor steward of the state'.

Not all his friends survived the year. One, whom he wished to place on an agrarian commission, died before he could do anything, merely saying that he was pleased at least to have outlived Domitian. Another, Silius Italicus, was too sick to travel to Rome. Then Verginius Rufus fatally slipped and fell while practising the speech of thanks he was to address to Nerva for making him his consular partner for AD 98. At his funeral, Tacitus delivered the eulogy – a sure indicator of his rise to prominence, representing the new generation whose time had come.

Tacitus was suffect consul in AD 97. About this time he composed his short biography of his father-in-law, Julius Agricola. Stressing the values of the non-political military man, the book appeared just as Nerva was reaching his decision – almost too late – about who should be the next emperor. In the autumn his hand was forced when the praetorians rioted: the new emperor would be Trajan, then governor of Upper Germany.

Trajan was in Cologne when Nerva died, on 28 January 98 AD. He received word of the emperor's death in February from his nephew Hadrian, who had been dispatched with the news. Secure enough in his position to feel no immediate need to go to Rome, Trajan took off for the Danube, having first summoned to his headquarters the praetorians who had rebelled against Nerva. The conspirators would never return to Rome, and it was not until the autumn of AD 99 that he himself ventured there.

In AD 100 Trajan was saluted by, among others, the younger Pliny, who was suffect consul for the year. The surviving version of his inaugural speech (which Pliny lengthened well beyond the original) paints a picture of a man fully attuned to the Vespasianic style of administration. Yes, there had been miraculous predictions of Trajan's future greatness, but he was pleasant enough, and accessible. He showed respect for the accomplishments of his senators, reduced inheritance taxes, and sponsored programmes to support boys in rural Italy. He had had a long senatorial career, was the son of a man who had also had a long career as well as an important place in Vespasian's administration, and he seems to have genuinely shared the value system that Pliny laid out at such length. Furthermore, he was the first emperor whose family roots were outside Italy – his father was from Spain – so he could be expected to support men from newer families as they entered the administration.

When Trajan arrived in Rome he was married to Pompeia Plotina, whose intellect and simple lifestyle Pliny held out as a model for all other women even though the couple, after many years of marriage, had no children. Pliny also praised Plotina's relationship with Ulpia Marciana, Trajan's sister. Marciana had a granddaughter, Sabina, who was married to Hadrian, the son of Trajan's cousin. Plotina's friendship with Marciana, underscored by the fact that they would both soon receive the title Augusta, redefined from the designation 'Madame Empress' to 'leading lady', was a crucial factor for the future.

Trajan's style, of which we have already seen something in his correspondence with Pliny, was thoughtful and showed respect for precedent. He plainly sought to define his own place in the tradition of 'good' emperors, and Pliny gives us a glimpse of his world view when he describes a rare occasion on which he joined the emperor for a business weekend in the country. There is no hint of the allegation made by Cassius Dio – on good information, he claimed – of an imperial fondness for drink and sex with boys (which Dio qualified by saying that he had never caused harm to anyone). Pliny wrote instead of his pleasure at witnessing the emperor's 'justice and dignity' and his modesty in private.

There were three cases on the docket for the weekend.

One involved a man from Ephesus who had been charged with treason by his enemies. He was acquitted. The next was a case that fell under the provisions of the Augustan adultery legislation. Here, the wife of a retired military tribune who was about to seek senatorial office had been found guilty of a liaison with a centurion (since centurions were usually equestrians, she was not stepping outside her social milieu). Trajan had cashiered the centurion, but now the aggrieved husband, who seemingly still loved his wife, was trying to avoid having her sentenced under the law, which would have required divorce and her forfeiture of the dowry she had brought to the marriage. In Trajan's view, the law was the law: he ordered that she suffer the penalty, issuing a statement to the effect that he trusted such cases would not be coming his way in future and that lust would not corrupt army discipline.

The third case involved the forgery of a will. The heirs (there were no children) claimed that several bequests added to the will at a later date had been faked. If the will was found invalid, the law decreed that the imperial *fiscus* receive property for which there was now no legal heir. In the event, two of Trajan's officials were charged with fraud:

> The accused were Sempronius Senecio, a Roman knight, and Eurythmus, a freedman and procurator of the emperor. The heirs, when the emperor was in Dacia [during his second war in the region], had written jointly asking him to conduct the inquiry. He took it up … When he found that some of the heirs were reluctant to appear out of fear for Eurythmus and intended to drop the case, he had very properly declared that 'he [Eurythmus] is not Polyclitus [Nero's freedman] nor am I Nero'. He had, however, allowed an adjournment, and now … he sat to hear the case. Only two of the heirs appeared, and asked that either all the heirs should be compelled to appear, since they were all responsible for the prosecution, or that they should be allowed to drop the case. When the lawyer for Senecio and Eurythmus said that his clients were left under suspicion if they were

not given a hearing, the emperor's reply was most impressive: 'I am not concerned so much with their position, as with the fact I am left under suspicion myself.'

(Pliny, *Letters* 6.31)

Trajan was 'under suspicion' because he had a financial interest in the outcome, but more interesting is his choice of words in summing up the situation: namely, that he was not Nero, and nor were his freedmen like Nero's. The point to which he was responding in the first instance, before conceding that an unresolved charge should not be allowed to hang over the defendants' heads if there is no corroborating evidence, was the fear people felt when they found themselves entangled with the emperor's subordinates.

Visitors to Rome today can see one narrative of Trajan's Dacian wars on the column that sits at the centre of the great forum he built. The images meld together, from one war to the next, portraying the emperor and his subordinates leading their troops to bring civilisation to the lands of the barbarians. We see Trajan in a variety of roles – rewarding his men, dealing with ambassadors and prisoners, bringing aid to his soldiers in need. The Roman army, too, is depicted in all its diversity building all the time as it marches on. Decebelus is variously seen hiding in the woods, surrendering, and finally committing suicide at the end of the second war (the consequence of his treacherous attacks on the Roman garrisons).

The cause of the conflict was Trajan's decision to cut the subsidies that Domitian had agreed to give Decebelus at the end of the war in AD 92. Decebelus, who probably depended on the distribution of Roman gold to keep his followers onside, retaliated by invading Roman territory. Trajan, probably anticipating trouble, had posted some experienced commanders to the area, and took to the field in person towards the end of AD 101. Leading an army of around 75,000 men, he had secured victory by the end of the following summer. In return for the continued existence of his kingdom, Decebelus agreed to surrender weapons, war engines and deserters, have the same friends and enemies as the Romans, and to stop recruiting from within imperial territory.

The peace treaty put Decebelus' regime under great stress, which he attempted to relieve by attacking Roman territory in AD 105. Trajan again took command of the Roman forces, determined this time to bring an

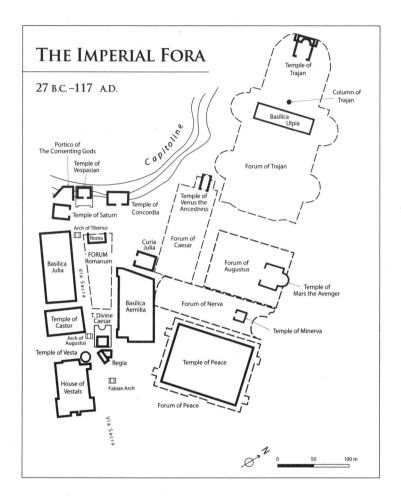

THE IMPERIAL FORA

27 B.C.–117 A.D.

Temple of Trajan

Column of Trajan

Basilica Ulpia

Forum of Trajan

Portico of The Consenting Gods

Temple of Vespasian

Capitoline

Temple of Venus the Ancestress

Temple of Concordia

Temple of Saturn

Arch of Tiberius

Rostra

FORUM Romanum

Curia Julia

Forum of Caesar

Basilica Julia

Via Sacra

Forum of Augustus

Temple of Mars the Avenger

Basilica Aemilia

Forum of Nerva

Temple of Minerva

Temple of Castor

T. Divine Caesar

Arch of Augustus

Temple of Vesta

Regia

Temple of Peace

House of Vestals

Fabian Arch

Forum of Peace

Via Sacra

N

0   50   100 m

end to the Dacian kingdom. Victory was declared in the autumn of the following year, when a Roman cavalryman, Tiberius Claudius Maximus, presented Decebelus' head to the emperor. A monument was built at Adamclisi, the site both of a great wartime victory and of an earlier monument of Domitian's commemorating the heroic dead of his wars. In both instances the point was to stress that the army, the upholder of the traditional virtues of the Roman people, was recruited from throughout the empire. Trajan transformed the kingdom into a new province.

At the same time Cornelius Palma, governor of Syria, was annexing the Nabataean kingdom of Arabia (roughly, modern Jordan): the logical conclusion to the process that Vespasian had initiated to turn eastern client kingdoms into provinces. The annexation of Dacia was, likewise, from a Roman viewpoint, the logical consequence of the problems that Decebelus had caused in the Danubian lands. The decisions to create provinces protruding north of the Danube (albeit with some goldmines) and stretching into the Arabian desert was typical of Roman understanding. For Rome, Dacia was defined both as the former realm of Decebelus and as an area bordered by the territories of the Quadi, the Marcomanni and the Sarmatians. A province with no pronounced natural boundaries might not make a great deal of sense in terms of a modern map, but Trajan did not use modern maps. Roman notions of geography were defined by borders – in this case the provincial border was placed at that of the Quadi. Ever since Appius Claudius crossed the straits into Sicily, geographical definitions of provinces had been based on the geopolitical realities that had existed before the Romans arrived.

The fact that Roman provinces were defined by pre-existing political structures reflects an important feature of Roman frontier policy. This was that, while decisions were shaped by local circumstance, they were made within a coherent framework. Trajan planned the second invasion of Dacia the way Claudius planned his invasion of Britain, or Tiberius resolved to give up the Augustan territory north of the Rhine. Vespasian had purposely shifted Vitellian legions towards the Balkans and the Balkan legions towards the Rhine, just as Domitian had decided that Agricola's conquests in Scotland had to go.

Similarly, all these emperors based the size of the Roman army – now twenty-eight legions – on their financial resources and the needs of the moment. They were capable of making large-scale strategic decisions because they had professional staff who could collect the necessary data. When Trajan resolved to give up the revenue from the 5 per cent inheritance tax on estates left by parents to their children or children to their parents, he would have known roughly how much money he was losing. Indeed, one of the more impressive pieces of imperial data collection figures in a commentary on the inheritance law by the third-century jurist Aemilius Macer, using an existing formula for the computation of annuity payments. The estimates are based on a reasonably accurate reckoning of life expectancy, which suggests the regular use of census data to estimate

26. The large imperial reception area at Hadrian's palace outside of Tivoli illustrates the grandeur with which the imperial government wished to impress its subjects.

income. The process of decision-making was largely reactive, but those reactions were based on experience and data.

Rationality, reliable data use and civility were all tenets of Trajan's administrative style, but so, too, was the sense of imperial magnificence. One of his first acts on returning to Rome in AD 99 had been to enhance the Circus Maximus, adding new rows of marble seating to Rome's most venerable entertainment venue. It was a way of introducing himself to the city's inhabitants and offering them a gesture of concern for their welfare. Then, in the wake of the Dacian wars, he planned something much more spectacular – the forum, of which his famous column was the centrepiece. Far bigger than the forums of earlier emperors, it was entered from the north end through a ceremonial gateway leading into the piazza where the column stands, flanked by public libraries, one for Greek, the other for Latin, abutting a massive basilica. South of the basilica was another large piazza entered through a triumphal arch supporting a statue of Trajan in his chariot. The piazza itself, with semicircular buildings (*exedrae*) on the east and west, had as its centrepiece a huge mounted statue of Trajan.

Work on the new forum was rapid – it was completed by AD 112. By this

27. Hadrian, emperor AD 117–38. As with Trajan's portrait (p. 379) the image projected is that of change. Hadrian is the first emperor to wear a beard as a sign of his appreciation of Greek cultural values.

time the composition of Trajan's inner circle was established, comprising a group of generals, some of them detectable in the panels of his column as regular companions. They included Licinius Sura, Sosius Senecio, Cornelius Palma (who had annexed Arabia), Marius Celsus and, towards the end of his reign, Lusius Quietus. Trajan promoted all these men to second consulships and honoured all except Quietus with statues in his forum. They were all members of 'new families'. Quietus was possibly a first-generation Roman, having been a tribal chieftain in North Africa before he came to Trajan's attention. Trajan also proclaimed the nature of his regime by deifying his sister Marciana, who died in AD 112. She was the first imperial sister to receive such honours and, for all his civility, Trajan evidently expected people to acknowledge a difference between their families and his. Plotina remained, meanwhile, immensely powerful in the palace, where she looked after the career of Hadrian.

A year after Marciana's death Trajan was on the move again. The reason was yet another quarrel over the Armenian succession. There was now a strongly pro-Parthian king on the throne, so Trajan decided to change the rules of the game. Dio suggests that he did this to win eternal military glory. That is possible, but unlikely. Otherwise, he appears to have retained until the end of his life the capacity to see things realistically. More likely, he decided that the dance the two empires had engaged in for more than a century was in need of some new steps.

By the end of AD 114 Trajan's armies had occupied Armenia. The next year he was following in the footsteps of Pompey and Lucullus, bringing his troops into northern Mesopotamia, where he turned the kingdom of Osrhoene into a province before advancing into Iraq, proceeding down the Euphrates to a position opposite the Persian capital of Ctesiphon on the Tigris. At this point he had a canal dug to connect the two rivers, making it far easier to transport his supplies, then captured Ctesiphon and established a new Mesopotamian province. As he journeyed south to the region of Mesene, at the mouths of the rivers, he learned that his plans for reconstructing the eastern frontier had fallen apart.

The prospect of Roman occupation disturbed networks that had existed since the Parthian kingdom had come into being and, thanks to an earthquake at Antioch in AD 115 in which Trajan himself had nearly been killed, the Jewish populations of Egypt and Palestine were filled with Messianic visions of the end of Roman rule. After Abgar of Osrhoene defeated a column under Appius Maximus Santra, and a failed effort to capture the city of Hatra in northern Iraq, Trajan gave up. Leaving Quietus to avenge the defeat in Osrhoene and then massacre the Jews of Palestine, he made a deal with the Parthian king Parthamaspates, abolished the new provinces and prepared to return to Italy. He would never make it. On 8 or 9 August AD 117 he died at Selinus in Cilicia, Plotina at his side.

Trajan had come to his deathbed without having named an heir. The obvious candidate from within the family was Hadrian – but *was* he the obvious candidate? Trajan had promoted many senior officials who might think themselves qualified for the job. It was even said that after he died, Plotina had a freedman slip into his bed, pretend to be him and give the necessary order to adopt Hadrian. She definitely signed Trajan's final letters to the Senate. Her ally was the praetorian prefect Attianus, and the key point of conflict was whether the palace would continue the practice of choosing the emperor, or whether the choice might be left to the Senate or a cabal of generals if the emperor himself had not spoken. It does seem that Trajan had not made up his mind and that some senior officers did not think the job should go to Hadrian. Within weeks of taking up office, Hadrian executed all four of Trajan's most senior officers, Celsus, Palma, Quietus and Nigrinus. He then wrote to the Senate saying that they had all been conspiring against him.

The murders of such senior officials silenced possible opposition, and Hadrian set about making his own mark on the empire. He built walls along some of its frontiers, which included extending the turf walls of the *limes* (borders) in Germany and in Britain creating the great stone wall that stretched from the mouth of the Tyne on the North Sea to the Solway Firth facing Ireland. Within a generation, people would be referring to the empire as a fortress of civilisation. Expansion was at an end. This, too, was a deliberate choice. The war with Persia had ended badly, and Dacia needed some readjustment (indeed, sections of the province were abandoned). Not surprisingly given the way he had opened his reign, Hadrian was a bit leery of successful generals. His relationship with the Senate would occasionally border on the frosty even as he sped up the process of transition, opening Rome's doors ever more widely to men from the provinces. He was especially keen on Greek culture and, in a major break with the persistently clean-shaven traditions of the Roman aristocracy, he grew a beard to signal his philosophical interests.

Above all, Hadrian liked to travel. He would rule for twenty-one years, until AD 138. Quite a lot of that time he spent away from Rome, though without a major war. He took the better part of a year to return from the east, arriving on 9 July AD 118. He stayed until the spring of AD 121, when he left for Gaul and Britain, where he began to construct the great wall that bears his name. From Britain he made his way back through Gaul to Spain, then sailed to Syria, where he engaged in some sort of negotiation with the Parthian king. He would be in Turkey and Greece until AD 125, then back to Rome. But he was off again in AD 128, visiting North Africa, Greece, Turkey, Syria, Palestine, Judaea, Egypt and the Balkans before returning to Rome four years later.

Subjects who got to know him learned that the best way to deal with Hadrian was to appeal to his taste for abstruse learning. Cities that could impress him with details of their distant past were more likely to gain his favour, and he established a major institution to reinforce the significance of the empire's Greek cultural heritage, the League of the Hellenes, based in Athens. Here he also, and with great pride, completed the vast temple to

Olympian Zeus, planned a mere 700 years earlier by the Athenian tyrant Pisistratus.

Hadrian had a significant impact on the course of Roman law when he standardised the praetor's edict, the document that still, as it had during the Republic, laid out the principles by which a praetor ran his court. So, too, in AD 134 he introduced changes to the scheduling of games that resulted in his masterminding a new calendar for the major festivals of the Greek world. At the same time he began promoting the designation of important cities within provinces as *metropoleis*, provincial centres with special privileges.

There was no question but that he liked the appearance of order and appreciated style. When a former imperial procurator, Gaius Julius Demosthenes, who lived at Oenoanda in the Lycian hills, faced local opposition to the month-long self-celebratory festival he wished to sponsor, Hadrian intervened so that he could get his way. A rhetorician, Polemo, so impressed him that he granted numerous favours to his adopted city of Smyrna (modern Izmir); and he had a great affection for entertainers, whose interests he favoured over those of the people who financed the games in which they performed (in one case, reversing a ruling of Trajan's).

But for all that he liked the appearance of order, Hadrian was not easy to get along with. Suetonius had risen in his service to the rank of secretary for Latin correspondence when he was suddenly sacked, along with his patron, the praetorian prefect Septicius Clarus. It was alleged that they were too close to Hadrian's wife Sabina. It was never clear why their relationship with the emperor's wife should have been an issue at this point, since both men would have been in Britain, and her relationship with Hadrian was sufficiently poisonous that she is unlikely to have been there as well. Others would tell stories of his ferocious temper, and Marcus Aurelius, whose ultimate succession to the imperial throne Hadrian would take steps to ensure, regarded him as exceptionally difficult.

However, none of this means that he was incapable of forming deep friendships. To those who shared his tastes, intellectual or physical – he loved hunting – he could be a good friend. One reason why he issued new regulations about the scheduling of the Greek games was that he wanted thereby to commemorate his deceased lover Antinous, who had died under mysterious circumstances while they were in Egypt in AD 130. They had been together for several years, but this did not make Hadrian's decision to encourage venues to include him in their celebrations of the imperial cult any less remarkable.

Hadrian had no empathy with or understanding of traditional Jewish culture, which led him to make two bad mistakes concerning Palestine. First, he expanded an imperial ban intended to prevent the castration of slaves, to include circumcision. Second, he founded a Roman colony, Aelia Capitolina, at Jerusalem, thereby demoting the city's Jewish heritage. The consequences, again of a distinctly apocalyptic aspect, proved exceptionally bloody, as the forces of Simeon Bar Kochba first captured Jerusalem and then, when they could not hold it, took to the hills around the Dead Sea, where they managed to resist Hadrian's massive armies.

Although his success in promoting his vision of a unified imperial culture based on eastern Mediterranean traditions was not total, there can be no doubt that Hadrian's perspective was genuinely Mediterranean. To illustrate his view that the emperor was the cultural director of his world there is no better exemplar than the palatial villa he constructed for himself in the hills near the modern town of Tivoli, twenty miles east of Rome.

This great palace, covering about half a square mile, was built to be the hub of government and the symbolic centre of the empire. 'He constructed at Tivoli an extraordinary villa, and in different parts were inscribed the names of the provinces and the most famous places such as the Lycaeum, the Academy, the Prytanion, the Canopus, the Poicile and Tempe' (*Historia Augusta, Life of Hadrian* 26). Of the famous places listed here, the Lycaeum, Academy and Poicile are in Athens (the first two being the homes of famous philosophic schools), the Canopus refers to Alexandria, and the Tempe to a famous valley in Thessaly. Here are the ideals of intellectual and artistic achievement that defined Hadrian's concept of classical culture assembled in the spectacular space required of an emperor. Here the court, free from the strictures of Rome, could be home to the civilised world, and it was from here that Hadrian conducted the business of government.

In AD 136 Hadrian's health began to fail. Unlike Trajan, Hadrian was not about to leave the issue of his succession open. In particular, he wanted to make sure that a nephew he especially disliked would not be in line for the job. So it was that he adopted a senator named Ceionius Commodus, whose son and teenage son-in-law he did like. In AD 137 he executed his unfortunate nephew (along with that nephew's grandfather, whom he also hated) for treason, while publishing a horoscope for the nephew proving that his demise was inevitable. Then things got difficult. Commodus was not a healthy man. He died in January AD 138, just as Hadrian's own health took a decided turn for the worse. He invited a man named Aurelius Antoninus to become his heir, with the proviso that he would adopt Commodus' son Lucius, and his teenage son-in-law, who would become the emperor Marcus Aurelius. Antoninus agreed to become heir apparent on 25 February. On 10 July, Hadrian died at Tivoli. A biographer said he died hated by all, which may not be far off the truth – but he had been very effective.

With some difficulty, Antoninus convinced the Senate to deify Hadrian. He was henceforth known as Antoninus Pius and reigned until AD 161. He and Marcus Aurelius, who ruled until AD 180, were remembered as two of Rome's finest emperors. They both, consciously, looked past Hadrian back to Trajan as their model. More importantly, both men understood the great forces that governed the empire: the need for peace; the need to bring Rome's former subjects into government; and the need for the Roman government to espouse values in which its subjects could believe. For more than forty years Antoninus and Marcus would succeed in these tasks. Our own concepts of rational thought, justice and equity owe much to their success.

31

WHAT HAPPENED

❦

Tacitus was still writing his *Annals*, his history of the Julio-Claudian era, when Hadrian became emperor, and he may well have visited him at his palace at Tivoli, which was constructed largely during his early years in power. He may even have visited the satirist Juvenal, who shared much of his outlook and would quote from his works. Their visions of Rome's history offer a broad insight into the processes that had shaped the world ever since Appius Claudius crossed from Rhegium to Messana. 'I am not unaware,' wrote Tacitus, that historians of the Republic could write of 'great wars, the sacks of cities, kings captured or routed, or, whenever they turned to internal affairs, the quarrels between consuls and tribunes, agrarian and grain laws, the struggles of the *optimates* and plebs, and liberty gone too far' (Tacitus, *Annals* 4.32.1). He, on the other hand, explored subjects 'seemingly of little import, from which greater things took their direction' (Tacitus, *Annals* 4.32.2).

One of Tacitus' subjects was the way emperors shaped the world in which they lived and the impact of their characters on the behaviour of the governing classes. Tacitus' world was one in which change came from the top down.

Tacitus' world was also one in which the imperial system was open to new talent, in which the future was not for Italians alone; a world in which imperial society would be shaped by Rome's historical openness to outsiders. The empire had grown because the Roman aristocracy had made itself useful to its Italian neighbours. It had stumbled when, as Tacitus perceived, the victorious alliance had turned into internal discord over the appropriation of the vast new resources. When Actium was fought in 31 BC, and long years of relative peace and prosperity followed, 'Who was left who could remember the old Republic?' he asked (Tacitus, *Annals* 1.3.7)?

The grand narrative of Roman history is of the development of a vast state that would endure for centuries, uniting different cultures, enabling conversations across time and space that continue to shape our thinking today. It is also the story of how a democracy tore itself apart and ultimately voted itself out of existence so that a monarchy could unite the world it had plundered. By the time Augustus died, the people, the sovereign body of state, had not just gone back to sleep – they had surrendered their power, their control over who would hold office, to a court bureaucracy. Juvenal wrote that the *populus*, who once decided matters of war and peace, were now content with food and entertainment, offered by imperial largesse.

The Republic could not solve the problem of its own success or devise a way to justify its own existence in the eyes of those enmeshed in its webs. Society's wealthy became wealthier, success was identified with self-interest rather than the public good, and, as Tacitus observed, '[T]here is an ancient and innate desire for dominance amongst mortals that matures and explodes with the power of empire; when resources are limited, equal standing is easily maintained, but with the world conquered, with rival cities and kings destroyed, there is leisure to covet wealth in safety ... after that only contests for supreme power' (Tacitus, *Histories* 2.38).

Notes on Sources

✦✦✦✦✦

General

Works listed here have influenced discussions across multiple sections of this book. For abbreviations other than those listed in the note on abbreviations used in the text shown at the beginning of this book, see the now standard list in the *Oxford Classical Dictionary* 3rd edition (Oxford, 1996).

General Surveys: F. W. Walbank, A. E. Astin, M. W. Frederiksen, R. M. Ogilvie, eds., *The Cambridge Ancient History*, 2nd ed., 7.2 *The Rise of Rome to 220 BC* (Cambridge, 1990); A. E. Astin, F. W. Walbank M. W. Frederiksen, R. M. Ogilvie, eds., *The Cambridge Ancient History* 2nd ed., 8 *Rome and the Mediterranean to 133 BC* (Cambridge, 1989); J. A. Crook, A. Lintott, E. Rawson, eds., *The Cambridge Ancient History* 2nd ed., 9 *The Last Age of the Roman Republic 146–43 BC* (Cambridge, 1994); A. K. Bowman, E. Champlin and A. Lintott, eds., *The Cambridge Ancient History* 2nd ed., 10 *The Augustan Empire 43 BC–AD 69* (Cambridge, 1996); A. K. Bowman, P. Garnsey and D. Rathbone, eds., *The Cambridge Ancient History* 2nd ed., 11 *The High Empire AD 70–192* (Cambridge, 2000).

Economic Structures: H. C. Boren, 'Studies Relating to the Stipendium Militum', *Historia* 32 (1983), 427–60; M. H. Crawford, *Roman Republican Coinage* (Cambridge, 1974); W. V. Harris, *Rome's Imperial Economy: Twelve Essays* (Oxford, 2011); S. Hin, *The Demography of Roman Italy* (Cambridge, 2013); D. Hollander, *Money in the Late Roman Republic* (Leiden, 2007); M. Kay, *Rome's Economic Revolution* (Oxford, 2014); W. E. Metcalf, *The Oxford Handbook of Greek and Roman Coinage* (Oxford, 2012); D. W. Rathbone, 'The Control and Exploitation of *ager publicus* in Italy under the Roman Republic', in J.-J. Aubert, ed., *Tâches publiques et enterprise privée dans le monde romain* (Geneva, 2003), 135–78; J. Rich, 'Lex Licinia, Lex Sempronia, B. G. Niebuhr and the Limitation of Landholding in the Roman Republic', in L. de Light and S. Northwood, eds., *People, Land and Politics: Demographic Developments and the Transformation of Roman Italy, 300 BC–AD 14* (Leiden, 2008), 519–72; S. T. Roselaar, *Public Land in the Roman Republic: A Societal and Economic History of Ager Publicus in Italy, 396– 89 AD* (Oxford, 2010); J. Tan, *Power and Public Finance at Rome*

264–49 BCE (Oxford, 2017). P. J. E. Davies, *Architecture and Politics in Republican Rome* (Cambridge, 2017).

Historiography: D. C. Feeney, *Caesar's Calendar: Ancient Time and the Beginnings of History* (Berkeley, 2007); R. Syme, *Tacitus* (Oxford, 1958); R. Syme, *Sallust* (Berkeley, 1964); F. W. Walbank, *A Historical Commentary on Polybius* 3 vols. (Oxford, 1957–79); F. W. Walbank, *Polybius* (Berkeley, 1972); T. P. Wiseman, *Unwritten Rome* (Exeter, 2008).

Imperialism: D. C. Braund, *Rome and the Friendly King* (London, 1984); P. J. Burton, *Friendship and Empire: Roman Diplomacy and Imperialism in the Middle Republic (353–146 BC)* (Cambridge, 2011); P. S. Derow, *Rome, Polybius and the East*, A. Erskine and J. C. Quinn, eds. (Oxford, 2015); D. Dzino, *Illyricum in Roman Politics 229BC–AD 68* (Cambridge, 2010); A. M. Eckstein, *Mediterranean Anarchy, Interstate War and the Rise of Rome* (Berkeley, 2002); J. L. Ferrary, *Philhellénisme et impérialisme: aspects idéologiques de la conquête romaine du monde hellénistique, de la seconde guerre de Macédoine à la guerre contre Mithridate* (Paris, 1988); E. Gruen, *The Hellenistic World and the Coming of Rome* (Berkeley, 1984); W. V. Harris, *War and Imperialism in Republican Rome* (Oxford, 1979); W. V. Harris, *Roman Power: A Thousand Years of Empire* (Cambridge, 2016); R. M. Kallet-Marx, *Hegemony to Empire: The Development of the Roman Imperium in the East from 148 to 62 BC* (Berkeley, 1996); D. Magie, *Roman Rule in Asia Minor to the End of the Third Century after Christ* (Princeton, 1950); S. Mitchell, *Anatolia: Land, Men, and Gods in Asia Minor* 1 (Oxford, 1993); A. N. Sherwin-White, *Roman Foreign Policy in the East 168 BC to AD 1* (London, 1984); F. W. Walbank, *Selected Papers: Studies in Greek and Roman History and Historiography* (Cambridge, 1985); F. W. Walbank, *Polybius, Rome and the Hellenistic World: Essays and Reflections* (Cambridge, 2002); G. Woolf, *Rome: An Empire's Story* (Oxford, 2012).

Italy: J. N. Adams, *Bilingualism and the Latin Language* (Cambridge, 2003); E. Bispham, *From Asculum to Actium: The Municipalization of Italy from the Social War to Augustus* (Oxford, 2007); M. H. Crawford, *Imagines Italiae: A Corpus of Italic Inscriptions* BICS Supplement 110 (London, 2011); M. Torelli, *Studies in the Romanization of Italy*, H. Fracchia and M. Gualtieri, eds. and tr. (Edmonton, 1995); M. Torelli, *Tota Italia: Essays in Cultural Formation of Roman Italy* (Oxford, 1999); A. Wallace-Hadrill, *The Roman Cultural Revolution* (Cambridge, 2008).

Social and Political Institutions: H. Beck, *Karriere und Hierarchie: Die römische Aristokratie und die Anfänge des cursus honorum in der mittleren Republik* (Berlin, 2005); H. Beck, A. Duplá, M. Jehne and F. Pina Polo, eds., *Consuls and* Res Publica*: Holding High Office in the Roman Republic* (Cambridge, 2011); T. R. S. Broughton, *The Magistrates of the Roman Republic*, 3 vols. (New York/Atlanta, 1951–86); P. A. Brunt, *Italian Manpower 225 BC–AD 14* (Oxford, 1971); P. A. Brunt, *The Fall of the Roman Republic and Related Essays* (Oxford, 1988); E. Dench, *Romulus' Asylum: Roman Identities from the Age of Alexander to the Age of Hadrian* (Oxford, 2005); F. Hinard, *Les proscriptions de la Rome républicaine* (Paris, 1985); L. Hodgson, Res Publica *and the Roman Republic: 'Without Body or Form'* (Oxford, 2017); A. Lintott, *The Constitution of the Roman Republic* (Oxford, 1999); F.

Millar, *The Roman Republic and the Augustan Revolution* (Chapel Hill, 2002); T. Luke, *Ushering in a New Republic: Theologies of Arrival at Rome in the First Century* BCE (Ann Arbor, 2014); C. Nicolet, *L'ordre équestre à l'époque républicaine (312–43 av J.-C.)* (Paris, 1974); C. Nicolet, *Le métier de citoyen dans la Rome républicaine* 2nd ed. (Paris, 1976); H. H. Scullard, *Roman Politics 220–150 BC* (Oxford, 1951); R. Syme, *The Roman Revolution* (Oxford, 1939); L. R. Taylor, 'Forerunners of the Gracchi', *JRS* 52 (1962), 19–27; L. R. Taylor, *Roman Voting Assemblies* (Ann Arbor, 1966); L. R. Taylor, *Roman Voting Districts* rev. ed. with additional material by J. Linderski (Ann Arbor, 2013); S. Treggiari, *Roman Marriage: Iusti Coniuges from the Time of Cicero to the Time of Ulpian* (Oxford, 1995); C. Williamson, *The Laws of the Roman People* (Ann Arbor, 2005).

Part I: War

The major primary sources for this period are: Polybius' *Histories*, once consisting of forty books of which only five books remain intact, which are readily available through the revised Loeb edition from F. W. Walbank and C. Habicht; Diodorus Siculus, for which there is now P. Goukowsky, *Diodore de Sicile: bibliothèque historique. Fragments*, Tome II, Livres XXI–XXVI (Paris, 2006); and Livy's *History of Rome*, Books 21–30 (for the Second Punic War), for which J. C. Yardley, *Hannibal's War* (Oxford, 2009) is a readily available translation. Livy's account is preserved in outline by the *Periochae* (summaries) for Books 16–20 (available in a Loeb edition and through J. D. Chaplin, *Rome's Mediterranean Empire, Books 41–5 and the Periochae* (Oxford, 2010)), and used in later sources such as Florus, Eutropius and Florus. Plutarch's lives of Marcellus and Fabius Maximus preserve some important details not available elsewhere (including evidence of a somewhat less negative tradition about Flaminius), and are readily accessible through I. Scott-Kilvert, *The Rise of Rome*, revised with notes by J. Tatum (London, 2013), as well as the older Loeb editions. The earliest Roman historians are now available in *FRH*; Greek historians whose work has not survived intact can be found through *FGrH*. There are a limited number of contemporary documents, of which the most important can be found in either *ILLRP* or *SVA*. J. Prag, 'Bronze rostra from the Egadi Islands off NW Sicily: the Latin inscriptions', *JRA* 27 (2014), 33–59 is a crucial addition. For a valuable collection of texts relating to diplomacy, see F. Canali de Rossi, *Le relazioni diplomatiche di Roma 2 Dall' intervento in Sicilia fino all'invasione annibalica (264–216 a.C.)*(Rome, 2007) and *Le relazioni diplomatiche di Roma 3 Dalla resistenza di Fabio fino alla vittoria di Scipione intervento in Sicilia fino all'invasione annibalica (215–201 a.C.)*(Rome, 2013).

General Introductions: A. Goldsworthy, *The Punic Wars* (London, 2000); D. Hoyos, *A Companion to the Punic Wars* (Oxford, 2011); D. Hoyos, *Mastering the West: Rome and Carthage at War* (Oxford, 2015) (which takes a somewhat rare, critical approach to Hannibal's generalship); N. Rosenstein, *Rome and the Mediterranean, 290 to 146 BC: The Imperial Republic* (Edinburgh 2012).

Carthage and the Western Mediterranean: J. Prag and J. C. Quinn, *The Hellenistic West: Rethinking the Ancient Mediterranean* (Cambridge, 2013); J. C. Quinn, ed., *The Punic*

Mediterranean: Identities and Identification from Phoenician Settlement to Roman Rule (Cambridge, 2014).

Cultural History: D. C. Feeney, *Beyond Greek: The Beginnings of Latin Literature* (Cambridge, MA, 2016); C. Watkins, 'Latin Tarentum Accas, the Ludi Saeculares and Indo-European Eschatology', in W. P. Lehman and H.-J. Jakusz Hewitt, eds., *Language Typology 1988: Typological Models in Reconstruction* (Philadelphia, 1991), 135–47.

Historiography: C. A. Baron, *Timaeus of Tauromenium and Hellenistic Historiography* (Cambridge, 2013); C. Champion, *Cultural Politics in Polybius' Histories* (Berkeley, 2004); E. Dench, *From Barbarians to New Men: Greek, Roman and Modern Perceptions of the People of the Central Apennines* (Oxford, 1995); J. Dillery, 'Quintus Fabius Pictor and Greco-Roman Historiography at Rome', in J. F. Miller, C. Damon, K. S. Myers, eds., *Vertis in Usum: Studies in Honor of Edward Courtney* (Munich and Leipzig, 2002), 1–23; A. Erskine, *Troy Between Greece and Rome: Local Tradition and Imperial Power* (Oxford, 2001); M. Gelzer, 'Nasicas Widerspruch gegen die Zerstörung Karthagos', *Philologus* 88 (1931), 261–99; M. Gelzer, 'Römische Politik bei Fabius Pictor', *Hermes* 68 (1933), 129–66; M. Gelzer, *Kleine Schriften* 2 (Wiesbaden, 1963), 39–72; M. Gelzer, *Kleine Schriften* 3 (Wiesbaden, 1964), 51–92 (central to the account of the outbreak of the Second Punic War in the text); B. Gibson and T. Harrison, eds., *Polybius and His World: Essays in Memory of F. W. Walbank* (Oxford, 2013); P. Pedech, *La méthode historique de Polybe* (Paris, 1964).

Punic Wars: B. Bleckmann, *Die römische Nobilität im Ersten Punischen Krieg: Untersuchungen zur aristokratischen Konkurrenz in der Republik* (Berlin, 2002); T. Cornell, B. Rankov and P. Sabin, eds., *The Second Punic War: A Reappraisal*, BICS Supplement 67 (London, 1996); S. Dimitriev, *The Greek Slogan of Freedom and Early Roman Politics in Greece* (Oxford, 2011); M. P. Fronda, *Between Rome and Carthage: Southern Italy during the Second Punic War* (Cambridge, 2010); J. F. Lazenby, *The First Punic War* (Palo Alto, 1996); C. Vacanti, *Guerra per la Sicilia e Guerra della Sicilia: il Ruolo delle Città Siciliane nel Primo Conflitto Romano-Punico* (Naples, 2012) (stressing the importance of the Syracusan connection).

Reading of the Roman Constitution in the Early Modern Period: D. Lee, *Popular Sovereignty in Early Modern Constitutional Thought* (Oxford, 2016); F. Millar, *The Roman Republic in Political Thought* (Boston, 2002); B. Straumann, *Crisis and Constitutionalism: Roman Political Thought from the Fall of the Republic to the Age of Revolution* (Oxford, 2016); R. Tuck, *The Sleeping Sovereign: The Invention of Modern Democracy* (Cambridge, 2016).

The Roman State: J. M. Bertrand, 'À propos du mot *provincia*: Étude sur le elaboration du langue politique', *Journal des Savants* (1989), 191–215; E. Bispham, '*Coloniam Deducere*: How Roman was Roman Colonization during the Middle Republic', G. Bradley and J. P. Wilson, eds., *Greek and Roman Colonization: Origins, Ideologies and Interactions* (Swansea, 2006), 73–160; F. Drogula, *Commanders and Command in the Roman Republic and Early Empire* (Chapel Hill, 2015); M. Gelzer, *The Roman Nobility*, R. Seager, tr. (Oxford, 1969); A. Giovannini, *Les institutions de la République romaine des origines à la mort d'Auguste* (Basel,

2015); K. J. Hölkeskamp, *Die Entstehung der Nobilität. Studien zur socialen und politischen Geschichte der Römischen Republik im 4. Jh v. Chr.* 2nd ed. (Stuttgart, 2011); J. Linderski, 'The Augural Law', *ANRW* 16.3 (Berlin, 1986), 2147–312; F. Münzer, *Roman Aristocratic Parties and Families*, T. Ridley, tr. (Baltimore, 1999); S. Northwood, 'Census and Tributum', in L. de Light and S. Northwood, eds., *People, Land and Politics: Demographic Developments and the Transformation of Roman Italy 300 BC–AD 14* (Leiden, 2008), 257–70; N. Rosenstein, Imperatores Victi: *Military Defeat and Aristocratic Competition in the Middle and Late Republic* (Berkeley, 1990); N. Terrenato, 'Private *Vis*, Public *Virtus*. Family Agendas during the Early Roman Expansion', in T. D. Stek and J. Pelgrom, eds., *Roman Republican Colonization: New Perspectives from Archaeology and Ancient History* (Rome, 2014), 45–59; A. Ziolkowski, *The Temples of Mid-Republican Rome and Their Historical and Topographical Context* (Rome, 1992).

Part II: Empire

The primary addition to the sources discussed in the previous section is the addition of Livy Books 31–45, readily accessible through J. C. Yardley, tr., with notes by W. Heckel, *The Dawn of the Roman Empire, Books 31–40* (Oxford, 2009) and J. D. Chaplin, *Rome's Mediterranean Empire, Books 41–5 and the Periochae* (Oxford, 2010), while J. Briscoe, *A Commentary on Livy Books XXXI–XXXIII* (Oxford, 1973), J. Briscoe, *A Commentary on Livy Books XXXIV– XXXVII* (Oxford, 1981), J. Briscoe, *A Commentary on Livy Books 38–40* (Oxford, 2008), J. Briscoe, *A Commentary on Livy Books 41–45* (Oxford, 2012) join Walbank's commentary on Polybius as invaluable guides through historical and historiographic issues for those connecting with the text in Latin. F. Canali de Rossi, *Le relazioni diplomatiche di Roma 4 Dalla 'liberazione della Grecia' alla pace infida con Antioco III (201–194 a.C.)* (Rome, 2014) offers an important collection of texts, with discussion. For the development of Roman relations in the east, see the documents collected in R. K. Sherk, *Roman Documents of the Greek East* (Baltimore, 1969); Sherk, nn. 2; 3; 40 are especially important for the events of the Third Macedonian War.

Cultural and Economic History: L. Ceccarelli and E. Marroni, *Repertorio dei santuari del Lazio* (Rome, 2011); F. Coarelli, ed., *Studi su Praeneste* (Perugia, 1978); F. Coarelli, '*I santuari del Lazio e della Campania tra I Gracchi e le Guerre Civili*', in M. Cébeillac-Gervasoni, ed., *Les 'bourgeoisies' municipals italiennes aux IIe et Ier siècles av. J.-C.*, Centre Jean Bérard, Institut Français de Naples 7–10 décembre 1981 (Naples, 1983), 217–36; F. Coarelli and P. G. Monti, *Fregellae 1: Le Fonti, La Storia, Il Territorio* (Rome, 1998); J. Elliott, *Ennius and the Architecture of the* Annales (Cambridge, 2013); J. A. Hanson, *Roman Theater-Temples* (Princeton, 1959); C. Howgego, 'The Supply and Use of Money in the Roman World 200 BC–AD 300', *JRS* 82 (1992), 1–31; A. M. Ramieri, *Ferentino dale origini all'alto medioevo* (Rome, 1995); C. Rowan, 'The Profits of War and Cultural Capital', *Historia* 62 (2013), 361–86; O. Skutsch, *The Annals of Q. Ennius* (Oxford, 1985).

Roman Imperialism: B. Bar-Kochva, *Judas Maccabaeus: The Jewish Struggle against the Seleucids* (Cambridge, 1989); J. Briscoe, 'Q. Marcius Philippus and Nova Sapientia', *JRS*

54 (1964), 66–77; P. J. Burton, *Rome and the Third Macedonian War* (Cambridge, 2017); M. Cottier, M. H. Crawford, C. V. Crowther, J.-L. Ferrary, B. M. Levick, O. Salomies and M. Wörrle, eds., *The Customs Law of Asia* (Oxford, 2009); B. Dreyer, *Die römische Nobilitätsherrschaft und Antiochus III (205 bis 188 v. Chr.)* (Hennef, 2007); A. M. Eckstein, *Rome Enters the Greek East: From Anarchy to Hierarchy in the Hellenistic Mediterranean, 230–170 BC* (London, 2008); R. M. Kallet-Marx, *Hegemony to Empire: The Development of the Roman Imperium in the East from 148 to 62 BC* (Berkeley, 1996); P. J. Kosmin, *The Land of the Elephant Kings* (Cambridge, MA, 2014); J. Ma, *Antiochus III and the Cities of Western Asia Minor* (Oxford, 1999); A. R. Meadows, 'Greek and Roman Diplomacy on the Eve of the Second Macedonian War', *Historia* 42 (1993), 40–60; J. S. Richardson, Hispaniae: *Spain and the Development of Roman Imperialism, 218–82 BC* (Cambridge, 1986); P. Thonemann, ed., *Attalid Asia Minor: Money, International Relations, and the State* (Oxford, 2013).

Roman Internal History: A. E. Astin, *The Lex Annalis before Sulla.* Collection Latomus 32 (Brussels, 1958); A. E. Astin, *Scipio Aemilianus* (Oxford, 1967); A. E. Astin, *Cato the Censor* (Oxford, 1978); L. Grieve, 'Livy 40.51.9 and the Centuriate Assembly', *CQ* 35 (1985): 417–29.

Part III: Revolution

For this period there is a major change in the source tradition, with the end of Polybius and Livy now preserved only through the *Periochae* and later users of his tradition (see Sources, Part I: War). At this point Appian becomes critically important, as does Plutarch and, in the later chapters of this section, Cassius Dio. There is an invaluable series of editions of Appian from the Budé series, with excellent commentaries; in English there is a Loeb translation. Plutarch is also well served in the Budé series; in English there is a Loeb edition, too. There is now an excellent Loeb edition of Sallust's *Histories* (complete) and a very helpful commentary and translation of Books 1–2 in P. McGushin, *Sallust: The Histories* 1 (Oxford, 1992). All of Cicero's speeches are available in Loeb editions. The discussion of the Asculum inscription in chapter 15 is based on N. Criniti, *L'Epigrafe di Asculum di Gn. Pompeo Strabone* (Milan, 1970).

Contractors and a Military-Fiscal Complex: These terms are borrowed from work on the early modern period. My understanding of this period is based on the application of work by C. Tilley, *Coercion, Capital, and European States AD 990–1992* (Oxford, 1992) as adapted through D. Parrott, *The Business of War: Military Enterprise and Military Revolution in Early Modern Europe* (Cambridge, 2012); J. Glete, *War and the State in Early Modern Europe: Spain, The Dutch Republic and Sweden as Fiscal-Military States, 1500–1660* (London, 2002).

Economic Structures: J. Andreau, *The Economy of the Roman World*, C. Kesler, tr. (Ann Arbor, 2015); C. T. Barlow, 'The Roman Government and the Roman Economy, 92–80 BC', *AJP* 101 (1980), 202–19; P. Garnsey, T. Gallant and D. Rathbone, 'Thessaly and the Grain Supply of Rome during the Second Century BC', *JRS* 74 (1984), 30–44; W. V. Harris,

'A Revisionist View of Roman Money', *JRS* 96 (2006), 1–24; J. Hatzfeld, *Les trafiquants Italiens dans l'orient hellénique* (Paris, 1919); J. Rich, 'The Supposed Roman Manpower Shortage of the Second Century BC', *Historia* 32 (1983), 287–331; N. Rosenstein, *Rome at War: Farms, Families, and Death in the Middle Republic* (Durham, 2013).

Foreign Affairs and the Social War: M. Dobson, *The Army of the Roman Republic: The Second Century BC, Polybius and the Camps at Numantia, Spain* (Oxford, 2008); H. Mouritsen, *Italian Unification: A Study in Ancient and Modern Historiography*, BICS Supplement 70 (London, 1998); D. S. Potter, 'Caesar and the Helvetians', in G. G. Fagan and M. Trundle, eds., *New Perspectives on Ancient Warfare* (Leiden, 2010), 305–30; S. T. Roselaar, ed., *Processes of Integration and Identity Formation in the Roman Republic* (Leiden, 2012).

Historiographic and Other Sources: H. van der Blom, *Cicero's Role Models: The Political Strategy of a Newcomer* (Oxford, 2010); D. C. Earl, *The Political Thought of Sallust* (Cambridge, 1961); E. Rawson, 'The First Latin Annalists', *Latomus* 35 (1976), 689–717; E. Rawson, *Roman Culture and Society* (Oxford, 1991), 245–71; T. P. Wiseman, *Clio's Cosmetics* (Leicester, 1979).

Intellectual and Cultural History: J. Becker and N. Terrenato, *Roman Republican Villas: Architecture, Context, and Ideology* (Ann Arbor, 2012); G. Bradley, *Ancient Umbria: State, Culture and Identity in Central Italy from the Iron Age to the Augustan Era* (Oxford, 2000); G. Bradley, E. Isayev and C. Riva, *Ancient Italy: Regions Without Boundaries* (Exeter, 2007); S. Capini and G. De Benedittis, *Pietrabbondante: Guida agli Scavi Archaeologici* (Campobasso, 2000); F. Coarelli, *Fregellae 2 Il Santuario di Esculapio* (Rome, 1986); T. Cornell, 'Cato the Elder and the Origins of Roman Autobiography', in C. Smith and A. Powell, *The Lost Memoirs of Augustus and the Development of Roman Autobiography* (Swansea, 2009), 15–40; G. Fagan, *Bathing in Public in the Roman World* (Ann Arbor, 1999); P. Gros, *L'architecture romaine du début du IIIe siècle av. J.-C. à la fin du Haute-Empire 2 Maisons, palais, villas et tombeaux* (Paris, 2001); M. Mogetta, 'A New Date for Concrete in Rome', 105 (2015), 1–40; E. Rawson, *Intellectual Life in the Late Roman Republic* (London, 1985); L. Robert, 'Catalogue agonistique des Romaia de Xanthos', *Revue Archeologique* 1978, 277–90 [L. Robert, *Opera Minora Selecta* 7 (Amsterdam, 1990), 681–94]; R. Roth, *Styling Romanization: Pottery and Society in Central Italy* (Cambridge, 2007); R. Scopacasa, *Ancient Samnium: Settlement, Culture, and Identity between History and Archaeology* (Oxford, 2015); N. Terrenato, *'Tam Firmum Municipium*: The Romanization of Volterrae and Its Cultural Implications', *JRS* 88 (1998), 94–114; N. Terrenato, 'A Tale of Three Cities: The Romanization of Northern Coastal Etruria', in S. Key and N. Terrenato, *Italy and the West: Comparative Studies in Romanization* (Oxford, 2001), 54–65; P. Zanker, *Pompeii Public and Private City*, D. L. Schneider, tr. (Cambridge, MA, 1998); M. Zarmakoupi, *Designing for Luxury on the Bay of Naples: Villas and Landscapes (c.100 BC–79 CE)* (Oxford, 2015).

Internal History: A. E. Astin, *Scipio Aemilianus* (Oxford, 1967); T. J. Cadoux, 'Catiline and the Vestals', *Historia* 54 (2005), 162–79; E. Gabba, *Republican Rome, the Army and the Allies* (Berkeley, 1976); T. W. Hillard, 'Scipio Aemilianus and a Prophecy from Clunia', *Historia* 54 (2005): 344–8; A. Lintott, *Judicial Reform and Land Reform in the Roman Republic*

(Cambridge, 1992); A. N. Sherwin-White, 'The Lex Repetundarum and the Political Ideals of Gaius Gracchus', *JRS* 72 (1982), 18–31; S. Sisani, *L'ager publicus in Età Graccana (133–111 A.C.) Una Rilettura Testuale, Storica e Giuridica della Lex Agraria Epigraphica* (Rome, 2015); C. Steel and H. van der Blom, *Community and Communication: Oratory and Power in Republican Rome* (Oxford, 2013); D. L. Stockton, *The Gracchi* (Oxford, 1979).

Part IV: Dictatorship

The enormous surviving corpus of Cicero's work is readily available in Loeb editions; the Loebs of Cicero's letters are by D. R. Shackleton Bailey, whose scholarly edition of Cicero's letters (Cambridge, 1965–80) is a masterpiece. There are excellent commentaries on many individual works, see especially A. R. Dyck, *A Commentary on Cicero, De Officiis* (Ann Arbor, 1997); A. R. Dyck, *A Commentary on Cicero, De Legibus* (Ann Arbor, 2004); A. R. Dyck, *Cicero, Catilinarians* (Cambridge, 2008); A. R. Dyck, *Cicero* Pro Roscio Amerino (Cambridge, 2010); H. Gotoff, *Cicero's Caesarian Speeches: A Stylistic Commentary* (Chapel Hill, 1977). For speeches of Cicero that have not survived, see J. W. Crawford, *M. Tullius Cicero: The Lost and Unpublished Orations* (Göttingen, 1984). The superb Budé series for Appian (in addition to the *Civil Wars*, see especially the volume on the *Mithridatica*) is joined by an equally excellent series of editions of Cassius Dio's *Roman History* Books 36–49. J. Rich, *Cassius Dio: The Augustan Settlement, Roman History 53–55.9* (Warminster, 1990) and P. M. Swan, *The Augustan Succession: An Historical Commentary on Cassius Dio's Roman History Books 55–56* (Oxford, 2004) are of great value for Dio's account, post-Actium.

There are numerous editions of Caesar's works, and readily available translations in the Loeb series. The editions used in this book are W. Hering, *Bellum Gallicum* (Leipzig, 1987) and C. Damon, *C. Iuli Caesaris Commentariorum libri III de Bello Gallico* (Oxford, 2015). For Sallust and Velleius Paterculus, see Sources, Part III: Revolution. Posidonius is cited from L. G. Edelstein and I. G. Kidd (eds.), *Posidonius*, vol. 1 *The Fragments* (Cambridge, 1989). For Asconius' commentaries on Cicero's speeches, B. A. Marshall, *A Historical Commentary on Asconius* (Columbia, MO, 1985) is invaluable. C. B. R. Pelling, *Plutarch Caesar: Translated with Introduction and Commentary*. Clarendon Ancient History Series (Oxford, 2011) is immensely useful, while M. Toher, *Nicolaus of Damascus: The Life of Augustus and The Autobiography* (Cambridge, 2017) makes an immensely important text for the last period of Caesar's life and 44 BC readily accessible.

General Introductions: C. Steel, *The End of the Roman Republic, 146–44 BC* (Edinburgh, 2013). On a more detailed level, three extremely important accounts of the period are: E. Gruen, *The Last Generation of the Roman Republic* (Berkeley, 1974); E. Meyer, *Caesars Monarchie und das Principat des Pompejus: innere Geschichte Roms von 66 bis 44 v, Chr.* (Stuttgart, 1922); T. Rice Holmes, *The Roman Republic and the Founder of the Empire* 2 (Oxford, 1923). The overall interpretation offered in the text owes a great deal to P. A. Brunt, *The Fall of the Roman Republic and Related Essays* (Oxford, 1988) and R. Syme, *The Roman Revolution* (Oxford, 1939).

Discussions of Significant Figures: M. Gelzer, *Pompeius* (Munich, 1949); M. Gelzer, *Caesar: Politician and Statesman*, P. Needham, tr. (Oxford, 1968); M. T. Griffin, ed., *A Companion to Julius Caesar* (Oxford, 2009); J. Osgood, *Turia: A Roman Woman's Civil War* (Oxford, 2014); R. Seager, *Pompey the Great: A Political Biography* 2nd ed. (Oxford, 2002); M. B. Skinner, *Clodia Metelli: The Tribune's Sister* (Oxford, 2011); D. L. Stockton, *Cicero: A Political Biography* (Oxford, 1971); K. Welch, *Magnus Pius: Sextus Pompeius and the Transformation of the Roman Republic* (Swansea, 2012).

Economic and Military Affairs: C. T. Barlow, 'The Roman Government and the Roman Economy, 92–80 BC', *AJP* 101 (1980), 202–19; L. De Light, *Peasants, Citizens and Soldiers: Studies in the Demographic History of Roman Italy 225 BC–AD 100* (Cambridge, 2012); B. W. Frier, 'Cicero's Management of His Urban Properties', *CJ* 74 (1978), 1–6; B. W. Frier, *Landlords and Tenants in Imperial Rome* (Princeton, 1980); E. Lo Cascio, 'Carbone, Druso e gratidiano: la Gestione della Res Nummaria a Roma tra la Lex Papiria e la Lex Cornelia', *Athenaeum* (1979); C. Virvoulet, *Tessara frumentaria: les procedures de la distribution du blé public à Rome à la fin de la République et au début de l'Empire* (Rome, 1995).

Equestrian Order: The view taken in the text, which stresses the role of the censors of 86 BC, is outside the mainstream of opinion. I feel that the divisions employed in the *lex Aurelia iudiciaria* of 70 BC pre-existed the censorship of that year, as the law is in the wind during the prosecution of Verres, at which point the censors of 70 BC had not carried out the *lectio senatus*, usually the first act of a censorship. Hence I feel that a definition of an *ordo equester* extended to people outside the eighteen centuries *equo publico* (the usage is attested in *Com. Pet.* 33; note also App. *BC* 1. 442; 482). I agree with T. P. Wiseman that the *tribuni aerarii* may have been equestrians who were registered outside the eighteen centuries and my understanding most closely tracks his in 'The Definitions of Eques Romanus in the Late Republic and Early Empire', *Historia* 19 (1970), 67–83 [= T. P. Wiseman, *Roman Studies* (Liverpool, 1987), 57–73]; my understanding of the chronology of 70 BC derives from J. L. Ferrary, 'Cicéron e la loi judiciaire de Cotta (70 av. J.-C.)', *MEFR* 87 (1975), 321–48.

Gallic Wars: K. Christ, '*Caesar und Ariovistus*', *Chiron* 4 (1974), 251–92; H. Delbrück, *Warfare in Antiquity*, W. J. Renfrew, tr. (Westport, CT, 1975); J. Thorne, 'The Chronology of the Campaign against the Helvetii: A Clue to Caesar's Intentions', *Historia* 56 (2007), 27–36; G. Walser, *Caesar und die Germanen: Studien zur politischen Tendenz römischer Feldzugsberichte*, Historia Einzelschriften 1 (Stuttgart, 1956).

General Political Structures: K.-J. Hölskeskamp, *Reconstructing the Roman Republic: An Ancient Political Culture and Modern Research*, H. Heitmann-Gordon, tr. (Princeton, 2010); F. Millar, *The Crowd in Rome in the Late Republic* (Ann Arbor, 1998); R. Morstein-Marx, *Mass Oratory and Political Power in the Late Roman Republic* (Cambridge, 2004); H. Mouritson, *Plebs and Politics in the Late Roman Republic* (Cambridge, 2001); C. Rosillo-López, *Public Opinion and Politics in the Late Roman Republic* (Cambridge, 2017); P. J. J. Vanderbroek, *Popular Leadership and Collective Behavior in the Late Roman Republic (ca. 80–50 BC)* (Amsterdam, 1987); T. P Wiseman, *New Men in the Roman Senate 139 BC–AD 14*

(Oxford, 1971); A. Yakobson, *Elections and Electioneering at Rome: A Study in the Political System of the Late Republic*, Historia Einzelschriften 128 (Stuttgart, 1999).

Historiography (Ancient) and Other Literary Issues: V. Arena, Libertas *and the Practice of Politics in the Late Roman Republic* (Cambridge, 2012); H. van der Blom, *Cicero's Role Models: The Political Strategy of a Newcomer* (Oxford, 2010); A. M. Gowing, *The Triumviral Narratives of Appian and Cassius Dio* (Ann Arbor, 1992); J. Hellegouarc'h, *Le vocabulaire Latin des relations et des partis politiques sous la République* (Paris, 1963); A. W. Lintott, *Cicero as Evidence* (Oxford, 2008); C. B. R. Pelling, 'Plutarch's Method of Work in the Roman Lives', *JHS* 99 (1979), 74–96; A. M. Riggsby, *Caesar in Gaul and Rome: War in Words* (Austin, 2006); C. Smith and A. Powell, *The Lost Memoirs of Augustus and the Development of Roman Autobiography* (Swansea, 2009), 65–85; H. Strasberger, *Caesars Eintritt in die Geschichte* (Munich, 1938); K. Welch and A. Powell, eds., *Julius Caesar as Artful Reporter* (London, 2008); T. P. Wiseman, *Catullus and His World: A Reappraisal* (Cambridge, 1985).

Internal Politics (before 59 BC): M. C. Alexander, *Trials in the Late Roman Republic 149 BC–50 BC* (Toronto, 1990); D. H. Berry, 'The Publication of Cicero's *Pro Roscio Amerino*', *Mnemosyne* 57 (2004), 80–87; B. W. Frier, 'Sulla's Propaganda: The Collapse of the Cinnan Republic', *AJP* 92 (1971), 585–604; M. T. Griffin, 'The Tribune C. Cornelius', *JRS* 63 (1973), 196–213; F. Hinard, 'Le "Pro Quinctio", un discours politique', *REA* 77 (1975), 88–107 [= *Rome, la dernière République*, 179–202]; F. Hurlet, *La dictature de Sylla: monarchie ou magistrature républicaine* (Turnhout, 1993); M. Lovano, *The Age of Cinna: Crucible of Late Republican Rome*, Historia Einzelschriften 158 (Stuttgart, 2002); P. Moreau, Clodiana religio: *un procès politique en 61 avant J.C.* (Paris, 1982); C. Nicolet, ed., Insula Sacra: *la loi Gabinia-Calpurnia de Délos (58 av J.-C.)* (Paris, 1980); S. I. Oost, 'Cyrene, 96–74 BC', *CPh* 58 (1963), 11–25; D. S. Potter, *Prophets and Emperors: Human and Divine Authority from Augustus to Theodosius* (Cambridge, MA, 1994); D. S Potter, 'Holding Court in Republican Rome (105–44)', *AJP* 132 (2011), 59–80; J. Reynolds, 'Cyrenaica, Pompey and Cn. Cornelius Lentulus Marcellinus', *JRS* 52 (1962), 97–103; M. A. Robb, *Beyond Populares and Optimates: Political Language in the Late Republic*. Historia Einzelschriften 213 (Stuttgart, 2010); F. Santangelo, *Sulla, the Elites and the Empire: A Study of Roman Policies in Italy and the Greek East* (Leiden, 2007); F. Santangelo, 'Roman Politics in the 70s BC: A Story of Realignments', *JRS* 104 (2014), 1–27; C. Steel, 'Rethinking Sulla: The Case of the Roman Senate', *CQ* 64 (2014), 657–68; A. Thein, 'Sulla the Weak Tyrant', in S. Lewis, *Ancient Tyranny* (Edinburgh, 2008), 238–47; F. J. Vervaet, 'The Lex Valeria and Sulla's Empowerment as Dictator (82–79 BCE)', *Cahiers Glotz* 15 (2004), 37–84.

Internal Politics and the Civil Wars (59–44 BC): P. A. Brunt, 'Cicero's *Officium* in the Civil War', *JRS* 76 (1986), 12–32; S. G. Chrissanthos, 'Caesar and the Mutiny of 47 BC', *JRS* 91 (2001), 63–75; P. J. Cuff, 'The Terminal Date of Caesar's Command', *Historia* 7 (1958), 445–72; G. K. Golden, *Crisis Management during the Roman Republic: The Role of Political Institutions in Insurgencies* (Cambridge, 2013); I. Gradal, *Emperor Worship and Roman Religion* (Oxford, 2002); H. Heinen, 'Kaiser un Kaisarion', *Historia* 18 (1979), 181–203; L. Keppie, *Colonization and Veteran Settlement in Italy 47–14 BC* (London,

1983); A. Lintott, 'Cicero and Milo', *JRS* 64 (1974), 62–78; H.-M. Ottmer, *Die Rubikon-Legende: Untersuchungen zu Caesars und Pompeius' Strategie vor und nach Ausbruch des Bürgerkrieges* (Boppard am Rhein, 1979); T. Rising, 'Senatorial Opposition to Pompey's Eastern Settlement: A Storm in a Teacup?' *Historia* 62 (2013), 196–221; C. Steel, 'The Lex Pompeia de Provinciis of 52 BC: A Reconsideration', *Historia* 61 (2012), 83–93; R. Syme, 'The Allegiance of Labienus', *JRS* 38 (1928), 113–25 [= *Roman Papers* 1, E. Badian, ed. (Oxford, 1979), 62–75]; W. J. Tatum, *The Patrician Tribune: Publius Clodius Pulcher* (Chapel Hill, 1999); L. R. Taylor, 'The Chronology of Caesar's First Consulship', *AJP* 72 (1951), 254–6; S. Weinstock, *Divus Julius* (Oxford, 1971).

Internal Politics and Civil Wars (44–36 BC): R. Alston, *Rome's Revolution: Death of the Republic and Birth of the Empire* (Oxford, 2015); H. Fritsch, *Cicero's Fight for the Republic: The Historical Background of Cicero's Philippics* (Copenhagen, 1946); E. Gabba, 'The Perusine War and Triumviral Italy', *HSCP* 75 (1971); J. Lobur, *Consensus, Concordia, and the Formation of Roman Imperial Ideology* (London, 2008); J. Osgood, *Caesar's Legacy: Civil War and the Emergence of the Roman Empire* (Cambridge, 2006); J. T. Ramsey, 'The Senate, Mark Antony, and Caesar's Legislative Legacy', *CQ* 44 (1994), 130–45; G. Sumi, *Ceremony and Power: Performing Politics in Rome between Republic and Empire* (Ann Arbor, 2005); A. Wright, 'The Death of Cicero: Forming a Tradition: The Contamination of History', *Historia* 50 (2001), 436–52.

Mithridatic Wars: A. R. Bellinger, 'The End of the Seleucids', *Transactions of the Connecticut Academy of Arts and Sciences* 38 (1949), 51–102; G. R. Bugh, 'Athenion and Aristion of Athens', *Phoenix* 46 (1992), 108–23; J. Camp, M. Ierardi, J. McInerney, K. Morgan, G. Umholtz, 'A Trophy from the Battle of Chaeronea of 86 BC', *AJA* 96 (1992), 443–55; J.-C. Gauger, '*Phlegon von Tralles Mirab. III: zu einem Dokument geistigen Widerstandes gegen Rom*', *Chiron* 10 (1980), 225–62; C. Habicht, *Athens from Alexander to Antony*, D. L. Schneider, tr. (Cambridge, MA, 1997); B. C. McGing, *The Foreign Policy of Mithridates VI Eupator, King of Pontus* (Leiden, 1986); E. Schürer, *A History of the Jewish People in the Age of Jesus Christ* 1 rev. ed., G. Vermes and F. G. Millar, eds.,(Edinburgh, 1973); R. Syme, *Anatolica: Studies in Strabo* (Oxford, 1995). For the number of victims during the massacre of 89 BC I have followed Cicero, *De imp. Cn. Pomp* 7; see also P. Goukowsky, *Appien: histoire romaine* vol. 7 (Paris, 2003), 152, n. 216. For the cloak of Alexander, see Appian, *Mith.* 577.

Parthia: P. Arnaud, 'Les guerres parthiques de Gabinius et de Crassus et la politique occidentale des Parthes Arsacides entre 70 et 53 av. J.-C.', in E. Daprowa, ed., *Ancient Iran and the Mediterranean World, Electrum* 2 (Warsaw, 1998), 13–34; J. Curran, 'The Ambitions of Quintus Labienus Parthicus', *Antichthon* 41 (2007), 33–53; E. Noé, 'Province, Parti e Guerra: Il Caso di Labieno', *Athenaeum* 85 (1997), 409–36; P. Roussel, '*Le miracle de Zeus Panamaros*', *BCH* 55 (1931), 70–116.

Spartacus: K. R. Bradley, *Slavery and Rebellion in the Roman World 140 BC–70 BC* (London, 1989); P. Piccinin, '*Les Italiens dans le "Bellum Spartacium"*', *Historia* 53 (2004), 173–99; Z. Rubinsohn, 'Was the *Bellum Spartacium* a Servile Insurrection', *Rivista di Filologia e di Istruzione Classica* 99 (1971), 290–99; A. Schiavone, *Spartacus*, J. Carden, tr. (Cambridge,

2013); B. D. Shaw, *Spartacus and the Slave Wars: A Brief History with Documents* (Boston, 2001); T. Urbainczyk, *Spartacus* (Bristol, 2004).

Social and Cultural Issues: G. W. Bowersock, 'A Date in the Eighth Eclogue', *HSCP* 75 (1971), 73–80; H. Evans, *Water Distribution in Ancient Rome: The Evidence of Frontinus* (Ann Arbor, 1994); E. Fantham, H. Foley and N. Kampen, *Women in the Classical World: Image and Text* (Oxford, 1994); P. M. Fraser, 'Mark Antony in Alexandria – A Note', *JRS* 47 (1957), 71–3; J. Griffin, 'Augustan Poetry and the Life of Luxury', *JRS* 66 (1976), 87–105; W. D. Lebek, 'Moneymaking on the Roman Stage', in W. J. Slater, ed., *Roman Theater and Society* (Ann Arbor, 1996), 29–48; K. Milnor, *Gender, Domesticity and the Age of Augustus: Inventing Private Life* (Oxford, 2005); R. G. M. Nisbet, *Collected Papers on Latin Literature*, S. J. Harrison, ed. (Oxford, 1995); J. Rüpke, *The Roman Calendar from Numa to Constantine: Time, History and the Fasti*, D. M. B. Richardson, tr. (Oxford, 2011); T. P. Wiseman, *The Roman Audience* (Oxford, 2015). The view of Caesar's forum in the text is borrowed from Davies, *Architecture and Politics in Republican Rome*, 247–9.

Part V: Monarchy

For the reign of Augustus, Cassius Dio's remains the primary narrative (see Sources, Part IV: Dictatorship for editions). He is now joined by Suetonius, *The Twelve Caesars* (numerous translations) and the greatest of the historians of ancient Rome, Cornelius Tacitus (numerous translations), whose *Annals* and *Histories* once covered the period from 14 to 96 AD (now preserved for the years 14–37, 47–66, 69–70 AD). His three shorter works are the *Dialogue Concerning Oratory*, *Agricola* (the biography of his father-in-law) and the *Germania* (again all available in numerous translations). Velleius Paterculus continues to offer insights into the reign of Tiberius. The Elder Pliny's *Natural History* (readily available through a Loeb edition) has a great deal to say about the period as a whole, while the letters of his nephew, the Younger Pliny, can be found in both Loeb and Penguin editions. D. Wardle, *Suetonius: Life of Augustus* (Oxford, 2014) is an immensely useful guide to the sources for the first part of this period, along with the commentaries on Dio, Rich, *Cassius Dio: The Augustan Settlement* and Swan, *The Augustan Succession* (see Sources, Part IV: Dictatorship). As documentary sources become vastly more common for this period, see the discussions in the editions cited. For the documents connected with funerals, see J. B. Lott, *Death and Dynasty in Early Imperial Rome* (Cambridge, 2012).

General Histories: R. Syme, *Tacitus* (Oxford, 1958) (see also under historiography); R. Syme, *The Augustan Aristocracy* (Oxford, 1986). P. A. Brunt, *Roman Imperial Themes* (Oxford, 1990) contains a great number of important studies, while F. Millar, *The Emperor in the Roman World* 2nd ed. (London, 1992) offers a crucial model for the way the Roman state worked; see also the essays collected in F. Millar, *Government, Society and Culture in the Roman Empire*, H. M. Cotton and G. M. Rogers, eds. (Chapel Hill, 2004).

Actium: R. Gurval, *Actium and Augustus: The Politics and Emotions of Civil War* (Ann

Arbor, 1995); P. Petsas, *Octavian's Campsite Memorial for the Actian War. Transactions of the American Philosophical Society*, n. 79.4 (Philadelpia, 1989).

Army and Military Affairs after the Civil Wars: P. Allison, *People and Spaces in Roman Military Bases* (Cambridge, 2013); P. Conole and R. D. Milns, 'Neronian Frontier Policy in the Balkans: The Career of Ti. Plautius Silvanus', *Historia* 24 (1983), 183–200; S. Dillon, 'Women on the Columns of Trajan and Marcus Aurelius and the Visual Language of Roman Victory', in S. Dillon and K. Welch, *Representations of War in Ancient Rome* (Cambridge, 2006), 244–71; W. Eck, '*Herrschaftssicherung und Expansion: Das römische Heer unter Augustus*', in G. Negri and A. Valvo, *Studi su Augusto: In occasione del XX centenario della morte* (Turin, 2016), 77–93; I. Haynes, *Blood of the Provinces: The Roman Auxilia and the Making of Provincial Society from Augustus to the Severans* (Cambridge, 2013); F. Lepper, *Trajan's Parthian War* (Oxford, 1948); F. Lepper and S. Frere, *Trajan's Column* (Gloucester, 1988); C. S. Lightfoot, 'Trajan's Parthian War and Fourth-century Perspective', *JRS* 80 (1990), 115–26; E. Luttwak, *The Grand Strategy of the Roman Empire* rev. ed. (Baltimore, 2016); R. McMullen, *Change in the Roman Empire: Essays in the Ordinary* (Princeton, 1990); F. G. Millar, 'Emperors, Frontiers and Foreign Relations, 31 BC to AD 378', *Britannia* 13 (1982), 1–23; T. Mommsen, *Res Gestae Divi Augusti* (Berlin, 1883); D. S. Potter, 'The Mysterious Arbaces', *AJP* 100 (1979), 541–2; D. S. Potter, 'The Inscription on the Bronze Hercules of Mesene: Vologaeses IV's War with Rome and the Date of Tacitus' *Annales*', *ZPE* 88 (1991), 277–90; D. S. Potter, 'Empty Areas and Roman Frontier Policy', *AJP* 113 (1992), 269–74; D. S. Potter, 'Emperors, Their Borders and Their Neighbors: The Scope of the Imperial Mandata', in D. L. Kennedy, ed., *The Roman Army in the East, JRA* Supplemental Series 18 (Ann Arbor, 1996), 49–66; E. Ritterling, 'Legio', *RE* 1216–18; M. P. Speidel, 'The Captor of Decebelus: A New Inscription from Philippi', *JRS* 60 (1970), 142–53; R. Syme, 'Some Notes on the Legions under Augustus', *JRS* 23 (1933), 14–33; B. Turner, 'War Losses and Worldview: Reviewing the Roman Funerary Altar at Adamclisi', *AJP* 134 (2104), 277–304.

Cultural History: M. T. Boatwright, *Hadrian and the City of Rome* (Princeton, 1987); M. T. Boatwright, *Hadrian and the Cities of the Roman Empire* (Princeton, 2000); G. W. Bowersock, *Greek Sophists and the Roman Empire* (Oxford, 1969); G. W. Bowersock, 'Historical Problems in Late Republican and Augustan Classicism', in *Le classicism à Rome aux Iers siècles avant et après J.C.* Fondation Hardt, Entretiens 25 (Geneva, 1979), 57–75; G. W. Bowersock, 'The Pontificate of Augustus', in K. A. Raaflaub and M. Toher, eds., *Between Republic and Empire: Interpretations of Augustus and His Principate* (Berkeley, 1993), 380–94; E. Gabba, *Dionysius and the History of Archaic Rome* (Berkeley, 1991); A. M. Gowing, *Empire and Memory: The Representation of the Roman Republic in Imperial Culture* (Cambridge, 2005); C. P. Jones, *Plutarch and Rome* (Oxford, 1971); R. Laurence, S. Esmonde Cleary and G. Sears, *The City in the Roman West c. 250 BC–c. AD 250* (Cambridge, 2011); C. Marek, *In the Land of a Thousand Gods: A History of Asia Minor in the Roman World*, S. Rendall, tr. (Princeton, 2016); R. McMullen, *Change in the Roman Empire: Essays in the Ordinary* (Princeton, 1990); D. S. Potter, 'Cultural Archaism and Community Identity: The Case of Xanthus and Paphos', Μελέται και Υπομνήματα Ιδρυματος Αρχιεπισκόπου Μακαρίου Γ΄ Κύπρου (Nicosia, 1994), 427–41; R. R. R. Smith, 'The Imperial Reliefs from the Sebasteion at Aphrodisias', *JRS* 77 (1987), 88–138; A. J. Spawforth, *Greece and the Augustan Cultural Revolution* (Cambridge, 2012), 18–26; R. J. Tarrant, 'Poetry and Power: Virgil's Poetry in Contemporary Context', in C. Martindale, ed., *The Cambridge Companion to Virgil* (Cambridge, 1995), 169–87; P. Veyne, *L'empire gréco-romain* (Paris, 2005); G. Woolf, *Becoming Roman: The Origins of Provincial Civilization in Gaul* (Cambridge, 1998); P. Zanker, *The Power of Images in the Age of Augustus* (Ann Arbor, 1987).

Economic Structures: P. F. Bang, *The Roman Bazaar: A Comparative Study of Trade and Markets in a Tributary Empire* (Cambridge, 2008); K. Hopkins, 'Taxes and Trade in the Roman Empire (200 BC–AD 400)', *JRS* 70 (1980), 101–25; P. Horden and N. Purcell, *The Corrupting Sea: A Study of Mediterranean History* (Oxford, 2000); A. Tchernia, *The Romans and Trade*, J. Grieve with E. Minchin, tr. (Oxford, 2016); P. Temin, *The Roman Market Economy* (Princeton, 2012).

Evolution of the Principate: A. R. Birley, *Hadrian: The Restless Emperor* (London, 1997); G. W. Bowersock, *Roman Arabia* (Cambridge, MA, 1983); G. W. Bowersock, 'Augustus and the East: The Problem of the Succession', in F. Millar and C. Segal, *Caesar Augustus: Seven Aspects* (Oxford, 1984), 169–88; P. A. Brunt, '*Lex de Imperio Vespasiani*', *JRS* 67 (1977), 95–111; E. J. Champlin, *Nero* (Cambridge, MA, 2005); A. Dalla Rosa, 'Dominating the Auspices: Augustus, Augury and the Proconsuls', in J. Richardson and F. Santangelo, eds., *Priests and State in the Roman World* (Stuttgart, 2011); W. Eck, 'The Administrative Reforms of Augustus: Pragmatism or Systematic Planning', in J. Edmondson, *Augustus* (Edinburgh, 2009), 229–49; W. Eck, '*Die Lex Troesmensium: eine Stadtgesetz für ein Municipium Civium Romanorum*', *ZPE* 200 (2016), 565–606 (evidence for emendation of the Lex Julia in AD 5); J.-L. Ferrary, '*À propos des pouvoirs d'Auguste*', *Cahiers du Centre Gustave Glotz* 12 (2001), 101–54 [reprinted in shortened form in Edmondson, *Augustus*]; H. I. Flower, 'The Tradition of Spolia Opima: M. Claudius Marcellus and Augustus', *CA* 19 (2000), 49–53; M. T. Griffin, *Nero: The End of a Dynasty* (London, 1984); H. Halfmann, *Itinera principum: Geschichte und Typologie der Kaiserreisen im Römischen Reich* (Stuttgart, 1986); O. Hekster, 'All in the Family: The Appointment of Emperors Designate in the Second Century AD', in L. de Blois, ed., *Administration, Prosopography and Appointment Policies in the Roman Empire* (Amsterdam, 2001), 35–49; O. Hekster, *Emperors and Ancestors, Roman Rulers and the Constraints of Tradition* (Oxford, 2015); P. Hermann, *Der römische Kaisereid* (Göttingen, 1968); R. A. Kearsley, 'Octavian and Augury: The Years 30–27 BC', *CQ* 59 (2009), 147–66; W. K. Lacey, *The Augustan Principate: The Evolution of a System* (Liverpool, 1996); C. Lange, *Res Publica Constituta: Actium, Apollo and the Accomplishment of the Triumviral Assignment* (Leiden, 2009); B. Levick, *Claudius* (London, 1990); B. Levick, *Tiberius the Politician* rev. ed. (London, 1999); B. Levick, *Vespasian* (London, 1999); J. F. Matthews, *Roman Perspectives: Studies in the Social, Political and Cultural History of the First to Fifth Centuries* (Swansea, 2010), 57–84; J. W. Rich, 'Augustus and the Spolia Opima', *Chiron* 26 (1996), 85–127; J. W. Rich and J. H. C. Williams, '*Leges et Iura P.R. Restituit*: A New Aureus of Octavian and the Settlement of 28–27 BC', *NC* 159 (1999), 169–213; G. D. Rowe, *Princes and Political Cultures: The New Tiberian Senatorial Decrees* (Ann Arbor, 2002); R. Syme, 'The Crisis of 2 BC', *Bayerische Akademie der Wissenschaften: Philosophisch-Historiker Klasse: Sitzungsberichte* 1974, 7, 3–34 [= *Roman Papers* 3 (Oxford, 1984), 912–36];

S. Thakur, 'Tiberius, the Varian Disaster and the Dating of *Tristia* 2', *MD* 73 (2014), 69–97; F. Vervaet, 'The Secret History: The Official Position of Imperator Caesar Divi Filius from 3–27 BCE', *AS* 40 (2010), 114–52; A. Wallace-Hadrill, 'Civilis Princeps: Between Citizen and King', *JRS* 72 (1982), 32–48.

Historiography: R. Ash, *Ordering Anarchy: Leaders and Armies in Tacitus' Histories* (Ann Arbor, 1999); D. S. Potter, 'The Greek Historians of Imperial Rome', in A. Feldherr and G. Hardy, eds., *The Oxford History of Historical Writing* 1, *Beginnings to AD 600* (Oxford, 2011); T. Rajak, *Josephus* 2nd ed. (Bristol, 2002); R. Syme, *Tacitus* (Oxford, 1958); R. Syme, 'Livy and Augustus', *HSCP* 64 (1959), 27–87 [= *Roman Papers* 1 (Oxford, 1979), 400–54]; A. Wallace-Hadrill, *Suetonius: The Scholar and His Caesars* (London, 1983); L. M. Yarrow, *Historiography at the End of the Republic: Provincial Perspectives on Roman Rule* (Oxford, 2006).

Imperial Administration: C. Ando, *Imperial Ideology and Provincial Loyalty in the Roman Empire* (Berkeley, 2000); G. W. Bowersock, 'Syria under Vespasian', *JRS* 63 (1973), 133–40; G. W. Bowersock, 'Hadrian and Metropolis', *Bonner Historia-Augusta-Colloquium 1982–83* (Bonn, 1985), 75–88; G. Burton, 'Proconsuls, Assizes and the Administration of Justice under the Empire', *JRS* 65 (1975), 92–106; D. Fishwick, *The Imperial Cult in the Latin West: Studies in the Ruler Cult of the Western Provinces of the Roman Empire* 1.1 (Leiden, 1987); B. W. Frier, 'Roman Life Expectancy: Ulpian's Evidence', *HSCP* 86 (1982), 213–51; M. T. Griffin, 'The Lyons Tablet and Tacitean Hindsight', *CQ* 32 (1982), 404–18; F. G. Millar, *The Roman Near East 31 BC–AD 337* (Cambridge, MA, 1995); S. Mitchell, 'The Treaty between Rome and Lycia of 46 BC', in R. Pintaudi, *Papyri Graecae Schøyen. Papyrologica Florentina* 35 (Florence, 2005), 166–259; C. Nicolet, *Space, Geography, and Politics in the Early Roman Empire* (Ann Arbor, 1991); S. R. F. Price, *Rituals and Power: The Roman Imperial Cult in Asia Minor* (Cambridge, 1984).

Senate and Equestrian Orders: P. A. Brunt, 'The Role of the Senate in the Augustan Regime', *CQ* 34 (1984), 423–44; S. Demougin, *L'ordre équestre sous les Julio-Claudiens* (Paris, 1988); F. Millar and C. Segal, *Caesar Augustus: Seven Aspects* (Oxford, 1984); R. J. Talbert, *The Senate of Imperial Rome* (Princeton, 1984).

Revolts: P. A. Brunt, *Roman Imperial Themes* (Oxford, 1990); W. Eck, *Rom und Judaea* (Tübingen, 2007); G. Gambash, *Roman and Provincial Resistance* (London, 2015); M. Goodman, *The Ruling Class of Judaea: The Origins of the Jewish Revolt against Rome AD 66–70* (Cambridge, 1987); A. Heinrichs, 'Vespasian's Visit to Alexandria', *ZPE* 3 (1968), 51–80; W. Horbury, *Jewish War under Trajan and Hadrian* (Cambridge, 2014); R. McMullen, *Change in the Roman Empire: Essays in the Ordinary* (Princeton, 1990); J. Nicols, *Vespasian and the Partes Flavianae Historia Einzelschriften* 28 (Wiesbaden, 1978).

The Life of Jesus: See G. Vermes, *Jesus the Jew* (New York, 1973), 21; the actual date of his birth was most likely 2 BC on the basis of Luke 3:1 and 3:23 stating that Jesus began his ministry at the age of 30 in the fifteenth year of Tiberius (29 AD). This is a significant statement because Luke did not recognise that it contradicted the date he selected for the birth of Jesus (6 AD) at 2:1. The error probably reflects the fact of variant traditions about Jesus' career.

LIST OF ILLUSTRATIONS

❦

Colour Plates

Black and White

ACKNOWLEDGEMENTS

While the formal genesis of this book goes back to the kind invitation of John Davey to contribute to the Profile History of the Ancient World, my interest in the subject extends many years in the past, to my tenure of the Salvesen Fellowship at New College, Oxford. There I had the pleasure of learning from Antony Andrewes, George Forrest, Robin Lane Fox and Geoffrey de Ste Croix. I was able to attend seminars at which Ronald Syme was present, and to learn from three Peters – Brunt, Derow and Fraser. It seems appropriate that the composition of this book should have been undertaken during Michaelmas Term 2015, when I had the honour of holding a visiting fellowship at New College, for which opportunity I am grateful to fellows of the College, as well as for the warm and congenial environment of the Senior Common Room. I owe a particular debt of gratitude in all this to Professor Andrew Meadows. I would also like to thank Hassan Hamed for making me feel very much at home. While in Oxford I had the further opportunity of having regular discussions with Fergus Millar, whose approach to the subject can be felt throughout this book (and more than a few others I have written). The draft was finished in Ann Arbor, where I have been able to benefit from the fellowship of many excellent colleagues, among them Sara Ahbel-Rappe, Basil Dufallo, Ben Fortson, Bruce Frier, Richard Janko, Lisa Nevett, Chris Ratté, Francesca Schironi, Gina Soter, David Stone and Nicola Terrenato. I am especially grateful to Nic for introducing me to Italy in ways that only he can, and to Marcello Mogetta for organising various expeditions with the Gabii crew that have enabled me to get to know the subject as I would otherwise never have done, and to both Nic and Marcello for answering countless queries. It is also a pleasure to thank Professor Ratté and Professor Burt Smith for help with illustrations. The book went to press in my tenure of the Ronald J. Mellor Professorship in UCLA's wonderful History Department. I am immensely grateful to all my colleagues in Los Angeles for their hospitality, especially to Professor David Phillips and to Jonathan Ebueng, without whose patient help I could not have functioned.

I am also grateful to Louisa Dunnigan, who took over the project for Profile when John retired, and especially to Heather Hughes at Harvard University Press and to Penny Daniel, for their help. Jan Dewitt and Parrish Wright lent aid with an early draft of the text, helping make the text more user-friendly, Tim Hart and James Faulkner provided very helpful comments at a later stage. It is also a pleasure to thank Sally Holloway for her copyediting of the manuscript. I have once again benefitted enormously from the assistance of Sue Philpott, master copyeditor, for improving the manuscript in countless ways. And to Jane

Delancy who drew the three plans of the Roman Forum with impressive speed and accuracy, eliminating structures for whose location there is no direct evidence.

None of this would have been possible without the support of my family, my wife Ellen and our daughters, Claire and Natalie (and Michael Schneider, who will be joining the family on a more formal basis). While I was writing this book, my father, who encouraged my early interest in the history of the ancient world, died, taking with him an unparalleled depth of knowledge of mankind's assorted foibles, but I am confident that my mother will be recognising some resonance with people she has known.

The book is dedicated to our dear friends Veronika Grimm and John Matthews.

Oxford
Ann Arbor
Los Angeles

INDEX

❦

and Cleopatra, 250, 280, 290–94; and
Domitius Ahenobarbus 280, 293–4;
and Julius Caesar 256–7, 271, 273; and
Parthians 281, 290–91; and Philippi
278; and Sextus Pompeius Magnus
280–83; as consul in 44 BC after Caesar's
assassination 272–4; debauchery of 290,
293, 296; descent from Hercules 296;
in 43 BC 275–6; marriage to Octavia
280, 290, 292–3, 317, 319; on Augustus'
personal habits 305; suicide 295
Antonius Pallas (imperial freedman) 338,
354
Antonius Primus (commander of *legio VII
Galbiana* in 69 AD) 369, 372–3
Aphrodisias (city in the province of Asia)
350–1, 415
Apollo (god)
and Augustus 296, 298; cult of, in Italy 38,
114; cult of, at Rome 70–71; oracle of at
Delphi 38, 62, 70, 91, 149
Appian of Alexandria (historian),
on Roman intervention in Illyria 45; on
Roman wars in Spain 116, 119; on the
Sullan Civil War 185
Appuleius Saturninus (tribune 103, 100 BC)
164–6, 177–8, 181, 192, 224, 232, 312
Arminius (German chieftain) 330,
347–8
Army, Roman,
cost 188–9, 287, 290, 327, 392; loyalty 173,
175, 177, 186, 190, 203, 263, 275, 279, 283,
366; mutinies 73, 190, 211–12, 226, 263,
274, 279, 283, 366; raised with private
resources 71, 176, 187–9, 199, 203, 250,
258; recruitment 62, 74–5, 117–18, 139,
160–61, 220, 345, 372, 391; scandals 94,
118–19, 156–7, 249; size 24, 27,46, 52–3,
59, 63–4, 74, 131, 189, 206, 246, 295, 345,
390, 392; standards, 160, 234, 291–2,
302–3, 335; tactics 28, 59–60, 72, 75, 85,
91–2, 131, 160, 162, 206, 226, 247, 258–61,
278; terms of service 78, 131, 195, 278,
314–16, 321, 327, 362, 389; training 75,
160–61, 204, 208–9

Athens (city in Greece) 39, 82, 149, 172, 183,
185, 281, 303, 310, 396, 398
Atilius Caiatinus, A. (consul 258, 254 BC)
27, 30
Atilius Regulus, M. (consul 267, 256 BC)
27–9
Atilius Regulus, C. (consul 235 BC) 46
Atilius Bulbus, G. (consul 245, 235 BC) 42
Atilius Serranus, C. (praetor 218 BC) 55–6
Attalus, generic name for a Greek king
88–9
Attalus I (king of Pergamon 241–197 BC)
70
Attalus III (king of Pergamon 138–133 BC)
129–30, 135
Augustus, Imperator Caesar (emperor 27
BC–14 AD)
administration of the city of Rome 302,
305, 325; administrative style 297, 326–31;
adoption by Julius Caesar 267, 272–3;
and cultural figures 280, 309–13, 341,
385; Civil war with L. Antonius 279–80;
Civil War with M. Antonius (32–30
BC) 292–5; Civil War with Magnus
Pius 280–83; Constitutional position
295, 299, 301–2, 305, 318, 322, 333, 342;
and Eastern Provinces 296, 303, 321;
and Parthia 302–3, 319, 335; Dynastic
plans 301, 308, 317–20, 331–2; illness
278, 300–301, 332; impact on the city of
Rome 296–7, 300, 313–14, 317; Philippi
campaign 278; reform of the Senatorial
and Equestrian Orders 306–7, 314, 322–
6; re-organises Roman army 295, 315–16,
327, 334, 336; rise to power 44–43 BC
273–6; ruler cult 333, 352–3; Secular
Games 307–8; sex life 277, 282, 305

B

Bacchus (god, Dionysus in Greek),
and Marius 162; dubious reputation
of his cult 88, 102, 296; suppression of
followers 102–3
Bath, public 114, 153, 348–9, 380
Brutus *see* Iunius Brutus